Empirical Methods for Artificial Intelligence

Paul R. Cohen

Empirical Methods for Artificial Intelligence

The MIT Press
Cambridge, Massachusetts
London, England

This book was set in Times Roman by Techbooks and was printed and bound in the United States of America.

CLASP for the Macintosh can be used for much of the analysis in *Empirical Methods for Artificial Intelligence*. CLASP for the Macintosh is a Common Lisp statistics package with broad descriptive and hypothesis-testing functionality, including tests of means, contingency tables, bootstrap and randomization methods, confidence intervals, analysis of variance and multiple regression. CLASP supports flexible exploratory data analysis, providing many powerful data manipulation functions and graphical options. Because CLASP is developed in Macintosh Common Lisp, one can easily compose new statistical functions from the base set described in the CLASP Reference Manual. Functions can be selected from menus or run directly from a Lisp Listener. CLASP for the Macintosh was developed by the Experimental Knowledge Systems Laboratory at the University of Massachusetts, which holds copyright, and is distributed by The MIT Press. It runs on all Macintosh computers from the SE series on; it requires at least 6 MB of memory beyond that claimed by the operating system. It is distributed with release notes, a manual, sample datasets, and utilities.

For ordering information, please contact Sales Department, The MIT Press, 55 Hayward Street, Cambridge, MA 02142, or via e-mail at mitpress-catalogs@mit.edu.

Library of Congress Cataloging-in-Publication Data

Cohen, Paul R.
    Empirical methods for artificial intelligence/Paul R. Cohen.
    p.   cm.
    Includes bibliographical references and index.
    ISBN 0-262-03225-2 (HC)
    1. Artificial intelligence—Research—Methodology. I. Title.
Q335.7.C64   1995
006.3′072—dc20   94-39316
                                                              CIP

Contents

Preface

When it was proclaimed that the Library contained all books, the first impression was one of extravagant happiness. All men felt themselves to be the masters of an intact and secret treasure....

As was natural, this inordinate hope was followed by an excessive depression. The certitude that some shelf in some hexagon held precious books and that these precious books were inaccessible, seemed almost intolerable. A blasphemous sect suggested that the searches should cease and that all men should juggle letters and symbols until they had constructed, by an improbable gift of chance, these canonical books. The authorities were obliged to issue severe orders. The sect disappeared, but in my childhood I have seen old men who, for long periods of time, would hide in latrines with some metal disks in a forbidden dice cup and feebly mimic the divine disorder.
—Jorge Luis Borges, *"The Tower of Babel,"* from *Labyrinths*

One writes a book for many reasons, some quite irrational. I will admit to three: First, I wanted a book on research methods because we have no curriculum in methods as other sciences do. My metaphor for this aspect of the book is the toolbox. Here are exploratory tools to help your eyes detect patterns in data, hypothesis-testing tools to help your data speak convincingly, and modeling tools to help you explain your data. Second, because our systems are increasingly embedded, complex, and sophisticated, we need a basis for designing new, more powerful research methods. I hope this book will convince you that statistics is one such basis. My metaphor for this aspect of the book is an imaginary class of "statistical microscopes" that disclose structures and behaviors in fairly complex systems. Third, it is time to revise some classical views of empirical artificial intelligence (AI) and to devote ourselves anew to others. For instance, it is no longer true that we can predict how a system will behave by looking at its code (unless it's very small); even if we could, let's remember that artificial intelligence once studied individual systems not for their own sake but in pursuit of general laws of intelligence. This goal has been maligned in the last two decades by the empirically inclined, and pursued abstractly by others. I think it's time for empirical researchers to resume the search.

This book was intended originally for graduate students, undergraduates, and researchers in artificial intelligence, but I discovered by teaching the material at the University of Massachusetts that it appeals to students in other areas of computer science as well. This isn't very surprising, as few undergraduates in computer science learn research methods, unlike their counterparts in psychology, chemistry, biology, and so on. I didn't call the book *Empirical Methods for Computer Science,* though, because most of its case studies are from AI, and some of its methods are particular to AI, and it doesn't include methods particular to other areas of computer science such as queueing models for network analysis.

Professors will want to allow one semester or two quarters to cover most of the material in lectures, although I expect it can be done in one quarter if advanced material in the appendixes is omitted. As to prerequisites, the book assumes nothing about the reader; the mathematical material is light and it is developed from first principles.

As I prepared the book I came to realize that my own training was a bit warped, emphasizing statistical hypothesis testing to the exclusion of every other aspect of empirical research. Because I want to avoid this mistake here, the book doesn't introduce hypothesis testing until Chapter 4, when it can be appreciated in the context of the broader empirical enterprise. A researcher should know how to look at data and encourage it to tell its story (Chapter 2) and how to design experiments to clarify and corroborate the story (Chapter 3) before submitting it to the blunt interrogation of hypothesis testing. I decided to present statistical hypothesis testing in two chapters, one devoted to classical, parametric methods (Chapter 4), the other to new, computer-intensive statistical methods based on Monte Carlo sampling (Chapter 5). The last four chapters focus on research strategies and tactics, and while each introduces new statistical methods, they do so in the context of case studies. Mathematical details are confined to appendixes. Chapter 6 is about performance assessment, and Chapter 7 shows how interactions and dependencies among several factors can help explain performance. Chapter 8 discusses predictive models of programs, including causal models. Finally, Chapter 9 asks what counts as a *theory* in artificial intelligence, and how can empirical methods—which deal with specific AI systems—foster general theories.

Behind every experimental or analytical tool is a scientist who views his or her subject through the lens of a particular collection of beliefs. Some of these concern the subject and some concern the science itself. Among the things I no longer believe about artificial intelligence is that looking at a program tells you how it will behave:

Each new program that is built is an experiment. It poses a question to nature, and its behavior offers clues to an answer. Neither machines nor programs are black boxes; they are artifacts that have been designed, both hardware and software; and we can open them up and look inside. We can relate their structure to their behavior and draw many lessons from a single experiment. We don't have to build 100 copies of, say, a theorem prover, to demonstrate statistically that it has not overcome the combinatorial explosion of search in the way hoped for. Inspection of the program in the light of a few runs reveals the flaw and lets us proceed to the next attempt.   (Newell and Simon, 1981, p. 36)

Much about this influential passage is true in specific situations, but not generally true, as it was in 1975. Although we can open up our artifacts and look inside, we no longer find this an easy way to relate their structure to their behavior. Increasingly we *do* require 100 repetitions—not of the code itself but of problems in samples— to demonstrate statistically that a program behaves as we hope. Increasingly, our characterizations of behavior are statistical, and the structures we induce to explain the behaviors are not programs but influence diagrams and other sorts of statistical models. Although it is true that we don't need statistics to tell us that a program is still crippled by the combinatorial explosion, we are unable to see subtler flaws unaided, and a few runs of the program might never reveal them. Let me relate an example: My students and I built a planner, called Phoenix, which maintains several internal representations of time. One of these representations is a variable called "time-in-seconds." In actuality, this variable stored the elapsed time in minutes, not seconds, because of a programmer's error. The planner worked fine—meaning the error wasn't obvious to anyone—even though some of its estimates were wrong by a factor of sixty. This was due in part to Phoenix's failure-recovery abilities: The error would cause a plan to fail, and Phoenix would fix it. Only when we looked at statistical patterns in the execution traces of failure recovery did we discover the error. Relating structure to behavior can no longer be done with the naked eye.

Another belief I no longer have is that each new program is an experiment that poses a question to nature. Too often I ask, What is the question?, and receive no answer. Paraphrasing David Etherington, researchers are adept at saying what they are *doing*, much less so at saying what they are *learning*. Even so, the program-as-experiment view has been influential and reiterated often, recently by Lenat and Feigenbaum (1987, p. 1177).

Compared to Nature we suffer from a poverty of the imagination; it is thus much easier for us to uncover than to invent. Premature mathematization keeps Nature's surprises hidden. . . . This attitude leads to our central methodological hypothesis, our paradigm for AI research:

Empirical Inquiry Hypothesis: Intelligence is still so poorly understood that Nature still holds most of the important surprises in store for us. So the most profitable way to investigate AI is to embody our hypotheses in programs, and gather data by running the programs. The surprises usually suggest revisions that start the cycle over again. Progress depends on these experiments being able to falsify our hypotheses; i.e., these programs must be capable of behavior not expected by the experimenter.

The empirical inquiry hypothesis is just that—a hypothesis. I want it to be true, but the evidence isn't encouraging. For example, when I surveyed 150 papers in the *Proceedings of the Eighth National Conference on Artificial Intelligence* (1990), I discovered that only 42 percent of the papers suggested a program had run on more than one example; just 30 percent demonstrated performance in some way; a mere 21 percent framed hypotheses or made predictions. Almost nobody "embodies hypotheses in programs," or "gathers data by running the programs." As to Nature and her surprises, very few papers reported negative or unexpected results.

Programs are not experiments, but rather, the laboratory in which experiments are conducted. Questions to nature are answered in the laboratory; building the laboratory and running a few things through it does not suffice. The empirical inquiry hypothesis can be true, but first we have to give up the idea that running a program is somehow so irresistible to Nature that she will drop her veils.

Which brings me to another belief I no longer have. I used to think experimental work would never add up to much because each experiment answers a single yes-or-no question, and it would take too long to understand anything this way. I was much influenced, as many were, by Allen Newell's "Twenty Questions" argument, which he addressed to a gathering of psychologists:

I was going to draw a line on the blackboard and, picking one of the speakers of the day at random, note on the line when he got his PhD and the current time (in mid-career). Then, taking his total production of papers like those in the present symposium, I was going to compute a rate of productivity of such excellent work. Moving, finally, to the date of my chosen target's retirement, I was going to compute the total future addition of such papers to the (putative) end of this man's scientific career. Then I was going to pose, in my role as a discussant, a question: Suppose you had all these additional papers . . . where will psychology then be? Will we have achieved a science of man adequate in power and commensurate with his complexity? And if so, how will this have happened via these papers I have just granted you? Or will we be asking for yet another quota of papers in the next dollop of time? (Newell, 1973, pp. 283–284)

If this line of argument applies equally well to artificial intelligence, then we should not rely unduly on the experiment as our engine of progress. But I don't think it necessarily applies to AI, or to psychology for that matter. First, the Twenty Questions argument, as its name implies, is directed to a particular class of empirical methods: statistical testing of mutually exclusive pairs of hypotheses—is system A equal to system B, yes or no? Does learning improve performance, yes or no? There is a place for hypothesis-testing in empirical AI (and two chapters of this book are devoted to it), but there is room for much more besides. Moreover, the Twenty Questions argument, by focusing on productivity in terms of research papers, obscures an essential distinction between the question you ask in an experiment and the question that motivated you to do the experiment. For example, among the psychologists at Newell's symposium were Lynn Cooper and Roger Shepard (1973), who presented data demonstrating that humans cannot mentally rotate images in constant time. The research question behind the experiment was whether humans code images in propositional or analog representations. Now, I agree that answering twenty experimental questions about mental rotation rates seems a modest contribution, but answering twenty research questions about how humans represent information is pretty good work. We need not fear the Twenty Questions argument if our studies are conducted to provide evidence about broader research questions.

I used to believe that these research questions ought to be precise, but now I see some fundamental advantages to including ill-defined terms in research questions, theories, and results. Here's one for illustrative purposes: *graceful degradation*. It means, roughly, that performance doesn't crash catastrophically when the going gets tough. In the early 1970s, Don Norman and Danny Bobrow formulated a theory of graceful degradation:

The principle of continually available output is a simple explanation of how increased use of computational resources can be reflected in performance. If a process using a fixed strategy did not provide an output until it was finished, then increasing resources would simply shorten the time required to get some output. But, if the process continually makes available its preliminary results, higher level processes can continually be making use of them. As increased resources allow the process to upgrade the quality of its output, the improvement can immediately be used by any other processes for which the output is relevant. In a similar fashion, processing overloads do not cause calamitous failure, but simply a decrease in performance. (Norman and Bobrow, 1974, p. 5)

In other words, performance will degrade (and improve) gracefully if processes make intermediate results available continuously, rather than waiting until they are "done." To my ear, this sounds like an early description of what we now call *anytime algorithms*. Indeed, the principle of continuously available output is the defining characteristic of anytime algorithms. But if we define anytime algorithms (or graceful degradation) any *more* precisely, we risk formulating theories that are less general than they could be. Norman and Bobrow (1974) believed their explanation of graceful degradation applied to "human information processing in general, and the lack of calamitous failure is one of the major distinctions between human performance and that of current artificial mechanisms." Today they might agree that anytime algorithms erase the distinction; they might formulate a general theory—graceful degradation requires continuously available output—and they might augment their psychological evidence for this theory with evidence from AI. All this is possible if graceful degradation and continuously available output are not too carefully defined. Distinctions are important, the scopes of theories must be bounded eventually, and formal theorems might one day take the place of imprecise theories; but too much precision too soon is not a good thing.

In sum, this book assumes some things about our science: We cannot explain the behavior of a program just by opening it up and perusing its structure; running a program does not constitute an experiment, programs are part of the laboratory apparatus with which we answer questions; experimental questions provide evidence about research questions, and experimental questions that aren't motivated by research questions are generally dull; research questions and theories will inevitably contain ill-defined terms if they are to have any generality. Finally, the formulation of general theories relating program behavior to architecture, tasks, and environments is our goal. Now, let's look in the toolbox.

Acknowledgments

It would have been impossible for me to write a book about empirical artificial intelligence if my colleagues were not willing to do this kind of research. Thus, my first debt is to the members of my research group. David Hart, who manages our lab, has been a resourceful ally and an insightful colleague from the start. Adele Howe, Scott Anderson, Marc Atkin, Robert St. Amant, Dawn Gregory, Tim Oates, and Lisa Ballesteros have worked with me to develop methods and tools. David Westbrook, Adam Carlson, Scott Anderson, and Matthew Schmill developed the CLIP/CLASP instrumentation and analysis package, which is distributed with this book. I am also very grateful to Victor Lesser for his continual encouragement, and to Keith Decker, Alan Garvey, Bob Whitehair, and other members of Victor's research group.

Bruce Porter, of the University of Texas at Austin, has shaped my thinking about empirical AI from the start. We organized a workshop together and we gave two tutorials on methodology at the National Conference on Artificial Intelligence. The workshop was supported by Helen Gigley at the National Science Foundation and Steve Cross at the Defense Advanced Research Projects Agency (DARPA). Since then, DARPA and Rome Laboratory, represented by Steve Cross, Northrup Fowler, and Lou Hoebel, have supported my research and provided impetus and encouragement for the development of empirical methods.

I thank William Gale, John Laird, Pat Langley, Elaine Rich, Glenn Shafer, and Mark Stefik for insightful, often challenging comments on early drafts of the book. The anonymity of other reviewers prevents me thanking them by name, but I am no less grateful for their efforts. I have a special debt to Dana Nau, at the University of Maryland, who taught a seminar from a draft of this book and provided me with detailed comments and suggestions.

Mike Sutherland, who directs the Statistical Consulting Center at the University of Massachusetts, served as a technical consultant for the book. Mike checked the math and helped with formalism, of course, but his greatest contribution was to help me understand applied statistics much better than I did when I started this book.

Several colleagues cheerfully sent me data to use in case studies. I thank Liane Acker and Bruce Porter, Wendy Lehnert and Joe McCarthy, Adele Howe, Ellen Riloff, David Aha, John Allen, Pat Langley, Stan Matwin, Anthony Barrett, Steve Hanks, and Dan Weld.

I thank Harold Cohen, author of the AARON program, for permission to reproduce the image in Chapter 9. A painting by AARON and Harold, which is reproduced on the cover, is from the collection of Robert and Deborah Hendel. I am grateful to them for allowing this painting, entitled "Meryl," to enliven my book.

Cynthia Loiselle made it possible to produce this book electronically. She defined the file structures, style macros, figure and table conventions, and countless other mechanisms with which we produced drafts of the book for courses, tutorials, and editing. She also translated the book from one format to another, provided a liaison to The MIT Press production staff, and gave insightful editorial advice. Peggy Weston helped me to construct the book's index and bibliography and has assisted me with a keen eye throughout the project. Matthew Schmill helped with the figures. David Westbrook wrote a program to make it easy to identify and insert index items.

When you start thinking about a book, it's good to talk to an enthusiastic publisher. Harry Stanton understood the purpose of the book immediately and signed me to Bradford Books/MIT Press. Teri Mendelsohn has advised me during production. I am especially grateful to Melissa Vaughn for dealing so flexibly with an electronic document in a world that relies on paper.

Three years ago Carole Beal urged me to start this book; today, with characteristic pragmatism, she told me to wrap it up. In the interim she gave me her intellect and scholarship, a lot of good ideas, and her unflagging encouragement. I dedicate this book as I dedicated myself, solely and always, to Carole Ruth Beal.

1   Empirical Research

Physicists ask what kind of place this universe is and seek to characterize its behavior systematically. Biologists ask what it means for a physical system to be living. We in AI wonder what kind of information-processing system can ask such questions.
—Avron B. Barr and Edward A. Feigenbaum, *The Handbook of Artificial Intelligence*,
Vol. 1, p. 11

Empirical methods enhance our observations and help us see more of the structure of the world. We are fundamentally empirical creatures, always asking, What is going on? Is it real or merely apparent? What causes it? Is there a better explanation? Great developments were born of microscopes, telescopes, stethoscopes, and other observational tools. No less important are "datascopes"—visualization methods—and techniques for drawing sound conclusions from data. Empirical methods cluster loosely into *exploratory* techniques for visualization, summarization, exploration, and modeling; and *confirmatory* procedures for testing hypotheses and predictions. In short,

empirical = exploratory + experimental.

Because empirical studies usually observe nondeterministic phenomena, which exhibit variability, both exploratory and experimental methods are based in statistics. Exploratory statistical methods are called, collectively, *exploratory data analysis*; whereas methods for confirmatory experiments go by the name *statistical hypothesis testing*. You can find any number of textbooks on the latter, very few devoted to the former. You might get the impression from these books and from scientific journals that *all* empirical work involves controlled experiments and hypothesis testing. But experiments don't spring like Athena fully formed from the brow of Zeus: They are painstakingly constructed by mortals who usually get it wrong first time, who require lengthy periods of exploration before formulating a precise experimental question, yet find themselves still amazed at Nature's ability to confound.

Even if experiments were easy, you should take a more encompassing view of empirical work for one reason if no other: experiments and hypothesis testing answer yes-or-no questions. You can reduce all your research interests to a series of yes-or-no questions, but you'll find it slow work. A more efficient approach is to flip back and forth between exploratory and experimental work, engaging in the latter only when the former produces a question you really want to answer.

Empirical methods and statistics are worth learning because a handful of each goes a long way. Psychologists, for example, know perhaps ten major statistical methods and a similar number of techniques for visualizing and exploring data; and they know perhaps two dozen important experiment designs.[1] With these methods they address thousands of research questions. We are AI researchers, not psychologists, but we too can expect a few appropriate methods to go a long way.

The American Heritage Dictionary[2] defines empirical and empiricism as follows:

Empirical   (1) Relying upon or derived from observation or experiment: empirical methods. (2) Relying solely on practical experience and without regard for system or theory.

Empiricism   (1) The view that experience, esp. of the senses, is the only source of knowledge. (2) The employment of empirical methods, as in science.

In this book, you should read empirical in its first sense and empiricism in its second sense. The other interpretations are too exclusive (Cohen, 1991). Down with empiricism (in its first sense); down with the equally exclusive view that theory is the only source of knowledge. Up with empirical studies informed by theories and theories informed by observations.

1.1   AI Programs as Objects of Empirical Studies

Our subject is empirical methods for studying AI programs, methods that involve running programs and recording their behaviors. Unlike other scientists, who study chemical reactions, processes in cells, bridges under stress, animals in mazes, and so on, we study computer programs that perform tasks in environments. It shouldn't be

---

1. I get these numbers from textbooks on statistics for psychologists and from books on experiment design such as Cook and Campbell 1979 and articles such as Bower and Clapper 1990 and Newell 1973.

2. *American Heritage Dictionary of the English Language*, American Heritage Publishing Co. Inc. and Houghton Mifflin Company, 1971.

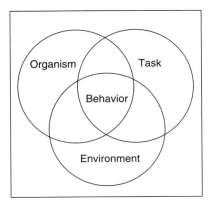

Figure 1.1   How the structure, task, and environment of an organism influence its behavior.

difficult: Compared with biological systems, AI systems are simple; compared with human cognition, their tasks are rudimentary; and compared with everyday physical environments, those in which our programs operate are extremely reduced. Yet programs are in many ways like chemical, biological, mechanical, and psychological processes. For starters, we don't know how they work. We generally cannot say how long they will take to run, when they will fail, how much knowledge is required to attain a particular error rate, how many nodes of a search tree must be examined, and so on. It is but a comforting fiction that building a program confers much understanding of its behavior. Predictive theories of program behavior are thin on the ground and no better than predictive theories of chemical, biological, mechanical, and psychological processes: at best incomplete and approximate, at worst vague or wrong.

Studying AI systems is not very different from studying moderately intelligent animals such as rats. One obliges the agent (rat or program) to perform a task according to an experimental protocol, observing and analyzing the macro- and micro-structure of its behavior. Afterward, if the subject is a rat, its head is opened up or chopped off; and if it is a program, its innards are fiddled with. Six components are common to these scenarios: agent, task, environment, protocol, data collection, and analysis. The first three are the domain of theories of behavior, the last three are in the realm of empirical methods. Behavior is what we observe and measure when an agent attempts a task in an environment. As figure 1.1 suggests, an agent's behavior is not due entirely to its structure, nor its environment, nor its task, but rather to the interaction of these influences.

Whether your subject is a rat or a computer program, the task of science is the same, to provide theories to answer three *basic research questions*:

■ How will a change in the agent's structure affect its behavior given a task and an environment?

■ How will a change in an agent's task affect its behavior in a particular environment?

■ How will a change in an agent's environment affect its behavior on a particular task?

1.2   Three Basic Research Questions

The three basic research questions all have the same form, so let's pick one to examine: How will a change in the agent's structure affect its behavior given a task and an environment? Bill Clancey and Greg Cooper asked such a question of the MYCIN system some years ago (Buchanan and Shortliffe, 1984, p. 219). They asked, how sensitive is MYCIN to the accuracy of its certainty factors? What will happen if each certainty factor, very precisely represented on the scale $-1000 \ldots 1000$, is replaced by the nearest of just seven values ($-1000, -666, -333, 0, 333, 666, 1000$)? When Clancey and Cooper ran the modified and unmodified versions of MYCIN and compared the answers, they found essentially no decrement in the adequacy of MYCIN's recommendations (see chapter 6 for details).

Clancey and Cooper's question was exploratory; their answer was descriptive. They asked, "What will happen if . . .?"; they answered with a description of MYCIN's performance. Question and answer belong in the lower left-hand corner of figure 1.2, the dimensions of which—understanding and generality—define a space of versions of the basic research questions and answers. Early in a research project we ask, "What will happen if . . .?" and answer, "Here's what happens. . . ." Later, we ask, "Does this model accurately predict what happens?" and "Does this model provide an accurate causal explanation of what happens?" Early in a project we ask short questions that often have lengthy descriptions of behavior as answers; later, the questions are lengthy because they refer to predictive and causal models, but the answers are short, often just "yes" or "no." This shift in balance characterizes progress from exploratory studies to experimental studies.

The progression is called "understanding" in figure 1.2 because descriptions—the low end of the dimension—require no understanding (you can describe leaves turning color in autumn without understanding the process); whereas prediction requires at least an understanding of the conditions under which behavior occurs (leaves turn color in the autumn, or when the tree is diseased, and turn more reliably after a period of intensely cold weather). In practice, the transition from description to prediction depends on identifying terms in the description that appear to have predictive power.

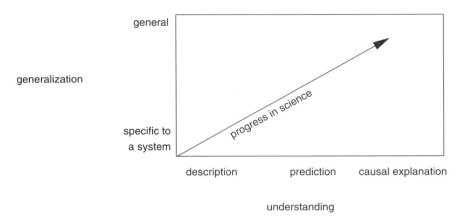

Figure 1.2   Generalization and understanding define a space of basic research questions.

This often involves a succession of descriptions: "leaves turn color in October," then, identifying a predictive feature, "leaves turn color when the weather turns cold." An important role of exploratory studies is to identify predictive features. What we aim for as scientists, however, is causal explanation: leaves turn color because chlorophyll, which masks other pigments, disappears. And not only causal explanations, but *general* causal explanations—why the leaves of aspen, maple, sumac, and oak (but not pine) change color in the autumn.

1.3   A Strategy for Answering Basic Research Questions

Clancey and Cooper did, in fact, offer a post hoc, informal causal explanation of their results. MYCIN's task was to prescribe therapy for all the organisms likely to have caused one or more infections. Inaccuracies in certainty factors affected MYCIN's judgments about the likelihood of organisms, but because most antibiotics kill many sorts of organisms, the chances are good that MYCIN will recommend an effective antibiotic even if it judges the likelihood of each organism incorrectly. Clancey and Cooper didn't generalize this explanation beyond MYCIN, but we can imagine how they might have done it. Here is a generalization in terms of features of a program's structure, task, environment, and behavior:

Suppose a program's task is to select actions to "cover" sets of situations. An instance of the task is a set S of situations. A feature of the environment is that during problem-solving, S doesn't change. A feature of the task is that it provides too little information for the program *to be certain whether a hypothesized situation h_i is in S. Another task feature is that S is relatively small. A feature of the program is that it can judge $Pr(h_i \in S)$, the likelihood that h_i is in S. Another program feature is that it can decide to cover only some h's (e.g., likely ones). The program selects actions to cover these. The actions have the interesting property that each deals with several h's. The only behavior of interest is whether the program selects "good" actions. A generalization of Clancey and Cooper's result is this: The program's behavior is robust against inaccurate estimates of $Pr(h_i \in S)$.*

The point of this long-winded exercise is to illustrate a central conjecture: General theories in artificial intelligence arise from *featural characterizations* of programs, their environments, tasks, and behaviors. Progress toward general theories depends on finding these features. Empirical methods, in particular, help us find general features by studying specific programs. The *empirical generalization strategy*, around which this book is organized, goes like this:

1. build a program that exhibits a behavior of interest while performing particular tasks in particular environments;

2. identify specific features of the program, its tasks and environments that influence the target behavior;

3. develop and test a causal model of how these features influence the target behavior;

4. once the model makes accurate predictions, generalize the features so that other programs, tasks, and environments are encompassed by the causal model;

5. test whether the general model predicts accurately the behavior of this larger set of programs, tasks, and environments.

Chapter 2 on exploratory data analysis addresses step 2. Chapters 3, 4, and 5, on experiment design and hypothesis testing address the testing part of steps 3 and 5. Chapters 6, 7, and 8, address the model formation parts of step 3. Chapter 9, on generalization, addresses step 4.

1.4 Kinds of Empirical Studies

Many researchers in artificial intelligence and computer science speak casually of experiments, as if any activity that involves building and running a program is experimental. This is confusing. I once flew across the country to attend a workshop on "experimental computer science," only to discover this phrase is shorthand for nonexperimental, indeed, nonempirical research on operating systems and compilers. We can distinguish four classes of empirical studies:

Exploratory studies   yield causal hypotheses that are tested in observation or manipulation experiments. To this end, exploratory studies usually collect lots of data, analyzing it in many ways to find regularities.

Assessment studies   establish baselines and ranges, and other assessments of the behaviors of a system or its environment.

Manipulation experiments   test hypotheses about causal influences of factors by manipulating them and noting effects, if any, on one or more measured variables.

Observation experiments   disclose effects of factors on measured variables by observing associations between levels of the factors and values of the variables. These are also called *natural* and *quasi-experimental* experiments.

Manipulation and observation experiments are what most people regard as proper experiments, while exploratory and assessment studies seem informal, aimless, heuristic, and hopeful. Testing hypotheses has the panache of "real science," whereas exploration seems like fishing and assessment seems plain dull. In fact, these activities are complementary; one is not more scientific than another; a research project will involve them all. Indeed, these activities might just as well be considered phases of a research project as individual studies.

The logic of assessment and exploratory studies is different from that of manipulation and observation experiments. The latter are *confirmatory*—you test explicit, precise hypotheses about the effects of factors. Exploratory and assessment studies suggest hypotheses and help to design experiments. These differences are reflected in methods and conventions for analyzing data. Manipulation experiments are analyzed with the tools of statistical hypothesis testing: *t* tests, analysis of variance, and so on. Results are outcomes that are very unlikely to have occurred by chance. Hypothesis testing is also applied to some observation experiments, but so are other forms of analysis. For example, it's common to summarize the data from an observation experiment in a regression model of the form

$$y = w_1 x_1 + w_2 x_2 + \ldots w_k x_k + C,$$

where y is called the response variable and $x_1 \ldots x_k$ are predictor variables. Typically, we'll appraise how well or poorly the regression model predicts y, but this is less a conclusion, in the hypothesis-testing sense, than an assessment of whether $x_1 \ldots x_k$ explain y. Not surprisingly, there are fewer conventions to tell you whether a regression model is acceptable. Obviously, a model that accounts for much of the variance in y is preferred to one that doesn't, all other things equal, but nobody will insist that predictive power must exceed some threshold, as we conventionally insist

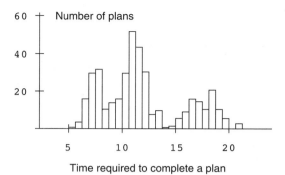

Figure 1.3   A frequency distribution.

that a result in hypothesis testing must have no more than a one-in-twenty chance of being wrong.

Data analysis for exploratory and assessment studies is freer still of conventions and definitions of significance. The purpose of these studies is to find suggestive patterns in data. For example, what does the distribution in figure 1.3 suggest to you? Suppose the horizontal axis represents the time required to complete a plan in a simulated environment and the heights of the bars represent the number of plans that required a particular amount of time: roughly thirty plans required 7.5 time units, more than fifty plans required 11 time units, and at least twenty plans required 18 time units to finish. These three peaks, or modes, suggest we are collecting data in three rather different conditions. Are we seeing the effects of three types of simulated weather? Three kinds of plans? Three different operating systems? Or perhaps there are just two conditions, not three, and the first "dip" in the histogram represents a sampling error. Are the modes equally spaced, or increasingly separated, suggesting a nonlinear relationship between conditions and time requirements? Why are more plans found in the second "hump" than in the first? Is it a sampling bias? Do fewer plans fail in this condition? These questions are representative of exploratory studies. They are answered by exploratory data analysis, which includes arranging and partitioning data, drawing pictures, dropping data that seem to obscure patterns, doing everything possible to discover and amplify regularities.

The strict standards of statistical hypothesis testing have no place here. Exploratory data analysis finds things in haystacks (data are rarely as clear as figure 1.3), whereas statistical hypothesis testing puts them under a microscope and tells us whether they are needles and whether they are sharp.

1.5   A Prospective View of Empirical Artificial Intelligence

A year or two before I started writing this book, I had the opportunity to sketch a vignette of artificial intelligence ten or twenty years hence. The following images stuck with me as I wrote the book, and will serve as a statement of purpose, or a destination.

Megan is an agent engineer, which means, as everybody knows, that she designs and builds agents. Agent engineers are in the news a lot because agents are increasingly responsible for the world infrastructure. As you can imagine, we hear about agents primarily when they fail. Just last week, an air-traffic agent failed and two airplanes collided on the runway. Other agent errors include a crash on the Fijian stock exchange, caused by an unanticipated partnership of trading agents; a billing problem involving all 19 million subscribers to the Los Angeles public library; and the tragic demise of two hundred BART passengers under the San Francisco Bay, caused by the incorrect reaction of a train-driver agent during an earthquake.

Megan works for Agent Failure Analysis Associates, and her job is to figure out why agents fail. Actually, they don't fail all that often. Some Luddites maintain that they are both dangerous and immoral, but most people acknowledge the essential role they play in today's increasingly interdependent world. For example, agents control the freeways, permitting a tenfold increase in capacity. Delays are newsworthy because they are so rare. Not everyone will read this news, of course, because their personal agents filter it from the newswires. This is a pretty harmless use of filtering but lately there has been concern that the public at large is permitting their agents to filter too much, so the principal of an informed populace that underlies our democracy is in jeopardy. The practice of having one's personal agent vote for one is a common concern among liberal intellectuals, although a recent spot-check found that liberal intellectuals are slightly more likely to engage in this practice than other segments of society (some things never change). Whatever the social costs of agents, there can be no doubt that energy management, transportation, and information management would be crippled without our sophisticated networks of agents. Which is why Megan's job is a desirable one by any standards.

Megan was educated at the prestigious Amherst Center for Human Agent Interaction. Life at the Center was extraordinarily exciting, if taxing. Classes in the first year included agent psychology, fundamentals of agent design, human-agent social theory, statistics, and experiment design, and, because she was particularly broadminded, she audited a class on agent ethics offered by the philosophy department. In her second year, Megan began to specialize in agent pathology. Megan graduated with honors about five years ago, and took her position with Agent Failure Analysis Associates. Her current assignment is to figure out why a video distribution agent has been sending subtly disturbing movies to the Amherst Rest Home.

Now let us ask how can get from where we are today to the era of Megan's education and professional development. The curriculum at the Amherst Center provides a convenient focus: What will the textbooks and the professors teach? Any answer is a challenge to us, because it is we who will make the discoveries and develop the tools that will eventually be filtered, organized and codified in Megan's textbooks. Some trends seem certain. Intelligent agents will become larger and more complex, they will learn much of what they know, they will interact with increasingly challenging environments, and they will work with other agents and humans.

By what methods will we study and develop intelligent agents? Today we find ourselves a bit short. We can say a program works, but we often don't know how to determine whether it works well or poorly, or whether it will work in different conditions. We can say a program works better than another, but we usually can't attribute the difference in performance to aspects of the programs' designs, or distinguish the influence of design differences from the influence of tasks, or detect interactions among tasks and designs. We can prove that a task is intractable, but we often can't say analytically or even empirically how difficult it is on average.

It is easy to imagine Megan's education and professional work are assisted by agents from earlier generations, as we are assisted by application programs incorporating earlier AI technology. Looking forward, we see programs that take on some of the responsibilities of human data analysts. Looking back, Megan might recognize these as the ancestors of her automated assistants. Today these programs induce regularities—even laws—from physical and biological data; in the future they should induce regularities and laws from data generated by AI systems. As an example, consider a program developed by Adele Howe (Howe, 1992) for what she calls failure recovery analysis (which I will call "agent diagnosis"). Howe's program analyzes execution traces of a planner called Phoenix, whose plans fail and are repaired during execution. Execution traces are just sequential records of failures and how they are fixed. Howe's program finds statistical anomalies in execution traces, patterns that suggest causal dependencies between failures and earlier repairs. These dependencies trigger diagnoses such as, "When part of a plan was repaired by changing the value of a shared variable, another part went unmodified, so the two parts had different expectations, which led to a failure due to inconsistent expectations." Currently, Howe's program finds dependencies by itself (see section 7.6) but she must help it generate explanations. In the near future, however, we will see an agent autonomously detect and diagnose pathological behavior in the Phoenix planner. It will be an agent diagnostician in both senses: a diagnostician of agents and an agent itself. This book is intended to provide some background knowledge for the task of building such agents.

2   Exploratory Data Analysis

A crude but useful distinction can be made between confirmatory experiments and exploratory studies. When experiments are reported in journals and proceedings, one gets the impression that the authors started with a clear question and breezed through the experiment to answer it. In reality, however, confirmatory experiments are the product of a sometimes lengthy process in which vague questions are refined to precise ones and pilot experiments that produce murky data are refined to produce crisp results. Exploratory studies, then, are the informal prelude to experiments. Exploratory studies are like working in a test kitchen whereas experiments are like recipes in cook books. One seeks an efficient, unambiguous procedure that others can follow to produce a distinctive result, but to get it one often must explore alternative procedures. Moreover, goals change: An idea for a sauce becomes a recipe for a soup, an exploration of why a robot bumps into walls becomes a predictive model of the conditions under which the robot is unable to attend to sensory interrupts. Exploratory studies start with a research question, an unexpected phenomenon, or simple curiosity about how a system will behave in particular conditions. They sometimes end with the realization that the question or phenomenon isn't worth continued study. Ideally, though, exploratory studies lead to confirmatory studies.

This chapter and the next discuss exploratory and confirmatory studies, respectively. The chapters are ordered this way to give a rough sense of what it is like to develop an unrefined idea into a polished, convincing result. I begin by discussing data—classes of data, transformations of data, and the fundamental idea that data represent reality. Then I describe ways to visualize and summarize univariate and joint distributions of data. The focus of the chapter, however, is techniques for finding patterns in data, specifically, hypothetical causal relationships between factors that eventually will be tested in experiments.

2.1 Data

The act that defines a project as *empirical* artificial intelligence is running a program and collecting data. The data might be execution traces, the percentage of correct answers, the time to complete a task, the trees generated by a search process, the number of times a process is interrupted, the frequency with which a piece of knowledge is used, or the difference between the program's answer and a human judge's answer. Data are sometimes collected while the program is running (e.g., execution traces) and sometimes are collected after the program has finished (e.g., the percentage of correct answers). In most experiments a program will be run more than once, and something will be slightly different on each trial. For example, the program might be given ten slightly different problems to solve.

Colloquially, a sample is just a collection of individuals, for instance, a collection of colleagues, brands of beer, or runs of a program. For the purpose of data analysis, however, a sample is a collection of measurements on individuals: hair color for a sample of five colleagues, or quality ratings of a sample of 20 imported beers, or the times required by a program to solve some problems. It is common to make many measurements of each member of a sample. For an individual run of a program you might measure run time, whether the answer was correct, how many times particular pieces of knowledge were used, and so on.

A measurement is associated with an individual—my hair color, or your height, or the run time of a particular version of a program. We also speak of hair color, height and run time as abstract entities called variables. In fact, hair color and run time are not variables, they are functions that map from individuals to data scales: run time (Version 1.0) = 3 seconds. Although I use the common terminology, it is important to remember that variable names denote functions that create representations of individuals. When credit-card companies collect information about you and me—credit rating, occupation, marital status, age, and so on—they are creating representations. The process is illustrated in figure 2.1. The vaguely round, lumpy object represents an individual named paul cohen. Rectangles represent factors, which are abstract characteristics of individuals. Variables, represented by circles, produce measurements of factors. For example, paul cohen is in dubious physical condition but is fortunate to enjoy a reasonable standard of living, as indicated by the variables height and weight, and income and occupation. (The introduction of factors seems to cloud the otherwise clear picture of variables as functions from individuals to values. Factors become important when we need to explain why particular combinations of values of variables, such as height and weight, are common.)

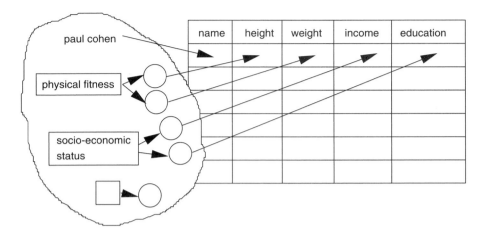

Figure 2.1 Viewing variables as functions that generate representations.

The previous example suggests that data can be organized in a data table in which columns are variable names and rows represent individuals. An example of a data table is shown in table 2.1, which represents thirty runs of an AI system that fights simulated forest fires. The system is called Phoenix (Cohen, Greenberg, Hart and Howe, 1989) and comprises a planner, called the fireboss, and a handful of simulated firefighters driving bulldozers; and the Phoenix environment, which is a simulation of fires in Yellowstone National Park. Every trial in the experiment involved setting one fire at the same location and letting the fireboss and firefighters try to contain it. The wind speed was fixed during a trial at one of three levels: high, medium, or low. A parameter called *RTK* determined how fast the environment could change relative to the speed at which the fireboss could think (*RTK* is described in more detail later). At the beginning of a trial, the fireboss picked a plan (*FirstPlan*) but sometimes this plan failed and another was selected. The variable *NumPlans* records how many plans had to be tried. At the end of a trial, the experiment recorded how much fireline was built by the bulldozers (*FirelineBuilt*), how much acreage was lost to fire (*AreaBurned*), whether the fire was successfully contained (*Outcome*), and how many simulated hours were required to contain the fire (*FinishTime*). Note that a successful outcome means that the fire is contained in less than 150 hours.

A column in a data table, such as the *FinishTime* column in table 2.1, is a distribution of values of one variable, also called a univariate distribution. One can also construct joint distributions of the values of two or more variables, to determine whether there is any relationship between, say, the amount of fireline built and finish time. A joint

Table 2.1   Data for thirty runs of the Phoenix system.

Trial	Wind Speed	RTK	First Plan	Num Plans	Fireline Built	Area Burned	Finish Time	Outcome
1	high	5	model	1	27056	23.81	27.8	success
2	high	1.67	shell	1	14537	9.6	20.82	success
3	high	1.00	mbia	3	0	42.21	150	failure
4	high	0.71	model	1	27055	40.21	44.12	success
5	high	0.56	shell	8	0	141.05	150	failure
6	high	0.45	model	3	0	82.48	150	failure
7	high	5	model	1	27056	25.82	29.41	success
8	high	1.67	model	1	27054	27.74	31.19	success
9	high	5	model	1	27056	24.92	28.68	success
10	high	1.67	mbia	1	21180	22.72	29.53	success
11	high	1.00	model	1	27056	31.28	34.62	success
12	high	0.71	mbia	3	0	81.74	150	failure
13	high	5	model	1	27056	23.92	27.86	success
14	high	1.67	shell	6	53336	84.43	117.57	success
15	high	1.00	shell	12	0	144.24	150	failure
16	high	5	shell	1	13956	9.39	18.52	success
17	medium	0.71	model	1	0	63.86	150	failure
18	medium	0.56	mbia	7	0	68.39	150	failure
19	medium	0.45	mbia	5	0	55.12	150	failure
20	medium	0.71	model	1	0	13.48	150	failure
21	medium	0.56	shell	4	42286	10.9	75.62	success
22	low	0.71	model	1	11129	5.34	20.69	success
23	low	0.71	shell	1	0	49.1	150	failure
24	low	0.71	shell	3	25288	4.03	51.54	success
25	low	0.71	mbia	2	0	37.01	150	failure
26	low	0.71	shell	2	19932	4.95	46.64	success
27	low	0.71	mbia	2	0	6.41	150	failure
28	low	0.71	mbia	2	24343	6.46	42.31	success
29	low	0.71	model	2	23059	6.06	55.82	success
30	medium	0.71	model	1	0	13.48	150	failure

distribution that includes a categorical variable or a variable with few values is called a partition; for example, the joint distribution of *FinishTime* and *WindSpeed* in table 2.1 is really three smaller distributions of *FinishTime*, one for each value of *WindSpeed*.

In sum, a data table represents a sample of individuals. Whereas psychologists and biologists usually populate samples with individual humans or mice, our samples usually comprise multiple runs of a system. Each row in a data table represents a single trial, each column represents a measurement. Measurements have distributions, and pairs or -tuples of measurements have joint distributions.

2.1.1   Scales of Data

Measurements are not all of the same kind; in particular, we can distinguish three common data scales:

Categorical Scale   Here, the measurement process assigns a category label to an individual. For example, the Phoenix planner either successfully contains a fire (*Outcome = succeed*) or does not (*Outcome = fail*). Categorical data are sometimes called nominal data when the value of a datum is a name.

Ordinal Scale   Ordinal data can be ranked, but no arithmetic transformations are meaningful. For example, the wind speeds in table 2.1 are ranked high, medium, and low, but we would not say that the difference between high and medium wind speed is equal to (or any arithmetic transformation of) the difference between a medium and low wind speed. In short, the distances between points on an ordinal scale are not meaningful.

Interval and Ratio Scales   The distances between data measured on an interval scale are meaningful; for example, we can compare differences in the amount of fireline built by bulldozers. Many data are measured on a ratio scale, in which case ratios among the data are also meaningful; for example, we can say one trial took half as long as another to contain a fire. A condition for ratio scales is that we know the zero point; for example, the melting point of glass is roughly 1.4 times as high as the melting point of silver, relative to zero degrees Fahrenheit, but roughly 1.3 times as high relative to zero degrees Kelvin.

Statistical analysis methods have been developed for all these kinds of data. Methods for categorical data are based on the distributions of individuals across categories, whereas methods for ordinal data are based on distributions of ranks, and methods for interval data and ratio data are based on distributions of real numbers. For convenience we often analyze one class of data as if it is another class. For example, wind speed is recorded as an ordinal variable (high, medium, and low) in table 2.1, when, in fact, the actual wind speed parameter in the Phoenix simulation takes ratio scale values such as 3 kilometers per hour.

2.1.2 Transforming Data

One can transform interval and ratio data into ordinal data, and ordinal data into categorical data. One way to effect the former transformation is to sort a distribution and replace each datum by its rank; for example, if the data are:

45   1   7   126   22   3   5   19

the sorted, ranked data are:

Sorted	1	3	5	7	19	22	45	126
Ranked	1	2	3	4	5	6	7	8

and the transformed data, that is, the ranks, are

7   1   4   8   6   2   3   5.

This transformation loses information, but it sometimes facilitates analysis. For example, developmental psychologists typically transform the chronological ages of children into ordinal values and then analyze the behaviors of children in age groups. The ordinal nature of the groups is preserved—all kids in one group are older than all those in another—but the age relationships within a group are ignored.

Analysts transform data in many ways, for many purposes; for example, logarithms of data are sometimes used to "spread out" a distribution that has many low values and few high values, and data collected over time are often "smoothed" with a moving-average transformation (see sections 8.3 and 2.5.2). When you play around with data, you might find a sequence of transformations that makes a pattern emerge, but leaves the queasy feeling that the data no longer represent reality. This is a visceral manifestation of the problems addressed by *measurement theory*.

2.1.3 Measurement Theory

Keep in mind that data represent reality, and relationships among data should somehow correspond to relationships in reality. In measurement theory, this is called the *representation problem*. Consider four people with the following heights:

Person	A	B	C	D
Height	72"	60"	68"	76"

Let's say "inches" is an interval scale, so differences are meaningful. If C stands on a block of wood that elevates her to the same height as D, then, because inches is an interval scale, we can determine the height of the block of wood by subtracting the height of C from the height of D. Moreover, we can infer that if B stands on the same block of wood, he will be as tall as C. We have established a representation of the world that permits us to make valid inferences about the world. But now let's transform our representation by ranking the heights:

Person	A	B	C	D
Height	2	4	3	1

This representation no longer captures one of the important relationships in the world, namely, the difference in heights. Inferences about these relationships are not guaranteed to be valid. For example, we *could* infer that the height difference between B and A is the same as the difference between C and D, but we would be wrong. Don't be fooled by the simplicity of the example; one must always ask whether transformations of data lead to incorrect inferences about reality.

Measurement theory is concerned with, among other things, which inferences about data are "protected" by particular data transformations. (See Coombs et al., 1970, and Suppes and Zinnes, 1963, for introductions to the topic.) We know for example that ordinal values are protected by any monotonic transformation, such as a log transformation, whereas interval values are not: if $x > y$ then $\log(x) > \log(y)$, but $(x - y) \neq (\log(x) - \log(y))$. The log transformation preserves order but not magnitude. A lively debate arose around proscriptions that particular arithmetic and statistical operations were permissible for particular data scales. Velleman and Wilkinson (1993) summarize the main points of the debate in a paper called, "Nominal, Ordinal, Interval and Ratio Typologies Are Misleading." Other authors find considerable heuristic value in the typologies (e.g., Hand, 1993). Our view is that numbers are representations for which scales provide weak interpretations. Thus, if we interpret the numbers 1,2,3 as ordinal, we will generally not compute their arithmetic average—just as we wouldn't compute the average of low, medium and high. And if we *do* compute an average of ordinal numbers, we will interpret it differently than averages of interval quantities.

It is tempting to think that one data scale provides a more "natural" representation of data than another, but this is like saying Monet's style of painting in 1880 more naturally represents landscapes than, say, Cezanne's style in 1870. Your representation of reality depends entirely on your purpose. For example, you might choose to represent paint colors categorically with their names, or as interval luminosity measurements. You might even treat luminosity as a continuous quantity, knowing all along that luminosity represents integer numbers of photons.

Our task is to construct good representations of reality—to collect and transform data in such a way that we see what is going on and avoid deluding ourselves. Every operation on a set of data—collecting it, transforming it, analyzing it, and presenting it—can obscure what is going on or mislead us. This fundamental point was nicely illustrated by John Tukey, the father of exploratory data analysis:

Given a sequence of numbers like this:

4   7   9   3   4   11   12   1304   10   15   12   13   17

we easily see that a reasonable smoothing of this sequence will increase slowly from near 5 to near 15, paying as little attention as reasonable to 1304.

1304 may be real, indeed very important, but it has nothing to do with a smooth curve. It ought to generate a very large residual, and leave the smooth fit as nearly alone as we can conveniently arrange to have it do.   (Tukey, 1977, p. 210)

On the one hand, the datum 1304 obscures a smooth trend, so we want to ignore it, and for the purpose of representing reality as a smooth trend, we should. We should not feel obliged to include all our data in a representation, we should feel free to set some aside. On the other hand, 1304 is in the data for a reason, and we don't know what it is, so we delude ourselves by ignoring it. Our representation of reality, then, has two parts: a smooth trend and a memo to ourselves to figure out what caused the extreme value.

2.2   Sketching a Preliminary Causal Model

When confronted with unusual data values, as in the previous example, we look for explanations: Why does a datum have the value 1304, when all the other values in the distribution are so much smaller? Common explanations are, for example, that a combination of conditions exposed a bug in the program just once, or a human erred in transcribing or editing the data, and so on. Even when we cannot say what caused the anomalous value, we assume that some factor (or factors) is responsible, and this faith extends to all data values, not only anomalies. As noted in chapter 1, a datum represents the influences of many factors, although we generally don't know what all the factors are, how much they influence the datum, or what to measure to estimate these influences. The purpose of exploratory data analysis is to develop and refine a causal model of data values. An early step in exploratory data analysis, therefore, is to sketch a causal model. This will serve as an agenda and a roadmap for exploratory

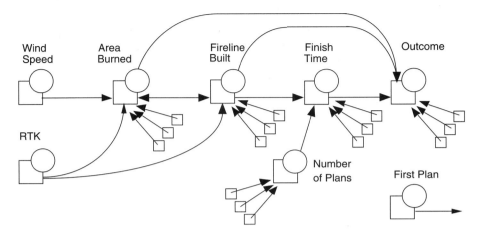

Figure 2.2   A preliminary causal model of the relationships among variables in table 2.1.

work, as well as a notepad and a summary of suspicions and beliefs about the causal relationships among factors represented by variables.

Often you can sketch a causal model before collecting data. This can help you design an exploratory study to collect the data you want. For example, before Dave Hart and I (Hart and Cohen, 1992) ran the exploratory study that produced table 2.1, we already had a rough model of causal relationships in the Phoenix system, illustrated in figure 2.2. At this stage of the game, however, all the causal relationships denoted by arrows were untested, mere guesses based on a limited understanding of how Phoenix works. Nor could we make the distinction, introduced in section 2.1, between factors and variables. Instead we noted the possibility of factors underlying variables with a box underlying a circle. To keep the following discussion parsimonious, we will speak of variables influencing each other (e.g., *WindSpeed* influences *AreaBurned*) but we really mean that *WindSpeed* represents something in the Phoenix environment that influences something else, represented by *AreaBurned*.

WindSpeed was set by us, the experimenters. *WindSpeed* probably influences the area burned by the fire, which might in turn influence the amount of fireline built by bulldozers. Reciprocally, *FirelineBuilt* might influence *AreaBurned*. We were pretty sure that *FirelineBuilt* would influence the finish time of the system, because building fireline takes time. We also expected the incidence of replanning (*NumPlans*) to influence *FinishTime*, because replanning and executing new plans takes time. And, because a successful trial was defined to be one in which the fire was contained in less than 150 simulated hours, we recognized that *FinishTime* would influence *Outcome*.

We expected *RTK*—the ratio of "thinking time" for the planner to "burning time" for the fires—to influence both *AreaBurned* and *FirelineBuilt*, but we thought the influence of *RTK* on *FinishTime* would probably be indirect, through *FirelineBuilt*. Finally, we thought that the choice of an initial plan (*FirstPlan*) might be important, but we had no idea how it would influence other variables. We also assumed that unmeasured factors would influence *AreaBurned*, *FirelineBuilt*, *NumPlans*, *Outcome* and *FinishTime*; but because *WindSpeed* and *RTK* were set by us and *FirstPlan* was selected randomly by the Phoenix planner, no unmeasured factors would influence these variables.

At the outset, a model like the one in figure 2.2 is probably wrong and certainly incomplete; for example, it includes no arc weights to represent the strengths of causal influences, indeed no representation of the functional relationships between factors. Moreover, one inevitably finds patterns in data that are not explained by measured variables. Like Sherlock Holmes's dog that didn't bark in the night, they hint at factors present but unmeasured. One might decide to pursue these influences, or not, depending on how well one's model accounts for the data.

2.3   Looking at One Variable

Once a sample of data has been collected, it is usually a good idea to look at the data several ways. It is dangerous to have too clear an idea of what you are looking for, because you might miss other things. In the following pages I will illustrate how Dave Hart and I explored the data generated in 343 runs of the Phoenix system, and in the process refined the causal model in figure 2.2.

2.3.1   Visualizing One Variable

A good place to start is with distributions of individual variables. A common visualization of univariate distributions is the *frequency histogram*, which plots the relative frequencies of values in a distribution. To construct a histogram, divide the range between the highest and lowest values in a distribution into several bins of equal size, then toss each value in the distribution into the appropriate bin. The height of a rectangle in a frequency histogram represents the number of values in the corresponding bin. For example, figure 2.3 represents the frequency histogram of *AreaBurned* in 215 runs of the Phoenix system. Only successful runs are represented, which is to say that records in the data table (of which table 2.1 is a fragment) for which *Outcome* = *fail* are not represented. In more than half the cases, between zero and ten acres

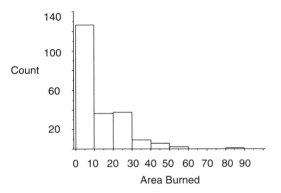

Figure 2.3   A frequency histogram of area burned (in acres) in 215 trials.

were burned; in thirty-five cases, between 10 and 20 acres were burned, and so on. The *mode* of the distribution, the range of values into which most data fall, represents trials in which fewer than ten acres were burned.

The choice of bin size affects the detail we see in a frequency histogram. Changing the bin size from ten to five, as in figure 2.4, illuminates things that were previously obscured. For example, the location of the mode is tightened up, and a gap in the range 15 to 20 is evident. Gaps are suggestive. Like footprints, they suggest that something was about, something influenced the factor we are measuring; in particular, something accounts for the fact that many fires burned less than 15 acres and more than 20 acres, but virtually nothing is seen in the 15- to 20-acre range. Gaps suggest two kinds of explanation. One possibility is that something has suppressed or censored particular values in a distribution; for example, if you look at the distribution of floor numbers in a sample of elevators, you'll find a gap or at least a dip at "13," because superstitious people prefer not to acknowledge a building's thirteenth floor.

A more common explanation of gaps is that the data on either side of the gap disclose unequal influences of another factor or combination of factors. For example, our informal causal model, described in figure 2.4, suggests that *WindSpeed* influences *AreaBurned*. Perhaps the data on the lower side of the gap represent low wind speeds and the other data represent high wind speeds. It is a simple matter to partition the distribution of *AreaBurned* by *WindSpeed,* yielding three smaller *conditional distributions*, one for each of the three wind speeds set in the experiment. Frequency histograms of these partitions (figure 2.5) appear to support our hypothesis: When the wind speed is low or medium, the area burned is less than 15 acres in all but four cases, but when the wind speed is high, the area burned exceeds 20 acres in all but 14 cases.

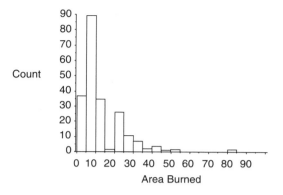

Figure 2.4   The histogram in figure 2.3, redisplayed with a smaller bin size, shows a gap.

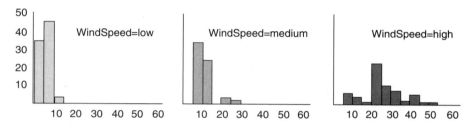

Figure 2.5   A partition of the distribution of *AreaBurned* by *WindSpeed*.

Thus, the gap in figure 2.4 leads to a hypothesis about a causal relationship between wind speed and area burned. As it happens, the relationship was not unexpected, it was part of our causal model of Phoenix before we ran the experiment (i.e., figure 2.2). But the three histograms in figure 2.5 do suggest something we didn't know or surmise in the original model, namely, that the influence of wind speed on area burned is not linear. Although *WindSpeed* is an ordinal variable with values low, medium and high in table 2.1, the actual settings in the experiment were interval values: 3, 6, and 9 kilometers per hour. Yet figure 2.5 suggests that the effect of changing the wind speed from 3 to 6 is much smaller than the effect of changing from windspeed from 6 to 9. I follow up this lead in the next section.

Before leaving the humble frequency histogram, it is worth noting that bin size affects not only the detail one sees in the histogram (particularly gaps) but also one's perception of the shape of the distribution. Figure 2.6 shows three different histograms of a single distribution, which contains 100 values between 60 and 84. The only difference between the histograms is bin size; yet when the bin size is 1.5, the

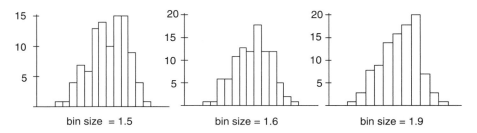

Figure 2.6   Changing bin size affects the apparent shape of a distribution.

histogram suggests a gap, and when the bin size is 1.6 the distribution not only appears free of gaps but also appears to be roughly symmetric, almost "bell shaped." Finally, when the bin size is 1.9 the distribution appears quite lopsided. Before drawing any conclusions about the shape of a distribution, you should try a few different bin sizes.

2.3.2   Statistics for One Variable

Visualizations such as frequency histograms help us think about some aspects of distributions, particularly gaps and shape, but they don't support other kinds of thinking. For example, to assert that wind speed has a nonlinear effect on area burned, given figure 2.5, we have to say something like this: "With a wind speed of 3 kph most fires burn between zero and ten acres. If we increase wind speed by 3 kph, most fires burn between five and 15 acres. Another increase of 3 kph yields a distribution in which fires burn between five and 55 acres, with many fires in the 20 to 35 acre range. The first 3 kph increase in wind speed appears to have a smaller effect than the second, so the effect of wind speed on area burned is nonlinear." This is an awkward way to state the case, and you can no doubt see a better way, such as, "The average areas burned at wind speeds of 3, 6 and 9 kph are 5.56, 11.12, and 25.56 acres, respectively. The linear increase in *WindSpeed* is not matched by a linear increase in *AreaBurned*, thus the effect of wind speed on area burned is nonlinear." The *mean* is a concise summary of one aspect of a distribution, namely, where its mass lies. Table 2.2 reports this and other statistics, computed for each of the three partitions of the distribution of *AreaBurned*, that is, for wind speeds of 3, 6, and 9 kph.

Sample Size   The sample size, denoted N, is the number of data items in a sample. In this case, 85, 67, and 63 fires were contained when the wind speed was 3, 6, and 9 kph, respectively. Fires are slightly more likely to be contained when wind speed is low.

Table 2.2   Statistics for the distribution of *AreaBurned*, partitioned by *WindSpeed*.

Summary statistic	Wind = 3 kph	Wind = 6 kph	Wind = 9 kph
Sample size (N)	85	67	63
Mean	5.56	11.12	25.56
Median	5.6	9.83	23.92
Mode	5 to 10	5 to 10	20 to 25
Skewness	1.385	1.51	1.794
Minimum	3.23	5.54	9.39
Maximum	12.35	26.41	84.43
Range	9.12	20.87	75.04
Interquartile range	2.42	3.96	7.82
Standard deviation	1.73	4.05	12.272
Variance	2.99	16.37	150.61

Mean   The arithmetic mean, denoted $\bar{x}$, is the average value—the sum of all the values in the sample divided by the number of values.

Median   If the values in the sample are sorted into a nondecreasing order, the median is the value that splits the distribution in half; for example, the median of the values (1 1 1 2 3 4 5) is 2 because half the values are greater than two and half are smaller. If N is even, the sample has two middle values, and the median can be found by interpolating between them or by selecting one of them arbitrarily.

Mode   The mode is the most common value in a distribution; for example, the mode of the distribution (1 2 2 3 4 4 4) is 4. If one's data are continuous, real numbers, then the mode is apt to be uninformative because of the very low probability that two or more data will have exactly the same value. But as noted earlier, real-valued data are often mapped into discrete numbers, by rounding or sorting into bins for frequency histograms. So when we say that the modal area burned is 5 to 10 acres, we mean that most fires burned between 5 and 10 acres. If we had selected a smaller bin size, the mode would be different; for example, most fires (9.4 percent of them) burned between 3.9 and 4.1 acres when the wind speed was 3 kph. Here, we have used a bin size of 0.2. Thus, the mode of a distribution depends on bin size.

  Although it is a contradiction in terms, we often speak of a distribution having two or more modes. This means the distribution has two or more values or ranges of values that are common. For example, the modes in figure 2.4 are 5 to 10 and 20 to 25. You might be surprised that we counted the latter as a mode, especially because it is less common than other values. The decision to characterize a distribution as bimodal

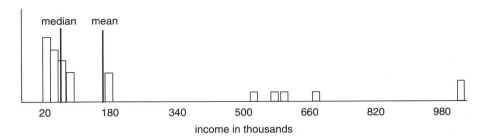

Figure 2.7   A highly skewed distribution.

(or multimodal) is subjective and equivalent to our earlier decision to characterize a region of figure 2.4 as a gap. We selected the peak between 20 and 25 as a mode not because it is the second most common value in figure 2.4 (it isn't), but because it is the biggest peak on one side of the gap.

The mean, median, and mode are measures of location or central tendency in a distribution. They tell us where the distribution is most dense. In a perfectly symmetric, unimodal distribution, the mean, median, and mode are identical. Most empirical distributions—those we get by running an experiment and collecting data— are neither symmetric nor unimodal, but, rather, are skewed and bumpy.

Skew   In skewed distributions the bulk of the data are at one end of the distribution. The distribution is said to have a long tail on the left or the right. If the bulk of the distribution is on the right, so the tail is on the left, then the distribution is called left skewed or negatively skewed, and the skew statistic is a negative number. Conversely, a right skewed distribution has a long tail on the right and a positive skew statistic. The distributions of the partitions of area burned by wind speed, shown in figure 2.5, are all positively skewed, and skew increases with wind speed. This is at least partly due to the presence of one extreme value in the high wind speed distribution, a value so large—84.43 acres—that it is left out of the histograms in figure 2.5.

In skewed distributions the median is often preferred to the mean as a measure of central tendency or location. This is because the mean can be shifted away from the body or densest part of the distribution by a few extreme values. For example, figure 2.7 shows a hypothetical distribution of incomes, the bulk of which is in the range between twenty and eighty thousand dollars. The median is at \$44,000 but the mean is roughly four times higher, \$178,000, due to the presence of five incomes above \$500,000. Incumbent administrations might prefer to report the mean national income because it paints a rosy picture, but everyone else recognizes that the mean does not represent the bulk of a skewed distribution, and they use the median, instead.

The median is said to be *robust* because its value is not distorted by *outliers*, values that are very large or small, and very uncommon. Conversely, the mean is *sensitive* to outliers: if you subtract one of the millionaires from the distribution in figure 2.7, the median drops just $500 while the mean decreases by $32,000. This is because subtracting a datum shifts the median up or down by at most the distance to the next highest or lowest score in the distribution; and because the median starts within the bulk of the distribution, it stays there when you subtract or add a datum. The mean, however, is more like the fulcrum of a balance beam, and might be shifted by a lot if you add or subtract an outlier.

Another robust alternative to the mean is the *trimmed mean*. The idea is to lop off a fraction of the upper and lower ends of a distribution, and take the mean of the rest. For example, if the sorted distribution is

0, 0, 1, 2, 5, 8, 12, 17, 18, 18, 19, 19, 20, 26, 83, 116

we can lop off the two smallest and two largest values and take the mean of the rest. In this case the trimmed mean is 13.75, smaller than the arithmetic mean of 22.75.

The remaining statistics in table 2.2 are measures of the dispersion, that is, how "spread out" the distribution is.

Maximum, Minimum, and Range   The maximum and minimum are just the largest and smallest values in a distribution, the range is the difference of the two.

Interquartile Range   The interquartile range is found by dividing a sorted distribution into four contiguous parts, each containing the same number of individuals. Each part is called a quartile. The difference between the highest value in the third quartile and the lowest value in the second quartile is the interquartile range. For example, if the sorted distribution is (1 1 2 3 3 5 5 5 5 6 6 100), then the quartiles are (1 1 2), (3 3 5), (5 5 5), (6 6 100), and the interquartile range is $5 - 3 = 2$. Contrast this value with the simple range, $100 - 1 = 99$, and you will see that the interquartile range is robust against outliers. Indeed, the interquartile range for high wind speeds (table 2.2) is much smaller than the range, and also the standard deviation.

Standard Deviation and Variance   The standard deviation is the most common measure of dispersion around the mean of a distribution. It is the square root of the variance, which is the sum of squared distances between each datum and the mean, divided by the sample size minus one. For a tiny sample of three values, (1, 2, 15), the mean is $(1 + 2 + 15)/3 = 6$, and the variance is

$$\frac{(1 - 6)^2 + (2 - 6)^2 + (15 - 6)^2}{3 - 1} = 61,$$

so the standard deviation is 7.81. Note that the variance is an average—just like the mean. It is the mean squared deviation between each datum and its mean.

Because they are averages, both the mean and the variance are sensitive to outliers. By sensitive, we don't mean tiny effects that only theoretical statisticians care about, we mean big effects that can wreck our interpretations of data. Earlier we mentioned an outlier in the distribution of *AreaBurned*, a single value of 84.43 in a distribution of 215 data. The mean of the distribution is 13.155, but if we discard the outlier the mean drops to 12.882, and the standard deviations with and without the outlier are 10.923 and 9.793, respectively. Suppose we wanted to test the hypothesis that the mean of *AreaBurned* is significantly different from 14.0 (using the *t* test described in section 4.4.6). It turns out that 12.882 is significantly different from 14.0 but 13.155 is not. In other words, the presence of a single outlier in a distribution of over 200 pieces of data can render some statistical comparisons insignificant. Outliers are discussed further in section 2.4.8.

2.4   Joint Distributions

Joint distributions, of which partitions are an example, sometimes show how one variable influences another. This section begins with joint distributions of categorical and ordinal variables. Later, the focus shifts to joint distributions of continuous variables.

2.4.1   Joint Distributions of Categorical and Ordinal Variables

It is usually a good idea to see whether some variables influence others. Independent variables are manipulated by experimenters and are expected to affect dependent variables. For example, in figure 2.2 two independent variables were *WindSpeed* and *RTK*, and one dependent variable was *Outcome*. *WindSpeed* is an ordinal variable, *RTK* is a continuous variable but we used only seven values in our study, so we treat it as ordinal, and *Outcome* is a categorical variable. How can we demonstrate influences of ordinal variables on categorical variables? All we know is whether a trial succeeds or fails, so all we can measure is the count or frequency of successes and failures.

We know, for starters, that Phoenix contained 215 fires successfully and failed to contain 128 fires. To assess whether a factor such as *WindSpeed* affects the distribution of successes and failures, I tabulated these outcomes in different wind speed conditions, as shown in table 2.3. What can you tell from this table? Most of the

Table 2.3   The joint distribution of *Outcome* and *WindSpeed*.

Wind Speed	Outcome=success	Outcome=failure	Totals
Low	85	35	120
Medium	67	50	117
High	63	43	106
Totals	215	128	343

trials at low wind speed succeeded, whereas roughly 60 percent of the trials at medium and high wind speeds succeeded. Apparently, *WindSpeed* does affect outcome: A disproportionate number of successes occur at low wind speeds. Note that this conclusion is not supported by table 2.3, alone, but requires the additional knowledge that *WindSpeed* is an independent variable, set by experimenters, and must therefore be "causally upstream" of the outcome of a trial. Table 2.3 does not tell us the direction of causal influence between *WindSpeed* and *Outcome*; all it tells us is that these variables are not independent.

Table 2.3 is called a *contingency table* because it shows how values of one variable are contingent on values of another. Contingency tables are not limited to two variables, nor do they need either variable to be binary; for example, in section 6.8 I cross-tabulated the number of integer scores in the range 1 through 5 assigned by each of ten judges. Many interesting statistical techniques have been developed for analyzing contingency tables (see sections 2.4.3, 7.6), but for now, let's focus on what can be learned from contingency tables just by looking carefully.

The pattern in a contingency table is often clearer if counts are expressed as proportions of the *row marginal counts*, also called *row margins*. For example, in table 2.4, the top-left cell contains 71 percent because 85 is 71 percent of 120. One can also divide by column marginal counts. Dividing by row margins estimates the probability of success or failure at each wind speed; dividing by column margins estimates the probability that the wind speed was low, medium or high on a successful or unsuccessful trial.

Let's be more precise about what's meant by a pattern or lack of pattern in a contingency table. Contingency tables, also called *cross-classification tables*, describe the joint distribution of sample data according to their classification by two or more variables. Each cell in a table corresponds to a unique combination of values for these variables. Because we are primarily interested in building causal models of a program's behavior, our contingency tables will often have one variable that measures an outcome, such as success or failure, and another that we believe influences the

Table 2.4   The distribution in table 2.3 expressed as percentages.

Wind Speed	Outcome=success	Outcome=failure	Totals
Low	71 percent	29 percent	120
Medium	57 percent	43 percent	117
High	59 percent	41 percent	106
Totals	215	128	343

outcome. Keep in mind, though, that contingency tables are simply representations of joint distributions, and do not themselves imply causal direction.

Consider some hypothetical survey data relating educational level (high school, undergraduate, postgraduate) to whether or not individuals are married, as shown in table 2.5. This table suggests that educational level and marital status are unrelated. There are roughly twice as many married as unmarried individuals, but this ratio is independent of educational level. Now imagine repeating the survey with a new sample of 300 individuals, distributed as shown in table 2.6. Here, too, marital status appears to be independent of educational level. Fewer individuals complete postgraduate work than college and fewer complete college than high school, but these numbers are distributed evenly over married and unmarried individuals. Now repeat the survey again with another sample of 300 individuals (table 2.7). At first glance, these results are more interesting, but on examination they provide no evidence that educational level influences marital status or vice versa. As in the previous tables we see a 2:1 ratio of married to unmarried individuals, and we see fewer individuals completing higher levels of education, but the 2:1 ratio is constant across levels of education.

Only in table 2.8 can a relationship be found between marital status and education. A causal interpretation of the data is that as educational level increases, the incidence of marriage drops to zero. Or perhaps lonely people who cannot find spouses go to graduate school. Perhaps education puts people off marriage, or perhaps married people cannot afford further education. The direction of causal influence is not clear (although you have your suspicions, as any good data analyst will). It *is* clear that marital status and education are not independent; thus the pattern in table 2.8 is called a *dependency*.

There is a nice graphical way to check by eye for dependencies. First build a contingency table, then draw a graph with cell proportions (not raw cell counts) on the y axis and one of the variables on the x axis. Cell proportions should be computed with respect to the marginal frequencies of the variable on the x axis. Now draw a

Table 2.5   Fewer individuals are unmarried than married.

Educational level	Unmarried	Married	Totals
Postgraduate	30	70	100
College	31	69	100
High school	33	67	100
Totals	94	206	300

Table 2.6   Fewer individuals are found at higher educational levels.

Educational level	Unmarried	Married	Totals
Postgraduate	25 (50 percent)	25 (50 percent)	50
College	50 (50 percent)	50 (50 percent)	100
High school	75 (50 percent)	75 (50 percent)	150
Totals	150	150	300

Table 2.7   Fewer individuals are found at higher educational levels, and more are married, but these are independent effects.

Educational level	Unmarried	Married	Totals
Postgraduate	16 (32 percent)	34 (68 percent)	50
College	35 (35 percent)	65 (65 percent)	100
High school	50 (33 percent)	100 (67 percent)	150
Totals	101	199	300

line for each level of the other variable, connecting the cell proportions. For example, starting with table 2.7, if educational level is on the x axis, then one line, labeled "unmarried" connects the cell proportions .32, .35, and .33, and another, labeled "married," connects the cell proportions .68, .65, and .67. Of course it isn't necessary to plot lines for both levels of marital status because the proportions in one determine the proportions in the other. When the variables in a contingency table are statistically independent, the line (or lines) will be horizontal. In figure 2.8, which corresponds to the "married" status in table 2.7, the independence of marital status and educational level is reflected in the flat line at roughly 67 percent. The location of the line on the y axis is irrelevant; because the percentage of married people (and thus unmarried people) is the same across all educational levels, neither variable influences the other.

Table 2.8   A dependency between educational level and marital status.

Educational level	Unmarried	Married	Totals
Postgraduate	50 (100 percent)	0 (0 percent)	50
College	75 (75 percent)	25 (25 percent)	100
High school	75 (50 percent)	75 (50 percent)	150
Totals	200	100	300

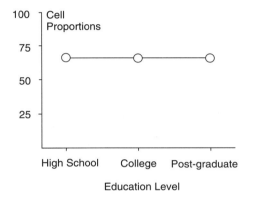

Figure 2.8   No dependency between education and marital status (corresponding to table 2.7).

Of course, if we put marital status on the x axis, we would plot three lines, one for each educational level. Provided we calculate cell proportions with respect to the variable on the x axis—marital status, in this case—the lines will still be horizontal (or nearly so). One will lie at roughly 16 percent, one at roughly 34 percent, and one at roughly 50 percent.

Figure 2.9, corresponding to table 2.8 isn't a flat line, however. Marital status and education are not independent. The way figure 2.9 is drawn suggests that the proportion of people at each level of education who are married is a negative function of education. Of course, you could have put marital status on the x axis and drawn three lines for the three different educational levels. These lines will not be parallel (try it yourself), indicating again that marital status and educational level are not independent.

Now let's try it with real data: by plotting the cell proportions in table 2.4 to see whether *WindSpeed* has an effect on *Outcome*. Because the proportions are calculated with respect to row margins, the row variable (*WindSpeed*) goes on the x axis. And

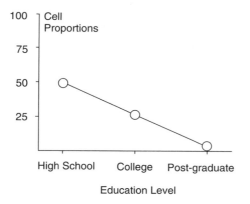

Figure 2.9   A dependency between education and marital status (corresponding to table 2.8).

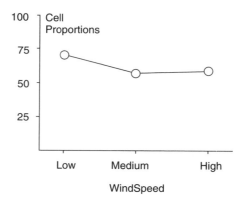

Figure 2.10   A small dependency (corresponding to table 2.4).

because the percentages of successes and failures sum to 100 percent, only one line needs to be plotted. The line in figure 2.10 is slightly kinked instead of flat, hinting at a small effect.

2.4.2   Contingency Tables for More than Two Variables

The story so far is that *WindSpeed* might have a small effect on *Outcome*. Why is the effect so small? Perhaps it is somehow dissipated or nullified by the factors "in between" *WindSpeed* and *Outcome* in the causal model in figure 2.2. For example, although we guessed *WindSpeed* influences *AreaBurned*, the influence might be slight,

Table 2.9   The joint distribution of *Outcome* and *RTK*.

	Outcome=success	Outcome=failure	Total
"slow thinking"			
RTK = 0.33	10 (33 percent)	20 (67 percent)	30
RTK = 0.45	14 (42 percent)	19 (58 percent)	33
RTK = 0.56	22 (55 percent)	18 (45 percent)	40
RTK = 0.71	54 (56 percent)	42 (44 percent)	96
RTK = 1.00	27 (63 percent)	16 (37 percent)	43
RTK = 1.67	38 (77 percent)	11 (23 percent)	49
RTK = 5.00	50 (96 percent)	2 (4 percent)	52
"fast thinking"			
Totals	215	128	343

in which case *WindSpeed* might have little effect on *Outcome*. Another possibility, which we will explore now, is that *WindSpeed* somehow interacts with another independent variable, *RTK*, in such a way that the effect of *WindSpeed* on *Outcome* depends on *RTK*.

RTK is the ratio of "thinking time" for the Phoenix planner to "fire burning time" in the Phoenix environment. *RTK* takes seven values, shown in the contingency table in table 2.9. It's pretty clear from this table that the proportion of successful trials rises gradually until *RTK* = 1.67 and then it reaches a ceiling.

Figure 2.11 is a plot of *RTK* against the proportion of successes, dropping the last coordinate for clarity. As noted earlier, it isn't necessary to also plot the proportions of failures. There can be little doubt that *RTK* affects the proportion of successes, but can you see more? Figure 2.12 suggests that the effect of *RTK* varies. As you increase the ratio of thinking time to acting time, increasing *RTK* from .33 to .71, the proportion of successes rises rapidly. Beyond *RTK* = .71 the proportion of successes increases more slowly.

Fitting lines to data can be a somewhat hallucinatory exercise, not unlike seeing animal forms in clouds or zodiacal figures in stars. Why, for example, did we fit two lines instead of one to the points in figure 2.11? Perhaps two lines fit the data better than one, but carrying this argument to an extreme would have us "fit" $N - 1$ lines to N points! In fact, there is a good reason to fit two lines: The Phoenix planner was developed by several graduate students over a period of two years at a single setting of the real-time knob: *RTK* = 1.0. We expected the planner to perform well at higher settings of *RTK* because these settings provide it more time to think. We suspected,

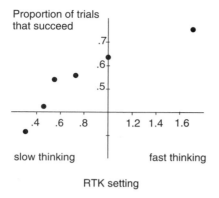

Figure 2.11   A plot of *RTK* against the proportion of trials that succeed.

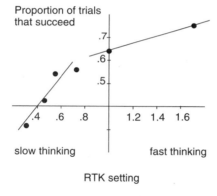

Figure 2.12   Fitting lines: *RTK* and the proportion of trials that succeed.

however, that the design of the planner had become "tuned" to one setting of *RTK* during its development. Intentionally or otherwise, Phoenix's developers probably made decisions that assumed *RTK* = 1.0. If so, we might expect a pretty serious change in performance at lower levels of *RTK*. This is why we draw two lines in figure 2.12. Clearly, when fitting lines to data, it helps to know something about the system one is modeling. This point is discussed further in section 2.4.4.

   The obvious question at this point is whether the effect of *RTK* on *Outcome* is independent of the previously demonstrated effect of *WindSpeed*, or whether *RTK* and *WindSpeed* somehow interact to determine *Outcome*. First let's simplify the situation by collapsing the seven values of *RTK* into two, as suggested by figure 2.12:

Table 2.10   A three-dimensional contingency table.

		Outcome =success	Outcome =failure	Total
RTK=Adequate	WindSpeed=low	30 (86 percent)	5 (14 percent)	35
	WindSpeed=medium	32 (80 percent)	8 (20 percent)	40
	WindSpeed=high	53 (77 percent)	16 (23 percent)	69
RTK=Inadequate	WindSpeed=low	55 (65 percent)	30 (35 percent)	85
	WindSpeed=medium	35 (45 percent)	42 (55 percent)	77
	WindSpeed=high	10 (27 percent)	27 (73 percent)	37

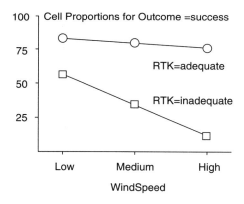

Figure 2.13   An interaction effect between *WindSpeed* and *RTK*.

Phoenix has adequate time to think if $RTK \geq 1.0$ and inadequate time if $RTK < 1.0$. The next step is to construct the three-dimensional contingency table in table 2.10, and plot cell proportions. Because successes and failures are exhaustive outcomes, it isn't necessary to plot cell proportions for both. Figure 2.13 does have two lines, however, one for *RTK = adequate* and one for *RTK = inadequate*. If these lines were parallel, it would mean the effect of *WindSpeed* on *Outcome* was the same at both levels of *RTK*. If the lines overlapped (i.e., if they were identical) it would mean *RTK* has no effect on *Outcome* at all. In fact, one line is higher than the other, indicating that overall, more trials succeeded when *RTK = adequate*. More importantly, the lines are not parallel, so the effect of *WindSpeed* on *Outcome* apparently depends on *RTK*. The top line has a shallow slope, suggesting *WindSpeed* has little effect on *Outcome* when *RTK = adequate*; but when the Phoenix planner has too little time to think, successes plummet as *WindSpeed* increases.

Table 2.11   The contingency table for *WindSpeed* and *Outcome* when *RTK = adequate*.

	Outcome = success	Outcome = failure	Total
WindSpeed=low	30	5	35
WindSpeed=medium	32	8	40
WindSpeed=high	53	16	69
Total	115	29	144

Table 2.12   The contingency table for *WindSpeed* and *Outcome* when *RTK = inadequate*.

	Outcome = success	Outcome = failure	Total
WindSpeed=low	55	30	85
WindSpeed=medium	35	42	77
WindSpeed=high	10	27	37
Total	100	99	199

2.4.3   Statistics for Joint Distributions of Categorical Variables

Our working hypothesis is that *WindSpeed* has little effect on *Outcome* when *RTK =
adequate*, but a considerable effect when *RTK = inadequate*. This section introduces
a statistic called chi-square that summarizes the degree of dependence that holds
between row and column variables in contingency tables (chi rhymes with pie, and
chi-square is denoted χ^2). Tables 2.11 and 2.12 represent the joint distribution of
WindSpeed and *Outcome* for adequate and inadequate *RTK*, respectively. If our
working hypothesis is correct, and we calculate χ^2 for these tables, we'd expect a
low value for table 2.11 a high value for table 2.12.

   Consider the top-left cell in table 2.11. It contains the frequency of a conjunctive
event: low wind speed and a successful outcome. The probability of a conjunct
$Pr(A \& B)$ is the product of the individual probabilities, $Pr(A)$ and $Pr(B)$ if A and
B are independent. If *Outcome* and *WindSpeed* are independent, the probability of a
success occurring when *WindSpeed = low* is:

$$Pr(Outcome = success) \times Pr(WindSpeed = low).$$

   We don't know the probabilities $Pr(Outcome = success)$ and $Pr(WindSpeed =
low)$ for Phoenix in general, but we can estimate them from the sample of trials in

Table 2.13   The expected frequencies f_e for table 2.11.

	Outcome =success	Outcome =failure	Total
WindSpeed=low	27.95	7.05	35
WindSpeed=medium	31.94	8.06	40
WindSpeed=high	55.1	13.9	69
Total	115	29	144

table 2.11. $\Pr(WindSpeed = low)$ is estimated from the row margin for low wind speed. As 35 cases out of 144 have low wind speed, we estimate

$$\Pr(WindSpeed = low) = \frac{35}{144} = .243.$$

Similarly, with the column margin, we can estimate

$$\Pr(Outcome = success) = \frac{115}{144} = .799.$$

This leads to the conjunctive probability

$$\Pr(Outcome = success \ \& \ WindSpeed = low) = .243 \times .799 = .194.$$

Don't forget, though, this is the estimated probability of the conjunct if and only if *WindSpeed* and *Outcome* are independent. Now we can derive the expected number of successes, denoted f_e for "expected frequency," when the wind speed is low, given that *WindSpeed* and *Outcome* are independent:

$$f_e = 144 \times \Pr(Outcome = success \ \& \ WindSpeed = low)$$

$$= 144 \times .243 \times .799 = 27.95.$$

An easier way to calculate f_e is simply to multiply the row and column margins and divide by the total number of trials:

$$f_e = \frac{35 \times 115}{144} = 27.95.$$

By this method we can obtain the expected count for every cell in table 2.11, under the assumption that *WindSpeed* and *Outcome* are independent. For example, the expected frequency of the second cell in the first row is $(35 \times 29)/144 = 7.05$. The entire table of expected frequencies is given in table 2.13.

All of the observed frequencies in table 2.11 are quite similar to the expected frequencies in table 2.13. The χ^2 statistic is a function of the differences between observed (f_o) and expected (f_e) frequencies:

$$\chi^2 = \sum \frac{(f_o - f_e)^2}{f_e}.$$

For the current example,

$$\chi^2 = \frac{(30 - 27.95)^2}{27.95} + \frac{(5 - 7.05)^2}{7.05} + \frac{(32 - 31.94)^2}{31.94}$$

$$+ \frac{(8 - 8.06)^2}{8.06} + \frac{(53 - 55.1)^2}{55.1} + \frac{(16 - 13.9)^2}{13.9} = 1.145.$$

Keep in mind that f_e is computed assuming the row and column variables are independent. Large values of χ^2 thus imply that the expected and observed cell counts are very different, that is, the observed frequencies differ from their expectations under the independence assumption. Large values of χ^2 suggest that the row and column variables are not independent. Of course, χ^2 could be large simply because a table has many cells, so a test of independence must take the number of cells into account. Such a test is described in chapter 6. Here it suffices to say that with published tables and computer statistics packages you can estimate the probability that the row and column variables are independent, given a value of χ^2 and the dimensions of a contingency table. This probability is .56 for table 2.11. If this probability was very low, we could say that the value of χ^2 is very unlikely under the assumption of independence, and we would be inclined to reject the assumption. You can see, however, that our value of χ^2 is not at all unlikely given the assumption of independence, so the assumption stands.

The story is different for the cases in which the Phoenix planner does not have adequate time to think, *RTK = inadequate,* represented in table 2.12. After calculating the expected frequencies as shown earlier, we obtain $\chi^2 = 15.795$, a much larger value than before. With statistical tables or software we can determine that the probability of obtaining a value of χ^2 this large by chance, under the assumption that *WindSpeed* and *Outcome* are independent, is less than .0004. Therefore, we can be fairly certain that *WindSpeed* and *Outcome* are not independent. The chi-square test gives us a formal, probabilistic statement of what we saw in figure 2.13: Wind speed has no statistically discernible effect on the success of a trial when the Phoenix planner has adequate time to think. But when the time is inadequate, wind speed has a big effect.

An Easy and Useful Special Case: Two-by-Two Table   One often wants to test for independence of two binary variables. The contingency table in this case will have four cells:

a	b
c	d

The χ^2 statistic in this case is just

$$\chi^2 = \frac{(ad - bc)^2 N}{(a + b)(c + d)(a + c)(b + d)},$$

where N is the sum $a + b + c + d$. For example, we can test the independence of *RTK* and *Outcome* with the following table (which is constructed from table 2.10 by summing three levels of *WindSpeed* per quadrant):

115	29
100	99

and the χ^2 statistic is:

$$\chi^2 = \frac{(115 \cdot 99 - 29 \cdot 100)^2 \cdot 343}{(115 + 29)(100 + 99)(115 + 100)(29 + 99)} = 31.314.$$

We will see in chapter 6 how to find probabilities for obtained values of χ^2, but you should know that for a two-by-two contingency table, the probability of obtaining $\chi^2 = 31.314$ when *Outcome* and *RTK* are not related is less than .0001. We can therefore conclude with very little probability of error that they are related.

Let us update figure 2.2, our causal model. We have learned several things, shown in figure 2.14. First, the effect of *WindSpeed* on *AreaBurned* is real, positive, and not linear. Second, the effect of *WindSpeed* on *Outcome* depends on *RTK*. Taken together these conclusions imply that when *RTK = adequate*, the Phoenix planner can cope with the increased acreage burned at higher wind speeds. We will now explore some other variables in table 2.1 in an attempt to explain why the Phoenix planner is robust when it has adequate time to think and brittle otherwise.

2.4.4   Visualizing Joint Distributions of Two Continuous Variables

A joint distribution of two continuous variables is a distribution of pairs of measurements, each pair representing one individual. These pairs can be treated as coordinates and plotted in two dimensions. For the following joint distribution, the height and weight of individual 1 can be represented as an x-y coordinate (72,180):

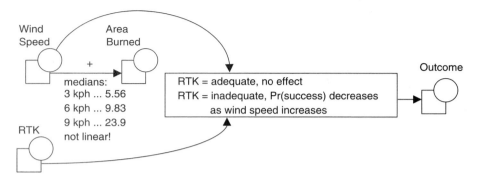

Figure 2.14   Some conclusions about the causal model in figure 2.2.

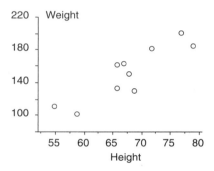

Figure 2.15   A scatterplot of a joint distribution of height and weight.

Individual	1	2	3	4	5	6	7	8	9	10
Height	72	68	66	67	79	59	55	66	69	77
Weight	180	150	160	162	184	100	110	132	128	200

The joint distribution of height and weight can be visualized in a scatterplot, as shown in figure 2.15. Each point in the scatterplot represents an individual. The scatterplot shows height and weight are related in this distribution: If an individual is short, then he or she is not very heavy, whereas if the individual is tall, he or she is not light.

Evidence of Independence in Scatterplots

Recall that our initial causal model of Phoenix left open the direction of causal influence between two variables (figure 2.2). On the one hand, the amount of area

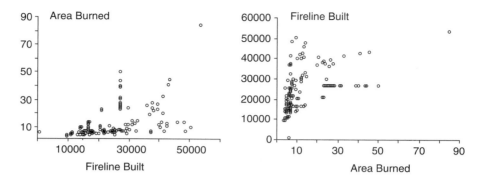

Figure 2.16   Two scatterplots of *AreaBurned* and *FirelineBuilt*.

claimed by a fire would seem to dictate how much fireline is built, because bulldozers have to build bigger boundaries to contain bigger fires. On the other hand, fires will grow to the size of the boundaries, so building a big boundary ensures a big fire. Thus we have two possible causal relationships: *AreaBurned* causes *FirelineBuilt* and *FirelineBuilt* causes *AreaBurned*. It is generally impossible to figure out the correct causal order given a single joint distribution or scatterplot (section 8.8), but we can sometimes find evidence that one factor does not cause another.

Two scatterplots of *AreaBurned* and *FirelineBuilt* are shown in figure 2.16. Both present the same data, the axes are merely reversed. One immediately sees an outlier point at *AreaBurned* = 84 and makes a mental note that the mean, standard deviation and range of the distribution will be inflated. Perhaps the most striking feature of the scatterplots is the line of points at *FirelineBuilt* = 27,050. A closer look at these points is shown in figure 2.17. They fall in a remarkably narrow range, with just ten meters separating the lowest value of *FirelineBuilt* from the highest. Ten meters is just .0008 of the interquartile range of the distribution of *FirelineBuilt*, so relative to the other points in the distribution, the ones in figure 2.16 can be regarded as a line, having essentially no variance around *FirelineBuilt*, but considerable variance around *AreaBurned*.

What does this line of points suggest? One interpretation is that, for these trials, the area burned has no influence on the amount of fireline built. Irrespective of the area of the fire, Phoenix builds a 27,055 ±5-meter fireline. More generally, a vertical or horizontal line of points in a scatterplot suggests that one variable has no influence on the other.

A scruffier line of points appears to be perpendicular to the one just described, running in figure 2.16 from *FirelineBuilt* = 9000 to *FirelineBuilt* = 28,000. Following the previous argument, this line suggests that irrespective of the amount of fireline

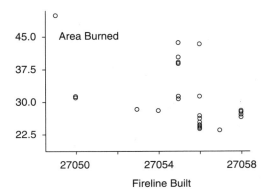

Figure 2.17   Blowing up the line of points in figure 2.16.

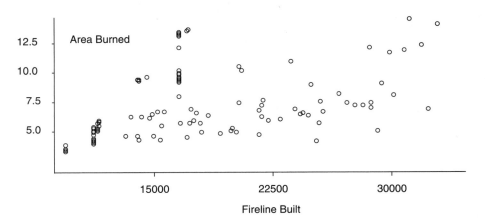

Figure 2.18   Blowing up another "line" of points in figure 2.16.

Phoenix builds, the fire burns a fixed amount of acreage. But when the scatterplot is expanded to show just these points, the "line" is illusory: *AreaBurned* ranges from less than four acres to more than twelve. The points in figure 2.18 cover 64 percent of the interquartile range of *AreaBurned*, so they can hardly be considered a constant value of that variable. (Had we used the range instead of the interquartile range for this calculation, then the points in figure 2.18 would cover only 11 percent of the range, because the range is inflated by the single outlier at *AreaBurned* = 84 acres.) The blown-up figure does disclose something, however: vertical lines at other values of *FirelineBuilt*, including two or perhaps three we had not seen before.

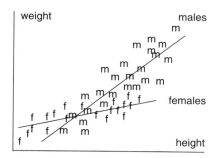

Figure 2.19   Point coloring shows that the relationship between two variables depends on a third.

2.4.5   Point Coloring to Find Potential Causal Factors

If in some conditions Phoenix builds a fixed amount of fireline, irrespective of the area burned, why does this not happen all the time? Which factors determine the conditions for this phenomenon? One method for answering such questions is called *point coloring*. It helps you see three variables simultaneously in a two-dimensional scatterplot and it sometimes explains patterns in scatterplots. For example, the individuals in a joint distribution of height and weight might be represented not by undifferentiated points, but by whether the individual is male or female, as in figure 2.19. On a computer screen, we might use two colors instead of the symbols "m" and "f," but either way, you'll agree that structure fairly leaps out of figure 2.19, but would be entirely obscured if every individual was represented by a single black dot. For example, if one draws a line through the long axis of the *m* points and a similar line for the *f* points, one sees that men are taller and heavier than women, but, more importantly, as women get taller their weight increases less rapidly than men. The relationship between height and weight is not the same for women as for men.

Point coloring helps to explain the lines in the scatterplot of *FirelineBuilt* and *AreaBurned*. In figure 2.20, I color the original scatterplot with *FirstPlan*, the variable that represents the plan Phoenix first adopts to try to contain a fire. You can see immediately that the vertical lines in the scatterplot all have one value of *FirstPlan*. When Phoenix tries the "model" plan first, it almost invariably ends up building 11,500, 17,000, or 27,000 meters of fireline. In other words, when Phoenix adopts the "model" plan, *AreaBurned* has no influence on *FirelineBuilt*. One question remains: Why are there three values of *FirelineBuilt*? It is a simple matter to answer this question by coloring the scatterplot again with another variable. This will show that the left line of points is made up exclusively of low wind speed trials, and the middle and right lines represent medium and high wind speed trials, respectively.

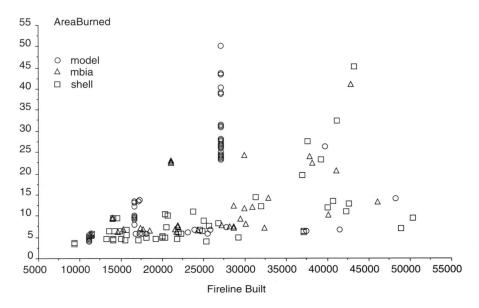

Figure 2.20   Coloring the scatterplot of *FirelineBuilt* and *AreaBurned* by *FirstPlan*.

Point coloring can quickly identify interesting combinations of variable values, but it works best when the coloring variables have relatively few values. If this isn't the case, you might bin a coloring variable first, and have a point's color or symbol denote bin membership.

In sum, point coloring has helped us refine our original causal model a little more, as shown in figure 2.21. We have strong evidence that *AreaBurned* doesn't influence *FirelineBuilt* when *FirstPlan* is "model"; rather, in this case, *FirelineBuilt* is determined by *WindSpeed* and *FirstPlan*. We still do not know the causal direction between *AreaBurned* and *FirelineBuilt* when *FirstPlan* is not "model."

2.4.6   Fitting Functions to Data in Scatterplots

One way to summarize the data in a scatterplot is with a function that relates x and y. For example, a straight line would seem to fit the scatterplot in panel A of figure 2.22 moderately well, so the function that relates x and y would have the familiar form $y = bx + a$. The task of linear regression is to find values for the slope and intercept parameters so that the resulting line is, by one criterion, the best fit to the data (section 8.2.1). You don't really need regression, though. For many purposes

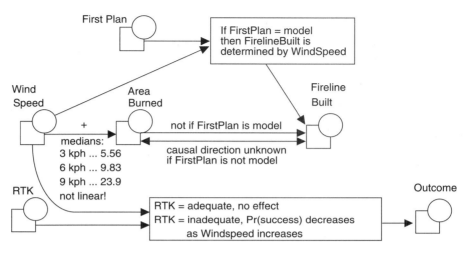

Figure 2.21   Further refinements of the causal model in figures 2.2 and 2.14.

it is just as informative to draw a line by eye, especially when you consider that such a line is probably more resistant to outliers. If you must fit lines algorithmically, you might consider a *robust procedure* for constructing a *three-group resistant line*, as described in section 5.3.4. The basic idea is to sort your points by *x*, divide them into three equal groups for low, medium, and high *x* values, take the *x* and *y* medians of the low and high groups, draw a line between these "median coordinates," and use the middle group to shift the line higher or lower on the y axis.

Often a straight line is not a good fit to data. A higher polynomial function or a piecewise fit would be better. Many statistics packages contain routines to find good nonlinear fits, and AI researchers have themselves developed function-finding programs for this purpose (Falkenhainer and Michalski, 1986; Zytkow, 1987; Langley et al., 1987; Nordhausen and Langley, 1990; Schaffer, 1990; Schaffer, 1991; Shrager and Langley, 1990; Rao et al., 1991). Panel C of figure 2.22 shows the fit of a quadratic function to the original data. Data analysts, however, will often try to transform data so a straight line fits the transformed data well. Panel B shows a linear fit after applying a logarithmic transform to *x* values. Panel D shows a quadratic function fit after applying the transform. Finally, panels E and F show two piecewise linear fits to the original data.

Which of these is the "best" fit to the data? If the criterion for a good fit is that the line passes near the points, then panels B, C, and D look good. If the criterion is parsimony, then panels C and D are not as good as panels A and B because they include a quadratic component. Additional components often complicate the task of

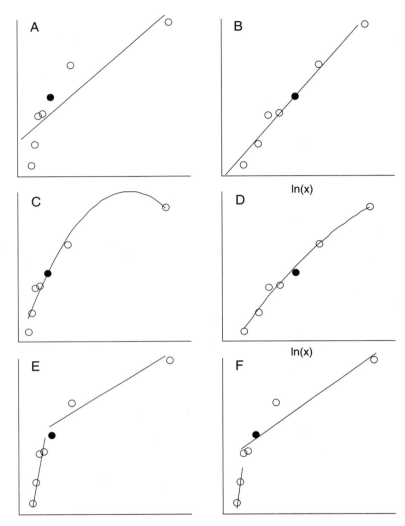

Figure 2.22   Six different fits to the same data.

interpreting a fit. If, for example, x and y were height and weight, it could be difficult to work "height squared" into an explanation of the data. Also, the function in panel C has a maximum, though no observed datum is in the vicinity. Should you try to explain it? (As it happens, the y axis represents percentages, so it will be difficult to explain the maximum in panel C, which exceeds 100.) The same argument can sometimes be made against transformations: what is the physical interpretation of ln(height) and what role does it play in an explanation of the data?

Knowing nothing about the processes that generated the data, we can evaluate the fits in panels A through F with weak criteria only. One thing you might know about the data is that some points are "special." For example, in physical experiments the freezing and boiling points of substances are special, and in figure 2.22 the darkened point is special. Alert readers might recognize it as $RTK = 1.0$; the data were presented first in table 2.9. What's special about $RTK = 1.0$ is that it was the default value of RTK during development of the Phoenix planner, so we expected performance on one side of this value to remain constant or improve, and performance on the other side to degrade. Note that panels A, B, C, and D all obscure this interpretation of the data. Panels A and B say performance improves linearly over the range of RTK and ln(RTK), respectively (although if you ignore the line in panel A you can still see nonlinear structure in the points, something that's mostly lost in panel B). Panel C implies that the qualitative change in performance occurs not at $RTK = 1.0$ but, rather, at $RTK = 3.75$. Panel D shows no qualitative change in performance at all; the curve is remarkably smooth. If you know points are special, however, you can fit functions piecewise between them, as in panels E and F. An interpretation of panel E is that performance changes qualitatively when RTK drops below its default value. Panel F offers a different interpretation: performance degrades gracefully, to a point, as RTK decreases, after which it collapses catastrophically. One can argue about which of these two interpretations is correct, but one at least has some interpretations to argue about.[3]

In sum, the purpose of fitting lines is to find a compact and interpretable functional representation of data. Even a little knowledge—knowing that points are special, for instance—makes it easier to achieve the second criterion. The subject of fitting lines is covered more in chapter 8, which is devoted to modeling.

2.4.7   Statistics for Joint Distributions of Two Continuous Variables

Although random scatter and vertical and horizontal lines in scatterplots suggest variables are independent, we usually are hoping for evidence of dependence or

---

3. I am indebted to Rob St. Amant for working out these examples.

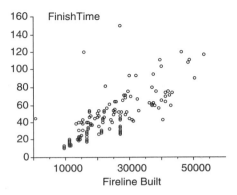

Figure 2.23 A scatterplot of *FirelineBuilt* against *FinishTime*.

association. For example, figure 2.23 shows that *FirelineBuilt* and *FinishTime* are not independent. If they were, any value of one variable would be equally likely to be paired with any value of the other. Instead, high values of one variable are very unlikely to be paired with low values of the other. Note that figure 2.23 does not say whether *FirelineBuilt* influences *FinishTime* or vice versa. We know that the former interpretation is the right one, because we know it takes time to build a fireline. Lacking this knowledge, however, we cannot infer a causal direction from the data in figure 2.23. On the other hand, a strong association between two variables certainly prompts us to look for a causal relationship between them. Thus, in an exploratory study, strong associations are a good source of causal hypotheses.

It looks as if the association between *FinishTime* and *FirelineBuilt* is pretty strong. At least for small values of *FinishTime* and *FirelineBuilt*, the points in figure 2.23 fall in a narrow corridor. Beyond *FirelineBuilt* = 35000, the relationship between *FirelineBuilt* and *FinishTime* is somewhat fuzzier.

A statistic that captures this notion of association is the *sample covariance* of x and y:

$$\text{cov}(x, y) = \frac{\sum_{i=1}^{n}(x_i - \overline{x})(y_i - \overline{y})}{n - 1} \tag{2.1}$$

Imagine a list of (x, y), coordinates:

$$((4, 2), (1, -3), (7, 10), (3, 0), (10, 15)).$$

If you sort this list by the x values, you get

$$((1, -3), (3, 0), (4, 2), (7, 10), (10, 15)).$$

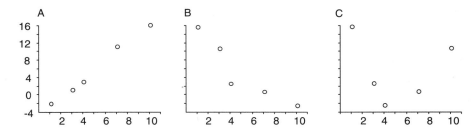

Figure 2.24   Positive, negative and nonlinear relationships between x and y.

Notice that the ascending x values are matched by ascending y values (figure 2.24a). The covariance in this case is 26.25. If ascending x values are matched with descending y values, as in the list $((1,15),(3,10),(4,2),(7,0),(10,-3))$ and scatterplot in figure 2.24b, then the covariance will be a relatively large negative number, in this case, -24.25. But if ascending (or descending) x values are matched with "jumbled" y values, as in the list $((1,15),(3,2),(4,-3)(7,0)(10,10))$ and the scatterplot in figure 2.24c, then the covariance will have small magnitude, in this case, -2.75. Thus the covariance is large (positive or negative) when the points in a scatterplot fall near a line, and small when they describe something other than a straight line. Covariance measures *linear association*.

   The trouble with covariance is that it can be an arbitrarily large positive or negative number, depending on the variances of x and y. The covariance of the data in figure 2.23 is 177,349, which certainly seems impressive; yet it represents a less clearly linear relationship than figure 2.24a, with its relatively small covariance. To standardize covariances and make them comparable, Pearson's correlation coefficient divides the covariance by the product of the standard deviations of x and y:

$$r_{XY} = \frac{\sum (x_i - \bar{x})(y_i - \bar{y})}{(n-1)s_x s_y}. \tag{2.2}$$

This statistic is always a number between -1.0, called a perfect *negative correlation*, and 1.0, a perfect *positive correlation*. The data in figure 2.23 have a correlation of .755—strong, but not outstanding. The scatterplot in figure 2.24a, represents a correlation of .995; the second, figure 2.24b, a correlation of $-.919$; and the third, figure 2.24c, which shows no linear relationship between x and y, a correlation of $-.104$. (Pearson's correlation coefficient is one of several, but is the most frequently used, so when we speak of correlations, we mean Pearson's, by default.)

   Despite the low correlation coefficient, x and y appear to be related in figure 2.24c. You could almost fit a parabola to the points. A low correlation does not mean x and

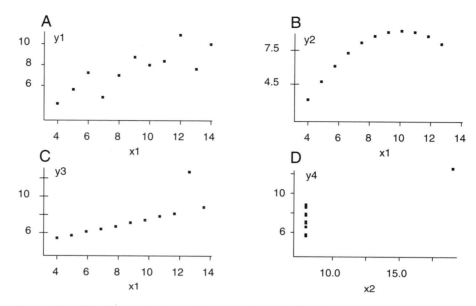

Figure 2.25   Why the correlation coefficient can be misleading (from Anscombe, 1973).

y are not associated, it just means they are not linearly associated. You should always look at a scatterplot before concluding variables are not associated, or, for that matter, that they are. In figure 2.25, Anscombe illustrates nicely the perils of inferring too much from correlations, alone (Anscombe, 1973, reproduced in Tufte, 1983). Case A is a linear relationship between *x* and *y*; case B is a distinctly nonlinear relationship. Case C appears to be a different linear relationship than case A; its slope is apparently less steep, yet the outlier in case C makes the relationships mathematically identical. If you ignore the outlier in case D, then no linear relationship exists between *x* and *y*. But if you include the outlier, then the correlation among *x* and *y* is identical to all the other cases, that is, $r_{xy} = .82$.

2.4.8   The Problem of Outliers

In two of Anscombe's examples, the correlation coefficient was distorted by a single point. Imagine 999 identical points, $x = 0$, $y = 0$, and a single point with higher values, say, $x = .001$, $y = .001$. Remarkably, this sample has a perfect correlation. It seems absurd to report a perfect linear relationship when 99.9 percent of the data sit on the origin. If all the points had zero values, the correlation would be undefined, because there can be no covariance where there is no variance. Unfortunately, the 999 points mark one end of a line and the remaining point marks the other end. The same thing happens, although less dramatically, in case D of figure 2.25. An outlier, then, is a point that is further from most of points than they are from each other. For instance, even though .001 is a very tiny distance from the other 999 points, it is a lot further from these points than they are from each other. A single outlier, far away, is dangerous because it appears to equation 2.2 to be the end of a line. But clusters of relatively nearby outliers can also distort the correlation badly.

One cannot do much about outliers except find them and, sometimes, remove them. A variety of procedures have been developed for the first step (see Emerson and Strenio, 1983; Cook and Weisberg, 1982), but the second requires judgment and depends on one's purpose. Consider, for example, the two outliers in the upper-left part of figure 2.23. Removing them increases the correlation from .755 to .832, a sizable increase when you realize that these two points are roughly 1 percent of the sample. If the correlation plays a central role in a model, you might remove the outliers on the grounds that you want a good estimate of the true correlation, and the outliers clearly cloud the picture. On the other hand, if all you want to know is whether two variables are associated, then a correlation of .755 serves the purpose.

Let us update the causal model of Phoenix with some correlation coefficients. To calculate the correlations I first removed from the data all cases in which *FirstPlan* is "model," because I know that in this case, *FirelineBuilt* is determined by *WindSpeed* alone. All the correlations in figure 2.26, then, are calculated from partitions in which *FirstPlan* is "mbia" or "shell."

The correlations are represented as dashed, undirected lines because, as we noted earlier, they do not themselves imply a causal direction. They do have heuristic value in suggesting causal hypotheses, especially hypotheses about independent and endogenous variables. Endogenous variables are those "downstream" of the independent variables. Because independent variables are set at the outset of the experiment, it is easy to interpret the correlation coefficient between, say, *WindSpeed* and *AreaBurned* as the strength of a causal relationship. Similarly, because I know *FirelineBuilt* is causally "upstream" of *FinishTime* I can interpret their correlation as a strength of causal association. In chapter 8, we will see that this interpretation of correlations is valid in some circumstances. For now, though, I will interpret the correlations heuristically: A strong correlation between two variables, one thought to be causally upstream of the other, suggests a causal link.

It is more difficult to interpret correlations between independent and dependent variables and correlations between endogenous variables. In particular, it's unclear whether to interpret them as evidence of direct or indirect causal influences. Does

AreaBurned directly influence *FinishTime*, or is the influence indirect, through *FirelineBuilt*? The correlations in figure 2.26 raise some other questions, as well:

- Is there really a direct effect of *RTK* on *FinishTime*, or does *RTK* instead influence *AreaBurned* and *FirelineBuilt*, and thus indirectly influence *FinishTime*? If the latter explanation is correct, why is the correlation of *RTK* and *AreaBurned* approximately zero (and so absent from figure 2.26)?

- Is the influence of *FirelineBuilt* on *FinishTime* direct, or indirect through *AreaBurned*?

- Why is the correlation between *WindSpeed* and *FirelineBuilt* approximately zero? This seems at odds with the apparent influence of *WindSpeed* on *AreaBurned* and the correlation between *AreaBurned* and *FirelineBuilt*. If a causal chain exists between *WindSpeed*, *AreaBurned* and *FirelineBuilt*, the lack of correlation between the ends of the chain is puzzling.

To answer these questions we need a method to estimate the strength of association between one variable and another while holding the influences of other variables constant. (This method is called *partial correlation*; see section 8.8). For example, we might find that *RTK* is uncorrelated with *FinishTime* when we hold the influences of all other variables constant, which means that the correlation in figure 2.26 ($r = -.56$) represents indirect influences of *RTK* on *FinishTime* through other variables. We also need a way to sum up multiple direct and indirect influences. These methods will be introduced in chapters 7 and 8.

Pearson's correlation is by no means the only statistic that measures association. Several other correlation coefficients have been proposed. Spearman's rank correlation coefficient is just like Pearson's except it uses the ranks of the values of variables, rather than the values themselves. It represents the strength of monotonic, not necessarily linear, association. Spearman's coefficient may be helpful in dealing with outliers because the tendency of a distant outlier to behave like the end of a line is diminished when distance is replaced by rank. Another rank correlation coefficient is called Kendall's tau. The idea is to count the number of times that the rank of y is what it should be (for a perfect correlation), given the rank of x. For example, if the rank of x is one, then, to have a perfect positive correlation, the rank of y should also be one; otherwise, somewhere in the data there is a higher-ranked x paired with a lower-ranked y, namely, with rank one. Kendall's tau is formed from the number of rank pairs that are consistent with a perfect correlation and the number of inconsistent pairs. Other correlation coefficients have been proposed, but Pearson's, Spearman's and Kendall's tau are the most common.

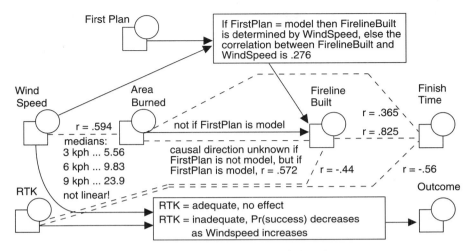

Figure 2.26   Further developments in the causal model of Phoenix.

The linear relationship between variables such as *FirelineBuilt* and *FinishTime* can be summarized by a straight line, or an equation for a line. One important part of exploratory data analysis involves fitting functions (such as straight lines, quadratics, exponentials, and so on) to data, and analyzing patterns in the residuals, the data that don't fit the rule. These activities result in functional models of data—models we can use to predict the values of dependent variables given independent variables. Because this chapter is already quite long, I will not discuss model-building and the analysis of residuals here, but postpone the discussion to chapter 8.

2.5   Time Series

One often wishes to track the value of a variable during a trial. For example, in a simulation of shipping, we might want to know how many ships are sitting in docks on each day of a simulation. The simulation used for the following examples is called TRANSSIM (see Oates and Cohen, 1994). Until now, I have focused on data collected just once per trial such as the area burned by a fire. The data table format was set up for this kind of data. Now I want to record the value of a variable several, perhaps hundreds, of times during a trial. I must extend the data table format (table 2.1) to include lists of data in some cells. These lists are called *time series*. It is usually assumed that the items in a time series are separated by a constant time interval; in case they are not, another list is included to show when each item was recorded.

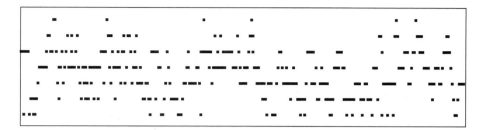

Figure 2.27   A scatterplot of time (x axis) against number of ships in docks (y axis).

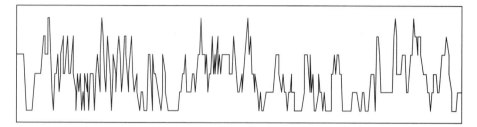

Figure 2.28   A time series of the number of ships in dock.

2.5.1   Visualizing Time Series

Time series are joint distributions where one variable is time. As such, they can be plotted as scatterplots. For example, figure 2.27 is a scatterplot of the number of ships sitting at docks on each of 646 days of a TRANSSIM trial. Note that data are plotted for a single trial, that is, a list from a single cell in a single row of a data table. Presumably, a different trial would produce a different scatterplot. Unfortunately, scatterplot representations of time series can be difficult to read, especially if many points are crammed close together on the time axis, and if, as in this example, *y* takes only integer values. It helps to "connect the dots," as shown in figures 2.28 and 2.29, which represent the number of ships in dock and the number of ships full of cargo and en route on each day, respectively.

These series plots (or lineplots as they are sometimes called) are better than scatterplots but it can still be difficult to see patterns in them. For example, can you see any correspondences between figures 2.28 and 2.29? Ships en route eventually have to dock, and ships in dock eventually leave for voyages, so one might expect peaks in one of the series to anticipate or follow peaks in the other. If you squint at figures 2.28 and 2.29 you might convince yourself that the curves correspond, but if you didn't expect such a relationship in the first place, it would not jump out of these pictures.

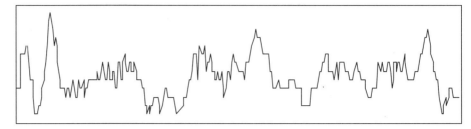

Figure 2.29   A time series of the number of ships en route.

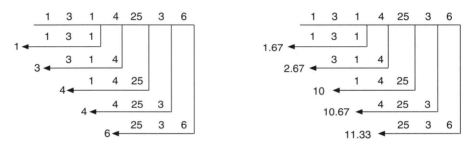

Figure 2.30   How to do median and mean smoothing (window size = 3).

2.5.2   Smoothing

The problem is that the series fluctuate so rapidly that trends and other features, if they exist, are obscured. The line in figure 2.28, for example, changes direction more than forty times in the first quarter of the series. Let us assume that these high-frequency fluctuations in values are due to random variance or noise, and see whether we can eradicate them by *smoothing* the series. The basic idea of smoothing is that the neighbors of a point often contain useful information about the true value of the point, above and beyond what the point itself says. To exploit this "neighbor information," every point in a series is replaced by an average of itself and its neighbors. Endpoints are handled separately; for example, they might be used as is, or averaged with their neighbor (see Tukey, 1977, for details.) The average need not be the arithmetic average, in fact, it is often better to use the median instead of the mean. In either case, values that are much bigger or smaller than their neighbors are "brought into line."

The most common mean and median smoothing techniques involve replacing the ith value in the series with the mean or median of the $i - 1$, i, and $i + 1$ values. These are called "3" smoovalues—a window of size 3. Figure 2.30 shows *3,median* and *3,mean smooths,* respectively, of the series 1 3 1 4

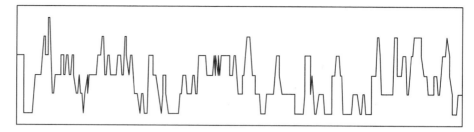

Figure 2.31   A median smooth of figure 2.28 (window size=3).

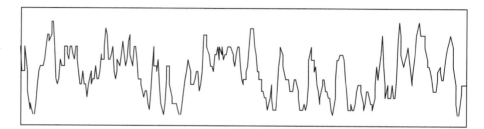

Figure 2.32   A mean smooth of figure 2.28 (window size=3).

25 3 6. You should verify that the value pointed to by the arrow that represents each window is the median or mean of the values within the window. In a median smooth, the second value in the series, 3, is replaced by 1, the median of the first three values (remember, end points are handled separately). The third value is replaced by the median of the second, third, and fourth values, and so on.

Note that the median smooth in figure 2.30 handles the outlier value, 25, differently than the mean smooth. Whereas the median smooth ignores the outlier, leaving only small values, the mean smooth gives the impression that the series contains three relatively high values, when in fact it contains only one. On the other hand, the median smooth creates *mesas* or short sequences of identical values; in this example the value is 4.

Figures 2.31 and 2.32 are 3,median and 3,mean smooths, respectively, of figure 2.28. The most notable difference between them is the mesas in the median smooth. Mesas can be handled by resmoothing, that is, smoothing the smoothed series again.

One can resmooth a sequence many times, with various sizes of windows and various kinds of averaging—not only median and mean smoothing, but also weighted smoothing in which each value in a window is multiplied by a weight. One can

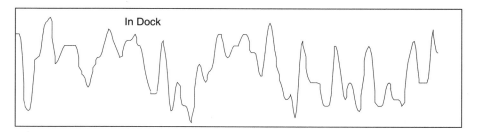

Figure 2.33   Smoothing figure 2.28 (*in dock*) with 4253H.

Figure 2.34   Smoothing figure 2.29 (*full en route*) with 4253H.

create long and complicated smoothing plans. For example, in Tukey's (1977), nota-tion 3R2H means "smooth the sequence with 3,median smooths repeatedly until the appearance of the series doesn't change with successive smooths (that's what the R means), then apply a 2,median smooth, and then a hanning operation (that's what the H means). A hanning operation multiplies the three values in a window by .25, .5, and .25, respectively, and sums the results. It is used to "clean up" a smooth by removing any leftover spikes. Hanning is familiar to researchers in computer vision who use it to smooth or "defocus" images. Interestingly, when the second of the three weights is a negative number, that is, 1, -2, 1, the operator computes the discrete version of the second derivative of the series, and can be used to sharpen, not smooth, the series (Cohen and Feigenbaum, 1982, pp. 211–214).

Smoothing plans have been developed for many kinds of data (Velleman and Hoaglin, 1981), but one that works pretty well in general is 4253H. This is four median smooths, with window sizes 4, 2, 5, and 3, followed by a hanning operation. The results of applying this plan to figures 2.28 and 2.29 are shown in figures 2.33 and 2.34.

Now we can return to the question that initiated this excursion: Does the number of ships in dock anticipate (or follow) the number of ships en route? By sliding

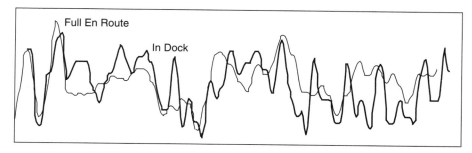

Figure 2.35   Shifting the *full en route* series left.

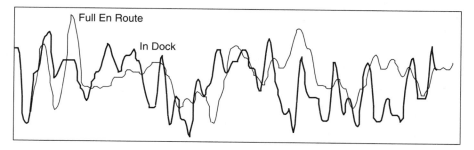

Figure 2.36   Shifting the *in dock* series left.

figures 2.33 and 2.34 over each other, we find alignments of the figures in which the series follow each other pretty closely. In figure 2.35, the *full en route* series is shifted to precede the *in dock* series by a few days. The curves overlap pretty well, which means that the *in dock* series anticipates the *full en route* series pretty well. (We shifted the *full en route* series backwards in time to get the overlap, so when the two series are synchronized again, high and low points in the *in dock* series are matched in the *full en route* series a few days later.) The *in dock* series is a *leading indicator* of the *full en route* series. In figure 2.36, the *in dock* series is shifted to precede the *full en route* series by a few days, but in this case the curves appear to overlap less. If the *full en route* series is a poorer indicator of the *in dock* series than the other way around, it is probably because ships en route take different amounts of time to reach ports where they have to wait for varying periods to get into a dock, whereas ships in dock are loaded and leave within a fairly narrow time window. Thus, once a ship is in dock we can predict fairly accurately when it will be full en route, but not the other way around.

2.5.3 Statistics for Time Series

Time series are joint distributions of time and another variable such as the number of ships in dock. We denote this other variable, v. A positive correlation between v and time indicates that the value of v increases over time; in other words, v has a positive trend. Conversely, a negative correlation between v and time indicates a negative trend. To assess whether a variable v_1 might be a good indicator or predictor of another variable v_2, we can compute a *cross correlation* between them. Let $v_1(i)$ and $v_2(i)$ be the values of variables 1 and 2 at time i. A cross correlation is simply the correlation of $v_1(i)$ and $v_2(i)$ at each time i. More generally, we can shift one series forward or backward in time and then compute a cross correlation; for example, correlating the values $v_1(i)$ and $v_2(i + 7)$ tells us whether the value of v_1 might be a good predictor of the value of v_2 seven time units hence. The amount we shift one series relative to another is called a *lag*.

Table 2.14 shows some cross correlations for the *in dock* and *full en route* series with lags ranging from -10 days to $+10$ days. Starting near the bottom of the table we see that when the lag is seven days—when values from the *in dock* series are correlated with values from the *full en route* series seven days later—the correlation is 0.303, which isn't striking but does promise some predictive power.

Table 2.14 Cross correlations between the series in figures 2.28 and 2.29 at several lags.

Lag in days	Cross correlation
−10	0.133
−9	0.129
−8	0.120
−7	0.111
⋮	⋮
−1	−0.214
0	−0.304
1	−0.183
⋮	⋮
6	0.253
7	0.303
8	0.278
9	0.244
10	0.236

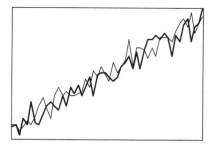

Figure 2.37   Two series with positive trend.

Conversely, the number of ships en route is a weak predictor of the number that will be in dock one week to ten days hence, as we can see from the low correlations associated with lags from −7 to −10. Note also the negative correlation at lag zero. This means that on any given day the number of ships in dock is negatively correlated with the number en route, which is what we would expect.

One must be wary that high cross correlations do not always mean one variable is a good predictor of another. In particular, if the trends of both variables are positive, then the cross correlation of the variables could be close to 1.0 (or if the trends are negative the cross correlation could be close to −1.0). To illustrate, I generated a series of numbers increasing from 0 to 100 in steps of 2; then I generated two other lists of random numbers distributed around zero and added each to the original series, yielding the two series shown in figure 2.37. The cross correlation of these series with zero lag is 0.942. This is high, but we know it means only that the values of both variables increase over time. Local peaks and valleys in one series are not matched synchronously or after some lag with peaks and valleys in the other, as they are in the *in dock* and *full en route* series.

When you find a high positive or negative cross correlation between series, therefore, you should check whether it is due to the general trends of the series. The easiest way to do this is to transform each series by *differencing*, replacing each value in a series by the difference of the value and its predecessor. This is a discrete version of subtracting the first derivative of the series (the trend) from the series, leaving the local peaks and valleys that were superimposed on the trend. Differencing the series in figure 2.37 gives figure 2.38 (the scales of the y axis are different in these figures), and, as you can see, there is no correspondence between peaks and valleys in the two series. Nor is the cross correlation between the two differenced series significantly higher than zero at any lag.

We sometimes want to use the current value of a variable to predict its value later, for example, we look at the weather in the morning to predict whether we will need

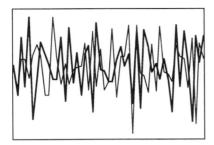

Figure 2.38   The series in figure 2.37 after differencing.

a coat later in the day. *Autocorrelation* measures the degree of association between values in a series separated by some lag. For example, if the series is

17   18   19   15   12   10   8

then a lag 2 autocorrelation is the correlation of these pairs:

(17, 19) (18, 15) (19, 12) (15, 10) (12, 8).

As always, end points are handled separately. The earlier proviso about trend holds for autocorrelations, too. For example, the lag 2 autocorrelation of one of the series in figure 2.37 is .897, whereas the lag 2 autocorrelation of the same series after differencing (figure 2.38) is just .181. This suggests that if you want to predict the value of the series two time units hence, you are better off using the general trend than the current value.

Trend can obscure interesting patterns in series. Consider the unsmoothed *in dock* series (figure 2.28). The autocorrelations for lag 1, 2, 3, and 4 are 0.67, 0.45, 0.22, and 0.31, respectively. One sees a typical autocorrelation pattern—high values initially, diminishing as lag increases. Evidently something else is going on, though, because the autocorrelation bounces at lag 4. When we difference the series to remove trend, these autocorrelations are -0.17, 0, -.48, and .36, and are much more instructive. They tell us if a dock loses some ships one day (a negative difference) then on the next day with a low probability it will gain some (indicated by the −.17 autocorrelation at lag 1); in three days it will quite probably have gained some (indicated by the autocorrelation −.48); and in four days it will lose some. Conversely, if the dock has just gained some ships then in one day it will have lost some (with low probability); in three days it will have lost some (with higher probability); and in four days it will have gained some. This strongly suggests that docks in the TRANSSIM simulator have a periodic "service cycle." (Interestingly, no comparable cycle shows up in the autocorrelations generated from the *full en route* series.) Note that the service cycle at docks is obscured if we look only at autocorrelations on the raw series; it becomes apparent only after the series is differenced.

Note also that the service cycle is short relative to the duration of the series, which is 646 days. This means smoothing obliterated the "bumps" in the series and, thus, evidence of the service cycle (e.g., compare figures 2.28 and 2.33). Smoothing removes high-frequency components from series because they are often noise. But sometimes, in this case for example, high-frequency components are meaningful. So, smooth the data for the clarity it brings to lower-frequency components, but use the original series or a differenced series, not a smoothed series, to find higher-frequency patterns.

2.6   Execution Traces

Although time series usually track quantities or continuous variables over time, such as the number of ships en route or the speed of a particular ship, we sometimes want to note instead the occurrence and duration of specific events over a period of time, such as when a ship finishes offloading its cargo or how long it takes each ship to traverse its route.

2.6.1   Visualizing Execution Traces

The simplest visualization of an execution trace is just a list such as this:

$$S_1^1 \ G_1^2 \ P_6^3 \ S_1^4 \ E_3^5 \ E_2^6 \ E_5^7 \ S_4^8 \ G_1^9 \ P_1^{10}.$$

Each capital letter denotes a type of activity. In the previous trace, for example, G stands for stating a goal, E for an external action such as moving from one place to another, S for sensing, and P for planning. Superscripts identify the times at which actions occurred (or simply the order in which they occurred) and subscripts identify types of actions, so A_1 is a different action than A_2, and A_1^1 is a specific instance of A_1.

Execution traces are easier to read if durations of actions are represented in a chart such as figure 2.39, which shows four classes of actions and several instances of actions from within each class, as well as their duration and order. One can sometimes detect patterns in execution traces represented this way; for example, it appears that sensing actions are more or less periodic and can run in parallel with external actions (E_3 and E_5). The chart also suggests that the third sensing action might have detected a

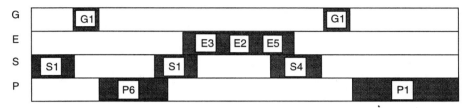

Figure 2.39   A chart representation of a behavior trace.

problem with the execution of a plan, because execution ceases, the goal is reasserted, and planning begins anew.

Another kind of visualization emphasizes not the actions in a trace but the transitions between actions. The simplest version of this idea is a transition table such as the one in figure 2.40. Each cell records the number of transitions from one type of item in a trace to another; for example, a fragment of a trace, ABABAB, would contribute 3 to the (A,B) cell in the table. Sometimes transition tables represent the transitions in a single behavior trace, in which case the total number of transitions is one minus the number of items in the trace. Sometimes the table represents the number of transitions that occur in a sample of several traces, a good idea if you want the table to describe "average" traces instead of a single, possibly anomalous trace. On the left hand side, figure 2.40 shows $91 + 3 + 45 + 1 + 3 = 143$ transitions from action A to another action, so the conditional probability of a transition to, say, C given that the current action is A is $45/143 = .31$. On the right hand side, figure 2.40 shows a *state-transition diagram* that includes all the transition probabilities calculated in this manner that exceed .1; the others are dropped for clarity. We can see that the system is very unlikely to take action D, for example, and if it does, the next action is apt to be A or D. If the next action is A, then the following one is twice as likely to be A than C. If action C does occur, then there is a good chance that the following action will be E, and the system could "settle" into a sequence of E's. I sketch a statistical analysis of state transitions in the next section.

Sometimes an execution trace is transformed before it is visualized, to get at a particularly important behavior. An example is a visualization called an *envelope*, which represents the progress of problem solvers, specifically, agents such as bulldozers and drivers in the Phoenix planner (Hart et al., 1990). Instead of visualizing all the actions of the agent, as in figure 2.39, an envelope represents the progress of the agent as a trajectory through a two-dimensional space. One dimension is time and the other is what has been achieved. Figure 2.41 shows a time-distance envelope for a bulldozer and driver. After a fast start, progress slows to the point that the agent is in jeopardy

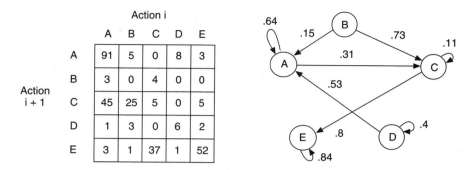

Figure 2.40   A transition table and a state-transition diagram corresponding to the table.

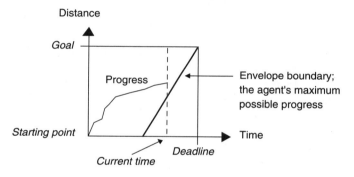

Figure 2.41   An "envelope" representation of progress.

of failing to achieve its goal by its deadline. At the current time, the agent must work at nearly maximum speed to make the deadline, and if it doesn't pick up speed soon, it will be too late.

One can design a practically limitless number of visualizations of execution traces, each to emphasize different aspects of behavior. For example, the state-transition diagram in figure 2.40 does not represent directly the order of actions in a trace. Figure 2.39 does, and it also shows the propensity of a system to repeat an action several times, but it is cumbersome and limited to a single trace. Surprisingly, visualizations of execution traces are rare in the artificial intelligence literature, perhaps because specific ones often must be implemented from scratch and involve graphics programming, whereas the more common histograms and scatterplots are easily generated with commercially available software. Tufte (1983; 1990) is a good source of ideas for visualizations.

2.6.2   Statistics for Execution Traces

Execution traces are series of categorical variables, so their statistics involve counting frequencies rather than operations on interval data. For example, it makes sense to find the modal (most frequent) action, but not the "mean action." If all we can do is count, then our only statistical options are those designed for frequencies. What follows is an illustrative sketch of how to find dependencies between events in execution traces. The topic is developed in more detail in chapter 6.

Consider again the transition table and state-transition diagram in figure 2.40. We can see that the probability of A following B is .15, but perhaps we want to know whether A follows B unusually often (or rarely) in a trace. One way to do it is to construct a contingency table to represent the number of times that A follows B, the number of times A follows something other than B (denoted $\overline{B}A$), the number of times something other than A follows B (denoted $B\overline{A}$), and the number of times something other than A follows something other than B (denoted $\overline{BA}$). This table can be constructed from the transition table in figure 2.40:

	A	$\overline{A}$	Totals
B	5	29	34
$\overline{B}$	102	164	266
Totals	107	193	300

Following B, the ratio of A to $\overline{A}$ is 5:29, but following $\overline{B}$ the ratio is 102:164, or roughly 5:8. So, does seeing B affect the probability of seeing A as the next event? Apparently it does: if you see B, the next observation is far less likely to be A than if you had seen $\overline{B}$. A chi-square test for a two-by-two table, described in section 2.4.3, confirms this. The χ^2 statistic is:

$$\chi^2 = \frac{(ad - bc)^2 N}{(a + b)(c + d)(a + c)(b + d)},$$

or, in the current case,

$$\chi^2 = \frac{(5 \cdot 164 - 102 \cdot 29)^2 \cdot 300}{(5 + 29)(102 + 164)(5 + 102)(29 + 164)} = 7.342.$$

The probability of obtaining such a large number by chance, given the assumption that the incidence of A is independent of the incidence of B, is less than .007. Therefore, we are safe concluding that a dependency holds between events A and B.

3   Basic Issues in Experiment Design

Most of the hypotheses tested in experiments are about causal relationships between factors. Sometimes the causal argument is implicit, but if one experiment doesn't address it, a subsequent experiment usually will. Suppose the hypothesis is that an information retrieval system, A, has a higher recall rate than a related system, A′. This hypothesis isn't explicitly causal, but unless it is just a wild, unmotivated guess ("gee whiz, perhaps A outperforms A′; one of them has to be best, right") there must be reasons for it. We must think A and A′ perform differently because one has features the other lacks, because they solve different problems, or they are constrained differently by their environments, and so on. An exploratory study might stumble upon a difference—or a murky suggestion of a difference—without intending to, but an experiment is designed to demonstrate a difference and the reasons for it.

Although experimental hypotheses have the form, "factor X affects behavior Y," experiments rarely test such hypotheses directly. Instead, factors and behaviors are represented by measured variables x and y, and an experiment seeks some sort of dependency between them. In a manipulation experiment, I manipulate x and record the effects on y. For the simple hypothesis A outperforms A′, x is the identity of the system, A or A′, and y is the performance variable, in this case, recall. For the hypothesis that A outperforms A′ because A has a larger dictionary, x is the size of the dictionary and y is recall, again. For the hypothesis that A outperforms A′ because A has a parser that handles compound nouns better, there are two x variables, the identity of the parser (x_i) and the prevalence of compound nouns in the test problems (x_j). I expect the effect of x_i on y to depend on x_j; for example, it shouldn't matter which parser is used if the test set includes no compound nouns. Whatever the hypothesis, a manipulation experiment tests it by manipulating x and recording the effect on y.

In an observation experiment one again tests a causal relationship between factor X and behavior Y, but one cannot find a variable x to manipulate directly. Your hypothesis might be that smoking causes lung cancer, but you cannot ethically manipulate whether or not people in a sample smoke. Your hypothesis might be that girls score higher on math tests than boys, but you cannot say to an individual, "for today's experiment, I want you to be a boy." In an observation experiment, the observed variable x is used to classify individuals in a sample, then y is computed for each class and the values compared. (It is hoped that individuals who differ on x also differ on factor X, but it doesn't always work out. Recall, for example, how various Olympic committees struggled to find appropriate observable indicators of gender.)

In manipulation experiments, x variables are called independent variables and y variables dependent variables. This terminology reflects the purpose of the experiment—to demonstrate a causal dependence between x and y. The same terms also apply in some observational experiments, although often x is called a predictor and y a response variable. Again, the terminology reflects the purpose of the experiment: if the goal is to see whether x predicts accurately the value of y—whether, for example, the number of cigarettes smoked per day predicts the probability of lung cancer—then the predictor-response terminology is more descriptive.

Manipulation and observation experiments produce two kinds of effects. Simple effects demonstrate that x influences y, while interaction effects show that x_i and x_j in concert influence y. For example, system A outperforms A$'$ (a simple effect) and the magnitude of the difference depends on the prevalence of compound nouns in test items (an interaction between the systems' parsers and the test material).

Although most experiments vary only two or three independent variables at a time, many more factors influence the dependent variable, as you can see by comparing young Fred and Abigail in figure 3.1. Your hypothesis might be that gender influences math scores but until you rule out the number of siblings, the parent's occupations, the child's height, and more, you can't be sure that gender—and not something else—is responsible for a simple effect on math scores. Nor can you be certain gender is the proximal influence; perhaps gender influences teachers' attitudes and the attention they pay to each child, which influences the child's confidence, and thus test-taking skills and math scores. Ruling out alternative explanations is the purpose of experimental control.

3.1   The Concept of Control

Like many children, I had a chemistry set. One day, mixing water and copper sulfate, I produced a beautiful blue-green liquid with which I tried to wash away some of the grime on my chemistry bench. It worked and I was convinced I had invented a new cleanser. My dad was unimpressed. He suggested I try water alone to see whether

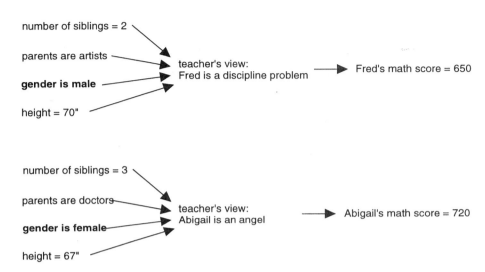

Figure 3.1   Dependent variables are influenced by many factors.

it cleaned as well as my new solution. What an awesome revelation. I insisted that water alone absolutely wouldn't work, but this only drew the noose tighter around my neck, because if you need a control condition, insisting that you don't only makes you look more foolish.

Perhaps you think that children make these mistakes but adults do not. Guess again. It can be very difficult to construct the right control condition, as a recent uproar in the AIDS research community attests. The following excerpt is from an article in the British weekly *New Scientist:*

> *The search for an AIDS vaccine was thrown into disarray last week with the disclosure of a "stunning" finding from experiments on monkeys carried out by Britain's Medical Research Council....*
>
> *The MRC researchers gave four macaques a vaccine based on human T cells that had been infected with SIV [a virus related to HIV, which causes AIDS] and then inactivated. When they gave these monkeys live virus, three out of four were protected. But the shock came from four other monkeys. The researchers gave these animals uninfected human cells of the same type as those used to create the vaccine. These cells had never seen SIV. To the team's amazement, when they gave the animals live SIV, two of them were protected....*
>
> *Some scientists were angry that the vital control experiment with uninfected cells had not been done earlier. But Jim Stott of the MRC countered that the need for such a control was not obvious at the beginning.... "It's terribly easy to say that afterwards," he said. "It would have been such a bizarre experiment to suggest. You have to try to save animals."* (*New Scientist,* 21 September, 1991, p. 14)

The *New Scientist* article is accompanied by a cartoon showing one macaque saying to another, "Perhaps we should be doing the research?" Let's examine what happened. Scientists developed a vaccine with two components, human cells and virus. They garnered evidence to suggest that the vaccine conferred immunity (three of four animals were protected). They assumed (with ample precedent from previous studies of vaccines) that the causative mechanism was a response to the virus, but in retrospect, they should have considered other hypotheses: The response could have been caused by the human cells and not the virus, or by human cells *or* the virus, or by an interaction between the agents. When it's spelled out this way, one cannot comprehend how the scientists—and their reviewers—simply assumed the virus was the causal agent and the T cells were not. Yet, as their spokesman said, "It would have been such a bizarre experiment to suggest." Clearly, the threat to experimental control was not technical competence; the scientists were perfectly capable of designing appropriate control conditions. The threat arose from something more pernicious. Controlled experiments do not control all possible alternative explanations directly, they control all *plausible* alternatives, so if something isn't plausible, it is controlled only indirectly through random sampling. The threat to control in this case was the *zeitgeist*, the collective beliefs of the field, which made human T cells an implausible cause of immunity.

Technically, however, the lesson is this: Before you claim x causes y, you must rule out all other possible causes of y, called *extraneous* variables. An extraneous variable (ev) is any variable other than the independent variable x that affects the dependent variable y. The most basic controlled experiment comprises two conditions, one called the *control* condition and the other the *treatment* condition, which are identical except for x. In particular, the extraneous variables in the treatment and control conditions are identical:

Treatment Condition : x & $ev_a, ev_b, \ldots, ev_k \rightarrow y_t$

Control Condition   : $ev_a, ev_b, \ldots, ev_k \rightarrow y_c$

If $y_t \neq y_c$, then x rather than $ev_a, ev_b, \ldots, ev_k$ influences y. However, we can't rule out the possibility that the effect $(y_t - y_c)$ is due to x acting in concert with one of the extraneous variables.

The story of the SIV experiment can be summed up this way:

Treatment Condition : virus & human T cells $\rightarrow$ immunity

And here's the control condition, which was run much later:

Control Condition   :   human T cells $\rightarrow$ immunity

Perhaps in the next round of experiments, human T cells will not be regarded as extraneous variables, but might be the focus, the hypothesized causal agent of immunity. I mention this to emphasize that the choice of independent variables is the researcher's choice. Nobody should tell researchers what causal factors to study, but nobody should listen to a researcher who asserts a causal association in the absence of an appropriate control condition.

3.1.1   What Is an Extraneous Variable?

In an ideal experiment, one controls all variables except the one that is manipulated, but in reality one can directly control very few variables. In figure 3.1, for instance, I list four variables besides gender that might account for math scores, and I could easily have expanded the list to include dozens more. To control for the possibility that parents' occupation affects math scores, I would have to compare Abigail, whose parents are doctors, with another child of doctors, not with Fred, whose parents are artists. In the extreme, I would have to compare Abigail with a sixty-seven-inch tall boy who has three siblings, doctors for parents, and is viewed by his teacher as "an angel." And if we could find such an individual, he probably wouldn't have been born in the same town as Abigail, or delivered by the same physician, or fed the same baby food, or dropped on his head on the same dark night that Abigail was. Agreed, this example seems a bit ridiculous, but you can't prove that these factors don't account for Abigail's math scores. So, if you take the definition of "extraneous variable" literally (i.e., extraneous variables are other possible causes) then the identity of the physician who delivered Abigail is an extraneous variable, and must be controlled in an experiment.

In practice, extraneous variables are not merely possible causes; they are plausible causes. It is plausible to believe that a teacher's view of a student influences her math scores; it is unlikely that the identity of the physician who delivered the baby who became the student influences her math scores. Thus, we distinguish extraneous variables from *noise* variables.

Experiments control extraneous variables directly, but noise variables are controlled indirectly by *random sampling*. Suppose we are concerned that a student's math scores are affected by how many siblings, s, he or she has. We can control s directly or let random sampling do the job for us. In the first instance, treating s as an extraneous variable, we would compare math scores of girls with $s = 0$ (no siblings) to scores of boys with $s = 0$, and girls with $s = 1$ to boys with $s = 1$, and so on. Alternatively, we can treat s as a noise variable and simply compare girls' scores with boys' scores. Our sample of girls will contain some with $s = 0$, some with $s = 1$, and so on. If we obtained the samples of girls and boys by random sampling, and if s is independent of gender, then the distribution of s is apt to be the same in both samples, and the effect of s on math scores should be the same in each sample. We cannot measure this effect—it might not even exist—but we can believe it is equal in both samples. Thus random sampling controls for the effect of s, and for other noise variables, including those we haven't even thought of.

The danger is that sampling might not be random. In particular, a noise variable might be correlated with the independent variable, in which case, the effects of the two variables are *confounded*. Suppose gender is the independent variable and s, the number of siblings, is the noise variable. Despite protestations to the contrary, parents want to have at least one boy, so they keep having babies until they get one (this phenomenon is universal; see Beal, 1994). If a family has a girl, they are more likely to have another child than if they have a boy. Consequently, the number of children in a family is not independent of their genders. In a sample of 1,000 girls, the number with no siblings is apt to be smaller than in an equally sized sample of boys. Therefore, the frequency distribution of s is not the same for girls and boys, and the effect of s on math scores is not the same in a sample of girls as it is in a sample of boys. Two influences—gender and s—are *systematically* associated in these samples, and cannot be teased apart to measure their independent effects on math scores. This is a direct consequence of relying on random sampling to control for a noise variable that turns out to be related to an independent variable; had we treated s as an extraneous variable, this confounding would not have occurred. The lesson is that random sampling controls for noise variables that are not associated with independent variables, but if we have any doubt about this condition, we should promote the noise variables to extraneous variables and control them directly. You will see another example of a *sampling bias* in section 3.3.

We hope, of course, that noise variables have negligible effects on dependent variables, so confounding of the kind just described doesn't arise. But even when confounding is avoided, the effects of noise variables tend to obscure the effects of independent variables. Why is Abigail's math score 720 when Carole, her best friend, scored 740? If gender was the only factor that affected math scores, then Abigail's and Carole's scores would be equal. They differ because Abigail and Carole are different: One studies harder, the other has wealthier parents; one has two older brothers, the other has none; one was dropped on her head as a child, the other wasn't. The net result of all these differences is that Abigail has a lower math score than Carole, but a higher score than Jill, and so on.

The *variation* in math scores within the sample of girls is assumed to result from all these noise variables. It follows, therefore, that you can reduce the variance (a measure of variation) in a sample by partitioning it into two or more samples on the

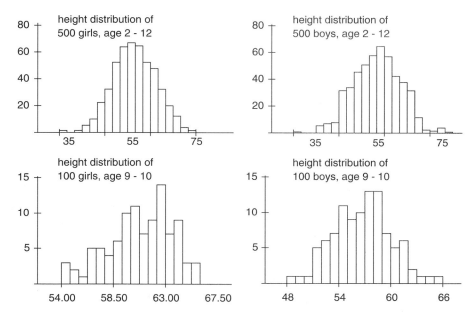

Figure 3.2   Distribution of heights for boys and girls at different ages.

basis of one of these variables, by promoting a noise variable to be an extraneous or independent variable. For example, figure 3.2 shows the distributions of the heights of boys and girls. In the top two distributions, the age of the children is treated as a noise variable, so, not surprisingly, the distributions have large variances. In fact, the variances are such that height differences between boys and girls are obscured. By promoting age to be an extraneous or independent variable—by controlling for age directly instead of letting random sampling control for its effect—we can reduce variance and see effects due to gender. The bottom two distributions represent boys and girls in the more tightly constrained nine-to-ten-year age bracket. They have smaller variances (compare their horizontal axes to those of the top two graphs) and we can now see that girls are taller than boys.

In sum, experiments test whether factors influence behavior. Both are represented by variables. In manipulation experiments, one sets levels of one or more independent variables, resulting in two or more conditions, and observes the results in the dependent variable. Extraneous variables represent factors that are plausible causes; we control for them directly by reproducing them across conditions. Noise variables represent factors we assume have negligible effects. They are controlled by random sampling, if the sampling is truly random. If noise factors turn out to have large effects, then variance within conditions will be larger than we like, and it can be reduced by treating noise variables as extraneous or independent (i.e., directly controlled) variables.

3.1.2   Control Conditions in MYCIN: A Case Study

MYCIN, developed at Stanford University by E. H. Shortliffe (Buchanan and Shortliffe, 1984) in the mid-1970s, was the first expert system to demonstrate impressive levels of performance in a medical domain. MYCIN's task was to recommend therapy for blood and meningitis infections. Because the cause of an infection was often unknown, MYCIN would first diagnose the cause and then prescribe therapy. Typically, MYCIN would ask a bunch of questions about a particular case and then suggest one or more therapies to cover all the likely causes of the infection. Sometimes, cases involved more than one infection.

Before reviewing how MYCIN was actually evaluated, consider how it might be. Stanford University is home to some of the world's experts on blood and meningitis infections, so perhaps we should show them a reasonable number of problems that MYCIN had solved and ask them what they think. Good idea, bad execution. Perhaps half the experts would say, "I think MYCIN is great," and the other half would say, "I think MYCIN is the thin end of a very dangerous wedge; computer diagnosticians, over my dead body!" A more likely scenario—seen often—is that the experts would be very enthusiastic and give glowing reviews, much the way that parents gush over their children. What we need is not opinions or impressions, but relatively objective measures of performance.

We might ask the experts to assess whether MYCIN offered the correct therapy recommendation in each of, say, ten cases. The experts would be told how to grade MYCIN when it offered one of several possible recommendations, and how to assign points to adequate but suboptimal therapy recommendations. This approach is more objective but still flawed. Why? It doesn't control for the prejudices of the experts. Enthusiastic experts might give MYCIN "partial credit" on problems that anti-MYCIN experts would say it failed.

A standard mechanism for controlling for judges' biases is *blinding*. In a single-blind study, the judges don't know whether they are judging a computer program or a human. MYCIN was evaluated with a single-blind study. Shortliffe asked each of eight humans to solve ten therapy recommendation problems. These were real, representative problems from a case library at Stanford Medical School. Shortliffe collected 10 recommendations from each of the eight humans, 10 from MYCIN, and the 10 recommendations made originally by the attending physicians in each case, for a

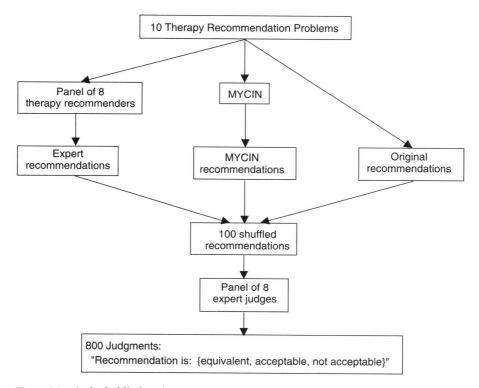

Figure 3.3   A single-blind study.

total of 100 recommendations. These were then shuffled and given to a panel of eight expert judges. Each judge was asked to score each recommendation as (1) equivalent to their own best judgment, (2) not equivalent but acceptable, or (3) unacceptable. This design, which controls for judges' bias by blinding them to the origin of the recommendations, is shown in figure 3.3.

You might think this design is an ironclad evaluation of MYCIN's performance. It isn't. The design as stated fails to control for two possible explanations of MYCIN's performance.

Imagine an expert system for portfolio management, the business of buying and selling stocks, bonds, and other securities for investment. I built a system for a related problem as part of my doctoral research. Naturally I wondered who the experts were. One place to look is a ranking, published annually, of pension-fund managers—the folks who invest our money for our old age. I learned something surprising: Very few pension-fund managers remain in the top 10 percent of the ranking from one year to the next. The handful that do could be considered expert; the rest are lucky one year, unlucky the next. Picking stocks is notoriously difficult (see Rudd and Clasing, 1982), which is why I avoided the problem in my dissertation research. But suppose I had built a stock-picking system. How could I have evaluated it? An impractical approach is to invest a lot of money and measure the profit five years later. A better alternative might be to convene a panel of experts, as Shortliffe did for MYCIN, and ask whether my stock-picking program picked the same stocks as the panel. As with the MYCIN judges, we face the problem that the experts won't agree. But the disagreements signify different things: When portfolio managers don't agree, it is because they don't know what they are doing. They aren't experts. Few outperform a random stock-picking strategy. Now you see the crucial control condition: One must first establish that the "experts" truly are expert, which requires comparing "experts" to nonexperts. Nonexpert performance is the essential control condition.

Surely, though, professors of medicine at Stanford University must be real experts. Obviously, nothing could be learned from the proposed condition; the professors would perform splendidly and the novices would not. Shortliffe didn't doubt the professors were real experts, but he still included novices on the MYCIN evaluation panel. Why?

Imagine you have built a state-of-the-art parser for English sentences and you decide to evaluate it by comparing its parse trees with those of expert linguists. If your parser produces the same parse trees as the experts, then it will be judged expert. You construct a set of test sentences, just as Shortliffe assembled a set of test cases, and present them to the experts. Here are the test sentences:

1. Bill ran home.
2. Jennifer ate ice cream.
3. The cat is on the mat.
4. Mary kissed John.

Because your program produces parse trees identical to those of the experts, you assert that your program performs as well as the experts. Then someone suggests the obvious control condition: Ask a ten-year-old child to parse the sentences. Not surprisingly, the child parses these trivial sentences just as well as the experts (and your parser).

Shortliffe put together a panel of eight human therapy recommenders and compared MYCIN's performance to theirs. Five of the panel were faculty at Stanford Medical School, one was a senior resident, one a senior postdoctoral fellow, and one a senior medical student. This panel and MYCIN each solved ten problems, then Shortliffe

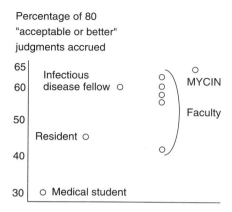

Percentage of 80
"acceptable or better"
judgments accrued

Figure 3.4   Results of the MYCIN evaluation.

shipped the solutions, without attribution, to eight judges around the country. For each solution that a judge said was equivalent or acceptable to the judge's own, Shortliffe awarded one point. Thus, each human therapy recommender, and MYCIN, could score a maximum of 80 points—for eight "equivalent or acceptable" judgments on each of the ten problems. The results are shown in figure 3.4. The expert judges actually agreed slightly more with MYCIN's recommendations than with those of the Stanford Medical School faculty.

By including novices on the MYCIN evaluation panel, Shortliffe achieved three aims. Two relate to control—ruling out particular explanations of MYCIN's high level of performance. One explanation is that neither MYCIN nor the experts are any good. Shortliffe controlled against this explanation by showing that neither MYCIN nor the experts often agreed with the novice panel members. This doesn't prove that MYCIN and the professors are better than the novices, but they are different. (If five professors recommend, say, ampicillin as therapy, and five novices give five different answers, none of which is ampicillin, then ampicillin isn't necessarily a better therapy, but which answer would you bet your life on?) Another explanation of MYCIN's performance is that Shortliffe gave MYCIN easy cases to solve. If "easy" means "anyone can do it," then the novices should have made the same therapy recommendations as the experts, and they didn't.

The third advantage of including novices on the evaluation panel is that it allowed Shortliffe to test a causal hypothesis about problem-solving performance in general, and MYCIN's performance in particular. Before discussing the hypothesis, consider again the results in figure 3.4. What is the x axis of the graph? It is unlabeled because the factors that determine performance have not been explicitly identified. What could these factors be? MYCIN certainly does mental arithmetic more accurately and more quickly than the Stanford faculty; perhaps this is why it performed so well. MYCIN remembers everything it is told; perhaps this explains its performance. MYCIN reasons correctly with conditional probabilities, and many doctors do not (Eddy, 1982); perhaps this is why it did so well. Even if you know nothing about MYCIN or medicine, you can tell from figure 3.4 that some of these explanations are wrong. The mental arithmetic skills of Stanford faculty are probably no better than those of postdoctoral fellows, residents, or even medical students; nor are the faculty any more capable of reasoning about conditional probabilities than the other human therapy recommenders, yet the faculty outperformed the others. To explain these results, we are looking for something that faculty have in abundance, something that distinguishes fellows from residents from medical students. If we didn't already know the answer, we would certainly see it in figure 3.4: knowledge is power! This is the hypothesis that the MYCIN evaluation tests, and that figure 3.4 so dramatically confirms.

Knowledge-Is-Power Hypothesis   Problem solving performance is a function of knowledge; the more you know, the better you perform.

To be completely accurate, figure 3.4 supports this hypothesis only if we define high performance as a high degree of agreement with the eight expert judges, but if Shortliffe didn't believe this, he wouldn't have used these judges as a gold standard.

Let's review the tactics discussed in this section:

■ To control for judges' bias, blind them to origin of the items they are judging. For example, do not tell them whether recommendations were produced by a program or a person.

■ To control for the possibility that high performance is due to easy problems, include a control group of problem solvers who can solve easy problems but not difficult ones. For example, if a student performs as well as faculty, then the problems are probably easy.

■ To control for the possibility that the "gold standard" against which we measure performance is not a high standard, include a control group that sets a lower standard. For example, if a chimpanzee throwing darts at the Big Board picks stocks as well as professional portfolio managers, then the latter do not set a high standard.

■ To test the hypothesis that a factor affects performance, select at least two (and ideally more) levels of the factor and compare performance at each level. For example, to test the hypothesis that knowledge affects performance, measure the performance of problem solvers with four different levels of knowledge—faculty, post-doc, resident, and student. Note that this is an observation experiment because problem solvers are classified according to their level of knowledge. It generally isn't practical to manipulate this variable because it takes so long to train people to expert levels. The knowledge-is-power hypothesis might also be tested in a manipulation experiment with MYCIN by directly manipulating the amount MYCIN knows—adding and subtracting rules from its knowledge base—and observing the effects on performance (chapter 6). In all these designs, it is best to have more than two levels of the independent variable. With only two, the functional relationship between x and y must be approximated by a straight line.

3.2   Four Spurious Effects

Good control conditions, like fine food and wine, are easy to admire and hard to produce. It helps to be aware of some common pitfalls.[4] Four effects are particularly relevant to experimental AI. They are called ceiling, floor, regression, and order effects, respectively, and *spurious effects*, collectively. Spurious effects suggest that a treatment is effective when it isn't, or suggest that a treatment isn't effective when it is. Ceiling and floor effects are sometimes easy to see, while regression and order effects can be quite subtle.

3.2.1   Ceiling and Floor Effects

Recall that MYCIN and human experts accrued roughly 65 percent of the available "acceptable or equivalent" scores from the panel of judges (figure 3.4). I concluded that MYCIN's performance was approximately equal to that of human experts. Now imagine that MYCIN and the human experts each accrued approximately 100 percent of the available "acceptable or better" scores. Can we conclude that MYCIN and human experts perform equally well? At first glance the answer is obvious: The program got the same score as the humans, so they perform equally. But this situation is qualitatively different from the one in which humans and MYCIN each got roughly 65 percent. In the latter case, 35 percent is available to demonstrate higher performance. If MYCIN was better than the humans, it could have a higher score. In the 100 percent case, if MYCIN is better, it cannot have a higher score, because both are "at ceiling."

---

4. Campbell and Stanley (1963) and Cook and Campbell (1979) discuss a dozen common problems in social science research. Not all are relevant to experimental methods in computer science, but these monographs are worth a careful perusal.

When one's hypothesis is Performance(A) $\geq$ Performance(B), if A and B achieve the maximum level of performance (or close to it), the hypothesis should not be confirmed, due to a ceiling effect. Ceiling effects arise when test problems are insufficiently challenging. Floor effects are just like ceiling effects but they are found at the opposite end of the performance scale. Imagine therapy recommendation problems that are so challenging that neither human experts nor MYCIN can solve them correctly.

Technically, a ceiling effect occurs when the dependent variable, y, is equal in the control and treatment conditions, and both are equal to the best possible value of y. In practice, we use the term when performance is nearly as good as possible in the treatment and control conditions. Note that "good" sometimes means large (e.g., higher accuracy is better) and sometimes means small (e.g., low run times are better), so the ceiling can be approached from above or below. A ceiling thus bounds the abstract "goodness" of performance. Floor effects occur when performance is nearly as bad as possible in the treatment and control conditions. Again, poor performance might involve small or large scores, so the "floor" can be approached from above or below.

Consider an example from the Phoenix project (section 2.1). Assume the performance variable y is the time required to contain a fire, so good scores are small, and the ceiling is the smallest possible score. The mean time to contain fires within a 50-km radius of the firebase is roughly twenty hours of simulated time. Suppose you have designed a new scheduling algorithm for the Phoenix planner, but unfortunately, it shaves only thirty minutes from the mean finish time. Distraught, you consult a Phoenix wizard, who tells you a bit about how long things take in the Phoenix environment:

Activity	Average time for the activity
Noticing a fire in the environment	2 hours
Deciding which plan to use	1 hour
Average bulldozer transit time from the firebase to any point in a 50 km radius	4 hours
Average time to cut one segment of fireline	6 hours

None of these activities involves scheduling. Each bulldozer cuts an average of two segments of fireline, so the average time to contain a fire is nineteen hours. The new scheduling algorithm therefore has very little room to show its superiority, because the old version of Phoenix required twenty hours, and any version requires at least nineteen hours. This is a ceiling effect, approached from above.

The most important thing to remember about ceiling and floor effects is how they arise. They arise not because a program in a control condition is very good (or bad) but because the program performs very well (or poorly) on a particular set of test problems. The fact that Phoenix's old scheduling algorithm takes only an hour longer than the minimum does not mean it is a good algorithm: A dozen uncontrolled factors might account for this performance, and its performance in a slightly different scenario might be considerably worse. Ceiling effects and floor effects are due to poorly chosen test problems.

3.2.2   How to Detect Ceiling and Floor Effects

If the maximum or minimum value of a dependent variable is known, then one can detect ceiling or floor effects easily. This strongly suggests that the dependent variable should not be open-ended; for example, it is easy to see a ceiling effect if y is a percentage score that approaches 100 percent in the treatment and control conditions. But the mere fact that y is bounded does not ensure we can detect ceiling and floor effects. For example, the acreage burned by fires in Phoenix is bounded—no fewer than zero acres are ever burned by a fire—so if two versions of the Phoenix planner each lost approximately zero acres when they fought fires, we would recognize a ceiling effect (approached from above). But now imagine running each version of the planner (call them P and P′) on ten fires and calculating the mean acreage lost by each: $\overline{y}_P = 50$ and $\overline{y}_{P'} = 49.5$. Does this result mean P′ is not really better than P, or have we set ten fires for which 49.5 acres is nearly the best possible performance?

To resolve this question—to detect a ceiling effect—it doesn't help to know that zero is the theoretical best bound on lost acreage; we need to know the *practical* best bound for the ten fires we set. If it is, say, ten acres, then P′ is no better than P. But if the practical best bound is, say, forty-seven acres, then the possible superiority of P′ is obscured by a ceiling effect. To tease these interpretations apart, we must estimate the practical best bound. A simple method is illustrated in table 3.1. For each fire, the least acreage lost by P and P′ is an upper bound on the practical minimum that would be lost by any planner given that fire. For example, P′ lost fifteen acres to fire 1, so the practical minimum number of acres lost to fire 1 is at most fifteen. The average of these minima over all fires, $400/10 = 40$, is an overestimate of the practical best performance. If this number was very close to the average areas lost by P and P′, we could claim a ceiling effect. In fact, one planner can contain any fire in the sample with, on average, ten fewer acres lost than the other planner. So we simply cannot claim that the average areas lost by P or P′ are the practical minimum losses for these fires. In other words, there is no ceiling effect and no reason to believe the alleged superiority of P′ is obscured.

Table 3.1   The acreage lost by fires fought by P and P′, and the minimum acreage lost.

Fire	1	2	3	4	5	6	7	8	9	10	Total
P	55	60	50	35	40	20	90	70	30	50	500
P′	15	50	50	75	65	40	60	65	40	35	495
Min	15	50	50	35	40	20	60	65	30	35	400

A dramatic example of ceiling effects came to light when Robert Holte analyzed fourteen datasets from a corpus that had become a mainstay of machine learning research. The corpus is maintained by the Machine Learning Group at the University of California, Irvine. All fourteen sets involved learning classification rules, which map from vectors of features to classes. Each item in a dataset includes a vector and a classification, although features are sometimes missing, and both features and classifications are sometimes incorrect. All datasets were taken from real classification problems, such as classifying mushrooms as poisonous or safe, or classifying chess endgame positions as wins for white or black. Holte also included two other sets, not from the Irvine corpus, in his study.

A typical classification learning experiment goes like this: A dataset is divided randomly into a training set (typically two-thirds of the items) and a test set (one third of the items). An algorithm learns classification rules from the training set, and with these rules attempts to classify the items in the test set. The proportion of correctly classified items is recorded, all classification rules are discarded, and the process is repeated. After, say, twenty-five iterations, the mean of the proportions is calculated. This is the *average classification accuracy* for the algorithm. (See section 6.10 for details on this and related procedures.) Table 3.2 shows the average classification accuracy computed by Holte for two algorithms on sixteen datasets. The first algorithm, C4, was at the time of Holte's study state-of-the-art. The other, 1R*, will be described momentarily. Note that the average classification accuracies for C4 and 1R* are just a bit more than two percentage points apart: C4 correctly classified 85.9 percent of the items in its test sets, whereas 1R*'s figure is 83.8. Following the logic of the previous section we must ask, is C4 hardly better than 1R*, or are we seeing a ceiling effect? To answer the question we can estimate the practical maximum average classification accuracy to be the average of the maxima of the classification accuracies in table 3.2. This estimate, 87.4, is not much larger than 85.9 or 83.8, so it appears that on average, the difference between an algorithm's performance and an estimate of the best possible performance is only two or three points. A ceiling effect seems to be lurking.

Table 3.2   Average classification accuracies for two algorithms, C4 and 1R*

Dataset	BC	CH	GL	G2	HD	HE	HO	HY
C4	72	99.2	63.2	74.3	73.6	81.2	83.6	99.1
1R*	72.5	69.2	56.4	77	78	85.1	81.2	97.2
Max	72.5	99.2	63.2	77	78	85.1	83.6	99.1

Dataset	IR	LA	LY	MU	SE	SO	VO	VI	Mean
C4	93.8	77.2	77.5	100	97.7	97.5	95.6	89.4	85.9
1R*	95.9	87.4	77.3	98.4	95	87	95.2	87.9	83.8
Max	95.9	87.4	77.5	100	97.7	97.5	95.6	89.4	87.4

The surprising thing about Holte's results is not the ceiling effect, but that 1R* is a much simpler algorithm than C4. Roughly speaking, 1R* bases its classifications on the single most predictive feature of the items to be learned, whereas C4 builds more complex classification rules with many features. Intuition tells us more features are better; for example, to classify mushrooms as poisonous or benign we might look at color, shape, odor, habitat, and so on. But in fact, the most predictive feature of mushrooms (odor) is an excellent basis for classification (see the MU column of table 3.2). C4's decision rules included six features of mushrooms (and 6.6 features on average, over all the datasets), but its average classification accuracy is less than 2 percent higher.

Holte's algorithm, 1R*, provides a powerful control condition for research on classification algorithms. Suppose your innovative algorithm achieves an average 86 percent classification accuracy. Until Holte's study, you didn't know how much of this score was purchased with your innovation. Now, however, you know that your idea is worth perhaps two or three percentage points, because 1R*, an utterly simple algorithm that lacks your idea, performs nearly as well.

If as we suspect the practical maximum classification accuracy for the Irvine datasets is roughly 87 percent, and the average performance of 1R* is roughly 84 percent, what does this mean for research on classification algorithms? Two interpretations come to mind: Perhaps the Irvine datasets are typical of the world's classification tasks, in which case the range of performance between the simplest and the most sophisticated algorithms is only two or three points (this interpretation is discussed further in chapter 9). Alternatively, C4 and other sophisticated algorithms might be at ceiling on the Irvine datasets, and the range of performance will not widen until more challenging datasets are introduced.

Table 3.3   Pre- and posttest score illustrating a regression effect.

Problem Number	6	14	15	21	29	36	55	61	63	84
Pretest Score	0	1	1	2	2	2	4	5	5	6
Posttest Score	5	6	4	1	8	12	2	2	6	19

3.2.3   Regression Effects

Consider the following hypothetical experiment: Dr. X runs a program on 100 test problems to get a baseline level of performance. Some of the results are shown in the "Pretest Score" row of table 3.3. The pretest scores are listed in ascending order, so problem number 6 has the lowest score (zero), problem 14 has the next lowest score, and so on. Dr. X then modifies the program to increase its performance. Because he wants a stringent test of these modifications, and he doesn't want the expense of running 100 more trials, Dr. X decides to test the modified program on the ten problems on which it previously performed worst, problems 6, 14, 15.... The performance of the modified program is shown in the "Posttest Score" row of table 3.3. Dr. X is delighted. You, however, are skeptical. You ask Dr. X a single question, and when he answers in the affirmative, you know he has made two related and inexcusable mistakes. What is the question?

The question is, "Does chance play any role in determining scores?" If it does, then rerunning the original program on problems 6, 14, 15, ... will produce different scores. And not only different scores, but higher scores! Let's start with problem 1, on which Dr. X's program scored zero. If zero is the lowest possible score, then when the original program is run again, it has no chance of attaining a lower score, but it has a chance of attaining a higher score. Thus, on the second attempt, Dr. X's program is expected to attain a score higher than zero on problem 1. Now consider problem 2. When the original program is run again, it has some chance of attaining a score lower than one, and some chance of attaining a score higher than one. If the first probability is smaller than the second, then Dr. X's original program is expected to attain a score higher than one on problem 2. And if the original program is expected to achieve higher scores simply by chance when it is run again, how can Dr. X be sure that the higher scores achieved by his modified program are due to the modifications instead of chance? Dr. X's first mistake is testing his program on problems whose scores have "nowhere to go but up."

The second mistake is best understood in terms of a model of scores. If chance plays a role, then each score can be represented as the sum of a true value and a chance value. Assume for a moment that the problems in Dr. X's test set are equally challenging, so his program ought to attain the same true value on each (i.e., the variance in scores is due entirely to the chance component). Then if Dr. X's original program attains a very low score on a problem, it is apt to attain a higher score next time it encounters that problem. Similarly, if the program first attains a very high score on a problem, then it is apt to attain a lower score on the next encounter. This means that if Dr. X reruns his original program on the ten highest-scoring problems, it will appear to magically become worse, and if he reruns the program on the ten lowest-scoring problems it will appear to magically improve. But this is no magic: It is a simple statistical artifact called *regression toward the mean.*

The best way to avoid regression effects is to run the same problems in both pretest and posttest. If the pretest involves 100 problems and you want to run only 10 in a posttest, then you should rank the problems by their pretest scores and select every tenth, or some such scheme to ensure a representative distribution of pretest scores. Be warned, however, that if you use a *t* test to compare samples of very disparate sizes (e.g., 10 and 100), you should treat marginal (i.e., barely significant) results with caution.

3.2.4 Order Effects

Level of performance on a series of tasks or on a composite task often depends on the order in which the tasks or subtasks are addressed. An example of an *order effect* is shown in figure 3.5. The Phoenix planner uses three general plans to fight simulated forest fires, called *model, shell,* and *mbia*. It begins work with one, but if the plan seems not to be working, it adopts another. (Sometimes it will select the same plan again, and update its parameters.) Thus, the first plan has three outcomes: successful containment of the fire (denoted S in figure 3.5), outright failure to contain the fire (F), or replanning (R). Sometimes a third attempt is made, but we will concentrate on the first two, here. It is striking that *model* does very well when it is the first plan (eighty-four success, fifteen failures, and fifteen replans) and *shell* and *mbia* do quite poorly, whereas the pattern is reversed for the second plan: *Model* does poorly when it is the second plan whereas *shell* and *mbia* do rather better. Figure 3.5 shows a clear order effect: The success of a plan depends on when the plan is tried.

Order effects can confound experiment results when different orders are systematically (and inadvertently) associated with treatment and control conditions. A set of exam problems might be completed more quickly in one order than another, because one problem might prepare you for another but not vice versa. So if a control group of students is presented test problems in a "good" order and the treatment group gets the problems in a "bad" order, then a positive effect of treatment might be washed

First Plan

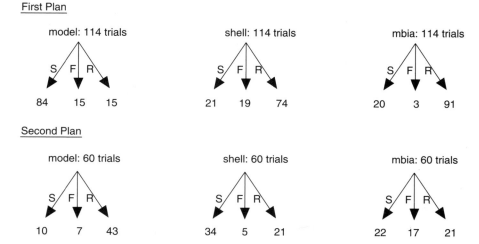

Second Plan

Figure 3.5   The success of a plan depends on when it is tried.

out by the effect of order; or, if the treatment group gets the "good" order, the effect of treatment (which could be zero) might appear larger than it really is.

Although the solution seems to be to present problems to the treatment and control groups in the same order, this does not control for the possibility that one group is more sensitive to order than the other. The treatment group, for instance, might have received training that makes them relatively insensitive to the order of presentation of standardized test problems. Then, if both groups get problems in a "bad" order, the treatment group will outperform the control group. You might think this is at it should be: The treatment group received training, and the effect of the training is demonstrated on the exam. But what should we conclude if both groups get problems in a "good" order and they perform equally? Should we conclude that the treatment is ineffectual? Clearly, if we select just one order to present problems to the treatment and control groups, we risk selecting an order that will not show the superiority of the treatment group.

If we knew which orders were "good" and which were "bad," then we could probably construct a "bad" order that highlights the treatment group. Unfortunately, we generally cannot anticipate order effects. This is because they arise from interactions among problems or tasks, and it is notoriously difficult to consider all such interactions. Virtually anything can create an order effect. For example, a program might have to garbage-collect twice if it performs tasks in a particular order, and just once if it adopts a different order.

Still, the idea of presenting problems in a single order to both treatment and control groups is appealing, so let's see whether it can be rescued. If the number of test problems is small, we could probably find a "bad" order that highlights the superiority of the treatment group. Then we could run the experiment and find a difference between it and the control group. Unfortunately, we don't know how much of the difference is due to the insensitivity of the treatment group to order, and how much is due to other skills imparted by the treatment. The only way to find out is to run both groups again, this time with problems presented in a "good" order.

I have discussed three problems:

1. Order effects can confound treatment effects if the treatment and control conditions present problems in different orders;

2. it is very difficult to anticipate order effects; and

3. even if we know about order effects, we cannot separate the effects of treatment into "insensitivity to order" and "other effects" if the treatment and control conditions present problems in a single order.

A single technique called *counterbalancing* avoids all three problems. The basic idea is to present problems in all possible orders to both the treatment and control groups. This avoids systematically associating "bad" orders with the control group and "good" orders with the treatment group (and vice versa). Counterbalancing renders irrelevant one reason for trying to anticipate order effects—to avoid systematically inflicting them on the treatment or control group. In fact, far from having to anticipate order effects, counterbalancing helps us discover them, thus problem 2 is moot. To see how counterbalancing helps us simultaneously discover order effects and solve problem 3, consider a simple case in which two problems, *a* and *b*, are presented to programs P1 and P2 in all possible orders, and measure the time to solve both is measured. Here are the results:

	P1	P2
Order *a*, *b*	10	15
Order *b*, *a*	12	20

Program P1 solves problems *a* and *b* more quickly than program P2, irrespective of the order of presentation, which, we discover, makes a difference. So P1 is better than P2. Part of this advantage is due to P1's ability to handle problems in any order, part is due to other factors. We can estimate the relative contributions of these parts (and solve problem 3) as follows: When problems are presented in the best possible order, P2's time is 150 percent of P1's, and in the other order, P2's time is 167 percent of P1's. The 67 percent advantage enjoyed by P1 in the second case is thus a sum:

17 percent due to P1's ability to handle problems in any order plus 50 percent due to other factors.

Unfortunately, counterbalancing is expensive. We generally cannot afford to present problems to both treatment and control groups in all possible orders. A set of just five problems yields $5! = 120$ orders. And it is frustrating to run a beautifully (and expensively) counterbalanced experiment only to find no order effects. For example, the fully counterbalanced, hypothetical experiment described earlier might have yielded these results:

	P1	P2
Order *a, b*	10	15
Order *b, a*	10	15

In this case counterbalancing tells us only that it is unnecessary. To minimize the expense of counterbalancing, researchers often approximate the technique by selecting just a few orders from among the many possible. For example, if the programs had to solve five problems, we might run an experiment with, say, ten randomly selected orders instead of the 120 possible:

	P1	P2
abcde	10	15
cbade	11	17
aecbd	10	14
dceab	13	20
bcaed	9	11
deabc	14	22
cadeb	10	15
dcbae	12	21
abdeb	11	14
baedc	9	15

If the results are all pretty similar, we might conclude that order effects are small or nonexistent. It appears in this example however, that whenever *d* is the first problem in the order, P2 gets a suspiciously high score. (In chapter 7 I describe a technique for automatically flagging suspicious associations between orders and scores.)

Although counterbalancing controls for order effects in the tasks that we, the experimenters, present to programs, many of these programs are designed to take most task-ordering decisions automatically beyond our control. In fact, programs such as planners exploit order effects by design. Counterbalancing is neither desirable nor even possible. It's one thing to counterbalance the order in which the Phoenix planner fights two fires, and quite another to counterbalance the order in which it selects plans, and virtually impossible to control the order in which it selects bulldozers to assign to the plans. To counterbalance tasks at all levels of planning, we would have to completely rewrite Phoenix's task scheduler, after which Phoenix would no longer be a planner. Counterbalancing should eliminate spurious effects. But if the difference between two versions of a planner is that one exploits constraints among tasks better than the other, then the effects of task order are not spurious, they are precisely what we hope to find in an experiment. Clearly, we must reserve counterbalancing for those situations in which order effects are spurious and potentially large enough to swamp or significantly inflate treatment effects. Even then, we probably won't be able to afford full counterbalancing, and will have to settle for a few orders, selected randomly.

3.3   Sampling Bias

Let's be optimistic and assume we have designed a sound experiment. Can anything else can go wrong? Unfortunately, yes: The data-collection procedure can introduce spurious effects called *sampling biases*. Imagine the following confession of an elementary school mathematics teacher: "I have resisted this conclusion for years, but I really don't think girls are good at mathematics. They rarely ask good questions and they rarely give good answers to the questions I ask." This confession disturbs you, so you ask to see a class for yourself. And what you find is that the teacher rarely calls on the girls. This is a sampling bias. The procedure for collecting data is biased against a particular result, namely, girls asking or answering questions well.

We encountered a subtle sampling bias in an experiment with the Phoenix system. The first hint of trouble was an obviously incorrect result, namely, wind speed and finish time were uncorrelated. We knew that higher wind speeds caused the fire to spread faster, which required more fireline to be cut, which took more time; so obviously wind speed and finish time ought to be positively correlated. But our data set included only successfully contained fires, and we defined success to mean that a fire is contained in 150 simulated hours or less. Suppose the probability of containing an "old" fire—one that isn't contained relatively quickly—by the 150-hour cutoff, is small, and this probability is inversely proportional to wind speed. Then at higher wind speeds, fewer old fires will be successfully contained, so the sample of successfully contained fires will include relatively few old fires fought at high wind speeds, but plenty of old fires fought at low wind speeds. Figure 3.6 is a schematic illustration of this situation (our sample contained 215 fires instead of

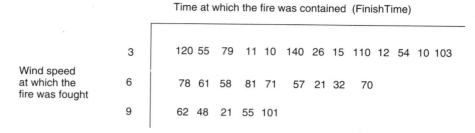

Figure 3.6   An illustration of sampling bias.

the 27 illustrated). Relatively few fires are contained at high wind speeds, and only one of these burned for more than 100 hours. In contrast, many fires are contained at low wind speeds and four of these burned for more than 100 hours. Clearly, old fires are under-represented at high wind speeds. Two opposing effects—the tendency to contain fires earlier at low wind speeds, and the under-representation of old fires at high wind speeds—cancel out, yielding a correlation between wind speed and finish time of approximately zero ($r = -.053$). Note, however, that one of these effects is legitimate and the other is spurious. The positive relationship between wind speed and finish time is legitimate; the negative relationship is due entirely to sampling bias.

The genesis of the sampling bias was the decision to include in our sample only fires that were contained by a particular cut-off time. Whenever a cut-off time determines membership in a sample, the possibility of sampling bias arises, and it is certain if time and the independent variable interact to affect the probability that a trial will finish by the cut-off time. It takes longer to contain fires at high wind speeds, so the independent variable (wind speed) has a simple effect on the probability that a trial will be included in a sample. But in addition, the effect of wind speed on this probability changes over time. As time passes, the probability of completing a trial decreases at different rates determined by wind speed. Because this interaction between wind speed and time affects the probability of completing a trial by the cut-off time, it is, by definition, a sampling bias.

It would help to have a way to detect sampling biases when they occur. A clue can often be found in frequency distributions of the dependent variable, y, at different levels of the independent variable, x. Before we show an example, let's consider a model of the effects of the independent variable. It is commonly assumed that x changes the location of the distribution of y but not its shape. This is illustrated schematically in figure 3.7. The effect of increasing values of x is to shift the mean of y, but not to change the shape of y's distribution. But what if changing x also changed

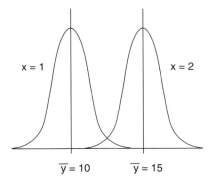

Figure 3.7   An effect of x changes the location of a distribution.

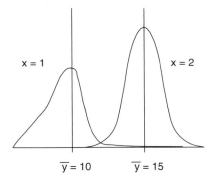

Figure 3.8   An effect of x changes the location and shape of a distribution.

the shape of this distribution, as shown in figure 3.8? The problem isn't only that the $x = 1$ curve includes fewer data points. The problem is that the $x = 1$ curve is not symmetric while the $x = 2$ curve is. This means that whereas $x = 2$ yields high and low scores in equal proportion, medium-to-high scores are disproportionately rare when $x = 1$. If $x = 1$ problems are simply more difficult than $x = 2$ problems, we would still expect to see a symmetric distribution for $x = 1$. Instead, it appears that x affects not only the score but also the probability of a relatively high score. This suggests the presence of another factor that influences membership in the sample and is itself influenced by x, in other words, a sampling bias.

Let us see whether the frequency histograms of finish time at different levels of wind speed disclose a sampling bias, as the previous discussion suggests. In figure 3.9, which shows the distributions, we see immediately that the slow wind

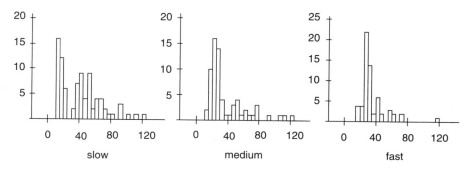

Figure 3.9   Distributions of finish times for three wind speeds, suggesting a sampling bias.

speed distribution has a shape very different than the others. Each distribution has a big mode in the 10 to 40 range, but the medium and fast wind speed distributions are pretty flat beyond their modes, whereas the slow wind speed distribution is bimodal. We expected wind speed to affect the locations of these distributions (in fact, the modal finish times are 10, 20, and 25 for slow, medium, and fast, respectively), but why should wind speed affect the shapes of the distributions? Well, as we know, wind speed interacts with time to affect the probability that a trial will be included in the sample. Thus, frequency distributions of a dependent variable at different levels of the independent variable suggest a sampling bias, if, as in figure 3.9, they have different shapes.

3.4   The Dependent Variable

A dependent variable represents, more or less faithfully, aspects of the behavior of a system. Often the dependent variable is a measure of performance such as hit rate or run time or mean time between failures. Some dependent variables are better than others. In general, continuous dependent variables such as time are preferable to categorical variables such as success or ordinal variables such as letter grades. It is easier to discern a functional relationship between x and y if values of x map to a continuous range of y values instead of discrete bins. Other criteria are: Dependent variables should be easy to measure; they should be relatively insensitive to exogenous variables (i.e., their distributions should have low standard deviations); and they should measure what you intend them to measure.

The latter criterion sounds trite, but remember, variables are representations and they can easily be misrepresentations (see section 2.1.3). Consider this simple but still

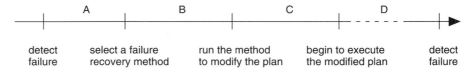

Figure 3.10   A timeline representation of failure recovery.

unresolved design question. Adele Howe added a failure recovery component to the Phoenix planner that allowed it to get out of trouble by changing its plans dynamically. She implemented several failure recovery methods. The obvious question is, which methods are best? If some accomplish more than others with comparable costs, then, clearly, they are better. Now, the only question is, how should the benefits of a failure recovery method be measured? The answer is not obvious. To illustrate the difficulty, look at the "timeline" representation of failure recovery in figure 3.10. A good failure recovery method should fix a plan quickly (i.e., C should be small) and should modify the plan in such a way that it runs for a long time before the next failure (i.e., D should be large). C and D, then, are measures of the costs and benefits, respectively, of failure recovery.

Unfortunately, plans can run for long periods making little progress but not failing, either; so large values of D are not always preferred. In fact, small values of D are preferred if the modified plan makes little progress. A good method, then, modifies a plan so it either runs for a long time before the next failure and makes a lot of progress, or fails quickly when it would probably not make much progress. The trouble is that we cannot assess the latter condition—we cannot say whether a failed plan might have progressed. Thus we cannot say whether a plan modification is beneficial when the modified plan fails quickly.

In rare instances one can analyze mathematically whether a dependent variable actually represents the aspects of behavior it is supposed to represent. A good example is due to Fayyad and Irani (1990), who asked, "What is a good measure of the quality of decision trees induced by machine learning algorithms?" Decision trees are rules for classifying things; for example, figure 3.11 shows a fragment of a tree for classifying animals. Decision trees (and the algorithms that generate them) are usually evaluated empirically by their *classification accuracy* on test sets. For example, the tree in figure 3.11 would incorrectly classify a penguin as a turtle, and so would achieve a lower classification accuracy score than a tree that classified penguins as birds (all other things being equal). Fayyad and Irani invented a method to judge whether an algorithm is likely to generate trees with high classification accuracy, without actually running lots of test cases. They proved that the number of leaves in a decision tree

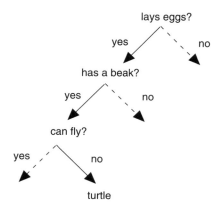

Figure 3.11   A small fragment of a decision tree for classifying animals.

is a proxy for several common performance measures; in particular, trees with fewer
leaves are likely to have higher classification accuracy than leafier trees:

*Suppose one gives a new algorithm for generating decision trees, how then can one go about
establishing that it is indeed an improvement? To date, the answer . . . has been: Compare the
performance of the new algorithm with that of the old algorithm by running both on many data
sets. This is a slow process that does not necessarily produce conclusive results. On the other
hand, suppose one were able to prove that given a data set, Algorithm A will always (or 'most
of the time') generate a tree that has fewer leaves than the tree generated by Algorithm B. Then
the results of this paper can be used to claim that Algorithm A is 'better' than Algorithm B.*
(Fayyad and Irani, 1990, p. 754)

Thus, Fayyad and Irani demonstrate that we sometimes can find a formal basis for the
claim that one dependent variable is equivalent to (or, in this case, probabilistically
indicative of) another.

3.5   Pilot Experiments

Some aspects of an experiment design cannot be pinned down before the experiment
is run. I once developed a model of the time required to contain several simulated
forest fires, fought in succession. My model said that, irrespective of the size or rate
of growth of the fires, they should be fought in order of their age, younger fires before
older ones. To test this rather surprising prediction, I designed the following *fully
factorial experiment*, an experiment in which all combinations of all levels of each
independent variable are represented:

Set two fires in a simulated forest. Fire A should be set H hours after fire B, so fire A is the youngest fire.

Fire A should grow {slowly, quickly}

Fire B should grow {slowly, quickly}

Fire A should be {small, large}

Fire B should be {small, large}

Fire A should be fought {before B, after B}

The experiment thus had $2^5 = 32$ conditions. My hypothesis was that in the sixteen conditions in which fire A, the youngest fire, was fought first, the time to contain both fires would be less than in the other sixteen conditions. It was clear before I ran the experiment that the time required to fight the fires would vary considerably across the conditions; for example, a pair of large, fast-growing fires would take longer to contain than one large and one small, slow-growing fire. Thus, it might be difficult to find evidence for the theoretical advantage of fighting the youngest fire first. In particular, I had no idea how to set the parameter H, the age difference between the fires, although my model said that the advantage of the youngest-first strategy ought to be proportional to H. Because the models we test in experiments are incomplete or imprecise, we often do not know how to set the values of independent variables to best see effects on dependent variables. How slow should "slow growth" be? How large is a "large" fire?

In such cases, one runs *pilot experiments* to find informative settings of experiment parameters. Pilot experiments also debug experiment protocols. With human subjects, for instance, one worries about the effects of fatigue. Computer programs don't suffer fatigue, but one often finds the experimental procedure takes longer to run than anticipated. Or when the program is heavily instrumented, the procedure can generate unexpected quantities of data. Or when garbage collection is uncontrolled, run times become uninterpretable. Or pieces of code that implement the experimental procedure can be buggy; for example, because fires are reported by watchtowers, which sometimes fail, I found in a pilot experiment that roughly half of my "youngest fire first" trials actually fought the oldest fire first.

Often, the only way to detect spurious effects and sampling biases is to run a pilot experiment. Floor effects and ceiling effects, remember, arise when test problems are too difficult or too easy for both the control and treatment conditions. It is difficult to predict these effects, but a pilot experiment can disclose them. Similarly, order effects and sampling biases are due to problems with the experiment protocol, and can be discovered in pilot data.

3.6   Guidelines for Experiment Design

When you design an experiment, consider the following items:

The Experimental Procedure   Often, the experiment is so simple that you'll assume you understand the procedure, but making it explicit helps to find spurious effects and sampling biases.

An Example of a Data Table   Lay out your data table with independent and dependent variables in columns. This shows you what is being varied and what data are being collected. Now consider the rows. How often will data be collected? At the end of each trial? At regular intervals? After significant events? Do you need a variable to time-stamp your data? If you can put hypothetical numbers in the table, so much the better, because then you can consider an example of your analysis.

An Example of Your Analysis   A common complaint from statistical consultants is that their clients collect reams of data with only a vague notion of how it will be analyzed. If you think through the analysis before running the experiment, you can avoid collecting too much or too little data and you often can find a better experiment design. These benefits are especially likely when your experiment is intended to find interaction effects, because these experiments inherently involve combinations of conditions, which complicate analysis and confuse humans.

A Discussion of Possible Results and Their Interpretations   What do potential results mean? It is very helpful, especially in complex designs, to sketch hypothetical results and see how you would explain them. Consider, for instance, a factorial experiment with two independent variables, x_1 and x_2, and a continuous dependent variable y. You plan to calculate the mean of y in each of four conditions defined by the combination of two values of each of x_1 and x_2. A useful trick is to plot some possible outcomes and see whether you can interpret the results, as shown in figure 3.12. In case A, x_1 clearly has an effect on y because mean y values are higher at $x_1 = 2$ than at $x_1 = 1$ at both levels of x_2. Similarly, mean y values are higher at $x_2 = 1$ than at $x_2 = 2$, irrespective of the values of x_1. In case A, x_1 and x_2 have independent effects on y. In contrast, in cases B and C, the effect of x_2 on y depends on the value of x_1 or vice versa. Your interpretation of cases B and C might be that the influence of x_1 on y is controlled or "gated" by x_2. The point is that sketches like figure 3.12 help you consider the possible outcomes of your experiment, often raising possibilities that you wouldn't have considered otherwise, and help to determine whether the experiment design can actually produce the results you are looking for.

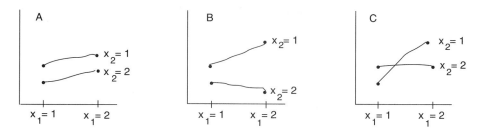

Figure 3.12   Rough sketch of potential outcomes of a two-factor experiment.

Now, What Was the Question Again?   Experiment design is a seductive activity, made more so by easy statistical analysis. You can design an experiment and an analysis that do not actually answer the question you initially asked. You should double check the potential results against the question. Do they answer the question? Nothing prevents you from changing the question if, while designing the experiment, you find one you'd rather answer, or one that better summarizes your research interest. Still, check whether the experiment answers your question.

3.7   Tips for Designing Factorial Experiments

In factorial experiments, every combination of levels of factors is sampled. For instance, an experiment to find effects of gender and age in high school might have six conditions: two levels of gender crossed with three grade levels. Some general tactics yield well-designed factorial experiments.

If an independent variable x is categorical, then the number of levels of x is generally determined by the number of "natural" categories (e.g., male and female), or by merging similar categories if the number of categories is very large (e.g., all occupations are merged into blue-collar, white-collar, etc.). If x is an interval variable, then your design should generally have more than two levels of x. This way, you have the opportunity to find a rough, functional relationship between x and the dependent variable y. It is more difficult to see functional relationships if x is ordinal, but it might still be worth having more than two levels of x, if only to check that y doesn't spike or drop unexpectedly for particular values of x.

It is often helpful to measure more than one dependent variable, so you can see how different aspects of a system behave in different conditions. For example, two common measures of performance for message understanding systems are *recall* and *precision*. Let's say perfect performance involves providing exactly one correct

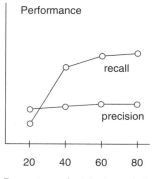

Figure 3.13   It is often useful to have more than one dependent variable.

answer to each of ten questions about a message. Recall is the number of correct answers divided by ten, and precision is the number of correct answers divided by the total number of answers. A system can get a high recall score by answering each question many ways, but its precision score will suffer. Alternatively, a system that doesn't answer a question unless it is sure the answer is correct might have a low recall score but high precision. By plotting both measures of performance, as shown in figure 3.13, you can see whether you have a "try everything" or a "conservative" system.

Factorial experiments often involve two or three independent variables, but rarely more. The great advantage of factorial designs is that they disclose interactions between independent variables; they show how the relationship between y and x_1 is influenced by x_2. Imagine there are two ways to parse messages: The first relies heavily on syntax and the second doesn't parse in the conventional sense but infers the message structure from semantics. We want to know which approach is most sensitive to vocabulary size. This is a classical two-factor design, with hypothetical results illustrated in figure 3.14. The first panel shows the semantic parser is always a bit better than the syntactic parser, and this advantage is roughly constant at all levels of vocabulary size. Vocabulary size doesn't affect the parsers differently; these factors don't interact. The second panel shows what are perhaps more realistic results: Successive levels of vocabulary size have diminishing influence on the performance of the syntactic parser and increasing influence on the performance of the semantic parser; in this case, the factors do interact.

In general, you can increase the sensitivity of an experiment by having your system solve the same set of problems in each condition. This way, you can be sure that

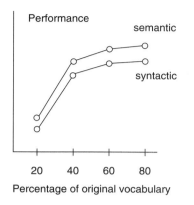
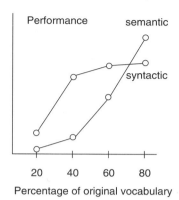

Figure 3.14 Factorial designs disclose that the influence of one variable on another sometimes depends on a third variable.

differences in performance across conditions are due to the factors that define the conditions and are not influenced by the problems that happen to be selected in each condition. If you select different sets of problems in each condition, there is always the possibility that, by chance, the problems in one condition will be easier than those in another. Recall, too, that the variance in a dependent variable can obscure differences between conditions, so we want to remove as many sources of variance—other than the independent variable—as possible.

It will simplify statistical analysis if each condition contains the same number of data. For example, each of the points in figure 3.14 might represent the mean performance on ten messages. The same messages might be tested in each condition, or each point might represent ten unique messages, but either way, it is best to have the points represent equal numbers of data.

The default hypothesis in statistical hypothesis testing is that no influence or effect exists; you reject this hypothesis only if you have strong evidence. Because the role of evidence is to demonstrate an influence, it is difficult to demonstrate no influence. For example, the precision score in figure 3.13 increases only a little as vocabulary size increases, and a statistical test might judge the increase to be insignificant. Should we therefore conclude that vocabulary size does not affect precision? Technically, we should not; statistical machinery was set up to find influences, not noninfluences. In practice, experiments are designed to demonstrate noninfluences (see section 7.3.1) but you should remember that it is much easier to fail to demonstrate an influence than it is to demonstrate one.

3.8   The Purposes of Experiments

Thus far, we have been concerned with experiment design decisions that clarify or obscure the results of experiments. Our focus now shifts to the results, themselves. There is a growing concern in some areas of AI that experimental results tend to be minor and uninteresting. In the area of machine learning, for instance, where experimental methods dominate the scene, several editorials and articles have urged researchers to not subjugate their research interests to the available methods (Dietterich, 1990; Porter, 1991). Too often, we fail to recognize the distinction between research questions and experimental hypotheses. Consider a hypothetical dialog between two AI researchers:

A   What are you doing these days?

B   I am running an experiment to compare the performance of a genetic algorithm to the performance of a backpropagation algorithm.

A   Why are you doing that?

B   Well, I want to know which is faster.

A   Why?

B   Lots of people use each kind of algorithm, so I thought it would be worth learning which is faster.

A   How will these people use your result?

At this point in the conversation we will learn whether the experimenter has a reason for comparing the algorithms besides discovering which is faster. Clearly, the experimental question is which is faster, but what is the underlying research question? Contrast the previous dialog with this one:

A   What are you doing these days?

B   I am comparing the performance of identical twins reared apart to the performance of identical twins reared together, and comparing both to nonidentical twins and ordinary siblings.

A   Why are you doing that?

B   Because identical twins are genetically identical, so by comparing identical twins reared together and apart, we can get independent estimates of the genetic and social contributors to performance.

A   Why do you want to do that?

B   Because the role of genetics in behavior is one of the great unresolved questions.

Here, the experimental question is undergirded by a much more important research question, namely, how much of our behavior is genetically influenced? One wouldn't attempt to answer the experimental question for its own sake, because it would be an enormously expensive fishing expedition, and because the experiment design makes sense only in the context of the research question.

Let us call experiments without underlying research questions *face value* experiments. They are not designed to provide evidence about research questions, but their results might be interpreted this way after the fact. Anything we learn about research questions from face value experiments is learned incidentally; uncovering such evidence is not the purpose of these experiments. The probability that incidental evidence will answer a research question is extremely small. Many things must be controlled, and much can go wrong in experiment design, so it is very unlikely that someone else's face value experiment would answer your research question. It follows that the results of face value experiments rarely interest anyone other than the people who ran them. Thus, generalization of the results of these experiments happens only by chance, after the fact. No wonder we hear the concern that experimental results are minor and unimportant.

When you design an experiment, consider its purpose. If it is not to provide evidence about a research question, then what? If your results are not intended to cast light on a research question, what are they for?

3.9   Ecological Validity: Making Experiments Relevant

Two friends go for a walk one fine summer afternoon and soon find themselves debating the pros and cons of experiments with AI systems. Fred says, "The kind of designs you describe are fine for psychology experiments, but AI programs are really complicated, and simple experiment designs won't tell us much." Fred's companion, Abigail, replies, "Humans are pretty complicated, too, but that doesn't stop psychologists studying them in experiments." Abigail thinks Fred is missing an important point; Fred isn't satisfied with her response. Abigail believes the complexity of AI programs generally does not preclude experimental control, so complexity doesn't bother her. She privately suspects Fred doesn't understand the concept of control because he often refers to the "huge number of factors that must be controlled." Abigail knows most of these factors can be treated as noise and needn't be controlled directly; she knows random sampling will do the job. Fred, on the other hand, believes that if you control all but one of the factors that affect a system's behavior (whether the control is direct or by random sampling), then only small results can be demonstrated.

(This argument is essentially Allen Newell's twenty questions challenge from the preface.) Fred also asserts that each small result applies only to the system within which it was demonstrated, and does not automatically apply to other systems.

Let us agree with Abigail: Complexity does not preclude control. Scientists have figured out how to exercise control in very complex physical, biological, social, and psychological experiments. Let us also agree with Fred and borrow a name for his concerns: Psychologists speak of the *ecological validity* of experiments, meaning the ability of experiments to tell us how real people operate in the real world. The concern has been voiced that psychology experiments, pursuing ever-higher standards of control, have introduced environments and stimuli that people never encounter, and tasks that people would never perform, in the real world. A scorching appeal for ecological validity is made by Neisser in his book *Cognition and Reality* (1976). Here is his description of tachistoscopic displays, which illuminate an image for a tiny fraction of a second:

Such displays come very close to not existing at all. They last for only a fragment of a second, and lack all temporal coherence with what preceded or what will follow them. They also lack any spatial link with their surroundings, being physically as well as temporally disconnected from the rest of the world.... The subject is isolated, cut off from ordinary environmental support, able to do nothing but initiate and terminate trials that run their magical course whatever he may do.... Experimental arrangements that eliminate the continuities of the ordinary environment may provide insights into certain processing mechanisms, but the relevance of these insights to normal perceptual activity is far from clear. (Neisser, 1976, p. 36)

Similar things are said about the environments in which AI systems do their work, and the work they do. Here is an analysis by Steve Hanks of two experiments with agents in the TILEWORLD environment (Hanks et al., 1993, p. 30; see also Pollack and Ringuette, 1990):

I think it's clear that these agents presented in these papers do not in and of themselves constitute significant progress. Both operate in extremely simple domains, and the actual planning algorithm . . . is feasible only because the testbed is so simple: the agent has at most four possible primitive actions, it doesn't have to reason about the indirect effects of its actions, it has complete, perfect, and cost-free information about the world, its goals are all of the same form and do not interact strongly, and so on.

The argument must therefore be advanced that these experimental results will somehow inform or constrain the design of a more interesting agent.... The crucial part of this extensibility argument will be that certain aspects of the world—those that the testbed was designed to simulate more or less realistically—can be considered in isolation, that is, that studying certain aspects of the world in isolation can lead to constraints and principles that still apply when the architecture is deployed in a world in which the testbed's simplifying assumptions are relaxed.

Neisser and Hanks are saying the same thing: The price of experimental control should not be irrelevant results, nor should control preclude generalization. It would be naive to suggest experimental control is nothing but technology, and the responsibility for minor, irrelevant, hard-to-generalize results rests with the researcher. Technologies and the cultures that adopt them encourage behaviors; sports cars encourage fast driving; statistics packages encourage data-dredging; and books like this one encourage well-designed experiments, which, if one isn't careful, can be utterly vacuous. This is a danger, not an inevitability. Knowing the danger, we can avoid it. Perhaps the best protection is afforded by the research questions that underlie experimental questions: If you have a reason for running an experiment, a question you're trying to answer, then your results are apt to interest other researchers who ask similar questions.

3.10   Conclusion

A single theme runs through this chapter: An experiment should tell us whether x (or several x's) truly influences y. It should not obscure the influence or suggest an influence where none exists. An experiment should be free of spurious effects and sampling biases. It should convince us that x and not something else influences y. It is difficult to design a controlled experiment free of spurious effects and sampling biases with a dependent variable that unambiguously represents a behavior of interest. Even if one gets this far, it is often hard to guess which experimental parameters—the values of independent variables and parameters of the experimental procedure—will most clearly demonstrate the effect of x on y. For this reason, researchers usually run pilot experiments. And all this machinery is pointless if one's experimental question isn't motivated by an interesting research question.

Now the bad news: Even when x truly influences y and one's experiment is perfectly designed and well motivated, the experiment might not demonstrate the influence. This is because x's influence on y is sometimes overwhelmed by the background noise of other influences. Separating the variance in y into components due to x and components due to everything else is the central task of statistical hypothesis testing, the subject of the next chapter.

4 Hypothesis Testing and Estimation

AI systems ought to behave properly in situations they haven't previously encountered. Diagnostic expert systems should handle novel combinations of symptoms, natural language systems ought to understand new stories, theorem proving systems should prove novel theorems, robot vision systems should steer robots down previously unseen roads, and so on. Statistical inference is one way to assess how systems will behave in untested situations. It is the process of drawing a conclusion about an unseen *population* given a relatively small *sample*. To the extent that a sample is representative of the population from which it is drawn, statistical inference permits generalizations of conclusions beyond the sample.

This chapter dissects some common statistical procedures to see how they work. Its focus is the intimate relationship between the *number* of data in a sample, the *variance* of the data, and our *confidence* in conclusions. Common sense tells us to be cautious of small samples and highly variable results. The statistical theory in this chapter tells us how cautious to be. Common sense also dictates that data should be representative of the population from which they are drawn, but statistical theory does not tell us how to get representative samples (the topic is deferred until chapter 9). Deferred, too, are discussions of many statistical procedures—analysis of variance, regression, path analysis, contingency table analysis, and more—because these are really just variations on the fundamental themes of hypothesis testing and parameter estimation. This chapter describes one version of the theory and practice of hypothesis testing and parameter estimation. It is the classical version, developed early in this century, and it purchases analytical solutions with the coin of parametric assumptions about populations. Chapter 5 describes another, more recent version, a movement in statistics toward computer-intensive procedures that make few, if any, parametric assumptions.

4.1   Statistical Inference

Statistical inference is inference from *statistics* to *parameters*. Statistics are functions on samples and parameters are functions on populations. Suppose two chess-playing programs, A and B, play a match of fifteen games. Program A wins ten games, draws two, and loses three. Thus, one statistic that characterizes this sample is the sample proportion of games won by A, $p = .67$. We can also imagine a "true" population proportion of games won by A in competition with B. This parameter, π, is a theoretical entity because the population of all possible chess games is too large to enumerate. Although we cannot know the exact, true value of π, we can estimate it with $p = .67$.

We are concerned with two kinds of statistical inference:

Hypothesis Testing   Answer a yes-or-no question about a population and assess the probability that the answer is wrong. For example, to test the hypothesis that one chess program is better than the other, first assume they are truly equal (i.e., $\pi = .5$), then assess the probability of the sample result $p = .67$, given $\pi = .5$. If this probability is very small, reject the assumption that the programs are equal.

Parameter Estimation   Estimate the true value of a parameter given a statistic. If $p = .67$, what is the "best" estimate of π, and how wide must one draw an interval around p to be confident that π falls within the interval?

Hypothesis testing asks, "How likely is a sample result given an assumption about the population?" And estimation asks, "What is the most likely value of a parameter, and what are likely bounds on the value of a parameter, given a statistic?" Before we address these questions, however, let's consider where statistics come from.

4.2   Introduction to Hypothesis Testing

For the last few years, researchers in Natural Language Understanding have participated in a competition to build message understanding systems that read and summarize newswire stories (MUC3, 1991). The performance of each system is measured in several ways; for example, *recall* is the proportion of the important parts of a news story that make it into the summary. If your system correctly identifies the location, the perpetrators, the victims, and a dozen other aspects of a story about a terrorist bombing, then its recall score will be high. Imagine running your system

Table 4.1   Recall scores in five trials of between eight and ten news stories.

Story number:	1	2	3	4	5	6	7	8	9	10	$\overline{x}$
Day 1	51	63	59	60	62	63	60	62	60	54	59.4
Day 2	49	53	54	64	66	42	45	69	61	50	55.3
Day 3	55	57	54	65	68	51	49	61			57.5
Day 4	52	61	63	49	44	56	65	63	42		55.0
Day 5	66	61	58	51	46	61	42	55	57		55.2

every evening on all the day's terrorist stories in the *New York Times*.[5] Every morning you tally its recall scores, which are proportions between 0 and 100 percent. We will call each evening's run a trial that produces a sample of recall scores. Table 4.1 shows the scores for five trials held on five successive days.

Each day's *New York Times* contains between eight and ten terrorist stories, thus, each trial garners between eight and ten recall scores. The frequency distribution of scores for the first day is shown in figure 4.1. Three stories got recall scores of 60, two got scores of 62, two got scores of 63, and three stories got scores of 51, 54, and 59, respectively. The last column of table 4.1 contains the mean recall score for each day's sample. The sample mean for the first day, which happened to be February 1, 1992, is

$$\overline{x}_1 = \frac{51 + 63 + 59 + 60 + 62 + 63 + 60 + 62 + 60 + 54}{10} = 59.4.$$

After careful analysis of many trials, you come to believe your program's performance would improve if it could handle pronouns better, that is, if it could identify the referents of words such as "he" and "she." You modify the program and run a new trial on ten terrorist stories from the June 1, 1992, *New York Times*:

$$\overline{x}_{new} = \frac{63 + 44 + 61 + 72 + 74 + 47 + 72 + 56 + 68 + 71}{10} = 62.8.$$

The higher score is gratifying, but is it really due to its better handling of pronouns? Perhaps the program is no better than it was, but the news stories on June 1, 1992, were somehow easier to analyse than those from previous days. How can you tell

---

5. Here, our example parts company with reality. Currently, recall scores are determined by hand-scoring each story's summary (Sundheim, 1991). This process is too time-consuming at present to do it on a daily basis.

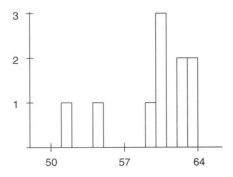

Figure 4.1   The frequency histogram of recall scores for trial 1.

which explanation is correct? You might run the program for several more days to see whether the higher scores persist, but you decide to test whether the modified program is superior, given only the June 1, 1992, sample of recall scores.

This is a classical *statistical hypothesis testing* problem. To solve it, first assume that the modified system is not better than the earlier version. This is your *null hypothesis*: Mean recall performance of the old system is equal to the new one. Next, determine the probability of obtaining a sample mean of 62.8, given the null hypothesis. If this sample mean is very unlikely, then the null hypothesis is probably wrong. Statistical hypothesis testing is like proof by contradiction, in which we negate a proposition and show that a contradiction follows, thereby proving the original proposition. Statistical hypothesis testing doesn't prove the null hypothesis false; rather, it bounds the probability of incorrectly asserting—based on a sample result— that the null hypothesis is false. For example, encouraged by the sample mean of 62.8, you might reject the null hypothesis and assert that your modified system produces higher mean recall scores than the previous version; statistical hypothesis testing bounds the probability that you are wrong.

The difficult part of statistical hypothesis testing is establishing the probability of incorrectly rejecting the null hypothesis. I will develop an informal approach here, then turn to formal techniques from classical statistics. Imagine you ran a single, unchanging version of your program every day from February 1 to May 31, a total of 120 days. On each day you obtain a mean recall score. Figure 4.2 shows the distribution of these means. On June 1, you modify the program to handle pronouns better and incautiously announce to your lab that henceforth, the program will achieve higher mean recall scores. A skeptical graduate student, who thinks pronouns are not very important, demands evidence that the modified program is really better. "Evidence," you say, "here's evidence: I will run the program tonight,

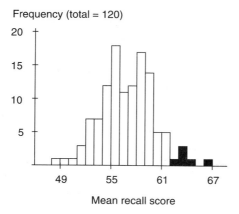

Frequency (total = 120)

Mean recall score

Figure 4.2   Frequency distribution of mean recall score for 120 successive trials of the "old" system.

and if it achieves a mean recall score greater than sixty, then everyone should be convinced that the program is really better." The skeptic points out that the old version of the program has already achieved scores greater than 60 on 16 of 120 days (as shown in figure 4.2), so there is a not inconsiderable chance (16/120 = .33) that it will do so again. In other words, if the program gets a score higher than 60 tonight, you won't know whether its performance is due to chance or to how it handles pronouns.

So you ask the student, "What score must the program achieve tonight to convince you that it is really improved?" The student answers, "The old version of the program achieved scores greater than 62 only six times in 120 trials (see figure 4.2). If the new version is not improved—if it is really no different than the old version—then the probability of achieving a score above 62 is 6/120 = .05. Given such a result, I will cease to insist that the new and old versions of the program are equal. Of course, they might be equal, your 'improvements' might be imaginary, and the sample result might be a fluke. But if the versions of the program are really equal, then the probability of achieving such a score by chance is only .05. If you achieve such a score, and I accept that the new program is improved, I stand only a 5 percent chance of being wrong." We know the rest of the story: You run the program on June 1 and obtain a mean recall score of 62.8, which is evidence enough (barely) to reject the null hypothesis that the new and old versions of the program have the same mean recall performance. You reject the null hypothesis "at the .05 level," meaning you acknowledge a 5 percent chance of being wrong.

4.3   Sampling Distributions and the Hypothesis Testing Strategy

Statistical hypothesis testing involves inferences about parameters, that is, populations. Its goal is not to show that a program performs well on today's sample of news stories, but, rather, to infer that it will do well on the population of unseen news stories. Let's define some terms:

NEW   The new version of the newspaper story understanding program.

OLD   The old version of the program.

μ_{NEW} The population mean recall score for *NEW*; the mean score obtained by running *NEW* on an infinite number of news stories.

μ_{OLD} The population mean recall score for *OLD*.

$\overline{x}_{NEW}$ The mean recall score obtained by running *NEW* on a single sample of news stories.

The hypothesis testing strategy is:

1. Formulate a null hypothesis and an alternative hypothesis, denoted H_0 and H_1, respectively:

   H_0: $\mu_{OLD} = \mu_{NEW}$;

   H_1: $\mu_{OLD} < \mu_{NEW}$.

2. Gather a sample of N news stories, run them through *NEW,* and calculate the sample mean recall score $\overline{x}_{NEW}$.

3. Assuming the null hypothesis is true, estimate the distribution of mean recall scores for all possible samples of size N run through *NEW.* Call this the *sampling distribution of the mean given H_0*, or, for brevity, the sampling distribution.

4. Use the sampling distribution to calculate the probability of obtaining the sample mean $\overline{x}_{NEW}$ given the null hypothesis.

5. If this probability is low, reject the null hypothesis in favor of the alternative hypothesis.

The only tricky part of this procedure is estimating the sampling distribution.

4.3.1   Sampling Distributions

In classical statistics, a sampling distribution is the distribution of a statistic calculated from all possible samples of a given size, drawn from a given population. Because sampling distributions represent all possible sample results, one can find the relative frequency, or probability, of a sample result or a range of sample results. Consider a sample of two tosses of a fair coin; let the number of heads be the sample statistic. The sampling distribution for this statistic is discrete. Its elements are zero, one, and two heads, with probabilities .25, .5, and .25, respectively.

Most sampling distributions are abstract, theoretical entities because the populations from which samples are drawn are generally very large or infinite, so distributions of all possible samples are likewise very large or infinite. Consequently, in classical statistics, most sampling distributions are estimated or determined analytically, not constructed. Exceptions include small discrete distributions, such as the coin-tossing example. If one draws many samples of a given size from a population, however, and calculates a statistic such as the mean for each, then the resulting *empirical sampling distribution* of the statistic will probably be quite similar to the theoretical sampling distribution. For example, the distribution of mean recall scores from 120 samples, each of which contains nine or ten newspaper stories (figure 4.2), probably looks quite similar to the theoretical sampling distribution of mean recall scores for all possible samples of ten newspaper stories.

Unfortunately, figure 4.2 is the empirical sampling distribution for means of the *OLD* system, whereas we want the sampling distribution for means for the *NEW* system; or, more precisely, the sampling distribution of $\overline{x}_{NEW}$ under the null hypothesis $\mu_{OLD} = \mu_{NEW}$. For now, assume that if the null hypothesis is true, that is, if *OLD* and *NEW* perform equally, then the sampling distribution of $\overline{x}_{NEW}$ is identical to the sampling distribution of $\overline{x}_{OLD}$. Thus, the sampling distribution of $\overline{x}_{NEW}$ is approximated by the empirical sampling distribution in figure 4.2.

Now let us repeat the five steps in the hypothesis testing procedure presented earlier:

1. Formulate a null hypothesis and an alternative hypothesis:

    H_0: $\mu_{OLD} = \mu_{NEW}$;

    H_1: $\mu_{OLD} < \mu_{NEW}$;

    Note that both hypotheses pertain to the population mean recall parameters μ_{NEW} and μ_{OLD}, not the sample mean recall statistic $\overline{x}_{NEW}$.

2. Gather a sample of ten news stories and run them through *NEW* to obtain a mean recall score $\overline{x}_{NEW} = 62.8$.

3. If H_0 is true, then the empirical sampling distribution of 120 samples of *OLD* (in figure 4.2) is probably very similar to the theoretical sampling distribution for *NEW*.

4. The probability of obtaining the sample mean recall score $\overline{x}_{NEW} = 62.8$ is easily found with this distribution. Only 6 samples out of 120 have means greater than or equal to 62, therefore, the probability of obtaining $\overline{x}_{NEW} = 62.8$ is less than $6/120 = .05$, if H_0 is true.

5. At this point, we have a choice. Under the assumption that *NEW* and *OLD* perform identically, $\overline{x}_{NEW} = 62.8$ is unexpectedly high. We can either maintain belief in H_0 and accept that the sample result is very improbable, or reject H_0 and accept that H_1 *might* be true. The probability of incorrectly rejecting H_0 is less than .05, small, but perhaps not small enough for a conservative researcher, especially as the sampling distribution was just a rough estimate, based on 120 cases, of the true, theoretical sampling distribution.

4.3.2   How to Get Sampling Distributions

The only unconventional aspect of the previous example involved estimating the sampling distribution of $\overline{x}_{NEW}$ from 120 samples. Classical statistical methods calculate sampling distributions exactly or estimate them analytically, and it is to these methods that I now turn. You haven't heard the last of empirical sampling distributions, though; chapter 5 is devoted to the topic.

Exact Sampling Distributions: The Sampling Distribution of the Proportion

Imagine tossing a coin twenty times and having it land heads sixteen times. Is the coin fair? Sixteen heads in twenty tosses seems, intuitively, an improbable proportion if the coin is really fair. To test this intuition, we need the sampling distribution of the proportion p under the null hypothesis that the coin is fair. It's easy to calculate exact probabilities for all the proportions p that could result from N coin tosses. These proportions are:

$$\frac{0}{N}, \frac{1}{N}, \ldots, \frac{N}{N}.$$

The probability distribution over these values, and thus the sampling distribution of p, is the well-known binomial distribution. The binomial is a discrete distribution of two parameters: N, the number of tosses, and r, the probability that a single toss will land heads. The probability of a particular sample proportion p, say $p = i/N$, is

$$\frac{N!}{i!(N-i)!} r^i (1-r)^{N-i}.$$

Assuming the coin is fair ($r = .5$), this formula becomes

$$\frac{N!}{i!(N-i)!} \, (.5)^N.$$

To test the hypothesis that the coin is fair, first assume the null hypothesis, $H_0 : \rho = .5$, the population proportion of heads is .5, then calculate the probability of the sample result $p = 16/20 = .8$:

$$\frac{20!}{16!(20-16!)} \, (.5)^{20} = .0046.$$

The sample result is so improbable that most researchers would reject the assumption that the coin is fair.

The binomial is a discrete probability distribution, which means it provides probabilities for exact outcomes such as sixteen heads. Continuous probability distributions, in contrast, provide probabilities for ranges of outcomes, such as the probability that the rainfall in Amherst in August, 1993, exceeds 3.12748 inches. In continuous distributions, the probability of a particular outcome (e.g., rainfall = 3.12748 inches) is zero, so hypotheses are tested by asking about the probability of a result at least as extreme as a particular result (e.g., at least 3.12748 inches of rainfall).

Estimated Sampling Distributions: The Sampling Distribution of the Mean

Unlike the sampling distribution of the proportion, the sampling distribution of the mean cannot be calculated exactly. It can, however, be estimated with the help of a remarkable theorem:

Central Limit Theorem   The sampling distribution of the mean of samples of size N approaches a normal distribution as N increases. If the samples are drawn from a population with mean μ and standard deviation σ, then the mean of the sampling distribution is μ and its standard deviation is $\sigma/\sqrt{N}$. These statements hold irrespective of the shape of the population distribution from which the samples are drawn.

The extraordinary thing about the central limit theorem is its scope. It says, draw samples from any population you like, and provided the samples are large (which usually means $N \geq 30$), the sampling distribution of the sample mean $\overline{x}$ is normal. Normal distributions are just familiar bell curves: They are easy to describe mathematically and they have only two parameters, the mean and standard deviation. The central limit theorem says if you know μ and σ, the mean and standard deviation of

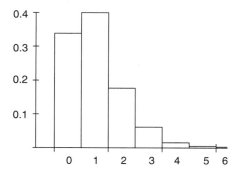

Figure 4.3   A skewed population distribution with $\mu = 1.0$ and $\sigma = .948$.

the population from which samples are drawn, and N is large, then you know the mean and standard deviation of the sampling distribution of $\bar{x}$ for samples of size N, and you know it's a normal distribution.

A simple experiment will illustrate the scope of the central limit theorem. The procedure is to draw samples from a severely skewed population distribution, calculate the mean of each sample, and then plot the distribution of these means. The population distribution is shown in figure 4.3. It is a discrete distribution from which one can draw integer values $0, 1, \ldots, 6$. The probability of drawing 0 is about .34 and the probability of drawing 1 is about .4, whereas the probabilities of drawing 5 or 6 are nearly zero. The mean and standard deviation of this distribution are $\mu = 1.0$ and $\sigma = .948$, respectively. Samples of five values are drawn at random from this distribution and their sample means $\bar{x}$ are calculated. For the purposes of this experiment, we'll estimate the theoretical sampling distribution of $\bar{x}$ with an empirical sampling distribution, obtained by Monte Carlo simulation of the sampling process (see section 5.1 for details). This distribution, which contains 300 samples, is shown in figure 4.4. It is not a normal distribution, a symmetric bell curve, but it is more symmetric than the original population distribution. The tendency toward normality is more pronounced in figure 4.5, an empirical sampling distribution for samples of size 20. In figure 4.6, where the sample size is increased to 50, the sampling distribution of $\bar{x}$ is very like a normal distribution. As the central limit theorem predicts, as N increases, the sampling distribution of $\bar{x}$ approaches normal irrespective of the shape of the original population distribution.

The central limit theorem also predicts the means and standard deviations of sampling distributions. Table 4.2 shows these predictions and the empirical means and standard deviations for the distributions in figures 4.4, 4.5, and 4.6. Incidentally, the close correspondence between the empirical values and the central limit theorem

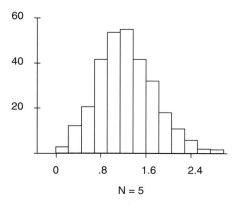

Figure 4.4   An empirical sampling distribution of the mean for 300 samples of $N = 5$ drawn from the population in figure 4.3.

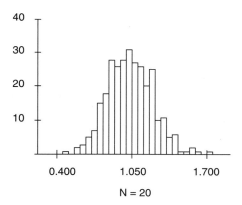

Figure 4.5   An empirical sampling distribution of the mean for 300 samples of $N = 20$ drawn from the population in figure 4.3.

predictions suggests empirical sampling distributions of even a small number (i.e., 300) of samples are good approximations to theoretical sampling distributions.

The Standard Error of the Mean and Sample Size

The standard deviation of the sampling distribution of the mean is often called the *standard error* of the mean and denoted $\sigma_{\bar{x}}$. According to the central limit theorem, the mean of the sampling distribution approaches the population mean μ as N increases,

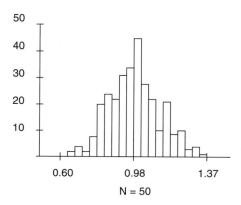

Figure 4.6 An empirical sampling distribution of the mean for 300 samples of $N = 50$ drawn from the population in figure 4.3.

Table 4.2 A comparison of empirical and theoretical sampling distributions.

	$N = 5$	$N = 20$	$N = 50$
Predicted mean	1.0	1.0	1.0
Empirical mean	.997	1.01	.99
Predicted standard deviation	.424	.212	.134
Empirical standard deviation	.449	.199	.133

hence the standard deviation of the sampling distribution represents uncertainty about μ; that's why it's called the standard error of the mean.

Some important intuitions about hypothesis testing are captured in the standard error of the mean. Formally,

$$\sigma_{\bar{x}} = \frac{\sigma}{\sqrt{N}},$$

where σ is the population standard deviation. Clearly, it's difficult to get accurate estimates of the mean if the population has large variance (σ), yet arbitrary levels of accuracy can be had by increasing the sample size N. Unfortunately, this tactic has diminishing returns; for instance, increasing N by 10 has a much larger effect on $\sigma_{\bar{x}}$ when $N = 10$ than when $N = 100$. Figure 4.7 plots $\sigma_{\bar{x}} = \sigma/\sqrt{N}$ for $\sigma = 1.0$ and values of N from 1 to 50. The marginal decrease in $\sigma_{\bar{x}}$ is very small after, say, $N = 20$. At the risk of oversimplifying a subtle issue, figure 4.7 suggests if you cannot draw a reasonably certain conclusion from a sample of size 20 or 30, then

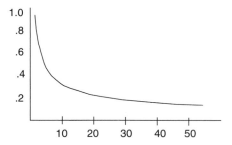

Figure 4.7   A plot of $\sigma_{\bar{x}} = \sigma/\sqrt{N}$ for $\sigma = 1.0$ as N goes from 1 to 50.

perhaps there is no conclusion to be drawn (see section 4.7 for further discussion of this issue).

Remarkably, standard errors of almost all statistics are hard to calculate or have no closed form expression. We do not know, for instance, the standard error of the median or the interquartile range. In fact, the sample mean is one of very few statistics for which we do know the standard error. This is one reason that classical statistical inference relies so heavily on the mean, even though it isn't as robust against outliers as, say, the median or the trimmed mean (chapter 2). The computer-intensive methods of chapter 5 make it possible to construct empirical sampling distributions and standard errors for many such statistics. Here, however, our focus is analytical tests of hypotheses, starting with hypotheses about means.

4.4   Tests of Hypotheses about Means

In unpredictable environments the best laid plans sometimes fail; in fact, occasional failures cannot be entirely prevented. Imagine a planner P that formulates and executes plans in such an environment. On each trial, P formulates and executes a plan. If the plan fails, P tries another. The trial ends when a plan succeeds. Let x denote the number of plan failures in a trial. Suppose figure 4.3, encountered earlier, is the population distribution of x. Plans execute to completion without failure ($x = 0$) on about 34 percent of the trials, and P squeaks by with just one failure in about 40 percent of the trials. At the moment it doesn't matter how we got this distribution—it might be a theoretical prediction, a large empirical sample, or a wild guess. All we need, at this point, are the parameters μ_P and σ_P, which we're willing to treat as the population or "long run" mean and standard deviation of x, respectively, for planner P. Let $\mu_P = 1.0$ and $\sigma_P = .948$.

Suppose a researcher develops a theory of why some planning problems are particularly difficult. She constructs twenty-five problems that ought to be very difficult for planner P, and, in fact, P fails frequently when it tries to solve them: The average number of failures per trial is $\overline{x}_{P,D} = 2.8$ (the subscript means "planner P solving Difficult problems"). Is this *significantly* higher than the population average, $\mu_P = 1.0$? Another way to ask the question is, "What is the probability that a sample of 25 perfectly ordinary problems will result in 2.8 failures per trial, on average, given that the population mean number of failures per trial is 1.0?" If this probability is very low, then the researcher's problems are probably not "perfectly ordinary," but are significantly more difficult than ordinary problems, as predicted. Here is a simple test of the null hypothesis that these problems are not significantly more difficult than those in the population in figure 4.3:

Let $Z = \dfrac{\overline{x}_{P,D} - \mu_P}{\sigma_{\overline{x}}}$. If $Z \geq 1.645$, reject H_0.

Before discussing why this test works, consider a related experimental question. Imagine that planner P is displaced to another environment where it formulates and executes a sample of $N = 25$ plans. Let $\overline{x}_{P,2} = 1.35$ be the mean failures per trial encountered by P in N trials in the new environment. As before, let $\mu_{P,1} = 1.0$ and $\sigma_{P,1} = .948$ be the population mean and standard deviation for P in its old environment. We are interested in whether the environments are significantly different in terms of failures per plan. Thus, the null and alternative hypotheses are $H_0 : \mu_{P,1} = \mu_{P,2}$ and $H_1 : \mu_{P,1} \neq \mu_{P,2}$, respectively. Here again is a simple test:

Let $Z = \dfrac{\overline{x}_{P,2} - \mu_{P,1}}{\sigma_{\overline{x}}}$. If $Z \leq -1.96$ or $Z \geq 1.96$, reject H_0

Now let us see how these tests work.

4.4.1   The Anatomy of the Z Test

To recap, a researcher suspects that planning problems with a particular feature are more difficult than "ordinary" problems. She tests planner P on $N = 25$ "difficult" problems and records $\overline{x}_{P,D} = 2.8$ failures per problem. To test whether difficult problems involve significantly more failures, first assert null and alternative hypotheses:

$H_0 : \mu_P = \mu_{P,D} = 1.0;$

$H_1 : \mu_P < \mu_{P,D}.$

Note that these are hypotheses about populations, about the "long run" behavior of P on ordinary and difficult problems. Of course, we don't know the mean of the population of difficult problems, only the sample mean $\overline{x}_{P,D} = 2.8$. We do know the parameters of the population of ordinary problems, however: $\mu_P = 1.0, \sigma_P = .948$. Now, if difficult problems don't cause any more plan failures than ordinary problems (H_0), we can assume that the sampling distribution of $\overline{x}_{P,D}$ is identical with the sampling distribution of $\overline{x}_P$. Said differently, given H_0, the distribution of mean failures per plan should be the same for ordinary and difficult problems. Thanks to the central limit theorem, we know that the sampling distribution of $\overline{x}_P$, and thus $\overline{x}_{P,D}$, is normal with mean μ_P and standard deviation

$$\sigma_{\overline{x}} = \frac{\sigma_P}{\sqrt{N}} = \frac{.948}{\sqrt{25}} = .19.$$

Given H_0, the expected mean number of failures on difficult problems is 1.0. (This is also the expected mean number of failures on ordinary problems.) But in 25 trials the observed mean number of failures is 2.8. Thus the sample result lies $\overline{x}_{P,D} - \mu_P = 1.8$ units above the mean of the sampling distribution. Dividing this difference by $\sigma_{\overline{x}}$ yields a *standard score* or *Z score*:

$$Z = \frac{(\overline{x}_{P,D} - \mu_P)}{\sigma_{\overline{x}}} = \frac{1.8}{.19} = 9.47.$$

Thus, the sample result $\overline{x}_{P,D}$ lies 9.47 standard deviations units above its expectation, the mean of the sampling distribution.

What is the probability of a sample result that diverges this much from its expectation? Look at any normal distribution, with any mean μ and standard deviation σ, and draw a vertical line through the horizontal axis at $x = \mu$. Because any normal distribution is symmetric, half its area will lie to the right of this line, so the probability of a sample result greater than μ is one half. Now draw a vertical line through $x = \mu + \sigma$. It happens that the area to the right of this line is .16, so this is the probability of a sample result greater than $\mu + \sigma$. Now draw a line through $x = \mu + 1.645\sigma$. Just 5 percent of the distribution lies to the right of this line. Finally, draw a line through $x = \mu + 9.47\sigma$. The fraction of the distribution that lies to the right of this line is very, tiny, essentially zero.

Thus, having assumed the null hypothesis and having derived a sampling distribution for $\overline{x}_{P,D}$, we determine that the probability of obtaining a sample result $\overline{x}_{P,D} = 2.8$ is practically zero. We can, therefore, reject the null hypothesis with essentially no probability of error. We can be extremely confident that the sample of twenty-five "difficult" problems, which produced $\bar{x}_{P,D} = 2.8$, wasn't drawn from the population of "ordinary" problems.

It isn't immediately obvious, but the simple Z statistic, given earlier, compiles all this reasoning. Recall,

$$Z = \frac{\bar{x}_{P,D} - \mu_P}{\sigma_{\bar{x}}},$$

and we said if $Z > 1.645$, we could reject the null hypothesis. The Z statistic essentially transforms the sampling distribution of a sample mean (i.e., $\bar{x}_{P,D}$) into another one, centered around zero, by subtracting its mean, μ_P, from every value in the distribution. This yields a new distribution with mean zero and standard error $\sigma_{\bar{x}}$. Dividing by $\sigma_{\bar{x}}$ expresses the distance between $\bar{x}_{P,D}$ and its expectation under the null hypothesis in terms of unit standard deviations; in other words, the sample result is placed on the horizontal axis of a *standard normal distribution* (or Z *distribution*) with mean zero and standard deviation one. Happily, we know everything there is to know about the standard normal. We know, in particular, that only 5 percent of the points in this distribution have Z scores greater than 1.645. Therefore, if

$$Z = \frac{\bar{x}_{P,D} - \mu_P}{\sigma_{\bar{x}}} \geq 1.645,$$

we know that the probability of $\bar{x}_{P,D}$ is .05 or less. But remember, this probability was derived under the null hypothesis. We assumed H_0 to derive the sampling distribution for $\bar{x}_{P,D}$, and, thus, the Z score. If the probability of the sample result is very low, then we are inclined to reject H_0.

The transformation of a sample result into a standardized Z score is illustrated graphically in box 4.1. The shaded area of the standard normal curve is called a *rejection region*. Conventionally, if a Z score falls in the lower or upper 5 percent of the sampling distribution, it is considered adequate evidence for rejecting the null hypothesis. If the sample result falls in a rejection region of 2.5 percent, it's usually considered good evidence against H_0; and if the sample result falls in a smaller rejection region, say .1 percent of the sampling distribution, it's considered strong evidence against H_0.

The previous example is called a *one-tailed test* because we accept only large values of $\bar{x}_{P,D}$ as evidence against the null hypothesis. Said differently, there's only one rejection region. "Difficult" problems are expected to produce more failures per trial, so the alternative hypothesis is $H_1 : \mu_{P,D} > \mu_P$. But in the other example introduced earlier, we have no such expectation. When planner P is displaced from environment

1 to environment 2, it might encounter more or fewer failures per trial, so the null and alternative hypotheses are:

$H_0 : \mu_{P,1} = \mu_{P,2}$;

$H_1 : \mu_{P,1} \neq \mu_{P,2}$.

The performance of P in environment 1 is known: $\mu_{P,1} = 1.0$, $\sigma_{P,1} = .948$, so assuming H_0, the standard error of the sampling distribution of $\overline{x}_{P,2}$ is $\sigma_{\overline{x}} = \sigma_{P,1}/\sqrt{N}$. Suppose we put P in environment 2 and collect a sample of twenty-five trials, during which P encounters $\overline{x}_{P,2} = 1.35$ failures per trial. Transformed to a standardized Z score, this is:

$$Z = \frac{\overline{x}_{P,2} - \mu_{P,1}}{\sigma_{\overline{x}}} = \frac{1.35 - 1.0}{.19} = 1.842$$

Should we reject H_0? Earlier, we decided to reject H_0 if the probability of the sample result was .05 or less. But in this example, we suspect $\mu_{P,2}$ is different from $\mu_{P,1}$ but we don't know whether $\overline{x}_{P,2}$ will be higher or lower than its expectation; it could be either. Therefore, we must consider two rejection regions, for unusually high and low values of $\overline{x}_{P,2}$. How big should these regions be? If we're comfortable rejecting H_0 when the probability of the sample result is .05 or less, then the rejection regions should bound the upper and lower 2.5 percent of the standard normal distribution, ensuring that the total probability of the sample result, be it high or low, is less than .05. This is called a *two-tailed test*.

As it happens, the Z scores that bound these rejection regions are -1.96 and 1.96, respectively, so if our sample Z score is more extreme than either, its probability is less than .05, and we can reject H_0. As it happens, $Z = 1.842$ does not fall into either rejection region so we cannot reject H_0. Interestingly, had this been a one-tailed test, we would have rejected H_0 at the conventional .05 level, because $1.842 > 1.645$. If we'd had the more specific hypothesis that P would encounter more failures in environment 2, then the sample result $\overline{x}_{P,2} = 1.35$ would have been sufficient evidence to reject H_0.

In sum, the Z test, so simple in form, really does three things simultaneously: It estimates the sampling distribution of the mean, it transforms the sampling distribution into a standard normal distribution, and it expresses the sample mean as Z standard deviations distance from its expectation under the null hypothesis. An amazing amount of work for such a little equation.

Box 4.1   Derivation of the *Z* Test

Assume you know the mean and standard deviation of a population Π_0. For concreteness, say $\mu_0 = 25$ and $\sigma_0 = 50$. Let $\bar{x} = 15$ be the mean of a sample of 100 items. The *Z* test assesses the probability that the sample was drawn from Π_0. The alternative is that the sample was drawn from a different population with a smaller but unknown mean, μ_1. Thus we want to run a one-tailed test. The null and alternative hypotheses are

$H_0 : \mu_0 = \mu_1$
$H_1 : \mu_0 > \mu_1$

Under H_0 the sampling distribution of $\bar{x}$ is normal with $\mu_0 = 25$ and $\sigma_{\bar{x}} = \sigma/\sqrt{N} = 50/\sqrt{100} = 5.0$, as shown here:

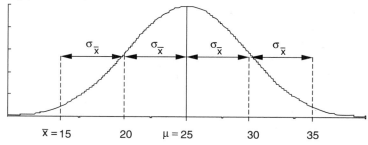

Each value in this distribution can be transformed into a *Z* score by subtracting μ_0 and dividing the result by $\sigma_{\bar{x}}$. This produces a standard normal distribution of *Z* scores, with mean zero and standard deviation one:

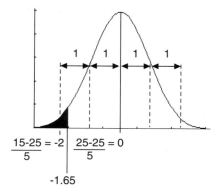

The shaded area contains 5 percent of the mass of the distribution, and is bounded by $Z = -1.65$. Note that the *Z* score corresponding to our sample mean is -2. This falls within the shaded area, so the probability of achieving this sample mean by chance, given H_0, is less than .05.

4.4.2 Critical Values

One often wants to know a value of the sample mean that would be sufficient to reject the null hypothesis at a particular confidence level p. All one requires is the standard score above (or below) which $100p$ percent of the standard normal distribution lies. For $p = .05$, the corresponding standard scores for a one-tailed test are 1.645 or -1.645, depending on whether we expect the sample result to exceed or fall below the mean of the sampling distribution; or 1.96 and -1.96 if we don't have any such expectations (i.e, if the test is two-tailed). It's easy to work backwards from $Z = \pm1.645$ or $Z = \pm1.96$ to find a *critical value* of the sample mean. Assume a one-tailed test in which $\bar{x}$ is expected to be less than μ; assume also $p = .05$. The formula for Z is

$$Z = \frac{\bar{x} - \mu}{\sigma_{\bar{x}}} = \frac{\bar{x} - \mu}{\sigma/\sqrt{N}},$$

therefore the critical value for $\bar{x}$ is

$$\bar{x}_{crit} = \mu - 1.645\sigma_{\bar{x}}.$$

For the example in box 4.1, if the mean and standard deviation of a population are $\mu_0 = 25$ and $\sigma_0 = 50$, respectively, and the sample size is 100, then

$$\bar{x}_{crit} = 25 - 1.645(50/\sqrt{100}) = 16.75.$$

In other words, if $\bar{x} \leq 16.75$, we can reject the null hypothesis at the .05 level.

4.4.3 *p* Values

This terminology—rejection at the .05 level—reflects residual uncertainty in our conclusions: the null hypothesis is rejected but it might be true. The probability of obtaining a particular sample result given the null hypothesis is called a *p value*. By convention, one usually doesn't reject the null hypothesis unless $p < .05$. This is the largest bound on p that most researchers will call statistically significant. Significant results are usually reported with p values; for example, "a Z test showed that algorithm A performed significantly better than algorithm B, $p = .015$." If you use a statistics package that gives exact values of p, then you should report these values provided they are less than .05. Some packages (and most available tables) give p values for only some critical values of the test statistic, typically those corresponding to probabilities of .05, .025, .01, .005, .025, and .001. In this case, you should report the smallest p value that your test statistic allows. Suppose $\mu_0 = 25$, $\sigma_0 = 50$, $N = 100$

and $\bar{x} = 16$, then

$$Z = \frac{16 - 25}{50/\sqrt{100}} = -1.8.$$

Because $-1.96 < Z < -1.645$, the smallest p value allowed by the test statistic is $p < .05$.

An exact value for p is not the exact probability of the sample result under H_0 unless the sampling distribution is discrete, because the probability of a particular sample result is zero. Exact values refer to the exact area of the sampling distribution bounded by the sample result as opposed to bounds on areas such as $p < .05$ or $p < .01$.

4.4.4 When the Population Standard Deviation Is Unknown

Until now, it has been assumed that the population standard deviation is known. This is rarely the case, so σ must be estimated from the sample standard deviation: $\hat{\sigma} = s$. (The hat above σ means "estimated".) Similarly, the standard error, or the standard deviation of the sampling distribution, is estimated as follows:

$$\hat{\sigma}_{\bar{x}} = \hat{\sigma}/\sqrt{N} = s/\sqrt{N}.$$

Z tests can be run as before, except with $\hat{\sigma}_{\bar{x}}$ instead of $\sigma_{\bar{x}}$:

$$Z = \frac{\bar{x} - \mu}{\hat{\sigma}_{\bar{x}}} = \frac{\bar{x} - \mu}{s/\sqrt{N}}.$$

4.4.5 When All Population Parameters Are Unknown

A common tactic is to compare a sample to an imagined null hypothesis distribution. You might say, "I would be very happy if my program's mean recall rate was 80 percent, so I'll run it on a sample of fifty newspaper stories and see whether its recall rate is significantly lower than 80 percent." In theory, you are testing whether the sample was drawn from a population of an infinite number of runs of a message understanding program with a mean recall rate of 80 percent. But unlike the population of, say, all *New York Times* stories, this one doesn't exist. In practice you are saying, "Suppose such a population does exist and its mean is 80; could my sample have come from it?" In practice you'll use s, the sample standard deviation, to estimate σ and $\sigma_{\bar{x}}$ and to run the test as previously described.

Because it is so simple and robust, the Z test provides quick heuristic estimates about whether results are significant, even when, technically, it shouldn't be used (see later discussion). Suppose your sample mean recall rate is 75 percent and the sample standard deviation is 5. Now for some quick mental arithmetic: The square root of the sample size is roughly 7, so the standard error is $5/7 \approx 1$, and so $Z = (75 - 80)/1 = -5$. Clearly, your sample mean recall rate is significantly lower than 80 percent. Back to the drawing board!

4.4.6   When N Is Small: The t Test

The sampling distribution of the mean approaches a normal distribution as sample size, N, approaches infinity. In practice, however, the sampling distribution of the mean is roughly normal even for relatively small sample sizes. If $N \geq 30$, you can be pretty sure that the sampling distribution is normal. But what about smaller samples, say, $N = 20$, or even $N = 5$? The sampling distribution of the mean for small N is called the t *distribution*, and it looks a lot like the normal distribution. It has heavier tails than the normal: More of the mass of the distributions is in the tails. Consequently, a sample result that's highly improbable when matched to a normal distribution is more likely when matched to the t distribution. Thus, Z tests on small samples risk rejecting the null hypothesis inappropriately, when Z exceeds 1.645, say, but the t value doesn't exceed the corresponding critical threshold.

To run a t test, do exactly what you would do to run a Z test. The test statistic is

$$t = \frac{\overline{x} - \mu}{\hat{\sigma}_{\overline{x}}} = \frac{\overline{x} - \mu}{s/\sqrt{N}}. \tag{4.1}$$

The only difference is that instead of comparing a Z score to a normal distribution, you'll compare a t score to the t distribution. The only catch is that t is actually a family of distributions, one for each value of N. If you run a t test by hand (instead of using a statistics package) you will have to look up the resulting t score in a table of t distributions, a fragment of which is shown in table 4.3. Each row in a t distribution is for a different number of *degrees of freedom* (a number closely related to sample size) and each column represents a p value.

For example, suppose you are a burglar, driving through an unfamiliar part of town, looking for evidence that the houses are worth robbing. One short cul de sac appears promising: It has just five parked cars, but they are quite expensive. In fact, the mean price of the cars is $\overline{x} = \$20,270$ and the standard deviation of this sample is $s = \$5,811$. The mean cost of cars in town is $\mu = \$12,000$. You think the cars in the cul de sac are significantly dearer than this, but being a sophisticated burglar with a strong background in empirical methods, you decide to test the hypothesis. The test

Table 4.3   A fragment of a table of *t* distributions.

Degrees of freedom	$t_{.05}$	$t_{.025}$	$t_{.01}$	$t_{.005}$
1	6.314	12.706	31.821	63.657
2	2.920	4.303	6.955	9.925
3	2.353	3.182	4.541	5.841
4	2.132	2.776	3.747	4.604
5	2.015	2.571	3.365	4.032
6	1.943	2.447	3.143	3.709
7	1.895	2.365	2.998	3.499
8	1.860	2.306	2.896	3.355
9	1.833	2.262	2.821	3.250
⋮	⋮	⋮	⋮	⋮
∞	1.645	1.965	2.330	2.570

statistic is

$$t = \frac{20270 - 12000}{5811/\sqrt{5}} = 3.18.$$

Now you look up $t = 3.18$ in the fragment of the *t* table in table 4.3. For this test (indeed, for any test involving one sample mean), the number of degrees of freedom is $N - 1$. Looking across the row of table 4.3 for four degrees of freedom, you see your sample result, $t = 3.18$, has a *p* value less than .025 but greater than .01. Evidently, the sample of cars on the cul de sac is significantly more expensive than the average car in town ($p < .025$). Were the cul de sac no different from other streets in town, the probability of finding five such expensive cars parked on it is less than .025.

The *t* test depends on one important assumption: The distribution from which the sample was drawn is normal. Automobile prices, of course, are not normally distributed: None is less than zero dollars and the distribution has a long right tail populated by Ferrari, Bentley, and so on. Thus, the previous test is technically invalid. The *t* test is pretty robust, however, and unless *N* is very small and the distribution is very skewed, and the derived *t* score is marginal, it can be trusted.

Three types of *t* tests are commonly run on means. One-sample *t* tests assess whether a sample was drawn from a population with known mean μ; alternatively, they test whether a hypothetical μ could be the mean of the population from which a sample was drawn. For instance, instead of comparing the prices of five cars to an actual population mean $\mu = \$12000$ you might have been thinking, purely hypothetically, that it wouldn't be worth your time or freedom to rob houses populated by people who can't afford more than, say, $12000, for a car. Irrespective of where you get μ, the one-sample t test is run with the test statistic given in equation 4.1. Some new developments are required for the two-sample and paired-sample t tests, discussed next.

4.4.7   Two-Sample t Test

Researchers often compare the means of two samples to see whether they could have been drawn from populations with equal means. Here are null and alternative hypotheses for a two-sample t test:

$H_0 : \mu_1 = \mu_2$;

$H_1 : \mu_1 \neq \mu_2$ (two-tailed test);

$H_1 : \mu_1 > \mu_2$ (one-tailed test);

$H_1 : \mu_1 < \mu_2$ (one-tailed test).

The logic of the test is identical to that of the others we have described, but the t statistic is slightly different. Recall that the estimated standard error for a one-sample t test is

$$\hat{\sigma}_{\bar{x}} = \sqrt{s^2/N} = \sqrt{\frac{\frac{\sum (x_i - \bar{x})^2}{N-1}}{N}} = \sqrt{\frac{\frac{SS}{df}}{N}}.$$

Note the new terminology: SS, called "the sum of squares," is the sum of the squared deviations of each datum in a sample from its mean. The term df stands for degrees of freedom; recall that a one-sample t test has $N - 1$ degrees of freedom.

In the two-sample case, we have two sample standard deviations with which to estimate the standard error of the sampling distribution of the difference of the means. The usual strategy is to pool the variances of the samples on the grounds that $\sigma^2_{x_1 - x_2} = \sigma^2_{x_1} + \sigma^2_{x_2}$. (It's interesting to consider why the variance of differences is the sum of the individual variances.) The pooled, estimated variance of the difference of means is:

$$\hat{\sigma}^2_{pooled} = \frac{SS_1 + SS_2}{df_1 + df_2} = \frac{(N_1 - 1)\, s_1^2 + (N_2 - 1)\, s_2^2}{N_1 + N_2 - 2}.$$

Note that this is just a weighted average of s_1^2 and s_2^2. Now the pooled, estimated variance of the sampling distribution of the difference of means is:

$$\hat{\sigma}_{\bar{x}_1 - \bar{x}_2} = \sqrt{\hat{\sigma}^2_{pooled} \left(\frac{1}{N_1} + \frac{1}{N_2} \right)}.$$

This estimated standard error has exactly the same form as in the one-sample test. It is the square root of the estimated variance of a population distribution divided by the sample size. In this case, however, we're interested in a population of differences, and we have two samples and thus two sample sizes. The t statistic for a two sample test is then

$$t_{\bar{x}_1 - \bar{x}_2} = \frac{\bar{x}_1 - \bar{x}_2}{\hat{\sigma}_{\bar{x}_1 - \bar{x}_2}}. \tag{4.2}$$

As an example, consider search algorithms A and B, and the number of nodes each expands before finding a goal node. Generate fifty random search trees, divide the set in half, and run each algorithm on a half (the case in which we run each algorithm on all the problems in a set is discussed in section 4.4.8).

1. Formulate a null hypothesis and an alternative hypothesis:

   $\mu_A = \mu_B$; equivalently $\mu_{A-B} = 0$;

   $\mu_A \neq \mu_B$; equivalently $\mu_{A-B} \neq 0$.

2. In $N_A = 25$ and $N_B = 25$ trials, the sample means for A and B are:

   $\bar{x}_A = 127, \ s_A = 33$;

   $\bar{x}_B = 131, \ s_B = 28$.

3. Determine the sampling distribution of the difference of the sample means given the null hypothesis. The mean of the sampling distribution is $\mu_{A-B} = 0$. The estimated standard error is derived from the pooled variance:

   $$\hat{\sigma}^2_{pooled} = \frac{(N_A - 1) s_A^2 + (N_B - 1) s_B^2}{N_A + N_B - 2} = \frac{(24)1089 + (24)784}{48} = 936.5.$$

   $$\hat{\sigma}_{\bar{x}_A - \bar{x}_B} = \sqrt{\hat{\sigma}^2_{pooled} \left(\frac{1}{N_A} + \frac{1}{N_B} \right)} = \sqrt{936.5 \left(\frac{1}{25} + \frac{1}{25} \right)} = 8.65.$$

   The test statistic is

   $$t_{\bar{x}_A - \bar{x}_B} = \frac{\bar{x}_A - \bar{x}_B}{\hat{\sigma}_{\bar{x}_A - \bar{x}_B}} = \frac{127 - 131}{8.65} = -0.46.$$

4. Look up the value of the test statistic in a t table to obtain a p value.

In this case, the number of degrees of freedom is $N_A + N_B - 2 = 48$. Without consulting a table of t distributions, we can be pretty sure that this value is not significant. For degrees of freedom in excess of 30, the t distribution is almost identical to the Z distribution. Recall, too, that critical values for Z for a two-tailed test are -1.96 and 1.96 to reject H_0 at the .05 level. Our test statistic, $t_{\bar{x}_A - \bar{x}_B} = -0.46$ is nowhere near -1.96. We cannot reject the null hypothesis. We have no credible evidence that A and B perform differently.

4.4.8 The Paired Sample t Test

It is often possible to design an experiment to boost the power of a test by controlling for the variance in test problems. The general idea is shown in table 4.4. Imagine testing two strategies, A and B, to see which confers better performance on a program. One approach, shown in table 4.4a, is to submit strategy A to problems $p_1 \ldots p_5$ and strategy B to problems $p_6 \ldots p_{10}$, then calculate means $\bar{x}_A$ and $\bar{x}_B$, and run a two-sample t test as above. A better approach is to run both strategies on the same set of problems, as shown in table 4.4b. For each problem, record the difference in performance between A and B, then calculate the mean $\bar{x}_\delta$ and standard deviation s_δ of these differences. The null hypothesis in this case is

$H_0 : \mu_\delta = 0$ or $H_0 : \mu_\delta = k$.

The latter form is used to test the hypothesis that the difference between the strategies is a constant other than zero. You can test this H_0 with a simple variant on the

Table 4.4 The design of t tests for two samples.

Trial	A	B
1	p_1	p_6
2	p_2	p_7
3	p_3	p_8
4	p_4	p_9
5	p_5	p_{10}
	$\bar{x}_A$	$\bar{x}_B$

Trial	A	B	$\delta = A - B$
1	p_1	p_1	
2	p_2	p_2	
3	p_3	p_3	
4	p_4	p_4	
5	p_5	p_5	
			$\bar{x}_\delta$

(4.4a) Two-sample t test.   (4.4b) Paired sample t test.

one-sample t test. The test statistic is

$$t_\delta = \frac{\overline{x}_\delta - \mu_\delta}{\hat{\sigma}_\delta}, \quad \hat{\sigma}_\delta = \frac{s_\delta}{\sqrt{N_\delta}}.$$

N_δ is the number of pairs, in this case, 5, and t is tested against a t distribution with $N_\delta - 1$ degrees of freedom.

One reason to prefer this test is that the variance due to test problems is minimized. The two-sample test associated with table 4.4a must contend with the variance in performance on ten test problems, whereas the paired sample test must contend only with the variance in differences in performance on five test problems. This tactic for boosting significance by reducing item variance shows up in slightly different guises in sections 7.3.2 and 7A.4.

4.5   Hypotheses about Correlations

The correlation coefficient usually serves as a descriptive statistic, but one can make inferences about correlations. For example, we might believe on the basis of a low correlation that two variables are independent, but, to be more certain, we want to test the hypothesis that their correlation is zero. To do so, we need the sampling distribution of the correlation coefficient, which is complicated. Two alternatives are to transform the correlation into another form that has a nicer sampling distribution, and to derive an empirical sampling distribution by Monte Carlo methods. We will discuss only the former approach because the latter is described in chapter 5.

Fisher's *r to z transform* produces a statistic the sampling distribution of which is approximately normal under the assumption that the variables are themselves normally distributed.[6] The statistic is

$$z(r) = .5 \ln \frac{1+r}{1-r}.$$

The mean and estimated standard error of the sampling distribution of $z(r)$ are

$$z(\rho) = .5 \ln \frac{1+\rho}{1-\rho}, \quad \hat{\sigma}_{z(r)} = \frac{1}{\sqrt{n-3}}.$$

The symbol ρ (rho) denotes the population correlation.

---

6. However, the test is reasonably robust against small deviations from this assumption (Olson, 1987).

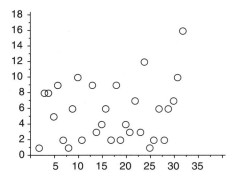

Figure 4.8 A scatterplot with a correlation of .14, which is not significantly different from zero.

Now we can run a Z test of the null hypothesis that the correlation of two variables is some number, $H_0 : \rho_{xy} = p$. The hypothesis that two variables are independent, for instance, is $H_0 : \rho_{xy} = 0$. Let's test the hypothesis that two variables, x and y, represented by the scatterplot in figure 4.8, are independent. The correlation between x and y is paltry, $r_{xy} = .14$. To see whether r_{xy} is significantly different from zero, first transform r_{xy} into $z(r)$ with Fisher's r to z transform:

$$z(r) = .5 \ln \frac{1 + .14}{1 - .14} = .141.$$

(As it happens, $z(r) \approx r$ for $-.4 < r < .4$.) Next, calculate the value of the estimated standard error of the sampling distribution of $z(r)$. There are thirty data points in figure 4.8, so $\hat{\sigma}_{z(r)} = 1/\sqrt{N - 3} = 1/27 = .192$. Now we can run a conventional Z test:

$$Z = \frac{z(r) - z(\rho)}{\hat{\sigma}_{z(r)}} = \frac{.141 - 0}{.192} = .73.$$

Clearly, the value of Z lies between the conventional critical values of -1.96 and 1.96, so we cannot reject the null hypothesis that x and y are independent.

It is equally easy to test the hypothesis that r is something other than zero. For instance, to test whether $r = .14$ is significantly different from $\rho = .4$, first calculate $z(.4) = .424$, then

$$Z = \frac{.141 - .424}{.192} = -1.47.$$

This value also is not significant. Evidently the scatterplot in figure 4.8 came from a population joint distribution of two variables that might be uncorrelated ($\rho = 0$) or might be weakly correlated ($\rho = .4$). There's not enough evidence in the sample for us to be more precise about ρ. It is to estimates of population parameters, and the uncertainty of these estimates, that we now turn.

4.6   Parameter Estimation and Confidence Intervals

One reason to collect a sample is to estimate the value of a parameter. As we just saw, the sample correlation $r = .14$ estimates the parameter ρ, although it turned out to be a pretty imprecise estimate: The sample might have been drawn from a population with $\rho = 0$, then again, it might have come from a population with $\rho = .4$. *Confidence intervals* provide one characterization of the accuracy of such estimates.

Imagine that we do not know the population mean μ but we collect a sample with $\bar{x} = 10.0$, which serves as an estimate of μ. Perhaps 10.0 is the exact, true value of μ, but, more likely, μ is a little larger or smaller than 10.0, that is, $\mu = \bar{x} \pm \varepsilon$. If ε is relatively small, then $\bar{x}$ is a good estimate of μ. Now imagine we know the true value of μ, and we pick a value of ε and collect thirteen samples to see how often $\mu = \bar{x} \pm \varepsilon$ is true. The results of this experiment are shown in the left panel of figure 4.9. The mean of each sample is represented as a circle in the center of a confidence interval of width 2ε. The heavy black line represents the true population mean, μ. Only one of the sample means (the sixth from the top) falls within ε of μ. If someone asked, "how confident are you that the true population mean falls within ε of your sample mean?," then for this value of ε you would have to say, "not confident at all!" Consider a much wider confidence interval, shown in the right panel of figure 4.9. In this case, every sample mean is within ε of μ. Comparing these pictures, you would suspect that even if we don't know μ, a wider confidence interval around the sample mean is more likely to contain μ than a narrow confidence interval. You can also see that if we reduce the confidence interval around the sample means in the right panel, then we will reduce the number of sample means that contain μ within their confidence intervals. For example, μ lies very close to the boundary of the confidence interval of three of the samples in the right panel of figure 4.9 (the fifth, seventh, and tenth from the top, respectively). Reducing ε would reduce the proportion of samples that contain μ within their confidence intervals from 100 percent (13 of 13) to 77 percent (10 of 13).

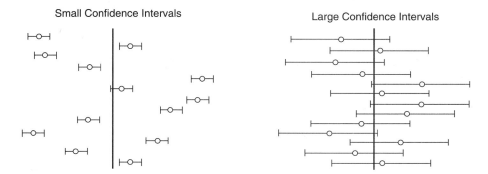

Figure 4.9   How wide should an interval be for us to be confident that it includes μ?

4.6.1   Confidence Intervals for μ When σ Is Known

The central limit theorem tells us that if we collect a very large number of samples of size N, then roughly 95 percent of their means will fall within a particular interval on either side of the population mean μ. The interval is 2×1.96 standard deviations of the sampling distribution of the mean. That is, $\bar{x} = \mu \pm 1.96\sigma_{\bar{x}}$ for 95 percent of the means $\bar{x}$. Conversely, if $\varepsilon = 1.96\sigma_{\bar{x}}$, then the confidence interval $\bar{x} \pm \varepsilon$ will contain μ in 95 percent of the samples we might draw. Thus, the 95 percent confidence interval about the mean is $\bar{x} \pm 1.96\sigma_{\bar{x}}$.

One must be clear about the interpretation of the confidence interval. When we say $\bar{x} \pm 1.96\sigma_{\bar{x}}$ is our confidence interval we do not mean $\Pr(\mu = \bar{x} \pm 1.96\sigma_{\bar{x}}) = .95$. The population mean μ is a constant and it makes no sense to speak of the probability that it has one value or another. In fact, a confidence interval says less about μ than $\bar{x}$: Not, "I am 95 percent sure about the true value of μ," rather, "I am 95 percent sure that this interval around $\bar{x}$ contains μ." The proper interpretation of a confidence interval, therefore, is shown in figure 4.9: wider confidence intervals are more likely to include μ. However, wide confidence intervals are confessions that we can't pin down a parameter very precisely given the sample. For instance, the 95 percent confidence interval around $z(\rho)$ from the previous section is:

$$z(\rho) = z(r) \pm 1.96\hat{\sigma}_{z(r)} = .141 \pm 1.96(.192) = -.235, .517.$$

Recalling that $z(r) \approx r$ for small r, we evidently can't pin down the population correlation ρ with any precision, given the sample in figure 4.8.

Because confidence intervals depend on standard errors, they are affected by sample size. As you might expect, we can construct tighter intervals with larger samples.

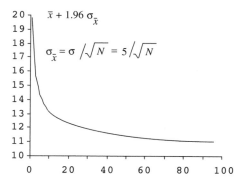

Figure 4.10   The width of a confidence interval depends on N.

This is shown in figure 4.10, where N increases from 4 to 100. The curve shows one half of the confidence interval for μ (i.e., $\bar{x} + 1.96\sigma_{\bar{x}}$), given a sample mean $\bar{x} = 10$ and a population standard deviation $\sigma = 5$. Note that the confidence interval narrows rapidly, so when $N = 20$, the 95 percent confidence interval for μ is roughly ± 2.

4.6.2   Confidence Intervals for μ when σ Is Unknown

If the population standard deviation σ is unknown, we estimate the standard error from the sample standard deviation: $\hat{\sigma}_{\bar{x}} = s/\sqrt{N}$. It would seem obvious that the 95 percent confidence interval for μ in this case should be $\bar{x} \pm 1.96\hat{\sigma}_{\bar{x}}$, but it isn't. The sampling distribution of the mean when we estimate σ is not a normal distribution but, rather, a t distribution. The point $x = 1.96\hat{\sigma}_{\bar{x}}$ bounds slightly more than 2.5 percent of the t distribution, as noted earlier, so $\bar{x} \pm 1.96\hat{\sigma}_{\bar{x}}$ is slightly narrower than a 95 percent confidence interval for μ, when σ is unknown.

We can easily find a coefficient $t_{.025}$ so that $\bar{x} \pm t_{.025}\hat{\sigma}_{\bar{x}}$ is in fact a 95 percent confidence interval. The coefficient is denoted $t_{.025}$ instead of $t_{.05}$ because the confidence interval is symmetric about $\bar{x}$, so the total probability of including μ is .95, but the probability of missing μ on either side of $\bar{x}$ is .025. The only complication in finding $t_{.025}$ is that t is a family of distributions, and you can see why. Imagine the sample size is very small, say, 3. How much confidence should we have in an estimate of the population mean from such a sample? Not much! The confidence interval should be pretty wide, all other things equal. As expected, $t_{.025}$ in table 4.3 is relatively large for $3 - 1 = 2$ degrees of freedom.

Of course, if a sample is moderately large ($N > 20$) it won't hurt to use a simple rule of thumb: The 95 percent confidence interval is approximately $\bar{x} \pm 2\hat{\sigma}_{\bar{x}}$.

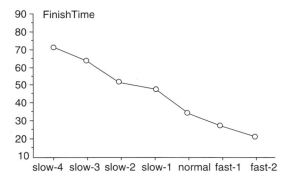

Figure 4.11   Mean *FinishTime* for seven values of *RTK*.

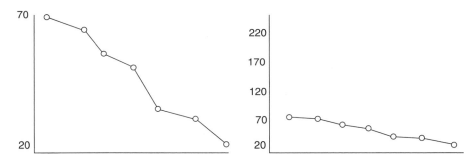

Figure 4.12   Apparently significant effects of an independent variable (x axis) on a dependent variable (y axis) look less significant when the scale of the y axis changes.

4.6.3   An Application of Confidence Intervals: Error Bars

Chapter 2 described the effects of a parameter called *RTK* that controls the rate at which the Phoenix planner thinks, relative to the rate at which fires burn in the Phoenix environment. *RTK* affects *FinishTime*, the time required to contain a fire, apparent in figure 4.11. Each point in this figure is the mean of *FinishTime* for a particular level of *RTK*; for instance, when Phoenix thinks very slowly (*RTK* = *slow-4*), mean *FinishTime* is about seventy simulation-time hours.

Figure 4.11 is less informative than it might be. Although *RTK* appears to influence *FinishTime*, appearances can deceive. For example, figure 4.12 shows two graphs like figure 4.11; the only difference being the scale of the y axes. But scale is arbitrary. Big effects seem smaller on a different scale. Just looking at figure 4.11, we can't tell, whether *RTK* really has a significant effect on *FinishTime*.

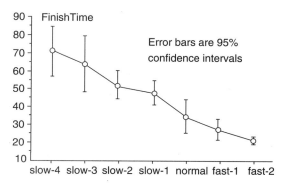

Figure 4.13   95 percent confidence intervals for the means in figure 4.11.

One can test whether *RTK* has a significant effect on *FinishTime* by running a one-way analysis of variance (see section 6.3.2), but there is an easier and sometimes more informative approach. Add error bars to the means in figure 4.11. Each bar represents the upper and lower bounds of a 95 percent confidence interval around its mean, as shown in figure 4.13. Now we can see several things. First, many means fall within the 95 percent confidence intervals of other means; for example, mean *FinishTime* for *RTK = slow-3* is well within the confidence interval for *RTK = slow-4*, suggesting that it doesn't matter whether Phoenix thinks very slowly or very, very slowly. Second, figure 4.13 suggests Phoenix performs differently when *RTK* $\geq$ *normal* than when *RTK* $\leq$ *slow-1*: Starting at *slow-4*, the second mean in each consecutive pair falls within the confidence interval of the first, except at the break between *slow-1* and *normal*. (You might recall the discussion in section 2.4.2 around the decision to break *RTK* into two groups at this boundary.)

Another thing to note in figure 4.13 is that the widths of the error bars generally decrease as *RTK* increases from *slow-4* to *fast-2*. This suggests the partitions of *FinishTime* by *RTK* get bigger (i.e., include more data) as *RTK* increases. This is true, in fact. The means in figure 4.13 represent 10, 14, 22, 54, 25, 38, and 50 trials, from left to right.

Before leaving this example, let's derive one of the seven confidence intervals in figure 4.13. The confidence interval for mean *FinishTime* for *RTK = normal* is as follows:

$$\overline{x} = 34.2, \; s = 23.5, \; N = 25$$

$$\hat{\sigma}_{\overline{x}} = 23.5/\sqrt{25} = 4.7$$

$$t_{.025} = 2.064, \text{ from a } t \text{ table with } N - 1 = 24 \; df$$

The confidence interval for μ is:

$$\bar{x} \pm t_{.025}(4.7) = 34.2 \pm 2.064(4.7) = (24.5, 43.9).$$

This interval, 24.5 to 43.9 is what appears as brackets around the mean *FinishTime* for *RTK = normal* in figure 4.13.

   The procedures for establishing confidence intervals and hypothesis testing are almost identical: Both require the standard error and sampling distribution of a statistic, and both find critical values of the statistic. It is tempting, therefore, to test hypotheses with confidence intervals. But beware; you can easily construct examples in which $\bar{x}_A$ falls outside the confidence interval around $\bar{x}_B$ and vice versa, yet a two-sample t test says $\bar{x}_A$ and $\bar{x}_B$ are not significantly different. (Try it for yourself with the following statistics: $\bar{x}_A = 106$, $s_A = 28.7$, $N_A = 100$, $\bar{x}_B = 99.13$, $s_B = 24.7$, $N_B = 100$.) This is because confidence intervals for means are estimated from standard errors of individual means, whereas the two-sample t test relies on the standard error of the difference between the means. Different sampling distributions and standard errors are involved. One can prove, however, that if the confidence intervals do not themselves overlap—if the upper bound of one is below the lower bound of the other—then a two-sample t test will say the means are different. In general, then, one shouldn't use confidence intervals to test hypotheses if the confidence intervals overlap.

4.7   How Big Should Samples Be?

Imagine a sample of 50 items with $\bar{x} = 20$ and $s = 5$, yielding an estimated standard error $\hat{\sigma}_{\bar{x}} = 5/\sqrt{50} = .71$. A t test rejects the null hypothesis that the sample was drawn from a population with mean $\mu_0 = 15$: $t = (20 - 15)/.71 = 7.04$. With 49 degrees of freedom, this is a highly significant result ($p < .001$). A sample of size 50 was sufficient to reject the null hypothesis at the .001 level; nothing is gained by collecting more data. But something is gained if our purpose is parameter estimation. The width of the .001 confidence interval around $\bar{x}$ is $\pm t_{.0005}(\hat{\sigma}_{\bar{x}}) = \pm 3.414(.71) = \pm 2.42$, but if we double the sample size and the sample variance doesn't increase (a reasonable assumption), then the confidence interval narrows: $\pm t_{.0005}(\hat{\sigma}_{\bar{x}}) = \pm 3.388(.5) = \pm 1.69$. Note that our confidence in the estimate doesn't change—it's a 99.9 percent confidence interval—but the range of the estimate changes by 30 percent. In hypothesis testing, by contrast, the only thing that changes when we increase sample size is our confidence in the conclusion, so if our sample is large enough to make us confident, nothing is gained by having a larger sample. In sum, for parameter estimation, samples should be as large as you can afford; for hypothesis testing, samples should be no larger than required to show an effect.

The previous comment suggests that samples can be "too big" for hypothesis testing, and indeed they can. First, the good news: Any real statistical effect, be it ever so small and obscured by variance, can be boosted to significance by increasing N. This is because the standard error of any statistic is reduced by increasing N. Now, the bad news: One can discover statistically significant but utterly meaningless effects in very large samples. And if data are essentially free, as they are in many AI experiments, then nothing prevents researchers from running trials until something shows up. Statistical reasoning, like any formal system, is concerned with the validity, not the importance or impact, of reasoning. The term "statistically significant" is not synonymous with meaningful, unexpected, elegant, insightful, or any other word we use to evaluate the contribution of research. Yet, when a researcher admits to running five thousand trials, one suspects that the result is either meaningless, or the experiment could have shown the same result with fewer data, or it is badly designed in terms of controlling variance, or all three. It would be nice to have techniques to assess objectively whether a result is meaningful or merely significant.

One class of techniques assesses the *informativeness* of results as follows: Assume we have run a two-sample t test and obtained a significant difference given samples A and B. Now we toss both samples into a bucket and calculate the mean of the bucket. We draw an item from the bucket and present it to a colleague, saying, "This item came from sample A (or B); please tell me whether its value is greater than the mean of the bucket." If the sample distributions overlap a lot, our colleague will perform poorly at this task. Said differently, samples A and B might be statistically different, but in practice they are indistinguishable in the sense that knowing the sample from which a datum is drawn doesn't help our colleague perform even a simple predictive task. For example, assume we have two samples with similar distributions that are, by merit of large sample size, significantly different:

Sample	$\overline{x}$	s	N
A	147.95	11.10	1000
B	146.77	10.16	1000
A & B	147.36		2000

A two-sample test returns $t = 2.468$ with 1998 degrees of freedom, $p < .05$. It turns out that 517 values in sample A exceed the grand mean of 147.36, whereas 464 values in sample B do. Thus, if we know which sample a datum comes from and we guessed that the value of the datum is above the grand mean, then we would be right 51.7 percent of the time if the datum is from sample A and 46.4 percent of the time if the datum is from sample B. But if we don't know which sample a datum comes from, and we guess its value is greater than the grand mean, then we will be right about 50 percent of the time. Thus, knowing the sample involves only a tiny reduction in the error in our guesses. Although the samples are statistically different, they are practically identical. It's fine to have derived a significant result, but what can we do with it? Very little.

We don't usually think of differences between means in terms of *predictive power*, but we really should. The whole point of statistical inference is to go beyond sample results to say something about populations, to predict future results. Unfortunately, some significant results confer very little predictive power. Fortunately, it's possible to measure the predictive power of a result, albeit roughly.

Suppose a system is exposed to tasks of types A and B. The population variances for performance on these tasks are σ_A^2 and σ_B^2, whereas the variance of performance for the population of both kinds of tasks is σ_P^2. One measure of the predictive power of a task type is the reduction in variance that results from specifying the task type, that is, $\sigma_P^2 - \sigma_A^2$ or $\sigma_P^2 - \sigma_B^2$. Let's assume that $\sigma_A^2 = \sigma_B^2 = \sigma_{P|task}^2$, then, following Hays (1973, p. 414) we can define the relative reduction in variance as follows:

$$\omega^2 = \frac{\sigma_P^2 - \sigma_{P|task}^2}{\sigma_P^2}.$$

If $\omega^2 = 0$, then $\sigma_P^2 = \sigma_{P|task}^2$, which means that the task type does not influence the variance of performance. If $\omega^2 = 1$, then $\sigma_{P|task}^2 = 0$, which means that the variance in performance on each task is zero, and, so, knowing the task type ensures perfect predictions of performance.

Of course, we cannot know ω^2 exactly because its components are population parameters, but we can estimate it in a variety of ways from samples. In particular, given two samples, each with the same true variance $\sigma_{P|task}^2$, an estimate of ω^2 is

$$\hat{\omega}^2 = \frac{t^2 - 1}{t^2 + N_1 + N_2 - 1}.$$

This is a rough estimate of the predictive power of knowing the sample from which a datum was selected. For example, for our previous samples,

$$\hat{\omega}^2 = \frac{2.468^2 - 1}{2.468^2 + 1000 + 1000 - 1} = .0025.$$

This means that $\sigma_{P|task}^2$ is probably very nearly equal to σ_P^2; in other words, knowing the task type confers almost no predictive power.

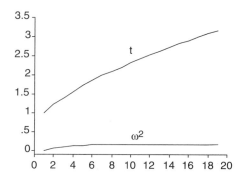

Figure 4.14   As N increases, $\hat{\omega}^2$ flattens out but t continues to increase.

Now suppose we draw two more samples as before, except that they contain only 100 items each. This time the means and standard deviations are slightly different, as expected, and t is 2.579, a bit bigger than before but not much. Now we find

$$\hat{\omega}^2 = \frac{2.579^2 - 1}{2.579^2 + 100 + 100 - 1} = .027.$$

Thus a similar value of t yields an order of magnitude more predictive power when the values of N are decreased by an order of magnitude. Not surprising, given the definition of $\hat{\omega}^2$, but still instructive: The fact that t is significant does not mean that the independent variable (the one that determines the sample) has any predictive relationship to the dependent variable, and the relationship depends inversely on the Ns, all other things being equal.

So, can N be too large? Yes, because increasing N boosts the probability of finding a significant difference between sample means, even though knowing the sample from which a datum was drawn has virtually no power to predict the datum's value. Here is a dramatic example: Assume equal sample sizes and let $\overline{x}_A = 18$, and and $\overline{x}_B = 19$, and let the sample size increase from 3 (per sample) to 50. Figure 4.14 plots t and $\hat{\omega}^2$, as they are defined above. What you see is that t increases steadily but $\hat{\omega}^2$ flattens out at around $N = 12$. Beyond $N = 12$, the predictive value of the independent variable does not increase.

4.8   Errors

The decision to reject H_0 is a binary decision and, like all binary decisions, it has two associated errors. One is the error of rejecting H_0 when H_0 is true, called a *type I error*, and the other is the error of failing to reject H_0 when H_0 is false, called a *type II error*. The probabilities of these errors are commonly denoted α and β, respectively:

$$\alpha = \Pr(\text{type I Error}) = \Pr(\text{Reject } H_0 \mid H_0 \text{ is true});\tag{4.3}$$

$$\beta = \Pr(\text{type II Error}) = \Pr(\text{Fail to reject } H_0 \mid H_0 \text{ is false}).\tag{4.4}$$

To reject H_0, you need an explicit decision rule based on the test statistic. For example, if the test statistic is Z, here is one decision rule:

Decision Rule 1 *Reject H_0 when $Z \geq 0$.*

Because Z measures the distance between $\bar{x}$ and the mean of the sampling distribution of $\bar{x}$, and this distribution is symmetric, it follows that half the sampling distribution lies above $Z = 0$, hence $\alpha = .5$ for this decision rule. Said differently, the probability of attaining a value of Z greater than zero given H_0 is .5, and, thus, $\alpha = .5$. Here is another decision rule:

Decision Rule 2 *Reject H_0 when $Z \geq 1.645$*

What is α for this rule? It's familiar: the probability of incorrectly rejecting H_0 when $Z \geq 1.645$ is .05 or less, so $\alpha = .05$.

It is less obvious how to assess β for a decision rule, because β refers to an infinite number of alternative hypotheses subsumed by "H_0 is false." Imagine we draw a sample with mean $\bar{x}$ and use it to test H_0, abiding by a decision rule that produces the type I error shown as dark shading in figure 4.15. Under H_0 the sampling distribution of $\bar{x}$ is normal with mean μ_0. Now, suppose H_0 is false and our sample is drawn not from a population with mean μ_0, but, rather, from a population with mean μ_1. Assuming the populations have equal variances, the sampling distribution for $\bar{x}$ under H_1 will have the same variance as the sampling distribution of $\bar{x}$ under H_0 (thanks to the central limit theorem). The sampling distribution of $\bar{x}$ under H_1 will be centered about μ_1, "shifted" to the left or right of the sampling distribution under H_0, but otherwise identical to it. Figure 4.15 shows three different values of μ_1, three sampling distributions of $\bar{x}$ given H_1. Recall that a type II error occurs when we fail to reject H_0 and H_0 is false. We won't reject H_0 unless our test statistic exceeds a critical value and falls in the rejection region (shaded black) in figure 4.15. Thus, the probability of a type II error, β, is the area to the left of the critical value under the curve for the sampling distribution for $\bar{x}$ given H_1. It is the light-shaded area in each panel in figure 4.15.

If β is the probability of failing to reject H_0 when we should, then $1 - \beta$ is the probability of rejecting H_0 when we should, and is often called the *power* of a test.

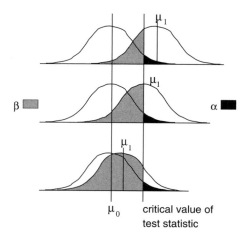

Figure 4.15   The probability of a type II error depends on the location of the sampling distribution under H_1.

You can see in figure 4.15 the relationship between α, β and $\delta = \mu_0 - \mu_1$, the difference between the means of the sampling distributions given H_0 and H_1:

- If α is fixed, then as δ decreases, β increases and the power of the test, $1 - \beta$, decreases (moving from the top panel in figure 4.15 to the bottom panel). This makes sense: It becomes more difficult to discriminate H_0 from H_1 on the basis of a sample mean $\overline{x}$ as δ gets smaller.

- If δ is fixed, then the only way to increase the power of a test, $1 - \beta$, is to increase α, the probability of a type I error, and the only way to decrease α is to decrease the power of the test. In the extreme, you could avoid type I errors altogether by never rejecting H_0, or you could avoid type II errors altogether by always rejecting H_0.

Practically, these tradeoffs limit the power of our tests. Both μ_0 and μ_1 are constants—we don't necessarily know μ_1, but it does have a value. And by convention we must fix α, usually at .05 or less. If $\delta = \mu_0 - \mu_1$ is relatively small, and α is fixed, then the power of a test can be quite small.

There is a way to escape. If the variances of the sampling distributions in figure 4.15 were smaller, more like those in the bottom panel in figure 4.16, then β would be smaller for a fixed value of α. Not surprisingly, you work this trick by increasing the sample size. Remember, the estimated standard error of the mean is $\hat{\sigma}_{\overline{x}} = s/\sqrt{N}$, so if you increase N, you decrease $\hat{\sigma}_{\overline{x}}$. In sum, if you want to decrease the probability of both type I and type II errors, increase your sample size.

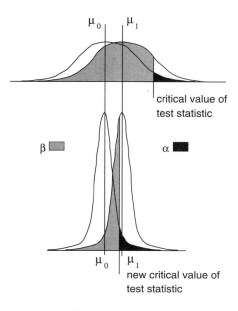

Figure 4.16   Increasing sample size decreases the estimated standard error of the mean, and increases power $(1 - \beta)$ for fixed values of μ_0, μ_1, and α.

4.9   Power Curves and How to Get Them

The power of a test depends on several factors:

- the α level of the test;
- the degree of separation between the null and alternative hypothesis distributions, denoted δ;
- the variance(s) of the population(s) from which sample(s) are drawn; and
- sample size, N, which affects the standard error of the sampling distributions under the null and alternative hypotheses.

Power curves plot power against changes in one of these factors. For example, for a fixed α and δ, we can plot the relationship between power and sample size. Alternatively, we could fix α and N and plot how power changes with δ. Figure 4.15 shows levels of power for three values of δ (each level corresponds to the unshaded area of the alternative hypothesis distribution), so figure 4.15 gives us three points on a power curve. Constructing power curves this way, however, is tedious. Computers provide an easier way, illustrated in procedure 4.1. For concreteness, the procedure shows how to construct a power curve for varying sample sizes, but it can be modified to produce power curves for any factor. Also, we will illustrate the procedure with a two-sample t test, but it can be adapted to find the power of any test. On each iteration, the procedure draws two samples from different populations, so H_0 should be rejected. Next, the procedure runs the two-sample t test and records whether H_0 was rejected. It repeats this process 1000 times, after which we know the fraction of 1000 tests that rejected H_0 when they should have. This is the power of the test for a particular setting of sample size (and fixed settings of all the other factors, such as α and δ). Then the procedure changes the setting of sample size and repeats the previous steps. When it is finished, the procedure has produced power levels for several values of sample size.

Procedure 4.1   Constructing Power Curves

i. Fix all but one of the factors that affect power; for example to construct a power curve for the influence of sample size on the two-sample t test, fix $\alpha = .05$; fix the variances of two populations A and B at σ_A^2 and σ_B^2; and fix the means of the populations at, say, zero and k, so that the mean of the sampling distribution of our test statistic (the difference of sample means) will be zero under H_0 and k under H_1. Thus $\delta = k$.

ii. Loop over values of sample size; for example, loop over values of N from 5 to 100 in steps of 5:

   a. Loop 1000 times:

      1. Draw a sample of size N from population A.

      2. Draw a sample of size N from population B.

      3. Run a two-sample t test on the samples and increment a counter C by one if the test rejects H_0.

   b. The power of the test for this value of N is $C/1000$, the fraction of 1000 tests that rejected H_0 when they should have.

By running several tests inside procedure 4.1, you can derive and compare power curves for each. Cohen and Kim (1993) did just this to compare three different tests for *censored data*. Censored data come from trials that are abandoned for some reason. For instance, a sample of run times might include three trials that were abandoned when they exceeded a threshold of 100 seconds: (18 27 100 51 12 100 100 19). Chapter 5 describes three tests for the difference of means of samples that

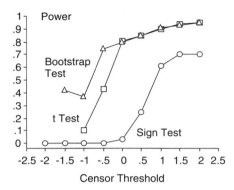

Figure 4.17   The power of three tests depends on the censoring threshold.

include censored data. One is the conventional two-sample *t* test, except that the censored values are discarded before the test is run. We won't describe the others here, but refer to them simply as the sign test and the bootstrap test. Each is a two-sample test. Figure 4.17 shows how the power of these tests depends on the *censoring threshold*. A low censoring threshold causes more items to be censored; for example, if the threshold was 20 instead of 100, the previous sample would not be (18 27 100 51 12 100 100 19) but (18 20 20 20 12 20 20 19). You can see the sign test is less powerful than the others, and that the bootstrap and the *t* tests have similar power. Note the characteristic rise in power as the censoring threshold increases.

4.10   Conclusion

The logic of hypothesis testing depends on sampling distributions and standard errors derived under the null hypothesis. Parameter estimation and confidence intervals also rely on standard errors. Remarkably, statistics has become indispensible in many fields on the basis of very few sampling distributions and standard errors. We know standard errors for means, correlations, ratios of variances, proportions, and that's about all. In the last decade, however, statisticians have shown how to estimate standard errors for any statistic, however peculiar, by simulating the process of sampling. These computer-intensive methods are discussed in the following chapter.

4.11   Further Reading

You can find in many excellent statistics texts more depth and breadth than is offered here. Hays 1973, and Winkler and Hays 1975 provide a good balance between theory and accessibility. Sokal and Rohlf (1981) cover more ground, although their presentation of fundamentals is perhaps less good than Hays's. Olson 1987 and Bohrnstedt and Knoke 1988 are elementary and very clear.

5   Computer-Intensive Statistical Methods

The classical approach to statistical estimation and inference is to derive the sampling distribution for a statistic and then calculate the probability of a sample statistic. Unfortunately, there are no analytical sampling distributions for many interesting statistics, such as the trimmed mean and the interquartile range; and other sampling distributions rely on assumptions, for instance, the t distribution assumes that samples are drawn from normal populations. For a long time, statistical practice was like carpentry with a hand axe—a good tool, capable of many things, but not exactly right for most tasks. In the mid-1980s, however, methods such as Efron's *bootstrap* made it possible to construct sampling distributions and standard errors for virtually any statistic, without making any troubling assumptions about sampling models and population distributions (Efron and Tibshirani, 1993). All these methods rely on computers to simulate the sampling process, so they are called, collectively, *computer-intensive statistical methods*. They are used primarily for parameter estimation and establishing confidence intervals and standard errors. Most of the examples in this chapter concern hypothesis testing.

We begin with an example that illustrates the logic of a computer-intensive test even though it could be run analytically without resorting to heavy computation. Imagine that someone shows you the result of two sequences of five coin tosses:

Sequence 1: Heads, Heads, Tails, Heads, Heads

Sequence 2: Tails, Tails, Tails, Tails, Heads

You are asked to distinguish two hypotheses:

H_0: A single fair coin produced both sequences

H_1: The sequences were not produced by a single fair coin

You could reject H_0 by demonstrating that, if it's true, the result is very unlikely. But what, exactly, is the result? You don't want the particular sample sequences to be the result because every sequence of heads and tails is equally unusual, so each has equal weight against H_0. The result you care about is the predominance of heads in Sequence 1 and tails in Sequence 2:

1. The result is four heads and one tail in Sequence 1 and four tails and one head in Sequence 2.

But perhaps you don't care which sequence has the heads and which has the tails:

2. The result is four heads and one tail in one sequence and four tails and one head in the other.

And perhaps you want to include more extreme results:

3. The result is four or more heads in one sequence and four or more tails in the other.

Clearly, before testing a hypothesis, you must first decide which characterizations of data count as results, noting that different results have different probabilities given H_0. I mention this because classical statistical hypothesis testing tells us which characterizations of data count as results: means, variances, correlation coefficients, and so on. If we are going to use computer-intensive procedures instead of classical ones, we must ask anew how to characterize data.

Given a result such as, "Four or more heads in one sequence and four or more tails in the other," you must assess the probability of obtaining it by chance if H_0 is true. Suppose you toss a fair coin ten times and on each toss, record whether it lands heads or tails. Here is one sample:

Order	1	2	3	4	5	6	7	8	9	10
Token	H	H	T	T	T	H	T	T	H	T

Call the first five items $S1^* = HHTTT$ and the second five $S2^* = HTTHT$. Now assess whether $S1^*$ and $S2^*$ match the result we just described. In this case, neither has four or more of either heads or tails, so this sample does not match the result. Note this failure and toss the coin ten times more, as before. Here is another sample:

Order	1	2	3	4	5	6	7	8	9	10
Token	H	H	H	T	H	T	T	T	T	T

This matches the result we have in mind: Four heads are in $S1^*$ and five tails are in $S2^*$. Note this success and toss the coin ten more times. In fact, repeat the process one thousand times. When you are done, you will have recorded m successes and $1000 - m$ failures. The probability of the sample result "four or more heads in one sequence and four or more tails in the other" is just $m/1000$. Implement this procedure and you'll probably find $m = 70$. Hence, the probability of the sample result is $p = 70/1000 = .07$. Actually, the *expected* value of m is 70. The procedure, being nondeterministic, will probably yield a slightly different value of m.

To recap, given the sequences:

Sequence 1: Heads, Heads, Tails, Heads, Heads

Sequence 2: Tails, Tails, Tails, Tails, Heads

you are asked to test whether a single fair coin produced both. In classical hypothesis testing, you would assert a null hypothesis—the coin is fair—and use the sample result as evidence against it. In many forms of computer-intensive hypothesis testing, the null hypothesis is "built into" the simulated sampling process: You simulate tossing a fair coin, so $p = .07$ is the probability of the sample result "four or more heads in one sequence and four or more tails in the other" under the null hypothesis. Most scientists won't reject the null hypothesis unless $p \leq .05$, so by this criterion the sample result is insufficient evidence.

The same result is obtained easily by analysis: The probability of four or more heads in a batch of five tosses of a fair coin is $6/2^5 = .1875$, and the probability of four or more tails is the same, so the probability of four or more heads in one batch followed by four or more tails in another is just $.1875 \times .1875 = .035$. Similarly, the probability of the inverse result—predominant tails in the first batch and heads in the second—is identical. Thus, the probability of four or more heads in one batch and four or more tails in the other is $2 \times .035 = .07$.

The advantage of computer-intensive techniques is that they construct probability distributions for sample results and estimate standard errors that cannot be derived analytically, or cannot be had without questionable assumptions. The previous example is not the kind of problem to which one would normally apply computer-intensive methods, but it serves to illustrate the steps in a computer-intensive hypothesis test:

1. Characterize the sample result and choose a sample statistic. In the example, the statistic took two values:

    1 if the number of heads in one sequence is 4 or 5 and the number of tails in the other sequence is 4 or 5; and
    0 otherwise.

2. Derive the sampling distribution for this statistic by simulating the process of selecting samples. For the example, the sampling distribution was: $\Pr(1) = .07$, $\Pr(0) = .93$.

3. Derive from the sampling distribution the probability of the sample result, in this case, .07.

This chapter describes three versions of this general idea: *Monte Carlo tests*, *bootstrap methods*, and *randomization tests*. In Monte Carlo methods, one knows the population distribution so it is easy to simulate sampling from it. In bootstrap and randomization tests, the population distribution is unknown, so one simulates the process of sampling by resampling from the sample.

5.1   Monte Carlo Tests

If you know the population distribution from which samples are drawn, but not the sampling distribution of a test statistic, you can test hypotheses with Monte Carlo simulations of the sampling process. The previous example simulated tossing a fair coin. Let us consider a case in which the sampling distribution of the test statistic cannot be derived analytically:

Your task is to evaluate a new policy for admitting students to graduate school in computer science. The faculty generally approves of the new policy, but is concerned it admits both well-prepared and poorly-prepared students, pointing to the interquartile range (IQR) of scores on a standardized test. Last year, before the policy changed, twenty-five incoming students took the test; their interquartile range was IQR = 6 points. This year's incoming class of twenty students has IQR = 8.5 points. Apparently there is more variation in scores under the new admission policy. The faculty realizes that the difference might be due to the test alone; perhaps last year's test was relatively easy, resulting in a ceiling effect and a narrow interquartile range.

As it happens, the test is administered nationwide. Last year the distribution of test scores was normal with a mean of 53 and a standard deviation of 6. This year the distribution of test scores was normal with a mean of 50 and a standard deviation of 5. You offer to test the hypothesis that the variation in preparation of this year's students (as measured by IQR) is not unusually high. You also agree to test whether there is more variation in the scores of this year's students than there was last year.

The classical approach to the first problem is to compare the sample result (IQR = 8.5) to the sampling distribution for IQR under the null hypothesis that this year's students were drawn from the same population as others in the nation. Unfortunately, the sampling distribution of IQR is unknown. It can be constructed empirically as follows.

Procedure 5.1   Monte Carlo Sampling: Interquartile Range

i.   Let R be a normal distribution with $\mu = 50, \sigma = 5$, (the parameters of this year's population). Let S be the original sample of size $N = 20$ students, and let IQR = InterquartileRange$(S) = 8.5$ be our sample statistic.

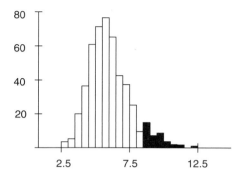

Figure 5.1   Monte Carlo sampling distribution of interquartile ranges.

ii.   Do $i = 1 \ldots K$ times:

    a.   Draw a *pseudosample* S_i^* of size N from R by random sampling.

    b.   Calculate and record $IQR_i^* = \text{InterquartileRange}(S_i^*)$, the value of the test statistic for pseudosample S_i^*.

iii.   The distribution of IQR^* is an empirical sampling distribution and can now be used to find the probability of obtaining the original sample result IQR under the null hypothesis.

We call S_i^* a pseudosample (and mark it with an asterisk) to distinguish it from the actual sample S of this year's students. It is a sample that "might have been," drawn from the specified population by random sampling. Procedure 5.1 draws pseudosamples of size twenty, rather than some other size, because IQR is expected to depend on sample size, so the sampling distribution of IQR should be constructed from pseudosamples of the same size as the original sample of students.

Procedure 5.1 can generate empirical sampling distributions for any statistic, of course, drawn from any known population. In general, $\theta = f(S)$ is our sample statistic (step i), and $\theta_i^* = f(S_i^*)$ is the ith *pseudostatistic* in the distribution of θ^* (step ii.b).

An empirical sampling distribution of the interquartile range, generated by procedure 5.1 for $K = 500$, is shown in figure 5.1. The darkened region of the distribution corresponds to forty scores greater than 8.5. So how unusual is the class you admitted this year? The probability that this year's class has an interquartile range of 8.5 or more is $40/500 = .08$. When you report this number, the faculty agrees that $IQR = 8.5$ is not significantly different from what would be expected by chance, but it is nearly significant, so the admission policy should be reviewed next year.

The faculty also wants to know whether this year's class has a higher interquartile range (8.5 points) than last year's class (6 points). To answer the question, adopt a minor variation of the earlier Monte Carlo procedure.

Procedure 5.2   Monte Carlo Sampling, Version 2

i   Let A and B be two populations with known parameters. Let S_A and S_B be the original samples of size N_A and N_B, respectively, and let $\theta = f(S_A, S_B)$ be a statistic calculated on these original samples.

ii   Repeat $i = 1 \ldots K$ times:

    a. Draw a pseudosample A_i^* of size N_A from A and a pseudosample B_i^* of size N_B from B.

    b. Calculate and record $\theta_i^* = f(A_i^*, B_i^*)$, the value of the test statistic for A_i^* and B_i^*.

iii   The distribution of θ^* can now be used to find the probability of obtaining the original sample result θ under the null hypothesis.

Instantiating this procedure for the current problem, let A stand for this year's population, with parameters $\mu_A = 50$, $\sigma_A = 5$; and likewise let $\mu_B = 53$, $\sigma_B = 6$, mimicking last year's population. Let $N_A = 20$, $N_B = 25$, and $K = 500$, as before, and let $\theta_i = \text{InterquartileRange}(A_i) - \text{InterquartileRange}(B_i)$.

By running procedure 5.1 with these settings, you obtain an empirical sampling distribution of 500 differences between interquartile ranges, as shown in figure 5.2. It is a simple matter to see whether the observed difference, $8.5 - 6 = 2.5$, is unexpectedly large. The darkened area of figure 5.2 represents forty-four values greater than or equal to 2.5. Thus, $44/500 = .088$ is the probability that your two samples will have interquartile ranges differing by 2.5 or more, given the populations from which they were drawn. Again, this probability is not low enough to reject—on the basis of these samples—the null hypothesis that the populations have equal interquartile ranges.

Monte Carlo sampling is very straightforward and easy to implement, yet it provides sampling distributions for any statistic. The distribution in figure 5.2 required less than one minute of computer time, so the technique is hardly expensive. Monte Carlo sampling does require a population distribution, however, which in many cases is unknown. In such cases you have only the original sample to work with. Remarkably, though, you can estimate a sampling distribution of a statistic from a sample.

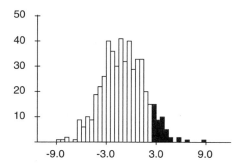

Figure 5.2   An empirical sampling distribution of the difference of two interquartile ranges.

5.2   Bootstrap Methods

If the population distribution is unknown, one can still generate an empirical sampling distribution for a statistic by Monte Carlo resampling from the sample, treating the sample as the population. To illustrate, consider the example of the interquartile range of test scores again, only now, imagine we don't know the population distribution of test scores. All we have is a single sample of twenty test scores. To construct a sampling distribution of IQR, simply draw pseudosamples S_i^* of size 20 from the original sample with replacement (i.e., returning each datum to the sample after it is drawn), calculating IQR_i^* for each. The resulting distribution of IQR^* is called the *bootstrap sampling distribution* of IQR. Bootstrap sampling distributions can be calculated for any statistic, and they assume nothing about the population, except that the sample is representative of the population. To illustrate the bootstrap procedure, I will develop an extended example around the problem of *censored* data. It is important to note, however, that the bootstrap is an extraordinary versatile procedure and is by no means limited to tests of censored data.

5.2.1   Bootstrap Sampling Distributions for Censored Data

It is sometimes necessary to abort a run of a program during an experiment because resource bounds are exceeded. Imagine running ten trials of a search algorithm, recording the number of node expansions required to find a goal node if that number is less than 5000, and otherwise abandoning the trial. A hypothetical sample distribution of the number of node expansions, x, is shown in table 5.1. Two of the trials were abandoned and the numbers we record in these cases (5000) are called censored data.

Table 5.1   A sample that includes two censored data.

Trial	1	2	3	4	5	6	7	8	9	10
Nodes	287	610	545	400	123	5000	5000	601	483	250

Censored data present no problems for descriptive statements about the sample, but they make it difficult to draw more general inferences. Provided we limit ourselves to the sample we can say, for example, that the mean number of nodes expanded in the previous ten trials is $\bar{x} = (\sum_{i=1}^{10} x_i/10) = 1329.9$. If we are disinclined to include the censored data in the average, then we can leave them out and simply report the mean number of nodes expanded after the censored data are discarded: $\bar{x} = (\sum_{i \neq 6,7}^{10} x_i/8) = 412.375.$[7]

We run into problems, however, when we try to generalize sample results. For example, it is unclear how to infer the population mean number of nodes that would be expanded by the previous algorithm if we ran other experiments with ten trials. Statistical theory tells us how to make this generalization if no data are censored: the best estimate of the population mean is the sample mean. But our sample includes censored data, and we should not infer that the population mean is 1329.9, because we do not know how many nodes the censored trials might have expanded if we had let them run to completion. Nor should we infer that the population mean of uncensored trials is 412.375. Statistical theory that explains the relationship between the mean of a sample that includes censored data and the mean of a population is described in Cohen (1959); Cox (1984).

Suppose we want to test the hypothesis that the mean number of nodes expanded by our algorithm is significantly less than 500, that is,

H_0: $\mu = 500$;

H_1: $\mu < 500$.

To run a conventional t test, we would calculate the mean of the numbers in the table above and compute a t statistic. The mean is

$$\bar{x} = \frac{287 + 610 + 545 + 400 + 123 + 5000 + 5000 + 601 + 483 + 250}{10} = 1329.9$$

---

7. In this example, the abandoned trials expanded more than ten times as many nodes as the others, which suggests that they are somehow different and not really comparable with the others, and should be left out of the sample.

and the t statistic is

$$t = \frac{\bar{x} - \mu}{s/\sqrt{N}} = \frac{1329.9 - 500}{1940.7/\sqrt{10}} = 1.352.$$

This value is not significant, so H_0 stands. It isn't clear, however, whether this test answers the question we asked. Whereas eight values in the sample represent the exact number of expanded nodes, the value 5000 denotes a lower bound on the number that would have been expanded had the algorithm run longer. We don't know why these values are so high, or how high they might have become, but we suspect they shouldn't be included in the analysis. There is also a good mathematical reason to set them aside. By including them in the sample, we ensure that the sampling distribution of $\bar{x}$ will have a very high estimated standard error $\hat{\sigma}_{\bar{x}}$, which is why the t statistic has such a low value. In general, a few outlier values can make it very difficult to get a significant value of t.

Our inclination, then, is to re-run the t test without the high values:

$$t = \frac{\bar{x} - \mu}{s/\sqrt{N}} = \frac{412.375 - 500}{178.56/\sqrt{8}} = -1.388.$$

This value of t is not significant, so again we fail to reject H_0. But perhaps our logic is flawed. Can we simply toss out the aborted trials and pretend our sample comprises eight trials instead of ten? Recall that standard errors depend on the sample size N. If we drop two cases from our sample, should $N = 8$ or $N = 10$ be used to calculate $\hat{\sigma}_{\bar{x}}$? By dropping two cases, the t test ends up comparing $\bar{x}$ to a sampling distribution for $N = 8$, when in fact the sample included ten cases. This is a more stringent test of $\bar{x}$ than is appropriate, because the standard error for $N = 8$ is larger than it is for $N = 10$. Later, we will show this difference has little practical impact, and in the process illustrate an important lesson about the bootstrap: The test one uses is less important than the size of one's sample (see section 5.5). Even so, it is instructive to derive a *bootstrap sampling distribution* of the censored mean.

The censored mean $\bar{x}_C$ is the mean of a sample that has been censored. For example, the censored mean of the data in table 5.1 is

$$\bar{x}_C = \frac{287 + 610 + 545 + 400 + 123 + 601 + 483 + 250}{8} = 412.375.$$

We'd like to test the hypothesis the population censored mean is less than 500:

H_0: $\mu_C = 500$;

H_1: $\mu_C < 500$.

Unfortunately, the sampling distribution of $\overline{x}_C$ under the null hypothesis is unknown. Recall the rough outline of the Monte Carlo procedure:

Repeat K times:

1. Draw a pseudosample S_i^* of size N from a population.
2. Calculate and record θ_i^* for this pseudosample.

If only we knew the population distribution of x, the number of nodes expanded by our search algorithm, then we could generate a sampling distribution of $\overline{x}_C$ this way. Unfortunately, all we have is one sample of ten values of x; we do not know the population distribution of x. We can treat our sample as if it is the population, however, and construct a sampling distribution by Monte Carlo sampling from the sample. Counterintuitive it may be, but this method works well. It works because the sample distribution is the best estimator of the population distribution. If the sample contains N data $x_1, x_2, \ldots x_N$, then the maximum likelihood estimator of the population distribution is found by assigning to each x_i the probability $1/N$ (Efron and Tibshirani, 1986).

Here again is our sample S:

Trial	1	2	3	4	5	6	7	8	9	10
Nodes	287	610	545	400	123	5000	5000	601	483	250

We can *resample* from S just as we would sample from a population. To construct a sampling distribution of a statistic, say $\overline{x}_C$, requires only a small modification to the Monte Carlo procedure:

Procedure 5.3   Bootstrap Sampling

Repeat $i = 1 \ldots K$ times:

i. Draw a bootstrap pseudosample S_i^* of size N from S by sampling with replacement as follows:
    Repeat N times: select a member of S at random and add it to S_i^*.
ii. Calculate and record the value of a pseudostatistic θ_i^* for S_i^*.

Here are three pseudosamples generated by this procedure:

	1	2	3	4	5	6	7	8	9	10	$\overline{x}_C^*$
S_1^*	610	601	610	483	483	610	287	5000	601	483	529.78
S_2^*	5000	601	250	250	5000	545	601	545	400	5000	456.0
S_3^*	250	287	400	400	123	545	601	250	545	545	394.6

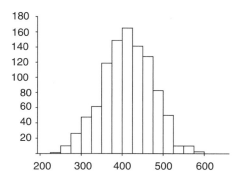

Figure 5.3   The bootstrapped sampling distribution for $\overline{x}_C^*$.

After drawing each, we calculate its censored mean, $\overline{x}_C^*$; for example, S_1^* contains nine values smaller than 5000 and their mean is 529.78, so $\overline{x}_C^*(S_1^*) = 529.78$.

Sampling with replacement ensures that a datum in the original sample might be selected several times for inclusion in a bootstrap sample; for example, 610 shows up three times in S_1^*, but just once in S. Similarly, items in S might not be selected for inclusion in a bootstrap sample; for example, 123 doesn't show up in S_1^*, and 5000 shows up just once instead of twice as in S. Resampling with replacement is justified in two rather different ways. First, if we resampled without replacement then every bootstrap sample S_i^* would be identical to S and every value of $\overline{x}_C^*$ for S_i^* would be identical to the original sample result, $\overline{x}_C$ for S. Clearly, this is no way to construct a sampling distribution of $\overline{x}_C^*$. Second, resampling with replacement is tantamount to assuming that the population (which we do not know) comprises the items in S, in the proportions that they appear in S, in essentially limitless quantities.

To construct a sampling distribution for $\overline{x}_C^*$ we simply run procedure 5.3 with a large value of K. Figure 5.3 shows the sampling distribution of 1000 values of $\overline{x}_C^*$ calculated from bootstrap samples. The mean of this distribution is 412.75 and its standard deviation is 60.1.

Bootstrap Sampling Distributions for H_0: Shift Method

Given this sampling distribution for $\overline{x}_C$, it would appear to be simple to test the hypotheses

H_0: $\mu_C = 500$

H_1: $\mu_C < 500$

The immediate inclination is to compare the sample result, $\bar{x}_C = 412.375$, to the sampling distribution in figure 5.3. This is wrong. Figure 5.3 is the bootstrapped sampling distribution of $\bar{x}_C^*$, not the sampling distribution of $\bar{x}_C^*$ under the null hypothesis. The Monte Carlo tests of the previous section were constructed by drawing samples from the null hypothesis population. In contrast, bootstrap samples S_i^* are drawn from a sample S that represents a population but not necessarily the null hypothesis population.

If figure 5.3 is not a sampling distribution of $\bar{x}_C^*$ under H_0, what is? The question can be answered only by assuming a relationship between the bootstrapped sampling distribution and the null hypothesis sampling distribution. For brevity, we will refer to these as S_{boot} and S_{H_0}, respectively. One common assumption is that S_{H_0} has the same shape but a different mean than S_{boot}. In this case, S_{H_0} is identical to the one in figure 5.3 except its mean is 500 (because $H_0 : \mu_C = 500$). The mean of S_{boot} is 412.75, so adding $500 - 412.75 = 87.25$ to every value in S_{boot} will transform it into S_{H_0}. Figure 5.4 is the result. We will use it to assess the probability of our original sample result, $\bar{x}_C = 412.375$, under H_0.

It transpires that 86 values in S_{H_0} are less than or equal to our sample result, $\bar{x}_C = 412.375$, so the probability of attaining this result by chance under H_0 is .086. This is not small enough to reject the null hypothesis. It is a simple matter to find a critical value for $\bar{x}_C$; just sort the K values in S_{H_0} and count off αK items from the front or the back of the list (or count off $(\alpha K)/2$ items from the front *and* the back for a two-tailed test). For example, our alternative hypothesis is $\mu_C < 500$, so we're looking for a small value of $\bar{x}_C$ to reject the null hypothesis. We sort the 1000 values in figure 5.4 into ascending order and count off $.05 \times 1000 = 50$ values from the front of the list. The 50th value is 395.75. Had our sample result been $\bar{x}_C \leq 395.75$, we could have rejected H_0 with $p \leq .05$.

Bootstrap Sampling Distributions for H_0: Normal Approximation Method

Another way to estimate S_{H_0} assumes the distribution of $\bar{x}_C - \mu_C$ is normal and that

$$Z = \frac{\bar{x}_C - \mu_C}{\text{standard error of } \bar{x}_C}$$

has a standard normal distribution. We bootstrap only to find $std.(S_{boot})$, the standard deviation of S_{boot}, which serves as an estimate of the standard error $\sigma_{\bar{x}_C}$. For the current example, $\hat{\sigma}_{\bar{x}_C} = std.(S_{boot}) = 60.1$. With this estimate, we can run a conventional Z test:

$$Z = \frac{\bar{x}_C - \mu_C}{\hat{\sigma}_{\bar{x}_C}} = \frac{412.375 - 500}{60.1} = -1.458.$$

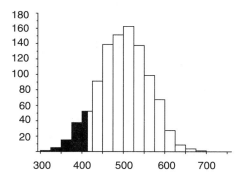

Figure 5.4 The sampling distribution derived from the bootstrapped distribution (figure 5.3) by the Shift method.

Under the null hypothesis, the probability of $Z \leq -1.458$ is .072. This jibes pretty well with the result from the shift method, where the probability was .086. Neither the shift method nor the normal approximation method allow us to reject the null hypothesis at the conventional .05 level. We can calculate a critical value for this level as follows:

$$-1.645 = \frac{\overline{x}_{crit.} - 500}{60.1}, \ \overline{x}_{crit.} = 400.853.$$

This, too, is close to 395.75, the critical value derived by the shift method. For completeness, let's find the critical value if we had run a t test on the eight uncensored data items (simply ignoring the censored ones). The critical value of t for $\alpha = .05$ and eight degrees of freedom is -1.86. Thus

$$-1.86 = \frac{\overline{x}_{crit.} - 500}{s/\sqrt{N}} = \frac{\overline{x}_{crit.} - 500}{178.56/\sqrt{8}}, \ \overline{x}_{crit.} = 382.57.$$

By these indications, it appears that the shift method, the normal approximation method and the t test all give similar results. This is not very surprising when we consider that the test statistic is a mean (albeit a censored mean for the bootstrap tests), so its sampling distribution is probably normal or something like it. We will develop this intuition further in section 5.5.

5.2.2 Bootstrap Two-Sample Tests

Two-sample and paired-sample t tests are general and robust methods to compare the means of two samples (secs. 4.4.7, 4.4.8), but computer-intensive methods are required to compare most other statistics across samples. Suppose we measure the time

Table 5.2   Hypothetical censored sample data for a comparison of two robots.

	1	2	3	4	5	6	7	8	9	10
Robot A	300	290	600	5000	200	600	30	800	55	190
Robot B	400	280	5000	5000	300	820	120	5000	120	400

required for robots A and B to perform navigation tasks. Now and then, a robot gets trapped in a cul de sac and bumps around, like a bumblebee against a windowpane, until the trial duration exceeds a threshold. Sample data are shown in table 5.2. Trials 3 and 8 are singly censored, meaning one or the other robot exceeds the time limit (5000, again), and trial 4 is doubly censored, that is, both robots exceed the limit. (To reiterate an earlier point: You can bootstrap any statistic whatsoever, you aren't limited to the censored mean. We illustrate it here for convenience and continuity, only.)

The general form of a two-sample test statistic is $\theta(S_A) - \theta(S_B)$, whereas a paired-sample statistic has the form $\theta(a_i, b_i)$ for $a_i \in S_A, b_i \in S_B$. For example, the two-sample t test involves the difference between sample means, $\overline{x}_A - \overline{x}_B$, whereas the paired-sample t test involves the mean difference between items paired across samples: $\sum_i (a_i - b_i)/N$. The following discussion begins with bootstrap two-sample tests; then, in section 5.3.2, we'll present a computer-intensive paired-sample test (though not a bootstrap test).

Suppose S_A and S_B are samples such as the robot data, above. One resampling procedure draws pseudosamples A^* and B^* from S_A and S_B, respectively:

Procedure 5.4   Bootstrap Sampling for a Two-Sample Test

i.   Let S_A and S_B be two samples of sizes N_A and N_B, respectively. Let $\theta = f(S_A, S_B)$ be a statistic calculated from these samples.

ii. Repeat $i = 1 \ldots K$ times:

    a. Draw a pseudosample A_i^* of size N_A from S_A by sampling with replacement.

    b. Draw a pseudosample B_i^* of size N_B from S_B by sampling with replacement.

    c. Calculate and record the value of $\theta_i^* = f(A_i^*, B_i^*)$, the value of a statistic for the two bootstrap pseudosamples.

iii. The distribution of θ^* can now be used with the shift method or the normal approximation method to find the probability of obtaining the original sample result θ under the null hypothesis.

Another scheme first merges S_A and S_B into a single sample S_{A+B}, then draws A^* and B^* from S_{A+B}.

Procedure 5.5   Bootstrap Sampling with Randomization for a Two-Sample Test

i.   Let S_A and S_B be two samples of size N_A and N_B, respectively. Combine S_A and S_B into a single sample, S_{A+B}. Note: This is not the union but rather the merge of S_A and S_B.

ii.   Repeat $i = 1 \ldots K$ times:

   a.   Draw a pseudosample A_i^* of size N_A from S_{A+B} by sampling with replacement.
   b.   Draw a pseudosample B_i^* of size N_B from S_{A+B} by sampling with replacement.
   c.   Calculate and record the value of $\theta_i^* = f(A_i^*, B_i^*)$, the value of a statistic for the two pseudosamples.

iii. The distribution of θ_i^* can now be used to find the probability of obtaining the original sample result θ under the null hypothesis.

The advantage of procedure 5.5 is that it yields an empirical sampling distribution of θ^* under H_0, whereas the distribution from procedure 5.4 must be shifted as described earlier to make it a sampling distribution under H_0. By sampling from S_{A+B}, procedure 5.5 enforces the implication of H_0 that a datum might as well have been produced by robot A as robot B. (This procedure is a hybrid bootstrap-randomization method; see section 5.3 for other randomization tests.)

Returning to our two-robot example, S_A and S_B are the data in the first and second rows of table 5.2, respectively, and S_{A+B} is the merge of all 20 data. Our test statistic, θ, is the difference of the censored means of S_A and S_B, obtained by throwing away the censored values (5000) and taking the difference of the means of the results, $\theta = -8.02$. The pseudostatistic θ_i^* is the difference of the censored means of bootstrap samples A_i^* and B_i^*. For $K = 1000$, procedure 5.5 yields the bootstrap sampling distribution shown in figure 5.5. The sample result $\theta = -8.02$ falls right in the middle of this distribution, nowhere near any reasonable rejection region. Evidently the censored trial durations for robots A and B are not significantly different.

5.2.3   Bootstrap Confidence Intervals

In chapter 4 we defined the confidence interval for the mean in terms of the standard normal distribution. The 95 percent confidence interval for the mean is

$$\bar{x} - 1.96\sigma_{\bar{x}} \leq \mu \leq \bar{x} + 1.96\sigma_{\bar{x}}.$$

With 95 percent confidence we believe the population μ mean falls within an interval $2 \cdot 1.96 = 3.92$ standard error units wide, centered around the sample mean. This definition works not only for the mean, but for any statistic whose sampling distribution

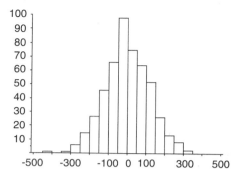

Figure 5.5   A bootstrap sampling distribution of the difference of censored means. The original data are in table 5.2; 1000 iterations of procedure 5.5 produced this distribution.

is normal. In general,

$$u - \sigma_u z_\alpha \le \upsilon \le u + \sigma_u z_\alpha.$$

That is, if the sampling distribution of a sample estimate u is normal with standard error σ_u, then with confidence $(1 - 2\alpha)$ a parameter υ falls in an interval $2 \cdot z_\alpha$ standard error units wide, centered around u.

If the sampling distribution of the correlation was normal, then the 90 percent confidence interval for the population correlation would be

$$r - (\sigma_r \cdot 1.645) \le \rho \le r + (\sigma_r \cdot 1.645).$$

In fact, the sampling distribution for the correlation is not normal, but confidence intervals for correlations can be constructed from bootstrap sampling distributions.

To begin, consider how to construct a bootstrap 95 percent confidence interval for a statistic that does have a normal sampling distribution, namely, the mean. Obviously, we don't need the bootstrap procedure in this case, but the example will be instructive. We would construct a sampling distribution from the means of, say, 1,000 bootstrap pseudosamples, sort them in ascending order, and find the 25th and 975th values. These would be the lower and upper bounds of the 95 percent confidence interval because 2.5 percent of the distribution lies at or below the 25th value, and 2.5 percent lies at or above the 975th. The procedure follows.

Procedure 5.6   Bootstrap Confidence Interval

i.   Construct a distribution from K bootstrap samples for a statistic u.

ii. Sort the values in the distribution.

Table 5.3   The original sample for the correlation example.

x	5	1.75	.8	5	1.75	5	1.75	1	5	1.75
y	27.8	20.82	44.12	29.41	31.19	28.68	29.53	34.62	20	41.54

iii. The lower bound of the $100(1 - 2\alpha)$ percent confidence interval is the $K\alpha$th value, and the upper bound is the $K(1 - \alpha)$th value in the sorted distribution.

Efron and Tibshirani (1991; 1993) note that if the sampling distribution of u is not normal, but there is a monotone transformation $\hat{\phi} = g(u)$ such that the sampling distribution of $\hat{\phi}$ is normal (with variance τ^2 for some constant τ), then procedure 5.6 still produces the desired $(1 - 2\alpha)$ confidence interval. It is not necessary to implement the transformation; it is only necessary that such a transformation exists. Said differently, if procedure 5.6 was run for the statistic $\hat{\phi} = g(u)$, then it would produce lower and upper bounds $\hat{\phi}_L$ and $\hat{\phi}_U$ for a confidence interval. These bounds are the same values we would get by running procedure 5.6 for the original statistic u and transforming the resulting bounds: $\hat{\phi}_L = g(u_L)$, $\hat{\phi}_U = g(u_U)$. This means that even if the sampling distribution of a statistic is not normal, but the aforementioned conditions are met, the bounds of, say, a 90 percent confidence interval are just the 5th and 95th percentile values of the sampling distribution.[8]

Now we will construct a 90 percent bootstrap confidence interval for the correlation. Our original sample is shown in table 5.3. Two variables, x and y have a sample correlation of $-.552$. A bootstrap sample is constructed by selecting ten x, y pairs from the original distribution with replacement; for example, table 5.4 shows one bootstrap pseudosample in which the pair 5, 27.8 occurs three times. The correlation for this pseudosample is $-.545$. Note that x and y data are not resampled as in a two-sample test (e.g., procedure 5.4 or 5.5); rather, x, y pairs are atomic items, resampled as in a one-sample t test (e.g., procedure 5.3). Resampling 1,000 times gives a bootstrap sampling distribution of the correlation, shown in figure 5.6. After sorting the values in this distribution, we find that the 50th value is $-.834$ and the 950th is $-.123$, so these are the upper and lower bounds of the 90 percent confidence interval of the correlation. Points outside the confidence interval are shaded.

The bootstrap is counterintuitive, as Diaconis and Efron (1983, p. 123) point out in their discussion of the bootstrapped standard error of the correlation:

---

8. See Efron and Tibshirani 1986 for procedures to construct confidence intervals for statistics for which other kinds of transformations into normal distributions are required.

Table 5.4   One bootstrap pseudosample drawn from the original sample in table 5.3.

x	5	1.75	1.75	5	1	5	.8	1.75	5	5
y	27.8	20.82	29.53	27.8	34.62	28.68	44.12	31.19	20	27.8

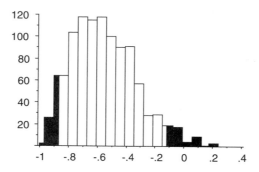

Figure 5.6   Bootstrap sampling distribution of the correlation. The original sample is shown in table 5.3. One thousand bootstrap samples were drawn.

At first glance this theoretical result seems paradoxical: it suggests that from the information in each sample one can derive a good approximation to the frequency distribution of the correlation coefficient for all real samples of the same size. It is as if statisticians had discovered the statistical analogue of the hologram, a pattern of light waves that is preserved on a surface. The scene from which the light waves are emitted can be reconstructed in great detail from the whole surface of the hologram, but if pieces of the surface are broken off the entire scene can still be reconstructed from each piece. Not every sample is like a broken piece of hologram, however: the good properties of the bootstrap are good average properties. Like any other statistical procedure, the bootstrap will give misleading answers for a small percentage of the possible samples.... The bootstrap does not always guarantee a true picture of the statistical accuracy of a sample estimate. What has been proved is that the bootstrap gives a good picture of the accuracy of the estimate most of the time.

In practice, the bootstrap works well in many situations, it works for many statistics—some of which are novel and task-specific, such as confidence intervals on barometric isobars—and it has the advantage of making no assumptions about underlying population distributions. Actually, it makes one assumption: The original sample is representative of the population. Another hypothesis-testing procedure, which does not require even this assumption, is discussed next.

5.3   Randomization Tests

Because the bootstrap treats samples as "proxies" for populations, it supports inferences about population parameters. Sometimes, however, it suffices to test hypotheses about samples without drawing any conclusions about populations. An archeologist might test whether males and females were segregated at two burial sites by showing that mean pelvis dimensions at the two sites are significantly different. No inferences are made about other sites, no "population mean pelvis difference" is inferred. The archeologist wants to know whether pelvises at two particular sites differ, not whether males and females were segregated in the population of burial sites. Of course, the archeologist might eventually want to assert that males and females were generally segregated in a particular culture, but the immediate question is whether the pelvises at two sites are significantly different.[9] Classical parametric tests and bootstrap tests answer this question indirectly by making inferences about the population mean pelvis difference. A more direct approach, called *randomization*, can tell us whether two samples are related without any reference to population parameters.

To illustrate randomization, let us modify an earlier example. Your faculty wants to know whether the performance of this year's students is significantly more variable (measured by the interquartile range) than the performance of last year's students. But instead of administering a standardized test for which population statistics are available, your department administers a home-grown test. It is given without modification to twenty-five students last year and twenty students this year, and the interquartile ranges of the samples were 6 and 8.5, respectively. The faculty wants to know whether these numbers are significantly different. Here is the sample of twenty-five scores from last year:

sample 1

48.35	53.93	55.48	45.67	52.82
49.47	57.00	53.61	57.69	51.34
44.98	54.70	59.32	51.70	50.73
46.84	63.13	52.50	49.67	54.07
44.96	48.68	53.94	59.00	50.92

And here are the scores from this year:

---

9. I am grateful to Mike Sutherland for this example.

sample 2

$$64.82 \quad 51.69 \quad 57.00 \quad 58.17 \quad 40.63$$
$$50.90 \quad 48.77 \quad 40.33 \quad 50.76 \quad 49.64$$
$$56.25 \quad 65.68 \quad 57.50 \quad 47.45 \quad 46.78$$
$$61.34 \quad 53.66 \quad 49.10 \quad 54.49 \quad 54.15$$

Let d_{IQR} denote the difference between the interquartile ranges of the samples, that is, $d_{IQR} = 6 - 8.5 = -2.5$. To determine the probability that this difference arose by chance, we need a distribution of the values of d_{IQR} that could arise by chance. Indeed, for the purpose of hypothesis testing, the distribution must be constructed under the null hypothesis that students' performance is no more variable this year than last. If H_0 is really true, then randomly swapping scores between the samples will hardly influence d_{IQR}. Said differently, H_0 asserts that there is no relationship between the variability of test scores and the constitution of the entering class, so if some of last year's students had been admitted this year, and vice versa, the variability of test scores would not be affected. Suppose we throw all forty-five scores into a hopper and shake them up, then divide them into a group of twenty-five called "last year's students" and a disjoint group of twenty called "this year's students." Under H_0, the interquartile ranges of these *randomized samples* should be approximately equal. In fact, this is a single iteration of the *approximate randomization* procedure:

Procedure 5.7   Approximate Randomization to Test Whether Two Samples Are Drawn from the Same Population

i.   Let S_A and S_B be two samples of sizes N_A and N_B, respectively. Let $\theta = f(S_A, S_B)$ be a statistic calculated from the two samples, such as the difference of the interquartile ranges of the samples. Let $S_{A+B} = S_A + S_B$, that is, the merge of S_A and S_B.

ii.   Do K times:

    a.   Shuffle the elements of S_{A+B} thoroughly.

    b.   Assign the first N_A elements of S_{A+B} to a randomized pseudosample A_i^* and the remaining N_B elements to B_i^*.

    c.   Calculate $\theta_i^* = f(A_i^*, B_i^*)$ and record the result.

iii. The distribution of θ_i^* can now be used to find the probability of the sample result θ under the null hypothesis that the samples are drawn from the same population.

Figure 5.7 shows a distribution of 500 values of d_{IQR}^*, generated by this procedure—a distribution of 500 differences of the interquartile ranges of two randomized samples A_i^* and B_i^*, of sizes 25 and 20, respectively, drawn without replacement from a

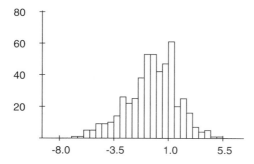

Figure 5.7 A distribution of d^*_{IQR} generated by procedure 5.7.

hopper that contains all 45 test score samples, above. The mean of the distribution in figure 5.7 is $-.343$ and its standard deviation is 2.08. If this year's test scores were significantly more variable than last year's, then d_{IQR} should be an unusually large, negative number. You can see readily that our original sample result, $d_{IQR} = -2.5$, is certainly not unusual—roughly one-fourth of the values of d^*_{IQR} lie below it—so we should not reject H_0 on this basis. The variability of test performance was apparently not significantly different last year and this year.

Procedure 5.7 is called approximate randomization because its K iterations do not exhaust the space of all possible assignments of elements of S_{A+B} to A^*_i and B^*_i. In contrast, we asked earlier for the probability that ten tosses of a single fair coin produced two sequences of five, one with at least four heads, the other with at least four tails. You can find the *exact* probability of this result by generating all outcomes of ten coin tosses, there being only 1,024 to consider. This is called *exact randomization*. The test-score example is considerably more complex: the number of distinct ways to draw twenty-five scores from forty-five (i.e., all possible sets A^*_i and B^*_i from S_{A+B}) is $45!/(25! \cdot 20!)$, a staggering number. Consequently, we cannot discover the exact probability of a sample result by generating all possible randomized samples. We must settle instead for a smaller distribution of results from relatively few randomized samples. This distribution provides an approximate probability for a sample result, so procedure 5.7 is called approximate randomization.

Approximate randomization can test a wide range of hypotheses, but it sometimes requires a little ingenuity to fit the hypothesis into the framework of procedure 5.7 (see Noreen, 1989, for several interesting examples). For the following examples, some new terminology will be helpful. Let $\theta^*[p]$ be the pth percentile value of the sorted distribution of θ^* values; for example, in a distribution of 500 values, $\theta^*[5]$ is the 25th value and bounds the lowest five percent of the distribution. Similarly,

$\theta^*[2.5]$ and $\theta^*[97.5]$ are the values of θ^* that bound the lower and upper 2.5 percent of the sorted distribution (conservatively, these numbers would be the 12th and 488th in the distribution in figure 5.7). Let θ^*_α be the critical value of θ^* for a one-tailed test. Clearly, $\theta^*_\alpha = \theta^*[100\alpha]$ or $\theta^*_\alpha = \theta^*[100 - 100\alpha]$, depending on whether the sample result θ must fall in the lower or upper tail of the distribution of θ^* to justify rejecting the null hypothesis. For example, if the lower tail is the rejection region and we desire a p-value of .05, then $\theta^*_{.05} = \theta^*[5]$; but if the upper tail is the rejection region, $\theta^*_{.05} = \theta^*[95]$. Similarly, for a two-tailed test with $p \leq .05$, the lower and upper bounds of the rejection regions are $\theta^*_{.025} = \theta^*[2.5]$ and $\theta^*_{.025} = \theta^*[97.5]$, respectively. Now let us consider some of the hypotheses we can test with procedure 5.7.

5.3.1   A Randomization Version of the Two-Sample *t* Test

For a test of the difference of two sample means, the original samples are S_A and S_B and the sample statistic is $\theta = \overline{x}_{S_A} - \overline{x}_{S_B}$. Procedure 5.7 will generate a distribution of $\theta^*_i = \overline{x}_{A^*_i} - \overline{x}_{B^*_i}$, the differences of the means of randomized samples. For a two-tailed test, with $p \leq .05$, we will reject the null hypothesis that S_A and S_B are drawn from the same population if θ falls in the upper or lower 2.5% of the distribution of θ^*, that is, if $\theta \leq \theta^*[2.5]$ or $\theta \geq \theta^*[97.5]$. For a one-tailed test we will use $\theta \leq \theta^*[5]$ or $\theta \geq \theta^*[95]$, depending on the direction of the alternative hypothesis.

5.3.2   A Randomization Version of the Paired Sample *t* Test

Recall that the test statistic for the paired sample *t* test is the mean difference between paired sample values: $\theta = \sum_{i=1}^{N}(a_i - b_i)/N$ for $a_i \in S_A, b_i \in S_B$. This means the "shuffle" operation in procedure 5.7 must be implemented differently for the two-sample and paired sample tests. Consider two robots, Alpha and Beta, who are competing in the Robotics Decathlon, a ten-event test of their skills. Their scores are shown in table 5.5.

The first row represents the event number, the second and third are Alpha and Beta's scores, and the fourth row is the difference between Alpha and Beta's score on each

Table 5.5   Decathlon scores for robots Alpha and Beta.

Event	1	2	3	4	5	6	7	8	9	10
Alpha	8	3	9	6	5	8	7	8	9	9
Beta	7	0	9	4	5	9	8	3	4	5
Difference	1	3	0	2	0	−1	−1	5	5	4

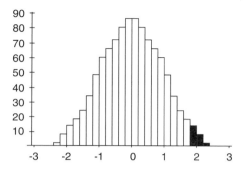

Figure 5.8   The exact sampling distribution of the mean paired difference for a ten-event competition between robots Alpha and Beta.

event. The mean difference between the scores, θ, is 1.8. We want to know whether this difference is significant. Under the null hypothesis that Alpha and Beta are equal, the score obtained by Alpha in an event might equally well have been achieved by Beta, and vice versa. The difference between Alpha's score and Beta's on the first event, for example, might equally well be 1 or -1. The distribution of θ^* is found by shuffling the members of each pair, such as the two scores on the first event, and calculating θ^*. In practice, shuffling means replacing each difference score d with $-d$, with probability one-half. For example, here is the result of one shuffle:

Event	1	2	3	4	5	6	7	8	9	10
Alpha	7	0	9	6	5	8	7	3	9	9
Beta	8	3	9	4	5	9	8	8	4	5
Difference	-1	-3	0	2	0	-1	-1	-5	5	4

In this case, the first, second, and eighth event scores were swapped and the difference scores were changed accordingly, yielding $\theta^* = 0$. The exact distribution of θ^* can be generated systematically when the number of pairs is small, as in this case. It is shown in figure 5.8. You can see that the original sample mean difference, $\theta = 1.8$, is relatively rare (means greater than or equal to 1.8 are shaded). In fact, only 24 of 1,024 means have values of 1.8 or more. Thus, we can reject the null hypothesis that Alpha and Beta are equal, with $p = .023$.

The randomization procedure really shines when we cannot estimate the sampling distribution of a statistic any other way. If the estimate can be derived mathematically, as with the two-sample and paired sample t tests, the only strong reason to run a randomization test is that the parametric assumptions that underlie the derivation are not met. (These assumptions include equal variance and sampling from normal

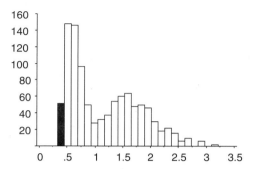

Figure 5.9   Ratio of two variances.

distributions, but the *t* test is quite robust, in any case.) In short, the two randomization versions of *t* tests that we have just described will rarely be superior to the conventional parametric tests, but they will not be inferior, either. Thus, we echo Noreen's (1989) advice to use them instead of ordinary *t* tests because they free us from worrying about parametric assumptions, and they are no less powerful.

It should be clear, however, that we can generalize the previous randomization procedures to other two-sample and paired-sample tests. We aren't limited to tests of differences of means. For example, note that Alpha seems to perform more consistently than Beta: The variances of their scores are 3.66 and 8.27, respectively, and the ratio of these variances is .442. Under the null hypothesis that Alpha and Beta's scores are equally variable, we would expect the ratio of their variances to be one. Is .442 an unusual value? To find out, we need the sampling distribution of the ratio of the variances under the null hypothesis.[10] For a two-sample test we simply replace the statement $\theta_i^* = f(A_i^*, B_i^*)$ with $\theta_i^* = (\text{var.}(A_i^*)/\text{var.}(B_i^*))$ in procedure 5.7. For a paired sample test, we get values of A_i^* and B_i^* by interchanging corresponding scores of S_A and S_B, then calculating $\theta_i^* = (\text{var.}(A_i^*)/\text{var.}(B_i^*))$ as before. We can run either approximate or exact randomization tests in either case. Figure 5.9 shows the exact sampling distribution of 1024 values of θ^* generated by the paired sample-procedure. The shaded block represents ratios of variances less than or equal to 0.442. There are fifty such ratios, so we can reject the null hypothesis that Alpha and Beta perform equally consistently, with $p \leq .05$. (In most situations you will want to shift the distributions S_A and S_B so their means are zero before generating a distribution of the ratio of their variances; see section 6.5.)

---

10. In fact, there is a parametric version of the two-sample test of equal variances (section 6.3.2) but it is not robust against violations of assumptions.

5.3.3   A Randomization Test of Independence

A parametric test of the hypothesis that the population correlation is some constant, $H_0 : \rho = k$, was presented in chapter 4. An alternative is to test the hypothesis that two samples are independent—drawing no inference about populations—given a statistic such as the sample correlation. For example, the correlation of the following numbers is $r = -.4$; are x and y independent?

x	1	2	3	4	5	6	7	8	9	10
y	54	66	61	44	60	55	51	45	63	52

If they are, there is no reason why a particular y value, say 54, should be associated with a particular x value. Thus, under the null hypothesis that x and y are independent, we can shuffle y values relative to x values (or vice versa) and calculate the resulting correlation. Here is the result of one shuffle:

x	1	2	3	4	5	6	7	8	9	10
y	61	55	54	44	63	52	51	60	45	66

In this case, $r^* = .037$. To test whether the original sample result $r = -.4$ is unusual under the null hypothesis that x and y are independent, simply repeat the shuffling process to get a distribution of r^*; then reject the null hypothesis if $r \leq r^*[2.5]$ or $r \geq r^*[97.5]$. The distribution of r^* can be constructed exactly if the number of shuffled arrangements is small, or by approximate randomization otherwise. Procedure 5.8 shows the approximate randomization version of the test.

Procedure 5.8   Approximate Randomization to Test Whether Two Samples of Variables are Related

i. Let S_A and S_B be two samples of size N (or two variables in a single sample). Let $\theta = f(S_A, S_B)$ be a statistic calculated from S_A and S_B, such as the correlation. Assign $A_i^* := S_A$ and $B_i^* := S_B$

ii. Do K times:
   a. Shuffle the elements of B_i^* thoroughly.
   b. Calculate $\theta_i^* = f(A_i^*, B_i^*)$ and record the result.

iii. The distribution of θ_i^* can now be used to find the probability of the sample result θ under the null hypothesis that the samples (or the variables) are unrelated.

5.3.4   Randomization for a Robust Statistic: The Resistant Line

A weakness of many statistics, particularly the mean, variance and correlation, is sensitivity to outliers. Computer-intensive methods make it possible to obtain standard errors for robust statistics such as the trimmed mean and the interquartile range. It is a simple matter to adapt procedure 5.8 to measures of association more robust than the correlation, such as Spearman's rank-order correlation. Here, however, we study a related problem; the least-squares regression line is very sensitive to outliers (section 8.2.1). We will illustrate a more robust way to fit a line to data and describe how to test whether the slope of the line is zero. For concreteness, imagine that on a succession of trials the differences between the scores of two robots appears to decrease as follows:

Event	1	2	3	4	5	6	7	8	9
Alpha	8	9	9	8	8	8	9	8	9
Beta	1	0	2	4	5	5	7	7	6
Difference	7	9	7	4	3	3	2	1	3

These data suggest that robot Alpha performs well on all trials and robot Beta improves on successive trials. Let us fit a line to the difference scores using the *three group resistant line technique* described by Emerson and Hoaglin (1983). First, the data are divided into three equal groups:

Event	(1 2 3)	(4 5 6)	(7 8 9)
Difference	(7 9 7)	(4 3 3)	(2 1 3)

Then the medians of each group are found:

Event	(2)	(5)	(8)
Difference	(7)	(3)	(2)

The medians are turned into coordinates: (2,7), (5,3), and (8,2). Call the values of the leftmost coordinate x_L and y_L, and the values of the middle and right coordinates x_M, y_M, x_R, and y_R, respectively. A line $\hat{y} = b(x - x_M) + a$ is fit as follows: b is the slope of the line through the leftmost and rightmost coordinates, that is,

$$b = (y_L - y_R)/(x_L - x_R) = (7 - 2)/(2 - 8) = -.833.$$

The intercept, a is

$$a = \frac{1}{3}[y_L - b(x_L - x_M) + y_M + y_R - b(x_R - x_M)].$$

For the current example,

$$a = \frac{1}{3}[7 - (-.833)(2 - 5) + 3 + 2 - (-.833)(8 - 5)] = 4.$$

So when $x = 6$, $\hat{y} = -.833 + 4 = 3.167$. The line fit by this method is called a three-group resistant line because it resists the influence of outliers.

It appears that Beta's performance is improving relative to Alpha's (their difference scores are decreasing), but we have no way to test whether the slope of the resistant line, fit to their differences, $b = -.833$, is significant. This is because we don't know the sampling distribution of b under the null hypothesis that the slope is zero. The solution is to construct an empirical sampling distribution for b with procedure 5.8. Under the null hypothesis, the difference between Alpha's and Beta's scores is constant over successive events (i.e., the slope of the resistant line is zero). Under this hypothesis, we can shuffle the difference scores relative to the event number; for example, the eighth difference score, 1, might equally well have been the first difference score. Here is the result of one shuffle, that is, several swaps among the difference scores:

Event	(1 2 3)	(4 5 6)	(7 8 9)
Difference	(4 3 7)	(2 3 3)	(7 1 9)

The slope of the resistant line that fits these points is $b^* = 0.5$. A distribution of 500 values of b^* is shown in figure 5.10. Unlike other sampling distributions we have considered, this one has relatively few discrete values. (Given how the resistant line method works, this is not surprising. Randomization assigns coordinates to three groups and b^* is the slope of the line that connects the "median coordinates" of the leftmost and rightmost group. Although there might be many ways to assign coordinates, many of the groups will have the same median x and median y values.) The mean of the distribution of slopes in figure 5.10 is 0.01, which is close to the value we expect given the null hypothesis of zero slope. Our sample result, $b = -.833$ is relatively rare; only ten slopes in the sampling distribution have this value (and it is the smallest in the distribution). Consequently, we can reject the null hypothesis that Alpha and Beta's difference scores are constant over trials. The probability that we are rejecting this hypothesis incorrectly is $10/500 = .02$.

Randomization tests are suited to hypotheses about arrangements of data and statistics that characterize the arrangements. Figure 5.11 is a hypothetical representation of the paths of two robots, Alpha and Beta, each of which is trying to reach the goal marked by a big X. All told, Beta appears to be the one that gets closest to the goal. This arrangement of data can be characterized by many statistics. For

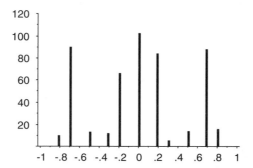

Figure 5.10   An empirical sampling distribution of the slope of the resistant line.

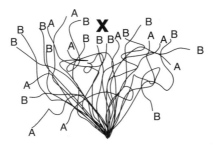

Figure 5.11   Paths forged by two robots, Alpha and Beta, as they attempt to drive from an initial location to the goal marked X.

example, we might measure the average Euclidean distance between each robot's final position and the goal, the variances of these Euclidean distances for each robot, or the average "kinkiness" of the robots' paths. We could compare the robots with any of these statistics; for example, δ might be the difference of the averages of the Euclidean distances between the goal and where each robot quits. An arrangement such as figure 5.11 is just one of many possible arrangements, and the value of δ that corresponds to figure 5.11 is but one of many possible values. Under the null hypothesis that the robots are equal, the rightmost path in figure 5.11, forged by Beta, might equally well have been Alpha's. By repeatedly shuffling the labels on paths and recalculating δ^*, we get a sampling distribution of δ^* under the null hypothesis that the robots are equal. The general framework of procedures 5.7 and 5.8 can obviously be extended to many statistics, including entirely novel ones.

5.4   Comparing Bootstrap and Randomization Procedures

Bootstrap and randomization procedures both generate the distribution of a statistic by resampling from the original sample; however, the bootstrap resamples with replacement whereas randomization resamples without replacement. Bootstrap resampling simulates or "stands in for" the process of drawing samples from a population. The original sample is assumed to be representative of the population. The frequency distribution of elements in the sample is assumed to mirror the population frequency distribution. Consider a sample in which half the elements are ones: $S = \{1, 2, 5, 1, 3, 1\}$. Given S, the best estimate of the relative frequency of ones in the population is .5. Resampling from S with replacement ensures that whenever we draw an element from S for a bootstrap sample S^*, the probability of getting a one is .5, just as it would be if we drew elements from an infinitely large population in which half the elements were ones. In this sense bootstrap resampling simulates the process of drawing elements from a population. Note that if we resampled from S without replacement, the probability of drawing a one would change on each draw. Clearly, this does not simulate sampling from an infinite population. Thus, randomization resampling, which draws elements from S without replacement, does not simulate the process of drawing elements from an infinite population. Note also that bootstrap resampling might produce a sample $S^* = \{1, 1, 1, 1, 1\}$, whereas randomization resampling will never produce a sample that contains more than three ones. Again, the bootstrap procedure simulates sampling from a population, whereas the randomization procedure does not.

Randomization tests whether a particular arrangement of data in S_A and S_B is unusual relative to the distribution of arrangements that might have arisen given the null hypothesis. For example, if $S_A = \{1, 1, 1\}$ and $S_B = \{2, 3, 5\}$, then we can easily find the probability of a statistic $\theta = \sum S_A - \sum S_B = -7$ by merging our original samples, $S_{A+B} = \{1, 1, 1, 2, 3, 5\}$, then repeatedly shuffling and sampling from S_{A+B} without replacement to get A_i^*, B_i^* and $\theta_i^* = \sum A_i^* - \sum B_i^*$. We would find that -7 is the most extreme value in the distribution of θ_i^*. This is not the distribution we would have generated by drawing samples A_i^* and B_i^* from a population or by bootstrapping, nor is -7 the most extreme conceivable result. Bootstrap sampling might produce $A_i^* = \{1, 1, 1\}$, $B_i^* = \{5, 5, 5\}$, $\theta_i^* = -12$, for example.

Randomization clearly does not produce sampling distributions, if by sampling distribution we mean "the distribution of all possible values of a statistic $\theta(S)$, where S is a sample of size N drawn from an infinite population." We speak colloquially of the sampling distributions generated by randomization, but they are not the same distributions as the bootstrap generates with the same data (the bootstrap distribution will have longer tails), nor are they the same as the theoretical sampling distributions of corresponding parametric tests. Because randomization does not produce sampling distributions in the conventional sense of the term, we cannot use randomized distributions to draw inferences about population parameters. In particular, we cannot construct confidence intervals with these distributions (see, e.g., Noreen, 1989, footnote 11, p. 19; p. 33).

In fact, we cannot use randomization to test hypotheses or to draw any inferences given a single sample. Resampling with replacement from S_{A+B} simply reproduces S_{A+B}. Thus, randomization always starts with at least two samples S_A and S_B that are merged and shuffled in S_{A+B} and resampled to produce A_i^* and B_i^* (procedure 5.7). Alternatively, the items in one sample or variable are shuffled with respect to the other (procedure 5.8). Either way, the two randomized samples will not be identical to the originals.

If the bootstrap procedure tests hypotheses and produces confidence intervals, whereas the randomization procedure cannot draw inferences about the population, why should we ever use randomization tests instead of bootstrap tests? One reason is that randomization tests are very powerful: They perform as well as parametric tests (e.g., t tests) when parametric assumptions are met, and they outperform parametric tests when parametric assumptions (e.g., normal populations, equal variances) are violated. Bootstrap tests, on the other hand, will in some circumstances make type I and type II errors (section 4.8) more often than parametric tests. For example, Noreen discovered that the one-sample t test outperformed the corresponding bootstrap test when the underlying population was normal. The effect was not very large. Having set $\alpha = .05$, Noreen expected roughly five percent of 1,000 t tests to incorrectly reject the null hypothesis. He found that when the sample size was 20, t tests rejected H_0 59 times, while the bootstrap rejected H_0 68 times. For larger samples, the bootstrap test was as accurate as the t test. (See the following section for another empirical demonstration of a related point.) When the underlying population was not normal—a situation in which the t test should do relatively poorly—the bootstrap and t tests were roughly equal (Noreen, 1989). In sum, bootstrap tests are somewhat less robust than randomization tests and parametric tests when the underlying assumptions of the latter are met.

This is not surprising if you consider the "inferential leaps" made by bootstrap tests and the lack thereof in randomization. Randomization answers the weak question of whether two samples are related, without assuming the samples are representative of the populations from which they are drawn, in fact, without making any inferences at all about populations. A bootstrap test, on the other hand, infers a sampling distribution S_{boot}, then shifts it or uses its variance to get a sampling distribution under the null hypothesis, S_{H_0} (section 5.2.1). Bootstrap tests, therefore, take two inferential leaps whereas randomization tests take none.

5.5   Comparing Computer-Intensive and Parametric Procedures

Computer-intensive tests such as randomization and the bootstrap are most desirable when no parametric sampling distribution exists for a statistic. Computer-intensive tests are also desirable when the assumptions that underlie a parametric test are violated and the test is not robust. For example, the F test for the equality of variances, described in chapter 6, is sensitive to violations of its assumptions, so a randomization version of the test (one version of which was described earlier in this chapter) is preferable. Many conventional tests are moderately robust, however, and in these cases, the strongest argument for computer-intensive tests is that they are no less powerful than the parametric ones and it isn't necessary to check whether parametric assumptions are met. Bootstrap tests are slightly less powerful than randomization and parametric tests run under ideal conditions, but the differences are generally very slight.

A small experiment will illustrate just how small the differences between parametric and bootstrap tests can be. We will focus on the parametric one-sample t test and the one-sample bootstrap test. We will draw a sample from a normal population and use it to estimate the standard error of the sampling distribution of the mean in the conventional way, that is, $\hat{\sigma}_{\bar{x}} = s/\sqrt{N}$. Then we will run 1,000 iterations of the bootstrap procedure to get a sampling distribution, the standard deviation of which is another estimate of the standard error, denoted $\hat{\sigma}_{\bar{x}}^b$. We will draw a second sample and calculate $\hat{\sigma}_{\bar{x}}$ and $\hat{\sigma}_{\bar{x}}^b$; then a third, and so on, until we have twenty pairs of estimated standard errors. The results of this experiment are shown in table 5.6. There are three pairs of columns. The first column in each pair represents the parametric estimate $\hat{\sigma}_{\bar{x}}$ for a sample. The second represents $\hat{\sigma}_{\bar{x}} - \hat{\sigma}_{\bar{x}}^b$ for that sample. For example, the first entry in the table is $\hat{\sigma}_{\bar{x}} = .3641$, and the second entry is $\hat{\sigma}_{\bar{x}} - \hat{\sigma}_{\bar{x}}^b = .0174$. Thus, the bootstrap estimate is $\hat{\sigma}_{\bar{x}}^b = .3641 - .0174 = .3467$. These pairs are sorted by the parametric estimate, with the highest at the top of the column and the lowest at the bottom. What you should notice about each pair of columns is that the range of parametric estimates is much larger than the range of the difference between parametric and bootstrap estimates. In the first pair of columns, for instance, the range of parametric estimates is $.3641 - .2286 = .1355$, while the range of $\hat{\sigma}_{\bar{x}} - \hat{\sigma}_{\bar{x}}^b$ is $.0353 - .0045 = .0308$. This means random sampling influences the variation in our estimates more than our choice between the bootstrap and parametric procedures.

Table 5.6   Parametric estimated standard errors and differences between parametric estimates and bootstrap estimates for samples of size 10, 20, and 30. Each pair is computed from a single sample.

N = 10		N = 20		N = 30	
Parametric standard error	Difference between standard errors	Parametric standard error	Difference between standard errors	Parametric standard error	Difference between standard errors
.3641	.0174	.2711	.0011	.2125	.0044
.3593	.0353	.2625	.0136	.2041	.0023
.357	.0296	.2622	−.0062	.2033	.005
.3548	.01	.2562	.0173	.2031	.0039
.3387	.02	.2498	.0146	.1985	−.0015
.3288	.0198	.2479	.0117	.1966	.0025
.3169	.019	.2426	.0093	.1964	.0011
.3106	.012	.2367	.0142	.1895	.0075
.3091	.0296	.2342	.0095	.1881	.0028
.3028	.012	.232	.0032	.1866	.0055
.2938	.0062	.2279	.0025	.186	.0015
.29	.0127	.2264	.0041	.1849	.0004
.2862	.0196	.2255	−.0003	.172	.0051
.2771	.0214	.2216	−.0004	.1705	−.0023
.2747	.0186	.2098	.0068	.1689	.0059
.2663	.0222	.2082	−.0051	.1659	−.003
.259	.0113	.2021	.0019	.156	−.0011
.241	.0045	.1917	.0064	.1498	−.0025
.2323	.0126	.1857	−.0019	.1462	−.0023
.2286	.0161	.1838	.0052	.141	.0022

Should you use a bootstrap test or a parametric t test? In this case, the difference is swamped by the variance in our samples.

Much more important than the test is the sample size. The second and third pairs of columns in table 5.6 are for larger samples, twenty and thirty items, respectively. The range of $\hat{\sigma}_{\bar{x}}$ drops to $.2711 - .1838 = .0873$ and then to $.2125 - .141 = .0715$; the range of $\hat{\sigma}_{\bar{x}} - \hat{\sigma}_{\bar{x}}^{b}$ also decreases. Imagine someone offers you a somewhat bizarre choice: You can test your hypothesis with a bootstrap test or a t test, as you please, or you can give up the freedom to select a test and have ten more data points. What is your answer? Based on the figures in table 5.6, take the data!

Let us recognize this little experiment was run under ideal conditions for the parametric t test: sampling from a standard normal distribution, calculating sampling distributions for the mean. When the assumptions of the t test are not so perfectly met, or when we want standard errors for unconventional statistics, we will want a bootstrap or randomization test. The point of the experiment is an important one, however: Random sampling and sample size may influence standard errors more than the methods we use to estimate them.

With this conclusion in mind, consider again the bootstrap test for censored means, described in section 5.2.1. The censored mean is the mean of what's left in a sample after censored values (those that exceed or fall below a threshold) are removed. For example, given the sample (287, 610, 5002, 545, 5725, 400, 123 , 601, 483, 250) and a censoring threshold of 5000, the censored mean is

$$\overline{x}_C = \frac{287 + 610 + 545 + 400 + 123 + 601 + 483 + 250}{8} = 412.375.$$

We suggested two ways to test a null hypothesis such as $H_0 : \mu_C = 500$; one was a bootstrap test, the other was to pretend the censored values never appeared and to run a one-sample t test on a sample with $N = 8$. We thought the latter test might be overly stringent because it has only seven degrees of freedom even though the original sample included ten data. In fact, the differences between the sampling distributions estimated by the t test and the bootstrap test are swamped by the variations in the samples themselves, as illustrated earlier.

The same story can be told about two-sample tests of the difference of censored means. One approach is to remove the censored data from both samples and run a conventional two-sample t test, pretending the censored data never existed. The other is procedure 5.4 from section 5.2.2. Cohen and Kim (1993) ran a series of experiments to assess the power of these tests in a variety of conditions. They varied the difference between the means of the populations from which the samples were drawn, the shapes of these populations, the sample sizes, and the censoring threshold. Even when the populations were uniform or highly skewed (which is bad for the t test), the t test and the bootstrap test had virtually identical power. All the factors that Cohen and Kim varied had considerable influence on power, but the choice of test—bootstrap or t—had virtually no impact. A representative power curve from these experiments is shown in figure 4.17.

All the examples in this chapter involve at least $K = 300$ pseudosamples, some more. Computers are becoming so powerful that, for most statistics, it makes little difference whether you generate 300 or 3,000 pseudosamples. Efron and Tibshirani

(1993, pp. 50–53) point out that for hypothesis testing, you can get a pretty good sense of whether H_0 is false from relatively few pseudosamples, and $K = 300$ is more than enough. For confidence intervals, however, you should construct as many pseudosamples as you can afford. This is because the bounds of confidence intervals fall in the tails of sampling distributions, where by definition there are relatively few items, hence relatively large uncertainty about where a bound truly lies. You can reduce this uncertainty by populating the tails more densely, by constructing 1,000 pseudosamples, for example.

5.6   Jackknife and Cross Validation

Before the bootstrap there was the *jackknife*, a technique invented by John Tukey (1958; 1977. See also Mosteller and Tukey, 1977, p. 135, and Efron and Tibshirani, 1993, pp. 133–152.) The jackknife estimates the sampling distribution of a statistic θ given a sample S as follows: Remove the first element of S and calculate θ for what's left, then remove the second element of S and calculate θ again, and so on until we have left out each element in S. Like the bootstrap, this procedure resamples from the original sample. And like the bootstrap, the jackknife can estimate the sampling distribution and standard error of any statistic. Efron and LePage (1992) describe the mathematical relationship between the jackknife and the bootstrap; pragmatically, the bootstrap performs better.

Generalizing the jackknife, we can leave out not one element but a subset of S, and calculate θ for what's left. This is called *cross-validation*. We describe cross-validation procedures in some detail in chapter 6. Weiss and Kulikowski (1989, pp. 26–39) compare cross-validation and bootstrap procedures. They prefer one or the other in different circumstances, but in general, both procedures work well.

5.7   An Illustrative Nonparametric Test: The Sign Test

Computer-intensive tests relieve the researcher of worries about underlying population distributions, but they are by no means the only such methods. Statisticians have developed a collection of *nonparametric* tests that, as their name implies, make no assumptions about population parameters. These tests are generally concerned with the likelihood of sample arrangements of data, given the number of arrangements that are possible. Thus, the sampling distributions they work with are usually exact distributions. The most common example is the binomial distribution, the exact

Table 5.7 Hypothetical censored sample data for a comparison of two robots, reproduced from table 5.2 above.

	1	2	3	4	5	6	7	8	9	10
Robot A	300	290	600	5000	200	600	30	800	55	190
Robot B	400	280	5000	5000	300	820	120	5000	120	400

distribution of the number of heads you can expect in N tosses of a coin with a known bias. Nonparametric tests and exact randomization tests are conceptually identical, although the latter construct sampling distributions by brute force and the former specify the sampling distribution in a closed-form expression.

It is difficult to see much justification for nonparametric tests now that Monte Carlo sampling and various forms of resampling are so easy. Many nonparametric tests are concerned with differences between means and medians in two or more samples, and they are less powerful than parametric or computer-intensive tests in these situations. On the other hand, it is worth knowing about some nonparametric tests simply because they specify interesting exact sampling distributions, thus saving one the embarrassment of constructing an approximate sampling distribution when the exact distribution is known. We will review just one nonparametric test here, to illustrate how these tests work, and because it has been adapted to the problem of censored data we discussed earlier.

Given paired samples, $S_A = (a_1 \ldots a_k)$, $S_B = (b_1 \ldots b_k)$, the sign of the difference $\text{Sign}(a_i - b_i)$ is positive if $a_i > b_i$ and negative if $a_i < b_i$. Assuming a and b are real, they should never be equal; in practice, there are several tactics for dealing with $a_i = b_i$ (see Hays, 1973). If S_A and S_B are drawn from the same population, then the probability is one-half that $\text{Sign}(a_i - b_i)$ is positive for any given pair. Let m be the number of N pairs with positive sign. The distribution of m under the null hypothesis that S_A and S_B are drawn from the same population is binomial. If m is unusually large or small, you can reject the null hypothesis.

Etzioni and Etzioni (1994) designed a version of the sign test for paired samples that include censored data. We will use an earlier example, a competition between robots A and B, to illustrate the test (table 5.7). Etzioni and Etzioni start with the idea that under the null hypothesis, one robot is just as likely as another to "win" a trial (i.e., perform a task more quickly), so the expected number of "wins" for one robot is half the number of trials. Singly censored data present no problem because the winning robot is obviously the one with the uncensored (i.e., smaller) execution time; for example, robot A wins trial three. Doubly censored data, such as trial 4, is problematic. We cannot say which robot won. Etzioni and Etzioni propose a conservative interpretation of doubly censored data: They count it as evidence for the null hypothesis. Suppose we are testing the hypothesis that robot A is faster than robot B. Then a "win" occurs when robot A completes a trial faster than robot B (e.g., trials 1,3). H_0 is that robot A and robot B are equally fast. H_0 will be rejected if the number of wins is unusually high. By counting each doubly censored pair as a "loss," Etzioni and Etzioni provide the following strong guarantee: If we reject H_0 given the censored samples, then we would also have rejected H_0 if the censored trials had been allowed to run to completion.

The test statistic is the number of wins, with doubly censored data counting as losses. Although the sampling distribution of this test statistic is not known, it is easy to show that comparing the test statistic to a binomial distribution provides the aforementioned guarantee. That is, if you are willing to reject H_0 because robot A won eight trials, and you counted the fourth trial as a loss for robot A, then you would be no less willing to reject H_0 if trial 4 had turned out to be a win for robot A. The probability of the sample result in table 5.7—eight wins in ten trials—given the null hypothesis that the robots perform equally, is .0547, marginally improbable enough to reject H_0.

The sign test, like many nonparametric tests, does not take account of the magnitudes of differences between the robots. For example, it is surely important that when robot A was faster, it was a lot faster, whereas robot B was only a little faster in trial 2. Ignoring this information with the resulting loss of power is the price we pay for the strong guarantee the test makes. In Cohen and Kim's experiments, described earlier, the sign test was not nearly as powerful as the bootstrap test for the difference of censored means (procedure section 5.5) or a conventional two-sample t test for censored samples (power curves for these comparisons are shown in section 4.8). However, these tests lack the strong guarantee of Etzioni and Etzioni's sign test.

5.8   Conclusion

Although there is no very compelling reason to run randomization and bootstrap tests for conventional statistics, it doesn't hurt, either. The results of bootstrap tests are general to the extent that the original sample is representative of the population, whereas the results of randomization tests are not general because they support no inferences about populations. Bootstrap tests seem ideal for researchers in artificial intelligence because they become very robust with large samples, which we can provide, and they do not require something we cannot provide, namely, knowledge about the sampling distributions of novel, perhaps task-specific, statistics, and the underlying populations from which our data are drawn.

5.9 Further Reading

An accessible introduction to the bootstrap is the *Scientific American* article by Diaconis and Efron (1983). Another short article, by Efron and Tibshirani (1991), covers much the same ground. Noreen (1989) provides a hands-on textbook on randomization and the bootstrap; Efron and Tibshirani's 1993 textbook, *An Introduction to the Bootstrap*, has more breadth and mathematical depth, yet remains very accessible. See also Efron and LePage 1992; Efron and Tibshirani 1986.

6   Performance Assessment

I wish I could be sanguine—that attention to performance analysis will follow automatically with maturity. But inattention to this matter has been a failing of research with AI programs from the start. The difficulties are clear. The programs, being complex, are always inadequate and incomplete. Direct perception into the program's structure leads its creators always to improvements that are eminently worthwhile. At the margin, it always seems a better decision to press on than to stop and analyze. Nor is the AI field strongly vocal on the necessity for analysis. Some of the most highly regarded efforts in AI (e.g., Winograd's thesis, 1971) are completely silent on the need for critical analysis of the program's structure against actual performance data. Finally, the complexity of programs mitigate against analysis directly, since there seems to be too many aspects to look at and it is so expensive per look.
—Allen Newell, *A Tutorial on Speech Understanding Systems.*

When AI researchers conduct experiments, the question they ask most often is, "Does it work?" Other questions, pertaining to when and how and why it works and fails, are less common although their answers contribute more to our understanding. This chapter focuses exclusively on performance assessment; specifically, how to measure performance and differences in performance. The business of explaining performance—tracking down the factors that affect performance and modeling their causal relationships—is postponed to chapters 7 and 8.

Colloquially, performance is an aspect of behavior that has some value; it often has both positive and negative aspects. For example, an information-retrieval system will find many texts for a user, which is good, but some will be irrelevant, which is bad. A learning algorithm might search an enormous space and find more regularity in data than any unaided human could, but requires hours and taxes the user's patience. An expert system that recommends appropriate drug therapies might get the underlying diagnosis wrong. The decision to measure one thing or another as a performance variable is often intuitive, and rarely is a strong argument made for or against a particular metric (but see section 3.4). Thus, the distinguishing characteristic of performance assessment is not performance—anything might be performance—rather, it is assessment. Assessment is concerned with how fast, how accurate, and how efficient our programs are. Performance assessment should not be the last word in empirical research—once we know how a system performs, we should turn our attention to why it performs that way—but it is an important and perhaps indispensable first step.

6.1   Strategies for Performance Assessment

My focus is on assessing performance in batches and repeated batches of trials. A batch is a collection of trials that are all run at roughly the same time, providing a snapshot of performance. For example, a dozen trials of a program on a particular day is a batch. Repeated batches are simply batches run at different times—one today, another tomorrow. Some treatment is usually interposed between the batches and the difference in performance between the batches is the measure of interest. For example, batches might be repeated at different stages of development of a program or after different amounts of training for a learning system.

Within a batch we often run several groups, corresponding to different systems, tasks, or environments. It's common to summarize and compare the performance of groups within a batch; for example, two group means can be compared with a *t* test. Things get slightly more complicated when we try to compare many groups; the underlying statistical methods are called *analysis of variance*. In some experiments, we make unrestricted pairwise comparisons among groups; in others, we select comparisons carefully to ensure they are independent of one another; and sometimes, we compare not only groups but also combinations of groups. These topics are discussed informally in this chapter, in the context of case studies. A more mathematical exposition is given in section 6.15.

When it comes to repeated batches, the first question is whether performance improves or otherwise changes. More specifically, we want to know how performance changes; for example, if a system is designed to learn from experience, what is the shape of the learning curve, the function that relates learning to performance? Our discussion will focus on assessing performance during learning and knowledge engineering. A common method is to run the same tests "before and after," thereby assessing the effects of changes to a system. If the tests can themselves be classified, then we can see whether different classes of performance change in different ways when we change a system. A statistical underpinning of this *classified retesting method* is contingency table analysis.

6.2   Assessing Performance in Batches of Trials

The simplest assessments of performance are descriptive statistics such as the mean and variance, or frequency histograms, scatterplots, and other visualizations described in chapter 2. For example, the mean classification accuracy of a decision tree might be 95 percent, or the median size of search trees might be 438 nodes. As assessments of performance, both measures lack something: We cannot tell whether 95 percent or 438 nodes are good, bad, or indifferent performance because we have no standard for comparison. (Although 95 percent sounds good, it means nothing if the test problems are unchallenging and result in a ceiling effect; see section 3.2.1.) Performance assessments usually involve comparisons between the system under examination and one or more standards. Sometimes the standards are straw men; for example, a system should outperform coin tossing on a binary-choice task. Sometimes the standards are experts such as physicians or chess grandmasters. Sometimes the standards are well-known, published results; for example, the famous planning problem called *Sussman's anomaly* can be solved in three moves, but many classical planning algorithms required four. Most often, however, one's standard is peculiar to and part of one's experiment design.

6.3   Comparisons to External Standards: The View Retriever

A study by Liane Acker and Bruce Porter (1994) at the University of Texas, Austin, involved three related standards. I will refer to this study extensively, so I'll introduce it in some detail. As part of her dissertation research, Liane Acker developed a program called the View Retriever that generates coherent explanations called *viewpoints*. From a very large knowledge base devoted to botany, the View Retriever selects facts to include in viewpoints. If the View Retriever selected everything in the Botany Knowledge Base about, say, photosynthesis, and strung these facts together in no particular order, then the resulting viewpoint would be incoherent; just as you would be judged incoherent if you burbled everything you know about hamburgers. The View Retriever is selective:

Intuitively, a viewpoint is a coherent collection of facts that describes a concept from a particular perspective. For example, three viewpoints of the concept "car" are: the viewpoint of "car as-kind-of consumer durable," which describes the car's price and longevity; the structural viewpoint, which describes a car's parts and interconnections; and the viewpoint "car as-having metal composition," which includes facts, such as the car's propensity to dent and rust, that are related to its composition. (Acker and Porter, 1994, p. 547)

Acker and her advisor, Bruce Porter, ran an experiment to test whether the View Retriever does in fact generate coherent viewpoints. They reasoned that the addition of a perspective, such as the "structural" perspective, would make viewpoints more coherent by filtering out facts that aren't relevant to the perspective, such as the car's cost.

The experiment design was straightforward: in one condition, a program generated random collections of facts about topics; in another condition, the View Retriever generated viewpoints by collecting facts relevant to particular perspectives. Both random collections and View Retriever viewpoints were translated by hand from their machine form (e.g., `flower location-of angiosperm-sexual-reproduction`) into simple English. Here is an example of a random collection of facts about flowers:

Flowers are the site of angiosperm sexual reproduction and metabolic reactions. They acquire materials, develop, metabolize, and degenerate. Flowers require nutrients. Two parts of the flower are the ground tissue and the perianth. Flowers tend to have symmetry.

And here is an example of a coherent View Retriever viewpoint:

The flower is the location of angiosperm sexual reproduction. The two main parts of the flower that are involved in reproduction are the androecium and the gynoecium. (The androecium surrounds the gynoecium.) The gynoecium is the location of embryo sac formation, and the androecium is the location of pollen grain formation. The androecium is the source of the pollen grain transfer, and the gynoecium is the destination. At the gynoecium, pollen grain germination and double fertilization occur.

Eight graduate students and two undergraduate seniors were asked to judge the coherence of random collections of facts and the viewpoints. On a five-point scale, 1 meant "incoherent" and 5 meant "coherent." Each judge saw six random collections of facts and twelve viewpoints. Thus, Acker and Porter obtained 60 judgments of random collections and 120 judgments of viewpoints.[11] In the same study, Acker and Porter included passages from botany textbooks, rewritten in simple English to make them stylistically comparable with viewpoints generated by the View Retriever. And as a further condition, Acker and Porter generated degraded viewpoints: ordinary View Retriever viewpoints in which sentences were replaced by random facts. For example, the fifth sentence above, from the View Retriever viewpoint ("The androecium is the source....") might be replaced by random fact such as "flowers need nutrients" to produce a degraded viewpoint. Acker and Porter varied the number of such substitutions so that some degraded viewpoints were quite similar to View Retriever viewpoints and some were mostly random facts, but we will treat all de-

---

11. Actually, not all the judges completed their assigned tasks, so the sample sizes were 59 and 118, respectively.

graded viewpoints as a single class, here. The experiment design therefore compared the View Retriever to three standards: textbook viewpoints, degraded viewpoints and random viewpoints.

These standards *bracket* the anticipated performance of the View Retriever, with textbook viewpoints expected to be as coherent or more coherent than View Retriever viewpoints, and degraded and random viewpoints expected to be less coherent. To see the value of bracketing, imagine Acker and Porter had limited themselves to a single standard, say, textbook viewpoints, and the mean judged coherence of textbook and View Retriever viewpoints had turned out to be indistinguishable. Until one shows that random viewpoints have a lower mean judged coherence, one cannot rule out the possibility that the judges are fools who will rate any collection of facts as coherent. Conversely, Acker and Porter could not claim that View Retriever viewpoints are coherent merely because they are judged more coherent than random viewpoints; it would still be necessary to compare them to good (i.e., textbook) viewpoints.

The means and standard deviations of coherence scores for Acker and Porter's conditions were:

	Mean	Standard deviation	N
Textbook viewpoints	4.241	.912	29
View Retriever viewpoints	3.754	1.383	120
Degraded viewpoints	2.847	1.375	59
Random viewpoints	2.627	1.413	59

What can we conclude from these results? Textbook viewpoints accrued the highest mean score (4.241) but is it significantly higher than the score for View Retriever viewpoints (3.754), or the other mean scores? Are degraded viewpoints significantly different from random viewpoints?

6.3.1   Introduction to Pairwise Comparisons of Means

One's first inclination is to answer these questions with *t* tests. As we'll see, this approach has some merit, especially when very few groups are to be compared, and the resulting *t* statistics exceed their critical values by a good margin. But imagine you have fifteen groups, hence $15(15-1)/2 = 105$ pairwise comparisons to contemplate. (A real example of this magnitude is discussed in section 6.4.) Suppose that unknown to you all the groups are drawn from the same population, so their population means are equal. Believe it or not, you are 99.5 percent certain to incorrectly reject this hypothesis if you run all 105 pairwise comparisons of the group means. To see why, pretend each pairwise comparison is a toss of a biased coin. On each toss, $\alpha = .05$ is the probability of "heads," which corresponds to the spurious result that the samples in the comparison are drawn from different populations. Conversely, when the coin falls "tails," you don't reject the null hypothesis and thus commit no error. Now, the probability of tossing tails m times is $(1 - \alpha)^m$, so $1 - (1 - \alpha)^m$ is the probability of at least one spurious result in m tosses. In 105 pairwise comparisons, the probability of at least one spurious result is $1 - (1 - .05)^{105} = .9954$. This is the probability of concluding incorrectly—at least once—that two groups are drawn from different populations. Obviously, it is also the probability of incorrectly rejecting the null hypothesis that all the groups are drawn from the same population.

We speak of the "null hypothesis," but really there are two kinds: the *experiment null hypothesis* says all fifteen population means are equal, and each *comparison null hypothesis* says one pair of population means is equal. The probabilities of incorrectly rejecting these hypotheses are denoted α_e and α_c for experimentwise and per-comparison errors, respectively. At the heart of the debate about how to handle pairwise comparisons is the relationship

$$\alpha_e \approx 1 - (1 - \alpha_c)^m,$$

where m is the number of pairwise comparisons. (This expression is approximate because all pairwise comparisons are not independent; see section 6A.2).

Many authors say the experimentwise error rate is the most important, so the per-comparison error rate, α_c, should be reduced until the experimentwise error rate is .05, or some other small value. You accomplish this by increasing the critical value that the difference between the means must exceed. Others say this standard can reduce α_c too much, to the point that a difference between means must be unrealistically large to be significant. As an extreme example, imagine your fifteen means are the average scores for fifteen kinds of viewpoints in an expanded version of Acker and Porter's experiment. Each mean is a number between 1.0 and 5.0, the minimum and maximum coherence scores. Suppose a per-comparison error of $\alpha_c = .05$ requires a pair of means to differ by 2.0 or more. Now, to achieve an experimentwise error of $\alpha_e = .05$, how much must you increase the critical value for the difference of these means? The Scheffé test, discussed later, requires the difference to increase by a factor of approximately $\sqrt{k - 1}$, where k is the number of means, overall. Since the old per-comparison critical value was 2.0, and there are 15 means, the critical value that guarantees $\alpha_e = .05$ is $\sqrt{15 - 1} \times 2.0 = 7.48$. Unfortunately, because the minimum and maximum mean scores are 1.0 and 5.0, respectively, no difference between means can possibly exceed 4.0. In other words, protecting the experiment null hypothesis makes it impossible to find any significant pairwise differences.

So the pitfalls of pairwise comparisons have been identified. You can protect the experiment null hypothesis by reducing α_c, but you will have more difficulty concluding that any two means are significantly different. Or, you can protect your ability to find differences between pairs of means, but you will increase the probability of incorrectly rejecting the experiment null hypothesis. Either way, you lose. Said differently, pairwise comparisons require you to decide whether you are most interested in experiment or comparison null hypotheses.

You might think the choice is easy because the experiment null hypothesis is often relatively uninteresting. You are more concerned with pairwise differences than with the experiment hypothesis that all population means are equal. Unfortunately, ignoring the experiment hypothesis leads to another pitfall, easily seen if you consider the coin-tossing analogy again. If the probability of incorrectly rejecting each comparison null hypothesis is α_c, then the expected number of such errors in m pairwise comparisons is $m\alpha_c$. For instance, in 105 pairwise comparisons with $\alpha_c = .05$, one expects to reject the comparison null hypothesis incorrectly $105 \times .05 = 5.25$ times. Again, this number is approximate because the comparisons are not independent. Unfortunately, you don't know which of your significant comparisons is in error. It could be any of them.

Or, you might try to dodge the whole issue by running only a few pairwise comparisons, reducing m in the previous equation. Typically, you won't know which comparisons are interesting until you have seen the experiment results, but if you say, "I intend to compare the samples with the highest and lowest means," then your de facto intention is to draw implicit pairwise comparisons among all the means, so the probability of incorrectly rejecting the experiment null hypothesis (which, recall, takes only one spurious result) is not reduced.

The problem of pairwise comparisons is not so easily avoided. In fact, there are only two kinds of solutions. First, you can run pairwise comparisons both ways, favoring α_e in one set of tests and α_c in the other, noting and discussing disparities in the results (see section 6.4). The second type of solution requires a shift in perspective. You might plan a set of comparisons in such a way that their results are statistically independent, which means a spurious result in one comparison implies nothing about any other, and the probability of a spurious result is the probability of being wrong once, only. You'll have to give up the experimentwise null hypothesis, because any spurious pairwise result causes it to fail, thus every such result involves being wrong at least twice. In return, you can ask a set of focused questions about your data, each of which has a known probability of error. The catch is, not all subsets of comparisons have independent results. In fact, you have to construct independent subsets carefully, which is why this approach is called *planned comparisons*. It involves more mathematics than we want to present at this juncture, but it is described in section 6A.2. Here we will focus on *unplanned* or *post hoc* comparisons, which, as the names imply, can involve any or all of the $k(k-1)/2$ possible comparisons, as you like, even after you've perused the data. Unfortunately, unplanned comparisons require us to favor either α_e or α_c.

How you resolve this tradeoff depends on the purpose of your experiment. For this reason, we defer further discussion of unplanned comparisons until we have considered a valuable statistical technique—analysis of variance—and two illustrative case studies.

6.3.2   Introduction to Analysis of Variance

Acker and Porter compared View Retriever viewpoints to three standards that were designed to represent levels of a factor that affects coherence judgments. Although Acker and Porter didn't name this factor, they believed it was related to the amount of "random stuff" in viewpoints. Textbook viewpoints presumably included no extraneous, unnecessary, irrelevant sentences, whereas degraded and random viewpoints comprised in part or in full randomly selected sentences. The question is whether this factor—the amount of random stuff in viewpoints—does in fact influence coherence judgments. The null hypothesis is it does not. More generally, the experiment null hypothesis—as opposed to specific hypotheses about comparisons of means—is that the population means of several groups are equal. *Analysis of variance* is a remarkably general, robust technique for testing this hypothesis. We will not dwell on the mathematics of the analysis of variance here, but rather give an informal account and refer the interested reader to section 6A.1 for details.

Suppose we run an experiment in which four algorithms are each tested on a set of five problems. The algorithms are denoted *A,B,C*, and *D*; their scores on the problems and means and standard deviations are shown in table 6.1. The data give the impression that performance depends significantly on the underlying factor, because the mean scores are quite different and the standard deviations are quite small. How can we formalize this impression?

First, merge all the data into a single sample of $N = 20$ trials and calculate the grand mean and grand variance, which are $\overline{x}_G = 7.0$ and $s_G^2 = 12.32$, respectively. The latter term is, of course, the sum of the squared deviation of each datum from the grand mean, divided by $N - 1 = 19$. It turns out that the deviation from the grand mean of the kth datum in the jth group, $(x_{jk} - \overline{x}_G)$, can be expressed as the sum of two deviations, the deviation of the datum from its own group mean, and

Table 6.1   A data table that appears to show a difference between groups.

		Algorithm	
A	B	C	D
3	6	7	8
2	4	9	10
2	7	12	11
4	5	11	9
1	7	10	12
$\bar{x} = 2.4$	$\bar{x} = 5.8$	$\bar{x} = 9.8$	$\bar{x} = 10$
$s = 1.14$	$s = 1.30$	$s = 1.92$	$s = 1.58$

the deviation of the group mean from the grand mean. For example, the first datum for algorithm A is 3.0, so

$$(x_{A,1} - \bar{x}_G) = (x_{A,1} - \bar{x}_A) + (\bar{x}_A - \bar{x}_G)$$

$$(3.0 - 7.0) = (3.0 - 2.4) + (2.4 - 7.0).$$

Moreover, given some assumptions, the sums of squared deviations are additive, too:

$$\sum_j \sum_k (x_{jk} - \bar{x}_G)^2 = \sum_j \sum_k (x_{jk} - \bar{x}_j)^2 + \sum_j (\bar{x}_j - \bar{x}_G)^2.$$

This means that the grand variance can be decomposed into two parts: The within-group part or the sum of squares within, $\sum_j \sum_k (x_{jk} - \bar{x}_j)^2$, represents the "background noise" in the data, whereas the between-group part or the sum of squares between, $\sum_j (\bar{x}_j - \bar{x}_G)^2$, represents the effect of being in one group or another. This makes sense: the within-group component sums deviations within groups, and so represents the part of the grand variance that is not due to differences between groups, that is, background variance; whereas the between-group component is the part of the grand variance that is due to the differences between groups. Intuitively, if the within-group component is small and the between-group component large, then we are inclined to say there is a significant effect of group. Formally, however, we must take one more step before claiming a significant result.

   If we divide the sums of squares by degrees of freedom, we get variances, or mean square deviations, MS_{within} and $MS_{between}$, for the within-group and between-group sums of squares, respectively. Under the null hypothesis that there is no effect of group, these terms should be equal. The sampling distribution of the ratio of two

Table 6.2 An analysis of variance tableau for the data in table 6.1.

Source	df	Sum of squares	Mean square	F	p value
Between	3	197.2	65.733	28.58	$p = .0001$
Within	16	36.8	2.3		
Total	19	234.0			

variances is known, given the null hypothesis that variances are equal; therefore, we can find the probability of obtaining the ratio

$$F = \frac{MS_{between}}{MS_{within}}$$

by chance if the null hypothesis is true. The expected value of F is 1.0 and large values speak against the null hypothesis. The critical value of F required to reject the null hypothesis can be looked up in a table of the F distribution, indexed with $j - 1$ and $N - j$ degrees of freedom, or some statistics packages will give it to you. In our example, $j - 1 = 3$ and $N - j = 16$, and the critical value required to reject the null hypothesis at the conventional .05 level is 3.24. As you'll see in table 6.2, our F value far exceeds the .05 critical value. In fact, if we reject the null hypothesis that algorithms $A, B, C,$ and D perform equally, the probability of being wrong is less than .0001.

The analysis of variance rests on some assumptions. First, the population distribution(s) from which groups are drawn are assumed to be normal. Second, these distributions are assumed to have the same variance. Third, the error components of the data in the groups are assumed to be independent. The analysis of variance is very robust against violations of the normality and equal variance assumptions (see, e.g., Keppel, 1973, pp. 74–77), especially if the group sizes are equal. Even for small, unequal group sizes, you have nothing to worry about if your F value is large enough to yield a small p value, say, .01 or less. The third assumption is more stringent, but it is generally not a problem unless the experiment design introduces a dependency between observations in groups (e.g., if groups represent performance after successive levels of training; see section 7A.5).

6.3.3   An Analysis of Acker and Porter's Data

Now we can return to the question that prompted the excursion into the analysis of variance. What should we make of Acker and Porter's results on the coherence of viewpoints? Here are their results again:

	Mean	Standard deviation	N
Textbook viewpoints	4.241	.912	29
View Retriever viewpoints	3.754	1.383	118
Degraded viewpoints	2.847	1.375	59
Random viewpoints	2.627	1.413	59

With a one-way analysis of variance we can test the null hypothesis that a factor (which we earlier identified as the amount of "random stuff" in viewpoints) does not affect coherence scores. An analysis of variance rejects this hypothesis:

Source	df	Sum of squares	Mean square	F	p value
Between	3	88.05	29.35	16.21	$p = .0001$
Within	261	472.61	1.811		
Total	264	560.66			

Clearly, the four types of viewpoints are not judged equally coherent.[12]

Analysis of variance tells us that all groups are not equal; it does not tell us which groups are better. For this, we must make pairwise comparisons of group means. Although many techniques have been developed, we will discuss only two here, *Scheffé tests* and *least significant difference* (LSD) tests. Scheffé tests protect the experiment null hypothesis and can make it difficult to demonstrate individual differences between means. LSD tests are at the other end of the spectrum: They do not make it more difficult than usual to demonstrate pairwise differences, but they do yield more spurious differences.

6.3.4   Unplanned Pairwise Comparisons: Scheffé Tests

Scheffé tests guard against the relatively likely event of finding at least one significant pairwise comparison in the $k(k-1)/2$ possible comparisons of k means. They guarantee that the experimentwise probability of incorrectly rejecting the null hypothesis is a small constant, say, $\alpha_e = .05$.

---

12. Liane Acker kindly sent me her data so I could run this analysis, but you can see that it could have been done with the group means, variances and N's, alone. With the group N's and means, a grand mean could be derived, and so $SS_{between}$ and $MS_{between}$; with the group variances and N's, sums of squares for each group could be derived, and so SS_{within} and MS_{within}.

To compare two groups means, $\overline{x}_1$ and $\overline{x}_2$, the Scheffé test statistic is

$$F_S = \frac{(\overline{x}_1 - \overline{x}_2)^2}{MS_{within}\left(\frac{1}{n_1} + \frac{1}{n_2}\right)(j-1)}, \tag{6.1}$$

where MS_{within} is taken from the analysis of variance table, n_1 and n_2 are the sizes of groups 1 and 2, and j is the number of groups. The critical value for this test—the value F must exceed for us to reject the null hypothesis—is the same as it is for the analysis of variance. You can look it up in a table of the F distribution with $j-1$ and $N-j$ degrees of freedom, where $N = \sum_{i=1}^{j} n_i$, if your statistics package doesn't provide it.

Let us compare textbook and View Retriever viewpoints with a Scheffé test. Their means are 4.241 and 3.754, respectively, and the number of coherence scores in each group were 29 and 118, respectively. From the previous analysis of variance we know $MS_{within} = 1.811$, and because there are four types of viewpoints, $j - 1 = 3$. The F statistic, then, is:

$$F_S = \frac{(4.241 - 3.754)^2}{1.811 \cdot \left(\frac{1}{29} + \frac{1}{118}\right) \cdot 3} = 1.016,$$

which, as you can guess, is not a significant difference (recall that the expected value of F under the null hypothesis of no difference is 1.0). This is good news for Acker and Porter: It means that although the analysis of variance rejected the experiment null hypothesis of equal means, there is no significant difference between the most coherent (textbook) viewpoints and those generated by the View Retriever program.

In contrast, the coherence score of View Retriever viewpoints is significantly different from that of degraded viewpoints. The mean coherence of degraded viewpoints is 2.847 and the number of such scores is 59, so the F statistic is

$$F_S = \frac{(2.847 - 3.754)^2}{1.811 \cdot \left(\frac{1}{59} + \frac{1}{118}\right) \cdot 3} = 5.9557$$

Consulting a table of the F distribution we find that the critical value for 3 and 261 degrees of freedom is roughly 2.6. This is clearly exceeded by the value we just derived, so we can reject the comparison null hypothesis. Again, this is good news for Acker and Porter: Not only are View Retriever viewpoints indistinguishable from textbook viewpoints, but they are also significantly better than degraded viewpoints. Because degraded viewpoints are constructed by substituting random sentences into View Retriever viewpoints, this result supports Acker and Porter's conjecture that the presence of "random stuff" in viewpoints affects their judged coherence.

6.3.5   Unplanned Pairwise Comparisons: LSD Tests

The Scheffé test is very conservative. Its purpose is to ensure a low probability of incorrectly rejecting even one comparison null hypothesis. Obviously, for large numbers of comparisons, the Scheffé test must make each very stringent. To balance protection of the experiment null hypothesis against sensitivity to pairwise differences, some authors suggest the following procedure. First run an analysis of variance. If the F statistic is significant, reject the experiment null hypothesis, and run pairwise comparisons with the usual per-comparison α_c level, such as .05. If the original F test is not significant, however, perform no pairwise comparisons. The logic of this procedure is that it decouples pairwise tests from the test of the experiment null hypothesis, permitting relatively sensitive pairwise tests—which threaten the validity of the experiment null hypothesis—only after the experiment null hypothesis has been rejected. This procedure is called the least significant difference (LSD) test. The test statistic for a pairwise comparison of two means, $\overline{x}_1$ and $\overline{x}_2$ is:

$$F_{LSD} = \frac{(\overline{x}_1 - \overline{x}_2)^2}{MS_{within}\left(\frac{1}{n_1} + \frac{1}{n_2}\right)}, \tag{6.2}$$

where MS_{within} is the mean square within from the analysis of variance and n_1 and n_2 are the sizes of groups 1 and 2, respectively. This F test has 1 and $N - j$ degrees of freedom, where $N = \sum_{i=1}^{j} n_i$ and j is the number of groups. Here is the test of the comparison between textbook and View Retriever viewpoints:

$$F_{LSD} = \frac{(4.241 - 3.754)^2}{1.811\left(\frac{1}{29} + \frac{1}{118}\right)} = 3.05.$$

Compared with a F distribution with one and $N - j = 264 - 3 = 261$ degrees of freedom, this difference is not quite significant at the $\alpha_c = .05$ level; textbook and View Retriever viewpoints are not significantly different.

Note that the F test is closely related to the familiar t test, as you can see by taking the square root of F in equation 6.2:

$$\sqrt{F_{LSD}} = t = \frac{\overline{x}_1 - \overline{x}_2}{\sqrt{MS_{within}\left(\frac{1}{n_1} + \frac{1}{n_2}\right)}}.$$

This formula is identical to the two-sample t test (section 4.4.7), except it uses MS_{within} instead of $\hat{\sigma}^2_{pooled}$ because MS_{within} is a better estimator, being based on all the groups in the experiment, not only the two being compared.

Table 6.3 Scheffé *F* and LSD *F* statistics for the View Retriever data. Asterisks denote significance at the $\alpha_c = .1$ level.

Comparison	Scheffé *F*	LSD *F*
Textbook vs. View Retriever	1.02	3.05*
Textbook vs. degraded	6.95*	20.85*
Textbook vs. random	9.32*	27.96*
View Retriever vs. degraded	5.95*	17.85*
View Retriever vs. random	9.19*	27.57*
Degraded vs. random	0.26	0.78

Note also the practical difference between the conservative Scheffé test and the less stringent LSD test. Comparing equations 6.1 and 6.2 shows that a significant difference between means in an LSD test need be only $1/\sqrt{j-1}$ as large as the difference required to give a significant result in Scheffé's test. This relationship is only approximate, however, because the LSD and Scheffé tests have different numbers of degrees of freedom, so aren't exactly comparable.

6.3.6   Which Test? Interpretations of "Conservative"

Given earlier comments about the pitfalls of pairwise comparisons, if you were in Acker and Porter's shoes, would you use Scheffé or LSD tests? If we adopt the conventional $\alpha_c = .05$ level of significance, then the tests agree perfectly and the question doesn't arise. If the criterion was weaker (e.g., $\alpha_c = .1$), the tests would disagree in one important and instructive case, shown in table 6.3. The difference between textbook and View Retriever viewpoints is arguably the most crucial of the six comparisons in Acker and Porter's experiment, because it compares the coherence of an AI program, the View Retriever, with the coherence of human textbook authors. If we say that the Scheffé test is the most conservative, so we will entrust to it this important comparison, then we are making a big mistake. The scientifically conservative approach is to say, "Our hypothesis was that View Retriever viewpoints would be judged equal to textbook viewpoints. The Scheffé test failed to find a difference between them, but the Scheffé test is very conservative. Because the LSD test, which adopts a per-comparison error rate of .1, found a difference, we do not feel we can claim that View Retriever and textbook viewpoints are equal in the minds of the judges." The statistically conservative test is not scientifically conservative in this case.

The problem is a general one: We sometimes want to "accept the null hypothesis," even though this is formally nonsense; failure to reject does not justify acceptance, because a test might fail for reasons that have nothing to do with the veracity of the null hypothesis. These reasons are summarized in the power of a test (section 4.9). Suppose a test fails to reject the null hypothesis and its power is .99. Then we may be certain that if the null hypothesis was false, the test would have told us. Conversely, if the power of a test is low, we should not "accept the null hypothesis" when we fail to reject it.

Thus it is important to run both kinds of tests and think carefully about how to interpret them when they disagree. Then at least you know which pairwise comparisons are at issue, and you can decide how you want to treat them, individually. Some statisticians might squawk at treating comparisons inconsistently—accepting some differences on the basis of LSD tests and rejecting others because their Scheffé tests are insignificant—but this strategy makes sense, because all comparisons are not equally meaningful.

6.4   Comparisons among Many Systems: The MUC-3 Competition

We turn now to one of the largest experiments conducted in artificial intelligence, the MUC-3 study. In 1990, the Defense Advanced Research Projects Agency sponsored a comparison of fifteen *message understanding systems* developed at universities and companies. These groups collectively constructed a set of training problems and another set of test problems, established what would count as the "right answer" on each, developed scoring criteria, and wrote code to automatically test and score their individual message understanding systems. The task domain for all the systems was preprocessed newswire stories about Latin American terrorist events. Figures 6.1 and 6.2 show a newswire story and the hand-coded *answer key template*. Message understanding systems processed stories (e.g., figure 6.1) and filled out *answer templates*, which were scored by comparing them with answer key templates. You can see that a message understanding system might make several kinds of mistake:

1. Failing to fill a slot; for example, failing to identify the TYPE OF INCIDENT of the story as a KIDNAPPING (slot 4 of the answer key).

2. Filling a slot incorrectly; for example, identifying the TYPE OF INCIDENT of the story as a MURDER.

3. Filling a slot with a spurious item; for example, filling the EFFECT ON HUMAN TARGETS (slot 18) with DEATH. (A slot for which the story provided no data is filled with a hyphen in the answer key.)

TST1-MUC3-0080

BOGOTA, 3 APR 90 (INRAVISION TELEVISION CADENA 1) – [REPORT] [JORGE SIERRA VALENCIA] [TEXT] LIBERAL SENATOR FEDERICO ESTRADA VELEZ WAS KIDNAPPED ON 3 APR AT THE CORNER OF 60TH AND 48TH STREETS IN WESTERN MEDELLIN, ONLY 100 METERS FROM A METROPOLITAN POLICE CAI [IMMEDIATE ATTENTION CENTER]. THE ANTIOQUIA DEPARTMENT LIBERAL PARTY LEADER HAD LEFT HIS HOUSE WITHOUT ANY BODYGUARDS ONLY MINUTES EARLIER. AS HE WAITED FOR THE TRAFFIC LIGHT TO CHANGE, THREE HEAVILY ARMED MEN FORCED HIM TO GET OUT OF HIS CAR AND GET INTO A BLUE RENAULT.

HOURS LATER, THROUGH ANONYMOUS TELEPHONE CALLS TO THE METROPOLITAN POLICE AND TO THE MEDIA, THE EXTRADITABLES CLAIMED RESPONSIBILITY FOR THE KIDNAPPING. IN THE CALLS, THEY ANNOUNCED THAT THEY WILL RELEASE THE SENATOR WITH A NEW MESSAGE FOR THE NATIONAL GOVERNMENT.

LAST WEEK, FEDERICO ESTRADA VELEZ HAD REJECTED TALKS BETWEEN THE GOVERNMENT AND THE DRUG TRAFFICKERS.

Figure 6.1   An example of a MUC-3 newswire story.

4. Filling a slot that is not applicable to the story. These slots are denoted by asterisks in the answer key. For example, the EFFECT ON PHYSICAL TARGET(S) is applicable in a bombing story but not in a kidnapping story.

5. Filling a slot with more than one item, when only one applies. For example, the HUMAN TARGET TYPES(S) of the story in figure 6.1 could be correctly reported as a GOVERNMENT OFFICIAL or POLITICAL FIGURE: "FEDERICO ESTRADA VELEZ" but not both.

Some stories involved several terrorist events; message understanding systems were required to differentiate between them and fill out an answer template for each.

It proved quite challenging to design summary performance scores, as documented by Nancy Chinchor, Lynette Hirschman, and David Lewis (1993) in a comprehensive report of the MUC-3 evaluation. The two major summary scores were recall and precision, each defined for an answer template as follows.

Recall   the number of slots in the answer template filled correctly, divided by the number of filled slots in the answer key template. A system could get a high recall score by flooding the answer template with items, hoping that some would match items in corresponding slots in the answer key template.

1.	MESSAGE ID	TST1-MUC3-0080
2.	TEMPLATE ID	1
3.	DATE OF INCIDENT	03 APR 90
4.	TYPE OF INCIDENT	KIDNAPPING
5.	CATEGORY OF INCIDENT	TERRORIST ACT
5.	PERPETRATOR: ID OF INDIV(S)	"THREE HEAVILY ARMED MEN"
6.	PERPETRATOR: ID OR ORG(S)	"THE EXTRADITABLES"/ "EXTRADITABLES"
7.	PERPETRATOR: CONFIDENCE	CLAIMED OR ADMITTED: "THE EXTRADITABLES"/"EXTRADITABLES"
8.	PHYSICAL TARGET: ID(S)	*
9.	PHYSICAL TARGET: TOTAL NUM	*
10.	PHYSICAL TARGET: TYPE(S)	*
11.	HUMAN TARGET: ID(S)	"FEDERICO ESTRADA VELEZ" ("LIBERAL SENATOR"/"ANTIOQUIA DEPARTMENT LIBERAL PARTY LEADER"/"SENATOR"/"LIBERAL PARTY LEADER"/ "PARTY LEADER")
12.	HUMAN TARGET: TOTAL NUM	1
13.	HUMAN TARGET: TYPE(S)	GOVERNMENT OFFICIAL/POLITICAL FIGURE: "FEDERICO ESTRADA VELEZ"
14.	TARGET: FOREIGN NATION(S)	–
15.	INSTRUMENT: TYPE(S)	*
16.	LOCATION OF INCIDENT	COLUMBIA: MEDELLIN (CITY)
17.	EFFECT ON PHYSICAL TARGET(S)	*
18.	EFFECT OF HUMAN TARGET(S)	–

Figure 6.2   An example answer template for the message in figure 6.1.

Precision   the number of slots in the answer template filled correctly, divided by the number of slot fillers. A system that fills slots with correct items only will have a precision score of 1.0. A system that floods slots with items will have a low precision score.

Note that recall and precision are opponent criteria because high recall demands lots of slot fillers and so increases the probability that some of them will be wrong, decreasing precision. A system might attain high recall or high precision relatively easily, but attaining both is difficult.

As an aside, one might be disappointed that only two scores were generated to describe the MUC-3 systems. In fact, other scores were developed, and other experiments were conducted in attempts to "look behind" the performance scores. If, however, you are limited to two performance scores, then you should strive to design opponent scores such as recall and precision. Said differently, if scores tend to be uncorrelated, then they provide independent information; conversely, if they are highly correlated then one is redundant.

Each of the message understanding systems was tested on a corpus of 100 messages that had been set aside, inaccessible, while the fifteen teams developed their systems. After months of development, the day dawned when each system was run once on the corpus of test messages, accruing one recall score and one precision score for each message. At the end of the day, Chinchor, Hirschman, and Lewis set out to compare each system to every other system on mean recall and precision. They did it by running exhaustive pairwise comparisons analogous to the LSD test of the previous section. That is, they made no attempt to protect the experiment null hypotheses that the population means were equal for recall (or precision).

Recall and precision were treated separately, so each pair of systems was compared twice, for different mean recall and precision scores, respectively. The comparison was by an approximate randomization version of the paired sample t test (section 5.3.2). In brief, the null hypothesis is that two samples were drawn from the same population, which implies that any datum might be drawn with equal probability into one sample or the other. Recall that in the paired sample t test, two systems each solve the same set of problems. Let's say that on problem 1, system A's score was 60 and system B's score was 70. Under the null hypothesis that the systems are equal, however, it is equally likely that these scores would be reversed. The difference between A and B, -10 points, might equally well have been 10 points. The sampling distribution of the mean difference between A and B is achieved by repeatedly shuffling and recalculating the mean difference, as in all randomization tests, except that shuffling involves reversing the sign of the difference score for each problem with probability .5.

Here then is Chinchor, Hirschman, and Lewis's procedure for pairwise comparisons of mean recall scores; the procedure is identical for mean precision scores.

Procedure 6.1   Approximate Randomization Paired-Sample Test of Differences of Means

i.   For systems I and J, make a list D of the differences between recall scores on each of 100 problems. The ith element of the list is the recall score for system I minus the recall score for system J on problem i. Denote the mean of these differences $\bar{x}_D$.

ii.   Set a counter C to zero.

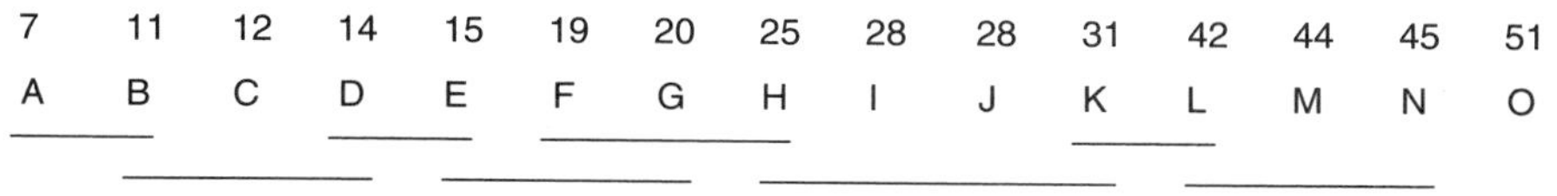

7	11	12	14	15	19	20	25	28	28	31	42	44	45	51
A	B	C	D	E	F	G	H	I	J	K	L	M	N	O

Figure 6.3 Pairwise comparisons of recall scores among fifteen message understanding systems ($\alpha_c = .05$). The top row is mean recall scores, the middle row is the systems that produced the scores, and the bars underline clusters of means that do not differ significantly at the $\alpha_c = .05$ level.

iii. Repeat 9,999 times:

    a. Create a list D^* as follows: For each element in D, change its sign with probability 0.5 and place it in D^*.

    b. Calculate $\overline{x}_{D^*}$, the mean of the elements of D^*.

    c. If $\overline{x}_{D^*} \geq \overline{x}_D$, increment C by one.

iv. $p = (C + 1)/(9999 + 1)$ is the probability of achieving a result greater than or equal to $\overline{x}_D$ by chance under the null hypothesis. That is, p is the probability of incorrectly rejecting the null hypothesis that systems I and J have equal population mean recall scores.

This procedure was run for all pairwise comparisons of the fifteen message understanding systems, a total of $15(15 - 1)/2 = 105$ comparisons on recall scores and 105 comparisons on precision scores. One way to represent these results is to cluster systems that are not significantly different at some level. Figure 6.3 shows the recall scores of the systems, which are labeled A to O. A bar beneath systems indicates they are not significantly different at the conventional .05 level. For example, system A does not differ from B, and B does not differ from C, but A differs from C. Notice that system O is significantly different from everything. Each system differed from 11.133 systems, on average, at the $\alpha_c = .05$ level.

Let us consider the validity of these results in light of our earlier discussions of pairwise comparisons. I said that conservative pairwise comparisons such as the Scheffé test guard against the event that one or more apparently significant pairwise differences is, in fact, spurious; but only by reducing the level for each comparison so much that the tests become insensitive to real differences. On the other hand, least-significant-difference (LSD) tests, of which the MUC-3 randomization tests are an example, are sensitive to differences between pairs of means but are virtually certain to produce some spurious pairwise comparisons if the number of comparisons is large. In short, we suspect that some of the differences indicated in figure 6.3 simply don't exist.

When I discussed Acker and Porter's pairwise comparisons, I suggested running both Scheffé and LSD tests to see where they disagreed, then dealing with the disagree-

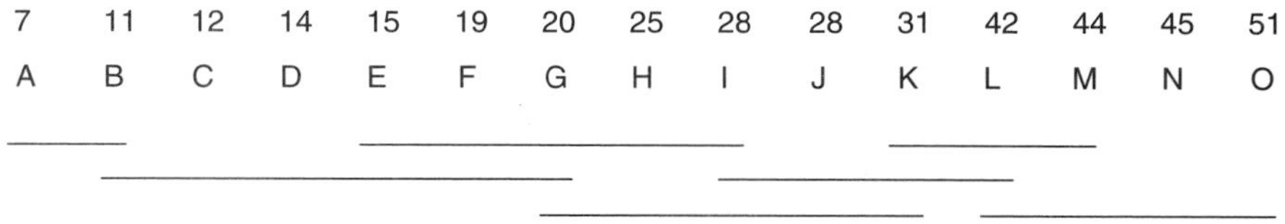

7	11	12	14	15	19	20	25	28	28	31	42	44	45	51
A	B	C	D	E	F	G	H	I	J	K	L	M	N	O

Figure 6.4 Pairwise comparisons of recall scores among fifteen message understanding systems ($\alpha_c = .0001$). The top row is mean recall scores, the middle row is the systems that produced the scores, and the bars underline clusters of means that do not differ significantly at the $\alpha_c = .0001$ level.

ments individually. This advice cannot be taken literally for the MUC-3 comparisons because Chinchor, Hirschman, and Lewis are committed to approximate randomization tests, while the Scheffé test is a conventional parametric one. Still, one can do something similar: one can redraw figure 6.3 for a much, much more stringent level. Because Chinchor, Hirschman, and Lewis' randomization procedure looped 9999 times, the most stringent nonzero α_c level is .0001. By restricting ourselves to differences this significant, we reduce the likelihood that one or more of the differences will be spurious, just as the Scheffé test does. Figure 6.4 shows bars under systems the recall scores of which do not differ according to this stringent criterion. Note that system A is still different from all systems other than B, but system O no longer stands alone: it shares top honors with systems L, M, and N. Each system differs from 8.8 others, on average.

By presenting the results of pairwise comparisons at conventional and stringent levels (e.g., $\alpha_c = .05$ and $\alpha_c = .0001$) we do not exactly avoid the pitfalls of pairwise comparisons but we see them more clearly. On average, each system differs from roughly eleven others at the $\alpha_c = .05$ level and roughly nine at the $\alpha_c = .0001$ level, so two comparisons per system are equivocal. This puts a number, albeit rough and heuristic, on the concern that some comparisons in figure 6.3 are probably spurious. Let's call this number the *criterion differential* for pairwise comparisons.

We can interpret the criterion differential as a measure of the sensitivity of the experiment: If it is large, then many significant differences at the $\alpha_c = .05$ level do not hold up at the $\alpha_c = .0001$ level, so the experiment produces many equivocal comparisons. If it is small, the criterion differential tells us the experiment differentiates systems unequivocally, or nearly so. It turns out that on *precision scores* (as opposed to recall scores, which we have just discussed), each MUC-3 system differed from 9.466 others, on average, at the $\alpha_c = .05$ level, and differed from only 5.2 systems at the $\alpha_c = .0001$ level; therefore, the criterion differential for pairwise comparisons of precision scores is 4.266. Clearly, the MUC-3 experiment provided a more sensitive test of recall scores than precision scores.

Between Scheffé tests and LSD tests lies a wide variety of methods for comparisons of means, including Tukey's Honestly Significant Difference test, Duncan's Multiple Range test, and others. Some tests work only for pairwise differences, some accommodate comparisons among combinations of means, some work by constructing continuous sets of indistinguishable means, and so on. Most statistics books describe several (see, for example, Sokal and Rohlf, 1981). The choice between them, or the decision to apply several and compare their results, depends on what you are trying to show. Sometimes you will want to protect the experiment null hypothesis, other times you will want sensitive tests of pairwise differences and you are willing to live with the probability that some apparently significant differences are not. Some comparisons require conservative tests, others don't. Sometimes you have just a few means, sometimes many. Typically, some pairwise comparisons are more important than others and should receive more attention.

In section 6A.2 you will find discussions of two other aspects of these tests. First, the notion of independent comparisons is discussed, then we look at comparisons of combinations of means. Remarkably, the sum of squares for the analysis of variance can be decomposed into independent parts that correspond to comparisons. You can say, for example, that the comparison between the means of groups *A* and *B* account for 27.3 percent of the between-group sum of squares, whereas the comparison between groups *C* and *D* accounts for another chunk of the sum of squares, and so on.

6.5   Comparing the Variability of Performance: Humans vs. the View Retriever

When I drive to work in the morning, I must choose between two routes: One takes twenty minutes and is relatively quiet, the other can be fast or slow, depending on traffic. On average the latter route is a probably little faster, but I rarely take it because I think it makes my travel time too unpredictable. Actually, I don't know whether travel times are really less predictable on one route or the other, but I know how to find out. Recall that the *F* distribution is the sampling distribution of the ratio of two variances under the null hypothesis that the variances are equal. To test whether travel time is more variable on one route than another, I could simply compare the ratio of the variances on the two routes to the *F* distribution. This will tell me the probability of attaining such a ratio by chance under the null hypothesis that the routes are equally variable.

An interesting application of this test pertains to Acker and Porter's data. Although textbook viewpoints and View Retriever viewpoints have indistinguishable mean coherence scores, the standard deviations of the two groups of scores appear to be different (.912 and 1.383, respectively). This suggests that the View Retriever system performed well on average but more erratically than human textbook authors. To test the one-tailed hypothesis that View Retriever viewpoints have more variable coherence scores than textbook viewpoints, we simply take the ratio of the variances:

$$F = \frac{(1.383)^2}{(.912)^2} = 2.3.$$

The critical value for rejecting the null hypothesis is indexed by a pair of degrees of freedom: the number of scores in each group, minus one. Because Acker and Porter collected 29 coherence scores for textbook viewpoints and 118 scores for View Retriever viewpoints, we look up the critical F value with 28 and 117 degrees of freedom. For $\alpha = .01$ this value is approximately 1.9, which is clearly exceeded by our test statistic. Thus we can reject the hypothesis that the coherence scores of textbook and View Retriever viewpoints are equally variable. With a small probability of error ($p < .01$) View Retriever viewpoints have more variable coherence scores.

The F test for equality of variances is used infrequently, perhaps because it is sensitive to violations of the assumption that the underlying population distributions are normal. (This is a less serious problem when the sample sizes are large, as in the previous example.) An alternative to the F test is a randomization version of the F test, following the approach we introduced in chapter 5, but with an interesting twist.

A conventional randomization test starts with two or more groups $g_1, g_2, \ldots$, and a test statistic, ϕ. The data in the groups are merged into a single list L, which is thoroughly shuffled and redistributed among "pseudo groups" $g_1^*, g_2^*, \ldots$. Then a statistic ϕ^* is calculated. Resampling from L yields the empirical sampling distribution of ϕ^* that we treat as a good estimate of the sampling distribution of ϕ under the null hypothesis that $g_1, g_2, \ldots$ are drawn from the same population. If we follow this procedure in the obvious way to get a sampling distribution for the F statistic, we run into a subtle problem.[13] Groups g_1 and g_2 might have identical variances but different means, in which case L will have a larger variance than either g_1 or g_2. We'd still expect the mean of the distribution of $F^* = g_1^*/g_2^*$ to be unity, but the variance of F^* will depend on the difference between the means. This is undesirable. We don't want a test of variances to depend on means, but the solution is simple. For each group j, replace each datum x_{jk} with $x_{jk} - \overline{x}_j$, ensuring that the means of the groups are zero but their variances are unchanged. Then merge the transformed groups into L and resample to find the sampling distribution of $F^* = g_1^*/g_2^*$, as usual.

---

13. I thank Tuomas Sandholm for pointing it out to me.

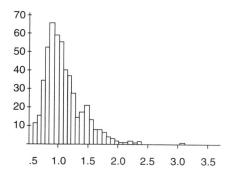

Figure 6.5   A sampling distribution of the ratio of two variances, produced by randomization.

A practical note: The purpose of this test is to show that one variance is larger than another, so if group g_1 has the larger variance, it must appear in the numerator of the F statistic, and you must be sure to put the variance of the corresponding pseudo group g_1^* in the numerator of F^*.

To test the hypothesis that View Retriever and Textbook viewpoint scores are equally variable, first shift the distributions of the scores so each has mean zero, then merge all the scores in a list L and shuffle it thoroughly. Because the original sample included 118 View Retriever viewpoint scores and 29 Textbook viewpoint scores, resampling assigns the first 118 scores in L to V^* and the remaining 29 scores to T^*. Calculate the variances of T^* and V^* and their ratio $F^* = var. (V^*)/var. (T^*)$. Repeat the resampling process 500 times. The distribution of 500 F^* scores is shown in figure 6.5. Its mean and variance are 1.08 and .098, respectively. Recall that the ratio of the sample variances for View Retriever and Textbook viewpoints is $F = 2.3$. How likely is this result under the null hypothesis that the variances are equal? Only two of the 500 values of F^* exceed 2.3, so the probability of a value at least this large is $2/500 = .004$ or less. The variance of textbook viewpoints is significantly smaller than the variance of View Retriever viewpoints.

6.6   Assessing Whether a Factor Has Predictive Power

In an earlier chapter I raised the possibility that a statistically significant result might have little or no predictive power (section 4.7). The problem can be succinctly illustrated in terms of the analysis of variance. If you know the group from which a datum is drawn, how much is your ability to predict the value of the datum increased?

Hays (1973, pp. 484–488) provides a simple estimate of the proportion by which the variance of the dependent variable is reduced as a result of knowing the group:

$$\hat{\omega}^2 = \frac{SS_{between} - (j-1)MS_{within}}{SS_{total} + MS_{within}}.$$

For example, imagine someone repeatedly draws coherence scores from Acker and Porter's data and asks you to guess their values. Each time, your best guess would be the grand mean coherence score. Over all, your summed, squared errors would be SS_{total} and your mean squared error would be the grand variance. Now imagine changing the game slightly: before you guess, you are told which group the datum was drawn from (e.g., textbook viewpoints). By what proportion does this information reduce your mean squared error? Following the formula, we estimate

$$\hat{\omega}^2 = \frac{88.05 - (3)1.811}{560.66 + 1.811} = .147.$$

Overall, the mean squared error in your predictions is expected to be reduced by nearly 15 percent as a result of knowing the group from which a datum was drawn. This does not seem like much, but it is evidence of a statistical relationship between the factor that underlies Acker and Porter's experiment—the amount of "random stuff" in the viewpoints—and coherence scores.

6.7   Assessing Sensitivity: MYCIN's Sensitivity to Certainty Factor Accuracy

By degrading parameters or data structures of a system and observing the effects on performance, one can run a kind of *sensitivity analysis*. Clancey and Cooper (Buchanan and Shortliffe, 1984, chapter. 10), who probed the sensitivity of MYCIN to the accuracy of its certainty factors, provide a good example. MYCIN was an expert system for prescribing antibiotics; certainty factors (CFs) were MYCIN's representation of its degree of belief in data, inference rules, and conclusions. MYCIN prescribed therapy for infections that it believed were likely, thus the concern that inaccuracies in CFs might affect therapy recommendations. Clancey and Cooper tested MYCIN's sensitivity to the accuracy of CFs by systematically introducing inaccuracy and observing the effects on therapy recommendations. Normally, MYCIN's CFs ranged from 0 to 1,000 (the scale was symmetric around zero, but it adds nothing to the following discussion to consider negative CFs). One can introduce uncertainty by mapping this scale to a coarser one, say 0 to 100. The mapping would eliminate the difference between, say, 910 and 919; both numbers would map to 91. Clancey and Cooper subjected MYCIN to much more radical treatments. The least radical mapping was from the original

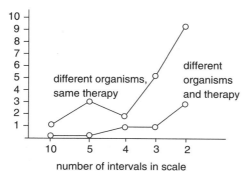

Figure 6.6 How MYCIN's diagnostic and therapy recommendation performance depends on the accuracy of certainty factors. (Source: Buchanan and Shortliffe, 1984, p. 219)

scale with 1,000 intervals to a scale with 10 intervals. They also tested MYCIN with mappings to scales with 5, 4, 3, and 2 intervals. In the latter case, for example, every positive CF was replaced by the closest of these numbers: 0, 500, and 1000.

In each of these cases, Clancey and Cooper ran MYCIN on a set of ten test problems that they had already solved with the original version of the program. They assessed two comparison measures. First, on how many of the ten problems did the roughened version of MYCIN prescribe the same therapy as the original version? Second, on how many of the problems did the roughened version of MYCIN attribute the infection to different organisms than the original version? The results of the experiment are shown in figure 6.6. When the CF scale included ten intervals, the roughened and original versions of MYCIN performed almost identically. Only in one case did the versions not agree on the causative organisms, but in this case they agreed on the therapy. When the number of intervals in the CF scale was reduced to three, the roughened version still performed pretty well. Although it misattributed the cause of the infection on half the cases, it disagreed with the original version only once on the subject of therapy. Only when the number of intervals was reduced to two did Clancey and Cooper find much effect; the diagnosis was wrong nine times and the therapy was wrong three times.

Clancey and Cooper were clever about two aspects of their experiment. They looked at five levels of roughening instead of just one or two, and they assessed two different measures of performance. Consequently, they found that one measure, correct diagnoses of organisms, degrades faster than the other, correct therapy recommendations. Although this result was not entirely unexpected, it does show clearly that MYCIN can recommend the right therapy even when it attributes an infection to the wrong organism, and, thus, it is insensitive to even relatively large inaccuracies in certainty factors.

6.8   Other Measures of Performance in Batches of Trials

So far we have focused on the means and standard deviations of continuous measures of performance, such as the scores given by judges. We have described case studies in which parametric and computer-intensive methods were applied to compare means and standard deviations. So far, so good, but keep in mind that means are relatively crude summaries of data. The mean tells us nothing about the distribution of our data besides location, that is, where the distribution sits on the horizontal axis. Consequently, if an experimental treatment changes a distribution but not the mean, then the effect of the treatment will not be detected with a *t* test or analysis of variance. Said differently, a treatment might affect the pattern of performance but not the average level of performance; or, the treatment might affect both, but the pattern of performance is what we really care about.

Acker and Porter's experiment illustrates different patterns of performance among human judges. Recall that each of ten judges saw several examples of four kinds of texts, and was asked to rate the coherence of the texts on a scale from one to five. As it happens, the mean scores assigned by the judges are quite variable. A one-way analysis of variance with *Judge* as the factor and *Score* as the dependent variable is highly significant ($p < .001$). But we are interested in the pattern of the judges' responses, specifically, in each judge's distribution of scores. The data for all ten judges is shown in table 6.4. Looking at the last two judges (J and K) we see that their pattern of responses are completely opposite: judge J thought nineteen texts were as good as could be, and judge K thought nineteen texts were awful. No wonder the analysis of variance found differences in judges' mean scores. The distribution of scores in table 6.4 is valuable because it helps us interpret the analysis of variance result and identifies judges who are judging by criteria different than others in the cohort.

Table 6.4   Distribution of scores for individual judges in Acker and Porter's experiment.

Score	Judge									
	A	B	C	D	E	F	G	H	J	K
1	0	1	9	5	5	7	1	2	0	19
2	5	2	5	6	4	1	5	1	0	2
3	6	7	2	6	10	6	2	2	4	2
4	14	8	2	8	9	6	6	12	7	2
5	5	12	12	5	2	10	11	13	19	5

It would be helpful to be able to identify anomalous patterns of performance automatically, with some statistical procedure. The chi-square test, introduced in section 2.4.3, will suffice. The steps of the test are, first, estimate the expected frequency in each cell under the assumption that the column factor *(Judge)* and the row factor *(Score)* are independent. Second, subtract the expected frequency in each cell from the observed frequency, square the difference, and divide it by the expected frequency. Third, sum these values over all the cells. Obviously, the result, denoted χ^2, will be a small number only if the observed and expected frequencies are similar. A large value of χ^2 suggests that the underlying assumption of the test—that the row and column factors are independent—is probably false. For table 6.4, $\chi^2 = 131.04$, $p < .0001$, that is, the probability of this result arising by chance under the assumption that judge and score are independent is virtually zero. The chi-square test has tipped us off to two or more significantly different patterns of response from the judges. It remains to find which judge or judges are responsible, although we can see that judge K is different simply by looking. An automatic, statistical procedure for finding judge K will be described in section 6.13.

6.9   Assessing Performance during Development: Training Effects in OTB

Most AI programs are under development for most of their lives, so we often want to measure effects of modifications. At first glance, it seems easy to compare versions of a program before and after modifications with *t* tests to see whether mean performance improves or declines. A few subtleties creep in, however, if we want to test whether performance changes significantly over a series of trials. In machine learning studies, for example, it is common to show learning curves of mean performance at different levels of training. One might be inclined to treat the level of training as a factor and run a one-way analysis of variance to see whether the factor has a significant influence on performance. This approach will produce positively biased results (Keppel, 1973, p. 464), however, so the probability of incorrectly rejecting the null hypothesis will be higher than indicated by the *p* value from an *F* test (see also section 7A.5). Statistical considerations aside, we are generally not satisfied with the naked assertion that training affects performance. We want to know many other things, including:

■ How much can performance be improved before it "flattens out?"

■ Does the amount of effort required to produce a unit improvement in performance change over the series of trials?

- When a program is modified, do we see improvements on many tasks or a few, or just one?

- What explains the shape of a learning curve?

- Do modifications to a system have different effects in different conditions?

A nice illustration of most of these questions is provided in research by Wendy Lehnert and Joe McCarthy on the *part-of-speech tagging* problem (Lehnert et al., 1993). Lehnert and McCarthy's program, called OTB, was trained on corpora of sentences to assign part-of-speech labels to words in test sentences. OTB acquired much of the knowledge it needed by counting frequencies of co-occurrences of word tags in sentences. Some knowledge, pertaining to special cases, was given to OTB by human knowledge engineers. I treat both as "training," and I will use the word throughout to refer to autonomous learning as well as human-mediated knowledge acquisition and software engineering in general.

The OTB part-of-speech tagger is a part of a larger system for automatically extracting information from newswire stories. OTB's job is to assign part-of-speech tags to a sentence before it is given to the CIRCUS parser (Lehnert, 1991). Because CIRCUS does not require very fine discriminations among parts of speech, OTB works with relatively few tags.

PREP (preposition)	INF (infinitive)	AUX (auxiliary)
CONN (connective)	NEG (negative)	REL (relative pronoun)
ART (article)	CONJ (conjunction)	PTCL (particle)
MODL (modal)	PUNC (punctuation symbol)	NM (noun modifier)
NOUN (noun)	VERB (verb)	PRES (present participle)
PASP (past participle)	GER (gerund)	ADV (adverb)
START, STOP (special symbols marking the beginning and end of sentences)		

For example, here is a newswire story with OTB's tags for each word in the story, and correct tags, assigned by a human tagger:

```
*START* THE GENERAL MOTORS CORPORATION AND ISUZU MOTORS LTD=
MAY PARTICIPATE IN A TRUCK MANUFACTURING PROJECT IN CZECHOSLOVAKIA
$COMMA$ A G=M= SPOKESMAN $COMMA$ JACK HARNED $COMMA$ SAID *END*
```

Story words:	*START*	THE	GENERAL	MOTORS	CORPORATION
OTB tags:	START	ART	NM	NM	NOUN
Human tags:	START	ART	NM	NM	NOUN

Story words:	AND	ISUZU	MOTORS	LTD=	MAY
OTB tags:	CONJ	NM	NM	NOUN	NM
Human tags:	CONJ	NM	NM	NOUN	MODL

Story words:	PARTICIPATE		IN	A	TRUCK	MANUFACTURING
OTB tags:	NOUN		PREP	ART	NOUN	NM
Human tags:	VERB		PREP	ART	NM	NM

Story words:	PROJECT	IN	CZECHOSLOVAKIA	$COMMA$
OTB tags:	NOUN	PREP	NOUN	PUNC
Human tags:	NOUN	PREP	NOUN	PUNC

Story words:	A	G=M=	SPOKESMAN	$COMMA$
OTB tags:	ART	NM	NOUN	PUNC
Human tags:	ART	NM	NOUN	PUNC

Story words:	JACK	HARNED	$COMMA$	SAID	*END*
OTB tags:	NM	NM	PUNC	VERB	STOP
Human tags:	NM	NOUN	PUNC	VERB	STOP

As you can see, OTB and the human scorer agreed pretty well, although they differed on four of the twenty-eight words in the sentence. In general, OTB's performance is better than this: It labels nearly 95 percent of the words in test sentences correctly. Remarkably, it achieves this level of performance with very little training. After describing how it works, we will document the studies Lehnert and McCarthy ran to explain aspects of OTB's performance.

Part-of-speech tagging is difficult because many words can function in two or more ways. For example, a surprisingly large fraction of the nouns can function as verbs: As I look around my office I see a table, a telephone, a light, a chair, a monitor, a cup, and several books; each of these nouns is also a verb. How, then, is OTB to know that the word "project" in the example above is a noun and not a verb? You and I rely on context: The article "a" leads us to expect a noun phrase, which allows us to interpret "truck" and "manufacturing" as modifiers of "project." OTB also relies on context, which it formalizes in terms of statistical dependencies between trigrams of tags. To illustrate, consider how OTB labels the words "general motors corporation."

These words constitute a gap, a sequence of one or more ambiguous or unknown words. OTB begins by identifying unambiguous words on either side of the gap, called anchors. In the sentence, above, the anchors are "the" and "and," which have unambiguous tags ART and CONJ, respectively. Next, OTB consults a database of tag trigrams that begin and end with ART and CONJ. Associated with each is its frequency in a set of training sentences. For example, here are the most common trigrams beginning with ART:

Trigram	Number of occurrences of the trigram in a training set
ART NM NOUN	418
ART NM NM	294

During its training, OTB encountered many other trigrams that begin with an article; for example, it came across 163 instances of ART NOUN PREP and 2 instances of ART NOUN CONN. The two trigrams listed previously, however, account for 61 percent of 1,001 three-word sequences in the training set that begin with an article.

Here are the most common trigrams ending in CONJ:

Trigram	Number of occurrences of the trigram in a training set
NM NOUN CONJ	160
NM NM CONJ	32

The approach to putting these trigrams together is straightforward: Leading trigrams are merged with trailing trigrams to span the gap between ART and CONJ, and the resulting bridge is assigned a score that sums the frequencies of all the trigrams it contains. All possible pairs of leading and trailing trigrams are considered, but some are pruned because they violate constraints; for example, although the leading trigram ART NOUN PUNC is fairly common in the training set, it is pruned from the set of trigrams to be merged because none of the ambiguous words in the gap (i.e., GENERAL MOTORS CORPORATION) is a punctuation mark. Here are the three five-tag sequences that OTB considered for GENERAL MOTORS CORPORATION, with their scores:

Trigram	Score (a sum of constituent trigram scores)
ART NM NM NOUN CONJ	294 + 944 + 160 = 1398
ART NM NM NM CONJ	294 + 569 + 32 = 895
ART NM NOUN NOUN CONJ	418 + 9 + 1 = 428

Constituent scores are simply the frequencies of the constituents in the training set:

Trigram	Score
ART NM NM	294
ART NM NOUN	418
NM NM NOUN	944
NM NM NM	569
NM NOUN NOUN	9
NM NOUN CONJ	160
NM NM CONJ	32
NOUN NOUN CONJ	1

Tag trigrams are only one source of information about ambiguous words in gaps. OTB also relies on word-tag frequencies and heuristics for repairing frequent tagging errors. Word-tag frequencies are simply the raw frequencies of word-tag pairs in the training set. For example, the word "general" was tagged as a noun modifier (NM) seven times and a noun three times in the training set. OTB simply added the word-tag scores for the bridging words to the tag trigram scores (more recent versions of the program weigh the word-tag and tag-trigram scores differently). For example, the total score of the ART NM NM NM CONJ interpretation of "THE GENERAL MOTORS CORPORATION AND..." is 895, the tag trigram score derived previously, plus 7 for the NM interpretation of GENERAL, 6 for the NM tag for MOTORS and 1 for the NM tag for CORPORATION, totalling 909.

Tag repair heuristics compensate for frequent tagging errors, and are hand-coded, as opposed to learned from a training set. For example, "to" is either a preposition (PREP) or an infinitive (INF) and the tag trigram VERB PREP VERB is very common, so when "to" is found in triples such as "agreed to form," it gets tagged as a preposition. In fact, in this context, "to" is an infinitive. OTB has 108 tag repair heuristics to seek out and correct such errors.

With this background we can see how Lehnert and McCarthy addressed many of the questions from the beginning of this section. Specifically,

■ How well does OTB perform and what are the confidence limits around its mean performance?

■ How does OTB's performance improve with training, and what explains the shape of its learning curve?

■ How does the effort required to obtain an increment in performance change?

■ What is OTB's expected asymptotic performance?

■ When OTB is modified, are there improvements on many tasks or a few, or just one?

■ What is the relative contribution of OTB's sources of knowledge, the tag trigrams, word-tag frequencies, and tag-repair heuristics?

The simplest way to answer the first question would be to repeatedly train and test OTB, then average the scores obtained during the testing phases and derive parametric confidence intervals as described in section 4.6.2. For example, imagine McCarthy and Lehnert had a corpus of 5000 sentences for which each constituent word had been hand-tagged by a human expert. Then, they might draw 500 sentences from the corpus, train OTB on 450, test it on the remaining 50, and repeat this process ten times, using up all the sentences in the corpus. At the conclusion of the experiment, they could average the performance scores obtained during each of the ten tests with fifty sentences and obtain confidence intervals. Overall, 4500 sentences would have been used for training and 500 sentences—none of which were in the training set—would constitute the test sets. The advantage of this scheme is its separation of training and test sentences; it guards against the possibility of training a system to respond correctly to idiosyncrasies of the training set. Unfortunately, the scheme is very expensive. In practical terms, hand-tagging 5000 sentences would have been excessive effort. There is a better way to use training sets.

6.10   Cross-Validation: An Efficient Training and Testing Procedure

A more efficient training and testing scheme, the one McCarthy and Lehnert chose, is called *k-fold cross-validation*. It requires a set of problem-solution pairs, which for OTB was 500 sentences, in which each word had been hand-tagged.

Procedure 6.2   k-fold Cross-Validation

i.   Shuffle the items in the training set.

ii. Divide the training set into k equal parts of size n; say, ten sets of size $n = 50$ sentences.

iii. Do $i = 1$ to k times:

    a. Call the ith set of n sentences the test set and put it aside.

    b. Train the system on the remaining $k - 1$ sets; test the system on the test set, record the performance.

    c. Clear memory, that is, forget everything learned during training.

iv. Calculate the average performance from the k test sets.

The reason to clear memory in step iii.c is to get k independent estimates of the effect of training. If there was any holdover from one of the k iterations to the next, then the estimates of performance obtained in each iteration would not be independent. OTB was tested with ten-fold cross-validation, that is, its original set of 500 sentences was divided into ten sets, and each was used nine times for training and once for testing. This is efficient in the following sense: We want to train a learning algorithm with all the available data, because its performance is expected to improve as it encounters more items. If we train on 500 items and immediately test on the same items, however, we will not find out how our algorithm performs on items it hasn't seen during training. Cross-validation allows us to train a system on almost all the items (450 of 500 for ten-fold cross-validation), test it on all the items, and still discover how the system performs on unseen items.

Cross-validation is a resampling technique that should remind you of bootstrap testing, discussed in chapter 5. The common idea that underlies these techniques is to estimate the true (population) performance by treating a sample as if it is the population and repeatedly drawing samples from it. A true bootstrap approach, of course, involves resampling with replacement. For a set S of size M (e.g., 500 hand-tagged sentences):

Procedure 6.3   Bootstrap Cross-Validation

i. Do k times:

    a. Draw M items from S with replacement, call this sample R.

    b. Find the items in S that do not appear in R, call these the test set.

    c. Train the system on the items in R; test it on the items in the test set and record the performance.

    d. Clear memory, that is, forget everything learned during training.

ii. Calculate the average performance from the k test sets.

To get good estimates of performance from bootstrap resampling, it is recommended that k should be at least 200 (Weiss and Kulikowski, 1989, p. 34); the bootstrap procedure thus involves a lot more computation than, say, a ten-fold cross validation. Weiss and Kulikowski report that both cross validation and the bootstrap procedure give good estimates of performance if the sample size is not small. They also discuss the relative merits of several other resampling procedures.

Procedures 6.3 and 6.2 test performance after a considerable amount of training (e.g., 450 training items per trial). To chart a learning curve, however, it is desirable to measure performance repeatedly as the amount of training is increased. For this purpose, Lehnert and McCarthy used a variant of cross validation:

Procedure 6.4   Incremental k-fold Cross-Validation

i.   Shuffle the items in the training set.

ii.   Divide the training set into k equal parts of size n, say, ten sets of size $n = 50$ sentences.

iii. Do $i = 1$ to k times:

    a. Call the ith set of n sentences the test set; call the remaining $k - 1$ sets of sentences the training set.

    b. Repeat 10 times:
Select one sentence at random from the training set, train the system on this sentence, test the system on the test set, and record the performance.

    c. Repeat 9 times:
Select ten sentences at random from the training set, train the system on these sentences, test the system on the test set, and record the performance.

    d. Repeat 7 times:
Select fifty sentences at random from the training set, train the system on these sentences, test the system on the test set, and record the performance

    e. Clear memory, that is, forget everything learned during training.

iv.   Calculate the performance for each level of training averaged over the k test sets.

Unlike the previous cross-validation procedures, this one tests OTB twenty-six times before training is completed, but it doesn't clear memory until then, so we get to see the cumulative effects of training. The procedure trains OTB on just one sentence, then tests it on all fifty from the test set; then it trains on a second sentence and tests again, and so on, until it has trained OTB on ten sentences. After that, the procedure adopts increments of 10 training sentences until OTB has trained on 100 sentences, and increments of 50 thereafter. Finally, the procedure clears memory, forgetting everything learned during training, and repeats itself.

At the end of the procedure, McCarthy and Lehnert average k performance measures taken after 1, 2, ..., 10, 20, ..., 100, 150, ...450 sentences of training, respectively. The performance measure is the proportion of the words in fifty test sentences that are correctly tagged. The vertical axes of figure 6.7 and figure 6.8 represent the means of $k = 10$ such measures. The 95 percent confidence intervals around these means are too small to show in the figures as error bars. Figure 6.7 shows the mean proportion of correctly tagged words after 1, 2, ..., 10 training sentences, and figure 6.8 shows the mean proportion after 10, 20, ..., 100, 150, ..., 450 training sentences. Two versions of OTB are shown in each figure, one that ran with tag repair heuristics and one that ran without.

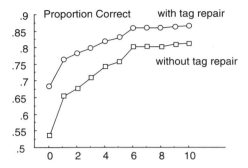

Figure 6.7   Mean proportion of correctly tagged words (vertical axis) after training on one to ten sentences (horizontal axis).

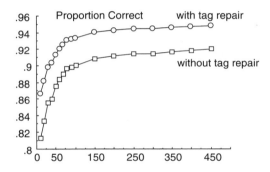

Figure 6.8   Mean proportion of correctly tagged words (vertical axis) after training on 10 to 450 sentences (horizontal axis).

Remarkably, after training OTB on a single sentence, it is able to correctly tag, on average, 53 percent of the words in a test set. With tag repair heuristics, this number jumps to about 68 percent. After just two training sentences, the average percentage of correctly tagged words is 56 percent, and by the time OTB has seen just ten training sentences, its performance level is over 70 percent.

6.11   Learning Curves

Figures 6.7 and 6.8 are called *learning curves*; they tell us much about how OTB benefits from training. Like learning curves for most systems (including humans) this one grows quickly at first and then flattens out. What explains this characteristic shape? One explanation is that the problems you learn to solve first are likely to be common problems. Learning to solve this kind of problem has a relatively big effect on performance, because a large fraction of the problems you will encounter later are of this type. Once you have learned to solve the most common types of problems, performance flattens out, because the only opportunities to improve performance come from relatively rare opportunities to learn to solve rare problems, and the knowledge gained is used rarely.

We can see exactly these phenomena at work in OTB. In its very first training sentence, the program encounters some extremely common, unambiguous words, including the articles ("a," "an," and "the"), the punctuation symbols, and the *START* and *END* symbols. If these comprise, say, 50 percent of the words in the average sentence, then OTB will achieve 50 percent correct performance after training on a single sentence. In the second and third sentences, OTB encounters other high-frequency, unambiguous words that by chance did not show up in the first sentence. When OTB encounters a common but ambiguous word in the first few sentences, its tag in the hand-coded sentences is most likely to be the most common tag for that word. This means OTB will probably give the word its most common tag when it is seen again, which also contributes to a rapid rise in performance.

It is sometimes possible to estimate the asymptotic performance of a learning system. In practical terms, the asymptote is where the learning curve flattens out. Deciding whether the curve is "really flat" can be tricky, although one approach is to fit a regression line or a resistant line to the supposed flat part and then see whether its slope is significantly different from zero, as described in section 8.4 or section 5.3.4. A simpler approach is to guess "by eye" the asymptotic level of a curve, but in some cases, such as figure 6.8, performance continues to improve, albeit slowly, even after 450 training sentences. The rate of improvement can be estimated by a regression line fit to the flattish part of the curve; for example, .0000232 is the slope of a line fit to the points in figure 6.8 (with tag repair) beyond 200 training sentences. Extrapolating, it would take about 2000 more training sentences to improve OTB's mean proportion correct to 100 percent. In fact, Lehnert and McCarthy suspect that OTB is limited by the accuracy of the human taggers who created the training set, and it probably won't achieve 100 percent accuracy until the human taggers do.

In summary, let's review how Lehnert and McCarthy answered some of the questions introduced earlier:

■ How well does OTB perform and what are the confidence limits around its mean performance? Mean levels of performance are found by k-fold cross validation, and show that OTB performs very well. Parametric confidence intervals on mean performance are very narrow, close to zero, in fact. This is not surprising, considering that the ten samples for ten-fold cross validation are drawn at random from a single population of 500 sentences; the probability that OTB would perform well on one sample and not another is very small.

■ How does OTB's performance improve with training, and what explains the shape of its learning curve? OTB's learning curve has a characteristic shape—an inverted "L"—due to a property of random sampling: The words OTB first learns to tag are the common words it is most likely to encounter. Thus it learns to solve common problems first, which produces big initial strides in performance.

■ How does the effort required to obtain an increment in performance change? Initially, a single training sentence will get OTB's performance into the 50 percent to 70 percent range, but after 90 training sentences, we expect OTB to require roughly 1,000 more to increase its performance by 2 percent.

■ What is OTB's expected asymptotic performance? This has yet to be established, though obviously it is between 95 percent and 100 percent. More important, the reasons performance flattens out are not fully understood and the point at which the flattening begins cannot yet be predicted. This is an important question because we would like to know how many training instances a program will need before we test it; and also because we want to predict how OTB will perform if we give it a different corpus of tagged sentences. To make such predictions, we must relate when the curve flattens out to characteristics of the corpus.

Lehnert and McCarthy's understanding of OTB's performance is clearly descriptive, as befits performance assessment. The next step is to understand how OTB's algorithms and the sentences in its corpora influence performance. Our attention, however, now shifts to performance assessment during knowledge engineering.

6.12 Assessing Effects of Knowledge Engineering with Retesting

Knowledge engineering is the process of adding knowledge to a system to improve its performance. These additions are made by hand, often with the assistance of a knowledge-acquisition interface, but not by automatic training as in the previous example. As before, we want to measure improvements in performance. One such experiment was run by Lehnert and McCarthy to assess the utility of 108 tag-repair heuristics, which, you'll recall, corrected common tagging errors due to relying on tag trigrams. The experiment simply compared OTB's performance with and without

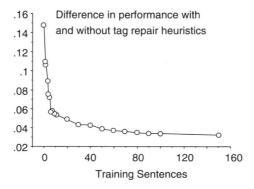

Figure 6.9   Difference in performance with and without tag repair heuristics.

its tag-repair heuristics. Studies of this sort are sometimes called *ablation* or *lesion* studies (Newell, 1975; Kibler and Langley, 1988), because they involve "cutting out" a component of a system (think of disconnecting a nerve pathway in a rat) to evaluate the role of that component.

Figure 6.9 shows the difference in performance for OTB with and without its heuristics (one simply subtracts the "without" curves in figures 6.7 and 6.8 from the "with" curves). Evidently, the advantage of tag repair heuristics is greatest before OTB has had much training. After fifty sentences the utility of tag repair heuristics is about four percentage points, and is independent of the level of training; suggesting that a constant number of words in the test sentences are misclassified by OTB, and, after fifty sentences, training evidently does nothing to fix the problem. If this is really the case, then Lehnert and McCarthy did the right thing to add special-case tag-repair heuristics instead of hoping that additional training would eventually correct OTB's classification performance.

What can we conclude from learning curves that are not parallel? If the curves are generated from an ablation experiment, then they should never actually cross, because this would mean that at some levels of training, a system does better without the ablated component than with it. If OTB's learning curves crossed it would mean tag repair heuristics actually hurt performance at some levels of training. If curves don't cross but aren't parallel then they might diverge or converge with the amount of training. OTB's curves converge (up to a point), so the advantage of tag repair heuristics evidently decreases with training. The other possibility—diverging curves—suggests some kind of reinforcing interaction between tag repair heuristics and other things OTB learns.

6.13   Assessing Effects with Classified Retesting: Failure Recovery in Phoenix

Software engineers, and knowledge engineers particularly, modify and test programs incrementally. This technique was used in the MYCIN project to assess the ramifications of changes to MYCIN's knowledge base. The MYCIN knowledge engineers "created an indexed library of test cases and facilities for running many cases in batch mode overnight" (Buchanan and Shortliffe, 1984, p. 156). In the morning, the knowledge engineers learned whether, as a result of modifications to its knowledge base, MYCIN was unable to solve problems it had previously solved successfully.

Here is a simple retesting tactic:

Procedure 6.5   Simple Retesting

i.   Run the system on all the problems in a corpus of test problems.

ii. The set *failures-1* contains the problems the system failed to solve correctly and the set *successes-1* contains the problems solved correctly.

iii. Modify the system.

iv. Run the system again on all the problems in the corpus.

v.   The set *failures-2* contains the problems the system failed to solve correctly and the set *successes-2* contains the problems solved correctly.

Every problem in the corpus can be classified by its membership in the four sets described in steps 6.5 and 6.5:

Continuing-successes are problems in *successes-1* and *successes-2*.

Continuing-failures are in both *failures-1* and *failures-2*.

New-successes are in *failures-1* and *successes-2*.

New-failures are in *successes-1* and *failures-2*.

Ideally, we want *new-successes* to include all the problems in *failures-1* and *new-failures* to be empty. In practice, a lot of training (and many iterations of the retesting procedure) might be required before a system solves all problems successfully, especially as modifications will often give rise to new failures.

If your dependent measure is not the number of correctly solved problems, but instead is a continuous variable such as run-time or, in Lehnert and McCarthy's example (1993), the percentage of words tagged correctly, then you should still try to construct sets analogous to *new-successes* and *new-failures*. Otherwise, you are apt to derive a relatively unenlightening result such as, "training increases the percentage of words tagged correctly." Results like this are sufficient for some purposes, but consider what happens if you design an experiment around an anticipated result that doesn't materialize. You scramble to explain the nonresult, which inevitably involves constructing retrospectively sets of problems on which performance was high and low. It is often easier to maintain these sets (or others with diagnostic power) during training.

One can better understand the effects of incremental program modifications by classifying test problems and tracking performance on problems in the individual classes. We call this *classified retesting*, or *blocking*, and illustrate it with a case study from Adele Howe's research with the Phoenix planner (Howe and Cohen, 1991). Often, a plan goes awry and *failure recovery methods* are applied to try to repair it or, in extreme cases, replace it. Initially, Phoenix had six failure recovery methods. Howe observed that they provided very expensive repairs to three kinds of failures. She designed two inexpensive methods specifically for these situations, anticipating that adding the new methods would reduce the overall cost of failure recovery. In the *six-method* condition Phoenix had its original six methods, and in the *eight-method* condition, it had these plus the new methods.

The result of the experiment was that the average cost of failure recovery did not change. A *t* test of the difference between mean costs in the two conditions turned up nothing. Fortunately, Howe classified failure recovery episodes by the type of failures that initiated them, and she computed average costs of failure recovery within each class. Thus, she was able to see that in the three problematic situations, the cost of failure recovery was reduced as expected, but in almost all the other situations, costs increased (figure 6.10). Because the increases offset the decreases, the new methods did not significantly change the mean cost of failure recovery.

These effects are surprising. The new methods somehow affected the costs of recovering from all failures, even though they were used only to repair failures *ner, prj*, and *ip*. Apparently, the new methods changed the state of Phoenix in such a way that it became more expensive to apply the old methods to other types of failures. Think of the new methods as cheap repairs to your car: They cost little and they fix the immediate problem, but they cause new problems that are expensive to fix later.

Although we have focused on changes in mean performance across classes, the classified retesting procedure applies to any difference measure. Perhaps the simplest is changes in the number of data in each class. For example, table 6.5 shows that Howe's treatment—adding two failure recovery methods to Phoenix—affected the relative frequencies of failures themselves. Some kinds of failures were more frequent in the six-method condition (specifically, *nrs, ccv, ccp*), some failures were roughly

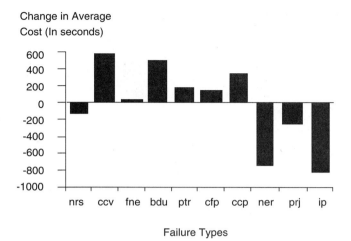

Figure 6.10 The addition of two new failure recovery methods decreased the cost of failure recovery in four failure situations but increased the cost in all other situations.

equally likely in both conditions (*ner, prj*), and some were more likely in the eight-method condition (*fne, bdu, ptr, cfp, ip*). Is this effect statistically significant? Any test of independence in a contingency table (e.g., the chi-square test, secs. 2.4.3, 6.8) will confirm that it is.

If the frequency of a particular type of failure, say *bdu*, is independent of the experimental condition, then the probability of a *bdu* failure should be the same in the six- and eight-method conditions. If failure types are indeed independent of experimental conditions, then the probability of a *bdu* failure in the six-method condition is:

$$\text{Pr}\,(Condition = \text{six-method} \times \text{Pr}\,(Failure = bdu).$$

In lieu of extrinsic knowledge about these probabilities, they are estimated from the marginal frequencies (margins, for short) of the contingency table. Because there are 1427 failures in the six-method condition and 2963 failures, total, the first

Table 6.5 Frequency of failures in the six-method and eight-method conditions.

	nrs	*ccv*	*fne*	*bdu*	*ptr*	*cfp*	*ccp*	*ner*	*prj*	*ip*	Total
Six-method	6	10	3	82	62	120	303	233	319	289	1427
Eight-method	3	5	7	122	76	143	232	246	321	381	1536
Total	9	15	10	204	138	263	535	479	640	670	2963

probability we want is $1427/2963 = .482$. Similarly, the probability of *bdu* failures is $204/2963 = .069$. If failure types are independent of conditions, then the probability of a *bdu* failure in the six-method condition is $.482 \times .069 = .033$, and the expected frequency of this event—given that there are 2963 failures, total—is $\hat{f}_{bdu} = .033 \times 2963 = 98.25$. A shortcut for this calculation is to multiply the row and column margins and divide by the total for the table: $(1427 \times 204)/2963 = 98.25$.

We test the hypothesis of independence by summing the deviations between these expected frequencies—derived by assuming independence—and the actual, observed frequencies. The χ^2 statistic sums

$$\frac{(f_{observed} - f_{expected})^2}{f_{expected}}$$

over the cells in a contingency table. Here, however, we take the opportunity to introduce a new but closely related test statistic:

$$G = 2 \sum_{cells} f_i \log \left(\frac{f_i}{\hat{f}_i} \right), \tag{6.3}$$

where f_i and $\hat{f}_i$ are the observed and expected frequencies, as defined previously. For table 6.5, the G statistic is:

$$G_H = 2 \left(6 \ln \left(\frac{6}{\frac{1427 \times 9}{2963}} \right) + 10 \ln \left(\frac{10}{\frac{1427 \times 15}{2963}} \right) + \ldots + 381 \ln \left(\frac{381}{\frac{1536 \times 670}{2963}} \right) \right)$$
$$= 34.166.$$

The subscript on the G statistic stands for "heterogeneity," or the extent to which the individual row or column proportions differ among themselves. For example, there are 50 percent more *bdu* failures in the eight-method condition, although *ccp* failures are more numerous in the six-method condition. In contingency tables, heterogeneity and nonindependence are the same and the statistic in equation 6.3 measures both. We add the subscript to G_H not because it is a different statistic but because we want to interpret it as the extent to which row or column proportions differ among themselves.

For a table with R rows and C columns, G is compared to a chi-square distribution with $(R-1)(C-1)$ degrees of freedom (in this case, nine). $G_H = 34.166$ is highly significant, which adds a statistical stamp of approval to what was obvious in table 6.5. Adding two new failure-recovery methods to Phoenix affected the relative frequencies of types of failures.

A more interesting question is which types of failures are most affected by the introduction of the two new methods. We asked the same question about the judges in Acker and Porter's experiment: We lacked a statistical method to identify judges who had different scoring criteria from the majority (section 6.8). Such a method would also give a statistical stamp of approval to the impression that *bdu* occurs less often than expected in the six-method condition and more often than expected in the eight-method condition (table 6.5). The method is simple. Expected frequencies are calculated as before, from the row and column margins, but we run *G* tests on individual columns (or rows) of the contingency table. Here is the test for the *bdu* failure:

$$G_{bdu} = 2 \left(82 \ln \left(\frac{82}{\frac{1427 \times 204}{2963}} \right) + 122 \ln \left(\frac{122}{\frac{1536 \times 204}{2963}} \right) \right) = 5.22.$$

Because there are only two entries in the *bdu* column, and they are constrained by the marginal sum 204, the column has only one degree of freedom. $G_{bdu} = 5.22$ is significant at the .05 level when compared to a chi-square distribution with one degree of freedom. Thus, the frequencies of the *bdu* failure in the six-method and eight-method conditions are significantly different than we'd expect by chance if *bdu* were independent of condition.

G statistics for all the failures types are shown in table 6.6. The frequencies of only three failures depend on the experimental condition: *ccp* occurs less often as a result of adding the new failure-recovery methods in the eight-method condition, but *bdu* and *ip* occur more often. Interestingly, the new failure-recovery methods were designed to provide cheaper recovery from three failures, including *ip*, and they did achieve this aim (see figure 6.10), but they also made *ip* occur more often.

Note that the individual statistics sum to G_H, the heterogeneity score for the entire table. This identity holds whenever expected frequencies are calculated from marginal frequencies, but not in general, as we'll see in section 7.6.

6.13.1   Expected Frequencies from Other Sources

Apparently, the incidence of failure *prj* is virtually identical in the six-method and eight-method conditions, so it appears to be unaffected by the new methods. This observation is more subtle than it seems at first, and it isn't obviously true. If you learned that Howe ran 100 trials in the six-method condition and 200 trials in the eight-method condition, would you still believe the frequency of *prj* is unaffected by the experimental condition? Let's hope not: The number of opportunities to fail is doubled in the eight-method condition but the number of failures remains constant, so the number of failures per trial is halved. Clearly we can't declare *prj* independent of the experimental condition on the basis of its equal distribution across conditions, alone. We must also decide that an equal distribution across conditions is what we'd

Table 6.6   *G* tests for all failures, using row and column margins as expectations.

Failure type	Six-method	Eight-method	G	Significance
nrs	6	3	1.25	n.s.
ccv	10	5	2.09	n.s.
fne	3	7	1.36	n.s.
bdu	82	122	5.22	$p < .05$
ptr	62	76	.58	n.s.
cfp	120	143	.68	n.s.
ccp	303	232	15.40	$p < .001$
ner	233	246	.04	n.s.
prj	319	321	.73	n.s.
ip	289	381	6.81	$p < .01$
Total (T)			34.166	

expect by chance. We have been content until now to use the marginal frequencies of the conditions as expectations. These are very roughly equal (1427 and 1536) so the *prj* column of table 6.5 contributes barely a sou to the overall G_H statistic calculated earlier. The implicit assumption of this approach must not be ignored. We are assuming that the Phoenix planner had as many opportunities to fail in the six-method condition as it did in the eight-method condition. Said differently, if we knew that one condition involved twice as many trials as another, we ought to use the *extrinsic frequencies* 1 and $\frac{1}{2}$ to derive expected frequencies rather than the intrinsic marginal frequencies 1427 and 1536.

In fact, Howe's experiment involved equal numbers of trials in the six-method and eight-method conditions. To derive a table of *G* statistics comparable to table 6.6, we substitute uniform extrinsic row frequencies for 1427 and 1536, then multiply the row and column margins and divide by the table total, as before. In practice, because the extrinsic row frequencies are uniform, we simply divide the column margin by the number of rows (two) to get expected frequencies. Thus, the test statistic for the *nrs* failure is

$$G_{nrs} = 2\left(6 \ln\left(\frac{6}{\frac{9}{2}}\right) + 3 \ln\left(\frac{3}{\frac{9}{2}}\right)\right) = 1.02.$$

This value is not significant; the occurrence of *nrs* failures is apparently independent of the experimental conditions. *G* statistics for the remaining failure types are shown in table 6.7.

Table 6.7   *G* tests for individual and pooled failure distributions.

Failure type	Six-method	Eight-method	G	Significance
nrs	6	3	1.02	n.s.
ccv	10	5	1.70	n.s.
fne	3	7	1.64	n.s.
bdu	82	122	7.89	$p < .01$
ptr	62	76	1.42	n.s.
cfp	120	143	2.01	n.s.
ccp	303	232	9.45	$p < .005$
ner	233	246	.035	n.s.
prj	319	321	.006	n.s.
ip	289	381	12.67	$p < .001$
Total (T)			38.177	
Pooled (P)	1427	1536	4.01	$p < .05$

Notice that we also report a *G* value for the marginal frequencies 1427 and 1536, testing the hypothesis that equal numbers of all types of failures occur in the six-method and eight-method conditions. Given uniform extrinsic row frequencies, the expected total frequency of failures in each condition is $(1427 + 1536)/2 = 1481.5$. The test statistic is

$$G_P = 2 \left(1427 \ln \left(\frac{1427}{1481.5} \right) + 1536 \ln \left(\frac{1536}{1481.5} \right) \right) = 4.01.$$

This test, like the others, has one degree of freedom because the two margins are constrained by the table total, 2963, so only one is free to vary. As it happens, we reject the null hypothesis that the total number of failures is independent of condition. Despite our earlier assertion that 1427 and 1536 are "very roughly equal," they are frequencies that are unlikely to occur by chance if failures are truly equally likely in the six- and eight-method conditions.

We have a new symbol, G_P, to denote a test of "pooled" or "packed" frequencies, in contrast to tests of individual failure frequencies such as G_{nrs}, or tests of the heterogeneity of frequencies. It's interesting (and no accident) that the sum of the individual *G* statistics in table 6.7, $G_T = 38.177$, is also the sum of the pooled and heterogeneity statistics, $G_P = 4.01$ and $G_H = 34.166$ (but for rounding errors). To grasp the meaning of these quantities, imagine sampling ten classrooms of students from biology, physics, and so on. Within each classroom you look at the number of males and females, and you also count the total number of males and females in all ten classrooms. G_P represents the deviation of these marginal male and female frequencies from an extrinsic expectation, such as equal proportions of males and females. G_H represents the summed effects of each classroom's deviation from the marginal totals. Thus, we describe the summed deviations of each classroom from an extrinsic expectation (G_T) in two steps: the deviation of the marginal totals from the extrinsic expectations, and the deviation of each classroom from the marginal totals.

G_P is far, far smaller than G_H, which means classroom proportions differ among themselves much more than the marginal totals differ from extrinsic expectations. A university administrator might boast that significantly more women than men attend classes ($G_P = 4.01$, $p < .05$), but he's papering over the fact that men and women don't attend all classes in these proportions: Some classes have many fewer women than men, while the pattern is reversed in other classes. In the following chapter we'll describe some powerful methods that exploit the relationship between G_H, G_P, and G_T.

6.13.2 Heterogeneity, Independence, and Goodness-of-Fit Tests

The analysis of contingency tables can be viewed from several perspectives, that is, we can give alternative interpretations to G statistics (or χ^2 statistics, for that matter). The heterogeneity interpretation of G goes like this: The null hypothesis is that the proportions in each row (or column) of a contingency table are identical, so G_H measures the extent to which the row proportions differ. This is a natural interpretation for experiments such as:

- We plan to test a system before and after modification, and we expect the proportion of errors on several classes of tasks to drop equally in the latter condition.

- We have several performance measures (e.g., number of correct diagnoses, number of correct therapy recommendations; see section 6.7), and we intend to roughen an important system parameter. We want to know whether roughening changes all performance measures equally.

Another interpretation of G is the familiar null hypothesis of independence, which is the natural interpretation for the following sorts of experiments:

- A dozen humans are recruited to judge the coherence of four kinds of explanations. We hope to show that the scores assigned to explanations are determined entirely by the quality of explanations, that is, the scores are independent of who assigns them.

- We want to know whether recall and precision are independent measures of performance. Assume we have scores for a system on a few dozen problems. If we divide the range of recall and precision into, say, five subranges, then we get a five-by-five contingency table, each cell of which contains the number of problems on which the system got a particular combination of recall and precision scores. An insignificant G statistic suggests that recall and precision are independent measures.

The heterogeneity and independence interpretations are very similar, and the expected frequencies for G are calculated from the row and column margins in both cases.

A third interpretation of G is called a *goodness-of-fit test*. Unlike the previous cases, the expected frequencies for a goodness of fit test may be specified or partly specified by an extrinsic distribution. Earlier, we constrained a single marginal distribution to be uniform. We can also constrain both marginal distributions, or even the cell contents themselves, as the following examples show:

- We run a system on equal numbers of five theorem-proving tasks (so the marginal distribution for tasks is uniform). In half the trials we leave out an important axiom from the task specification, and in the remaining trials we add 10, 20, 30, 40, or 50 superfluous axioms with equal probability. Hence the marginal distribution for available information is (.5, .1, .1, .1, .1, .1). The cells of this five-by-six contingency table contain the number of theorem-proving tasks that the system completes within some time limit.

- After an experiment, we observe that the latency or length of time between failures is not uniform, in fact it appears to be a symmetric distribution, perhaps binomial. We divide the range of latencies into, say, ten bins and construct a contingency table with ten columns and a single row. The cells contain the latencies we observed in our experiment. The expected frequencies that we need to calculate G come directly from a binomial distribution with $N = 10$ and $p = .5$.

In the first example we have extrinsic expectations for row and column marginal frequencies, in the second we have expectations for each cell frequency. Both test how well observed data fit extrinsic distributions, which is why they're called goodness-of-fit tests.

All of these tests can be run with G and χ^2 statistics, but χ^2 is not quite additive, so the decomposition of contingency tables is easier with G tests. All these tests can be extended to multiple factors, to contingency tables with more than two dimensions. The patterns of dependency in three-way and higher tables provide for a richer variety of hypotheses; for example, we can test whether two factors are independent provided a third is not allowed to vary. Multiway tables are discussed in the following chapter.

Finally, let us note that heterogeneity, independence, and goodness-of-fit can be tested in other ways. If you have continuous data and you don't want to bin it, then you can test independence by testing whether a correlation coefficient is equal to zero (secs. 4.5, 5.3.3). This is probably a preferable way to test the independence of recall and precision. Goodness-of-fit to continuous distributions is commonly tested with the Kolmogorov procedure, which is described in most statistics textbooks (e.g., Sokal and Rohlf, 1981).

6.14   Diminishing Returns and Overfitting in Retesting

When assessing performance during retesting, watch out for two phenomena. One is *diminishing returns*, that is, the first modifications to a system improve performance a lot, while later modifications result in successively smaller improvements. The *marginal utility* of modifications decreases. This phenomenon is especially apparent in knowledge-based systems because much of their knowledge is for relatively rare special cases. Perhaps 80 percent of the inferential work of a knowledge-based system is done by 20 percent of the knowledge; once this core knowledge is in place, the marginal utility of adding another piece of knowledge is quite small. We saw this effect in Lehnert and McCarthy's learning curves. Ultimately, adding one piece of knowledge might add just one problem to *new-successes*, and it might add one or more problems to *new-failures*.

The second phenomenon is called *overfitting*. If you improve a system until it can solve correctly every problem in a corpus, then you will probably "tune" your system to the corpus so its performance on problems outside the corpus actually begins to decrease. Many corpora contain errors or noise masquerading as structure, so as algorithms learn to solve all the problems in such a corpus, they learn errorful things that hurt performance on problems outside the corpus. If knowledge is added to a system by hand and is known to be correct, then one might suppose overfitting cannot happen. Knowledge engineers rarely anticipate all the situations in which knowledge might be applied, however, and it is quite common to add knowledge to fix a very specific problem, only to find that it leads to wrong conclusions in new situations.

Lynette Hirschman designed an experiment to disclose overfitting if it occurs. The design, illustrated in figure 6.11, is a variant on the simple retesting design. A second corpus has been added with the stipulation that the system developer cannot see the *contents* of the sets *successes-1B, failures-1B,* and so on, but he or she is told the cardinality of these sets. Overfitting shows up as small improvements on corpus *A* at the expense of performance on corpus *B*. For example, if both *new-successes-1A* and *new-failures-1B* grow slowly, and *new-successes-1B* doesn't grow, then we have overfitting.

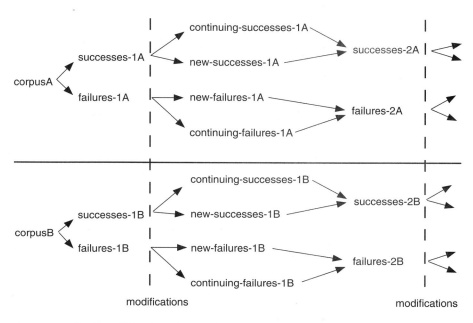

Figure 6.11   Design of Hirschman's experiment.

6.15   Conclusion

A batch of trials provides a snapshot of the performance of a program at a single point in its development. The simplest single-batch experiment involves a single measure of performance and a single factor; for example, we might test whether the recall performance of a message understanding system depends on whether it processes messages syntactically or semantically. We have encountered several tactics that improve on this basic scheme.

■ If you intend to assess the performance of your system by comparing it to standards, use several. The standards should have different levels of a factor that you can interpret as an explanation of your program's performance. For example, you will recall from chapter 3 that the MYCIN research team compared the program to four levels of medical expertise, from medical student to internationally recognized experts. Acker and Porter used the same tactic—and three standards—to show that an organizing principle (called viewpoints) could enhance the judged coherence of explanations.

- Try to find bracketing standards. Your program's anticipated performance should exceed at least one standard and fall short of another.

- Many AI experiments collect just one performance measure, such as run time or the number of correct responses. This is a shame because compared to the overall cost of experiments, the marginal cost of additional performance measures is nil. If you intend to collect relatively few measures, however, make sure they are not redundant. One tactic is to run a pilot experiment, collect measures, and calculate their correlation. If measures are highly correlated, you might not need all of them. Another tactic is to collect opponent measures such as recall and precision in the MUC-3 study.

- Even a single measure of performance can yield quite a lot of information, if you look beyond its mean. For example, the variance of performance in Acker and Porter's experiment showed that although their program had roughly the same mean performance as human experts, it didn't perform as consistently. Similarly, a chi-square test of the distribution of judges' score showed that judges had different scoring biases.

- Although many experiments collect information just once at the end of a trial, some collect information throughout the trial in the form of execution traces. We discuss the analysis of execution traces in sections 7.5 and 7.6.

- If you want to compare in a post-hoc manner the performance of many systems, or the performance of one system in many conditions, you will have to choose between experimentwise and per-comparison errors. We discussed two tactics for dealing with the problem. First, run an analysis of variance and make unconservative (e.g., LSD) comparisons only if the analysis is significant. Second, run every comparison twice, with unconservative and conservative procedures, and make careful individual decisions about the comparisons that are significant by one criterion but not the other, recognizing that not all comparisons are equally meaningful.

- Recognize, too, that the statistically conservative test might not be the scientifically conservative one, particularly if the goal of the experiment is to not reject the null hypothesis. The scientifically conservative conclusion of Acker and Porter's study is that their program might be different from human experts, but a statistically conservative test makes it difficult to find this difference.

- Use the criterion differential to summarize the number of pairwise comparisons that might be spurious given less conservative tests.

- Roughening experiments involve degrading something that is hypothesized to affect performance, measuring performance at several levels. Clancey and Cooper degraded an aspect of MYCIN's inference abilities, and Acker and Porter degraded the output of their program by adding random facts. Looking at several levels of roughening is, of course, a good idea.

■ Cross-validation makes efficient use of training and test items. A system can be trained on almost all items and tested on all items, and still we can tell how the system performs on items it didn't encounter during training.

■ An incremental version of cross-validation can be used to construct learning curves.

■ It is sometimes informative to fit a line to the slowly increasing part of a learning curve and extrapolate how many more training instances will be required to achieve a particular level of performance. A bootstrap test of the slope of the line might be used to decide whether it is effectively flat. Alternatively, one might test a pair of points on learning curves with a *t* test to see whether one is more than, say, 1 percent higher than another. If not, by this criterion one might declare the curve "flat."

■ To explain why the learning curve flattens out at a particular point, it is usually necessary to collect data in addition to the performance measure.

■ Classified retesting provides some such data. When applied repeatedly, it produces separate learning curves for classes of test items. The characteristics of test items used to construct classes should help explain observed differences in the learning curves. To display a single iteration of classified retesting, show positive and negative difference scores by class as in figure 6.10.

■ In addition to raw and mean difference scores, it is often informative to look at how class-membership changes in the classified retesting procedure. The frequency distribution over classes will often change.

■ Overfitting is a common problem in training studies. Hirschman's experiment is one way to disclose overfitting during knowledge engineering.

Appendix: Analysis of Variance and Contrast Analysis

6A.1   One-Way Analysis of Variance

Imagine going to a school and drawing five students from each of three classrooms. Each takes a quiz, the results of which are shown in table 6A.1. The means and

Table 6A.1   Quiz scores for five students in three classes.

	Class 1	Class 2	Class 3
	14.9	11.1	5.7
	15.2	9.5	6.6
	17.9	10.9	6.7
	15.6	11.7	6.8
	10.7	11.8	6.9
$\bar{x}$	14.86	11	6.54
s^2	6.812	.85	.233

variances of the scores for each classroom are shown in table 6A.1; for instance, the mean score for classroom 1 is $\bar{x}_1 = 14.86$. Individual scores are denoted $x_{j,k}$ where j is a classroom and k a student. The grand mean and variance of all the scores are $\bar{x}_G = 10.8$ and $s_G^2 = 14.638$, respectively.

Each score in table 6A.1 can be represented as a sum of two numbers, the grand mean and a random component. Thus, the first score in classroom 1 is

$$x_{1,1} = \bar{x}_G + e_{1,1} = 10.8 + 4.1 = 14.9.$$

Another representation of the same information focuses on the *deviation* of a score from the grand mean:

$$e_{j,k} = (x_{j,k} - \bar{x}_G).$$

The deviation can itself be expressed as a sum of two numbers, the deviation of $x_{j,k}$ from its class mean $\bar{x}_j$, and the deviation of the class mean from the grand mean:

$$e_{j,k} = (x_{j,k} - \bar{x}_j) + (\bar{x}_j - \bar{x}_G).$$

The first deviation, $(x_{j,k} - \bar{x}_j)$, is called the *within-group component* and the second, $(\bar{x}_j - \bar{x}_G)$, is the *between-group component*.

The total deviation of the first score in classroom 1 from the grand mean is:

$$e_{1,1} = (14.9 - 14.86) + (14.86 - 10.8) = .04 + 4.06 = 4.1.$$

Interestingly, the greater part of $e_{1,1}$ is the between-group component; in fact, the within-group component is almost zero. In other words, the deviation of a score from its group mean is smaller than the deviation of the group mean from the grand mean. An extreme version of this pattern is illustrated in table 6A.2, which shows that every student in a classroom performs identically, while the classes themselves

Table 6A.2   No within-group variance.

	Class 1	Class 2	Class 3
	15	11	6
	15	11	6
	15	11	6
	15	11	6
	15	11	6
$\overline{x}$	15	11	6
s^2	0	0	0

Table 6A.3   No between-group variance.

	Class 1	Class 2	Class 3
	17	11	22
	26	13	14
	9	18	12
	11	18	8
	12	15	19
$\overline{x}$	15	15	15
s^2	46.5	9.5	31.0

perform differently. Table 6A.2 shows a clear effect, unobscured by individual differences within a classroom, of being in one classroom or another, and it suggests a rule:

If group membership influences scores, then the between-group components of deviations will be larger than the within-group components.

An equally extreme example has unequal scores within a group but equal group means, as shown in table 6A.3. Although students in each classroom vary, the classrooms are equal overall—there is no effect of classroom membership. This example, too, suggests a rule:

If group membership has little effect on scores, then the between-group components will be no larger than the within-group components.

The overriding impression one gets from the original classroom data in table 6A.1 is that the within-group components are small relative to the between-group components.

Most of the former are in the range -1.0 to 1.0, whereas the latter are 4.06, .2, and -4.26, respectively. These data resemble table 6A.2, which shows an effect of classroom, more than table 6A.3, which doesn't.

In sum, one can claim an effect of a factor such as classroom membership if between-group components are larger than within-group components. This is the fundamental idea of analysis of variance. We turn now to a more formal description of analysis of variance.[14]

Foundation of One-Way Analysis of Variance

The analysis of variance is aptly named: It decomposes the variance in data and shows how much of it is due to random variations and how much is due to the influence of a factor. Consider again the deviation of a score from its grand mean: $e_{j,k} = (x_{j,k} - \overline{x}_G)$. Now, square each deviation, sum the squares, and divide by the total number of items in all the groups. This yields the sample grand variance:

$$s_G^2 = \frac{\sum_j \sum_k (x_{j,k} - \overline{x}_G)^2}{N - 1} = \frac{SS_{total}}{df_{total}}.$$

The numerator is called the *total sum of squares* and represents the sum of the squared deviations of each data item from the grand mean; the denominator is called the *total degrees of freedom*.

Having seen that an individual deviation has two components, it will come as no surprise that the sample variance also has two components. Because

$$(x_{j,k} - \overline{x}_G) = (x_{j,k} - \overline{x}_j) + (\overline{x}_j - \overline{x}_G),$$

it follows that

$$\sum_j \sum_k (x_{j,k} - \overline{x}_G)^2 = \sum_j \sum_k (x_{j,k} - \overline{x}_j)^2 + \sum_j \sum_k (\overline{x}_j - \overline{x}_G)^2$$

$$+ \left(2 \sum_j \sum_k (x_{j,k} - \overline{x}_j) \sum_j \sum_k (\overline{x}_j - \overline{x}_G) \right).$$

The last term equals zero because if you successively subtract the mean of a group from each item in the group, the sum of the differences is zero.

---

14. We will consider two- and three-factor analysis of variance in the following chapter, confining ourselves here to single-factor designs.

Thus the sample variance (or, rather, its numerator, SS_{total}) is decomposed into two sums of squared deviations:

$$SS_{total} = SS_{between} + SS_{within};$$ (6A.1)

$$SS_{within} = \sum_j \sum_k (x_{j,k} - \overline{x}_j)^2;$$ (6A.2)

$$SS_{between} = \sum_j n_j (\overline{x}_j - \overline{x}_G)^2.$$ (6A.3)

Here, n_j denotes the number of items in group j. Because the between-group component of each item in a group is a constant (i.e., $\overline{x}_j - \overline{x}_G$), multiplying by n_j is equivalent to summing this constant over all members of a group. If the groups are of equal size, n may be moved outside the sum, of course.

Dividing these sums of squares by their degrees of freedom gives us "mean square" deviations, that is, variances:

$$MS_{between} = \frac{SS_{between}}{df_{between}} = \frac{\sum_j n_j (\overline{x}_j - \overline{x}_G)^2}{j - 1};$$ (6A.4)

$$MS_{within} = \frac{SS_{within}}{df_{within}} = \frac{\sum_j \sum_k (x_{j,k} - \overline{x}_j)^2}{N - j}.$$ (6A.5)

$MS_{between}$ or "mean squares between," has $j - 1$ degrees of freedom, where j is the number of groups. This is because the mean of the group means is the the grand mean, so only $j - 1$ group means are free to vary, given the grand mean. Similarly, the items within a group are constrained by the group mean, so only $n_i - 1$ items in the ith group are free to vary. It follows that MS_{within}, or "mean squares within," has $\sum_{i=1}^{j} (n_i - 1)$ degrees of freedom, which is equal to $N - j$.

Hypothesis Testing with One-Way Analysis of Variance

The null hypothesis is that population group means are equal. Returning to our previous example,

H_0: $\mu_{classroom1} = \mu_{classroom2} = \mu_{classroom3}$

H_1: Not H_0

Note that the alternative hypothesis does not specify which means are larger or smaller, only that they are not all equal. In this sense the alternative hypothesis for a one-way analysis of variance is like that for a two-tailed t test.

MS_{within} is an unbiased estimate of the population variance, and remarkably, its value does not depend on whether the null hypothesis is true. To convince yourself of this, imagine adding 1000 to each item in one of the groups in table 6A.1, say, classroom 1. The resulting table would certainly suggest a strong effect of being in classroom 1, yet the variance of scores in classroom 1 wouldn't change. (Adding a constant to each item in a distribution doesn't change its variance.) By the same logic, MS_{within} wouldn't change, either. By adding constants to groups, it's possible to introduce or remove effects, rendering H_0 true or false, without ever changing MS_{within}.

If H_0 is true, then $MS_{between}$ also is an unbiased estimate of population variance because there is no reason for the group means to deviate from the grand mean more than individual scores deviate from their group means. Thus, H_0 implies $MS_{between} = MS_{within}$. If H_0 is false, however, $MS_{between}$ will be large relative to MS_{within}. The ratio

$$F = \frac{MS_{between}}{MS_{within}}$$

has an expected value of 1.0 under the null hypothesis, but will exceed 1.0 if the null hypothesis is false. If the sampling distribution of F under H_0 was known, we could ask, "What is the probability of obtaining a particular value of F by chance if H_0 is true?" Small probabilities speak against H_0 as always. Note that $MS_{between}$ and MS_{within} are variances—sums of squares divided by degrees of freedom—so F is a ratio of variances, and under H_0 these variances are equal. The desired sampling distribution is therefore the distribution of the ratio of two variances under the assumption that they are equal. This distribution is known. It's called F in honor of R. A. Fisher, who invented the analysis of variance. Actually, there isn't one F distribution but many, each indexed by two parameters, the degrees of freedom for $MS_{between}$ and MS_{within}.

To test the hypothesis that several group means are equal, one first calculates $SS_{between}$ and SS_{within}, then divides these by $j - 1$ and $N - j$, respectively, to get $MS_{between}$ and MS_{within}, as shown in equations 6A.2 to 6A.5. Next, one calculates F and compares it to the F distribution with $j - 1$ and $N - j$ degrees of freedom to find the probability of obtaining a value greater than or equal to F by chance under the null hypothesis. If the probability is low (e.g., $p < .05$) the null hypothesis is rejected.

From the data in table 6A.1, sums of squares are as follows:

$$SS_{between} = 5 \times ((14.86 - 10.8)^2 + (11.0 - 10.8)^2 + (6.54 - 10.8)^2)) = 173.3;$$

$$SS_{within} = (14.9 - 14.86)^2 + \ldots + (10.7 - 14.86)^2 + \ldots + (11.1 - 11.0)^2 + \ldots$$
$$\ldots + (6.9 - 6.54)^2 = 31.5.$$

Mean squares are:

$$MS_{between} = \frac{SS_{between}}{j-1} = \frac{173.3}{2} = 86.7;$$

$$MS_{within} = \frac{SS_{within}}{N-j} = \frac{31.5}{12} = 2.6.$$

Finally, $F = 86.7/2.6 = 32.97$. The $\alpha = .05$ critical value for an F distribution with 2 and 12 degrees of freedom is 3.89. This is clearly exceeded by $F = 32.97$, so the null hypothesis—that the classrooms have equal mean scores—can be rejected.

When you run an analysis of variance in a statistics package, you will usually find the results printed in a characteristic "tableau." Here is the tableau for the classroom data in table 6A.1:

Source	df	Sum of squares	Mean square	F	p value
Between	2	173.3	86.7	32.97	$p \leq .0001$
Within	14	31.5	2.6		
Total	16	204.9			

The first column lists the sources of variance in the data: between-group variance, within-group variance, and total variance. Remember that the one-factor analysis of variance partitions the total variance into two parts, which is why the total sum of squared deviations ($SS_{total} = 204.9$) is itself the sum of squared deviations between groups ($SS_{between} = 173.3$) plus the sum of squared deviations within groups ($SS_{within} = 31.5$). Dividing the sums of squares by their degrees of freedom yields mean squares and an F ratio. The probability of attaining such a large value of F under H_0 is nearly zero ($p \leq .0001$).

6A.2   Contrasts, or Comparisons Revisited

Chapter 6 introduced two methods for comparing pairs of means, the Scheffé and LSD tests. Here we generalize the notion of a comparison to weighted sums of several means. For instance, a researcher might wish to compare the mean of one classroom with the average of the means of two others. This more general kind of comparison is called a *contrast*. Contrasts pose the same difficulties as ordinary comparisons of means: The probability that a single contrast is spurious is, say $\alpha_c = .05$, but running several contrasts elevates the experimentwise probability that at least one is spurious (i.e., $\alpha_e > .05$). So as with ordinary comparisons, it's worth running contrasts both with conservative tests that protect experimentwise error, such as the Scheffé test, and with less stringent t tests. But this is getting ahead of the story; first let's see how to construct contrasts.

Recall Acker and Porter's experiment, in which they compared textual explanations called *viewpoints* from their View Retriever system with viewpoints from textbooks and with degraded and random viewpoints. Suppose Acker and Porter had run two contrasts:

C_1: View Retriever viewpoints with textbook viewpoints.

C_2: Combined textbook and View Retriever viewpoints with combined degraded and random viewpoints.

If the View Retriever works as anticipated, then its viewpoints should be roughly equal to the textbook viewpoints (C_1). And textbook and View Retriever viewpoints combined should be better than degraded and random viewpoints combined (C_2). One might prefer the second comparison to be between View Retriever viewpoints and combined degraded and random viewpoints, leaving textbook viewpoints out of the picture. As we will see shortly, this contrast is not independent of the first. Let $\bar{x}_T, \bar{x}_V$, $\bar{x}_D$, and $\bar{x}_R$ denote the mean coherence scores for textbook, View Retriever, degraded and random viewpoints, respectively. Then, the contrasts between the means can be expressed as weighted sums. For example, contrast C_1 is:

$$C_1 = (1)\bar{x}_T + (-1)\bar{x}_V + (0)\bar{x}_D + (0)\bar{x}_R$$

and contrast C_2 is:

$$C_2 = (.5)\bar{x}_T + (.5)\bar{x}_V + (-.5)\bar{x}_D + (-.5)\bar{x}_R.$$

Note that in these contrasts (in fact, in all contrasts) the weights on the means sum to zero.

The two-sample t test is of course a contrast; in fact, C_1 represents a t test between textbook and View Retriever viewpoints. Recall that the t statistic, like other test statistics, has a characteristic form:

$$t = \frac{\text{difference of sample means}}{\text{standard error of the difference of sample means}}.$$

The only impediment to generalizing the t test to include both C_1 and C_2 is, as always, finding the appropriate standard error term. Because a contrast is a weighted sum, the standard error of a contrast is related to the variance of a weighted sum. For a sum

$$C = w_1\bar{x}_1 + w_2\bar{x}_2 + \cdots + w_j\bar{x}_j$$

the variance of C is given by

$$\sigma_C^2 = w_1^2\sigma_{x_1}^2 + w_2^2\sigma_{x_2}^2 + \cdots + w_j^2\sigma_{x_j}^2.$$

We generally do not know all these parametric variances, but assuming the group means are for independent, random samples drawn from populations with a common mean μ, we can estimate the variance of a contrast from sample variances:

$$\hat{\sigma}_C^2 = \sum_{i=1}^{j} w_i^2 s_{x_i}^2.$$

Further assuming the groups share a common population variance, and recalling that the definition of MS_{within} implies $s_{x_i}^2 = MS_{within}/n_i$, we can express $\hat{\sigma}_C^2$ as:

$$\hat{\sigma}_C^2 = MS_{within} \sum_{i=1}^{j} \frac{w_i^2}{n_i}. \tag{6A.6}$$

Now, a contrast can be tested with a conventional t test:

$$t = \frac{C}{\sqrt{\hat{\sigma}_C^2}} = \frac{C}{\sqrt{MS_{within} \sum_i \frac{w_i^2}{n_i}}}. \tag{6A.7}$$

For a simple two-group contrast, such as the comparison between textbook and View Retriever viewpoints, this formula is identical to the two-sample t test:

$$t = \frac{C_1}{\sqrt{\hat{\sigma}_{C_1}^2}} = \frac{(1)\bar{x}_T + (-1)\bar{x}_V + (0)\bar{x}_D + (0)\bar{x}_R}{\sqrt{\hat{\sigma}_{C_1}^2}}$$

$$= \frac{\bar{x}_T - \bar{x}_V}{\sqrt{MS_{within} \sum_i \frac{w_i^2}{n_i}}}$$

$$= \frac{\bar{x}_T - \bar{x}_V}{\sqrt{MS_{within} \left(\frac{1}{n_T} + \frac{1}{n_V} \right)}}.$$

The number of degrees of freedom for the test is $N - j$, which in this case is $n_T + n_V - 2$, just as in the two-sample t test. Other contrasts, such as C_2 are equally straightforward:

$$t = \frac{C_2}{\sqrt{\hat{\sigma}_{C_2}^2}} = \frac{.5\bar{x}_T + .5\bar{x}_V - .5\bar{x}_D - .5\bar{x}_R}{\hat{\sigma}_{C_2}^2}$$

$$= \frac{\frac{\bar{x}_T + \bar{x}_V}{2} - \frac{\bar{x}_D + \bar{x}_R}{2}}{\sqrt{MS_{within} \left(\frac{.25}{n_T} + \frac{.25}{n_V} + \frac{.25}{n_D} + \frac{.25}{n_R} \right)}}.$$

For Acker and Porter's data, t evaluates to

$$t = \frac{\frac{4.241+3.754}{2} - \frac{2.847+2.627}{2}}{\sqrt{1.811 \left(\frac{.25}{29} + \frac{.25}{118} + \frac{.25}{59} + \frac{.25}{59} \right)}} = 6.75, \tag{6A.8}$$

with $N = (29 + 118 + 59 + 59) - 4 = 261$ degrees of freedom. This value of t is highly significant: the combined coherence scores for textbook and View Retriever viewpoints are significantly different than the combined scores for degraded and random viewpoints.

Square equation 6A.7 generalizes the LSD test for a pair of means (introduced in equation 6.2) to any contrast:

$$F_{LSD} = t^2 = \frac{C^2}{\hat{\sigma}_C^2} = \frac{C^2}{MS_{within} \sum_i \frac{w_i^2}{n_i}}. \tag{6A.9}$$

Similarly, the Scheffé test for any contrast is

$$F_S = \frac{C^2}{\hat{\sigma}_C^2 (j - 1)} = \frac{C^2}{MS_{within} \sum_i \frac{w_i^2}{n_i}(j - 1)}, \tag{6A.10}$$

where j is the total number of groups; four in Acker and Porter's experiment. Thus one can run conservative Scheffé tests and less stringent LSD tests for any contrast, not only pairs of means.

The Scheffé test guards against spurious contrasts given the "worst case scenario" in which all possible contrasts are pursued. As such, it is very conservative, but not unrealistically so, because often one doesn't know which contrasts are interesting until one sees the data. That's why these contrasts are called *unplanned comparisons*. If you plan before running your experiment to compare particular groups, however, you'd do it directly and save yourself the relatively uninformative effort of the analysis of variance. Analysis of variance precedes unplanned comparisons but is redundant given planned comparisons. This is the orthodox view.

The image evoked by "planned comparisons" is one of a pious researcher who would no sooner peek at data than inside the wrapping of his Christmas presents. We imagine this saintly individual posting a letter to the local newspaper, announcing exactly which comparisons will be drawn once the experiment has been run and asking for volunteers to witness that these and no others are conducted. In practice, researchers run all sorts of comparisons after looking at their data, including so-called planned comparisons. Purists pretend to be shocked because, if you can look at your data first, you can usually spot some comparisons that are apt to be significant. Purists say planned comparisons are like call-pocket pool: You must identify the pocket before the ball falls into it; how else can one control for lucky shots?

A more realistic interpretation of planned comparisons is this: Only some subsets of comparisons are independent, so if you want your conclusions to be independent, you had better plan your comparisons. Sets of independent contrasts are called *orthogonal contrasts*.

Imagine three numbers $a = 6$, $b = 9$, and $c = 27$ and their differences, which for concreteness are $c - b = 18$, $b - a = 3$, and $c - a = 21$. Notice that two differences constrain the third—you can always add two equations, or subtract one from another, to get the third. If a, b, and c are group means, then the difference between one pair of means is independent of the other pairwise differences, but as soon as you know one difference, the remaining two are not independent of each other. Suppose your first comparison is between b and a, and you find $b - a = 3$. This information tells you nothing about the other pairwise differences, so your first pairwise comparison is independent of any other. Your second pairwise comparison will determine the third, however, so the second comparison is not independent of any other. In general, for j groups, only $j - 1$ comparisons can be mutually independent.

Fortunately, for groups of equal size there is a simple test of orthogonality. Unequal group sizes complicate matters, but are discussed in (Keppel, 1973). Two comparisons are orthogonal if the products of their coefficients sum to zero:

$$\sum_j w_{1j} w_{2j} = 0.$$

For example, here are three mutually orthogonal comparisons of four means:

$$C_1 : (1)\overline{x}_1 + (-1)\overline{x}_2 + (0)\overline{x}_3 + (0)\overline{x}_4;$$

$$C_2 : (0)\overline{x}_1 + (0)\overline{x}_2 + (1)\overline{x}_3 + (-1)\overline{x}_4;$$

$$C_3 : (.5)\overline{x}_1 + (.5)\overline{x}_2 + (-.5)\overline{x}_3 + (-.5)\overline{x}_4.$$

The first and second comparison are orthogonal because

$$\sum_j w_{1j} w_{2j} = (1 \cdot 0) + (-1 \cdot 0) + (0 \cdot 1) + (0 \cdot -1) = 0.$$

You can work out the other sums to convince yourself that all pairs of comparisons are orthogonal.

Orthogonal contrasts can be tested for significance with the formula given earlier:

$$F = \frac{C^2}{\hat{\sigma}_C^2} = \frac{C^2}{MS_{within} \sum_{i=1}^{j} \frac{w_i^2}{n_i}}.$$

There is nothing wrong with formulating the test this way, but it obscures a very elegant identity: The sums of squares for orthogonal comparisons themselves sum to $SS_{between}$. This means that a significant effect of a factor (i.e., a significant ratio $F = MS_{between}/MS_{within}$) can be broken down into orthogonal, one degree of freedom components, each of which can be tested for significance. Whereas the *omnibus F* statistic assesses whether all group means are equal, orthogonal contrast *F* tests decompose the omnibus result into particular group comparisons.

Procedurally, one first finds the sum of squares for a contrast. The formula is

$$SS_C = \frac{C^2}{\sum_{i=1}^{j} \frac{w_i^2}{n_i}}.$$

Next, one transforms SS_C into a mean square, MS_C, by dividing by the number of degrees of freedom for the contrast. In fact, contrasts always have one degree of freedom, so $SS_C = MS_C$. Finally, one tests the significance of the comparison with an *F* test:

$$F = \frac{MS_C}{MS_{within}}. \tag{6A.11}$$

Let's run through these steps with the classroom data presented in table 6A.1. The classroom means were $\bar{x}_1 = 14.86$, $\bar{x}_2 = 11.0$, and $\bar{x}_3 = 6.54$ and the analysis of variance tableau was:

Source	df	Sum of squares	Mean square	F	p value
Between	2	173.3	86.7	32.97	p = .0001
Within	12	31.5	2.6		
Total	14	204.9			

Here are two orthogonal comparisons, classroom 1 against classroom 2, and classroom 3 against the average of classrooms 1 and 2:

$C_1 : (1)\bar{x}_1 + (-1)\bar{x}_2 + (0)\bar{x}_3$;

$C_2 : (.5)\bar{x}_1 + (.5)\bar{x}_2 + (-1)\bar{x}_3$.

The sums of squares for these comparisons are:

$$SS_{C1} = \frac{C_1^2}{\sum_i \frac{w_i^2}{n_i}} = \frac{(14.86 - 11.0)^2}{\frac{1}{5} + \frac{1}{5}} = \frac{14.9}{.4} = 37.25;$$

$$SS_{C2} = \frac{C_2^2}{\sum_i \frac{w_i^2}{n_i}} = \frac{\left(\frac{(14.86+11.0)}{2} - 6.54\right)^2}{\frac{.25}{5} + \frac{.25}{5} + \frac{1}{5}} = \frac{40.83}{.3} = 136.1.$$

Table 6A.4   Analysis of variance for the classroom data including orthogonal comparisons. (All the F statistics are significant.)

Source	df	Sum of squares	Mean square	F
Between	2	173.3	86.7	32.97*
C_1	1	37.25	37.25	14.33*
C_2	1	136.1	136.1	52.35*
Within	12	31.5	2.6	
Total	14	37.4		

These sums of squares have one degree of freedom each, so $MS_{C1} = SS_{C1}/1 = SS_{C1}$ and likewise for $MS_{C2} = SS_{C2}$. Now run F tests:

$$F_{C1} = \frac{MS_{C1}}{MS_{within}} = \frac{37.25}{2.6} = 14.33;$$

$$F_{C2} = \frac{MS_{C2}}{MS_{within}} = \frac{136.1}{2.6} = 52.35.$$

You can look up each of these values in a table of F distributions; the degrees of freedom are 1 (for the comparison) and 12 (for MS_{within}). Both F values are highly significant, so both null hypotheses fail. Classrooms 1 and 2 perform differently, and classroom 3 performs less well than the average of classrooms 1 and 2 (C_2). These analyses are added to the tableau for the analysis of variance shown in table 6A.4.

Note that $SS_{between}$ from the original analysis of variance is the sum of the sums of squares for the orthogonal comparisons:

$$SS_{between} = SS_{C1} + SS_{C2} = 37.25 + 136.1 = 173.35.$$

The larger of the two effects is C_2. It seems classrooms 1 and 2 differ more from classroom 3 than they differ from each other.

We could also run orthogonal contrasts on Acker and Porter's data, specifying $j - 1 = 3$ orthogonal comparisons, then computing sums of squares and F statistics for each. The four groups are not equal in size (ranging from 29 to 118), however, so the sums of squares for the comparisons will not total $SS_{between}$.

The questions answered by orthogonal contrasts are much more focused than those answered by analysis of variance alone. Some authors, such as Rosenthal and Rosnow (1985), argue that the omnibus F test is uninformative and should give way to *contrast analysis* in most settings. In fact, you aren't limited to orthogonal contrasts, they just decompose variance into independent components, which is often appealing. Nothing stops you from running nonorthogonal contrasts; just remember that your results aren't independent. Rosenthal and Rosnow draw hardly any distinction between orthogonal and nonorthogonal contrasts, and they recommend the same tests for both. This is not an orthodox view, however. Many authors assume that if contrasts aren't planned in advance of the experiment as orthogonal tests, then they must be exhaustive comparisons of the kind described in section 6.4 and they should be run with Scheffé tests or something else that preserves α_e. In light of the vast middle ground of nonorthogonal, nonexhaustive contrasts, however, Rosenthal and Rosnow's position makes a lot of sense: it's perfectly valid to run a few nonorthogonal comparisons with the F test in equation 6A.11, which is really just an LSD test.

7   Explaining Performance: Interactions and Dependencies

It is good to demonstrate performance, but it is even better to explain performance. Why, for example, does a vision-based navigation system perform well in the lab but poorly outdoors? Why does a machine learning algorithm perform well on some standard datasets but not others? Why are some planning problems particularly difficult to solve? Rarely is behavior explained by a single factor. Consider, for example, MYCIN's expert level of therapy recommendations, popularly attributed to its medical knowledge. By all indications, MYCIN's knowledge was the primary factor affecting its performance, but it was not the only one: The task itself was forgiving in the sense that MYCIN could get the therapy right even when its diagnosis was wrong; and the accuracy of MYCIN's certainty factors also had a small influence on diagnosis and therapy recommendations (section 6.7). A key question is whether these factors interact. Independent one-factor experiments could demonstrate the influence of more or less forgiving tasks and more or less accurate certainty factors; but a pair of one-factor experiments will not show, for example, that the accuracy of certainty factors has a much bigger influence in unforgiving cases than in forgiving ones. To demonstrate *interaction effects* such as this one, we must run two-factor or multifactor experiments.

The concept of interaction is so important that it merits another example. Age and gender are not independent influences on self-confidence. Girls and boys both start out overconfident relative to their objective performance on most tasks, but as they grow older, boys remain overconfident and girls become less so. A single one-factor experiment could show an effect of age (the mean confidence level drops); another could show an effect of gender (boys are more confident than girls, on average). But it takes a two-factor experiment to show that the effect of age on confidence depends on gender.

We care about interactions because we want explanations, and we usually can't construct them from the results of one-factor experiments. We can demonstrate experimentally that x affects or doesn't affect y, but this doesn't explain their relationship.

Of course, explanations are sometimes obvious: If x is the average branching factor of a search and y is the number of nodes searched, and y increases with x, then there isn't much to explain. But what if y doesn't increase with x, or it increases surprisingly slowly, or it increases in some trials but not others? Now we have some explaining to do: Another factor, z, is brought into the picture. It explains the relationship between x and y to the extent that it influences the relationship—to the extent that x and z interact. You can demonstrate relationships with one-factor experiments, but you usually need two or more factors, and interactions, to explain relationships.

7.1   Strategies for Explaining Performance

Suppose a researcher in the education school administers math and history tests to two classes of students, one from Amherst High School and one from neighboring Northampton. He arranges the scores in a two-by-two table, where columns represent the school district and rows represent the test subjects—math and history. Each cell in the table contains the scores of the students who belong in that cell; Amherst students who took the history test, for example. A *two-way analysis of variance* of this data will tell the researcher whether Amherst students equal Northampton students and whether math scores equal history scores, and also whether differences between math and history scores depend on the school district.

If, on the other hand, our researcher recorded each student's grade on each test, then he'd have a two-by-two-by-five contingency table, with rows and columns representing school district and test subject, and, in the third dimension, the grades A,B,C,D, and F. Each cell in the contingency table contains not several scores, but a single count or frequency; for example, one of the cells will contain the number of students from Amherst who got an A on the math test. With this table, the researcher can tell whether grades and school district are independent, whether grades and test subject are independent, and whether a dependency between grades and test subject depends on school district. In other words, he can test roughly the same hypotheses with analysis of variance and with contingency table analysis.

This chapter begins with some examples of two- and three-way analysis of variance, emphasizing interaction effects. It surveys three common uses of analysis of variance: looking for interactions to help explain relationships; looking for no interactions, in order to show relationships are independent or additive; and adding factors to an analysis to "mop up" variance and show the effects of *other* factors more clearly. The second part of the chapter begins with a simple example of *contingency table analysis* to find dependencies among actions in a sequence, then addresses a more complex version of the same problem, and concludes with an example of a general three-factor analysis. As in the previous chapter, this one emphasizes case studies; statistical details are postponed to section 7A.

7.2   Interactions among Variables: Analysis of Variance

Recall that the Phoenix testbed is a simulator of forest fires in Yellowstone National Park and a planner that tries to contain the fires by directing semi-autonomous simulated bulldozer agents. The planner tries to minimize the loss of acreage, but its plans sometimes go awry when the wind speed and direction changes, or the fire hits a patch of grassland, or burns uphill. This section shows how to find interactions among factors that explain the loss of acreage.

Graphs are a good way to begin. Put the performance variable, *AreaBurned*, on the vertical axis, and one factor such as *WindSpeed* on the horizontal axis, as shown in figure 7.1. Add another factor (denoted F) and plot the mean levels of *AreaBurned* for each combination of levels of the factors. For example, when $F = 1$ and *WindSpeed=high*, roughly twenty-five acres are burned, on average. Now draw lines between means with the same level of factor F. If the lines aren't parallel, the factors interact. This is apparently what is going on in figure 7.1. When $F = 1$, *AreaBurned* increases gracefully with *WindSpeed*; but when $F = 2$, *AreaBurned* increases slowly until *WindSpeed=medium*, then shoots up dramatically. Apparently, the effect of *WindSpeed* on performance depends on F, so both factors are required to explain performance. More importantly, it won't suffice to look at their effects in separate experiments, because their effects are not independent. This is what is meant by an interaction effect.

You know by now that apparent effects aren't necessarily significant in a statistical sense. Graphs like figure 7.1 are indicative and indispensible, but not sufficient to convince us that one mean, a combination of means, a relationship between means differs from another. These are jobs for analysis of variance.

7.2.1   Introduction to Two-Way Analysis of Variance

In the simplest *two-way factorial design* the levels of two factors are completely crossed, so all combinations of levels are present and every datum represents a unique task or individual—tasks or individuals don't appear in more than one condition. This design is called *two-way factorial without repeated measures*. For example, a cell of adolescent boys contains individuals who belong to the group of boys (gender is the

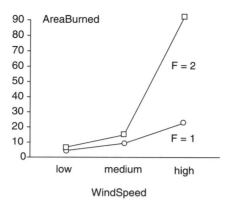

Figure 7.1   The relationship between wind speed and area burned degrades gracefully when $F = 1$ but not when $F = 2$.

Table 7.1   Design for a two-way factorial analysis of variance without repeated measures.

	Boys	Girls	Group means:
Preschool	$\overline{x}_{Pre,Boys} = 10$	$\overline{x}_{Pre,Girls} = 8$	$\overline{x}_{Pre} = 9$
SchoolAge	$\overline{x}_{Sch,Boys} = 9$	$\overline{x}_{Sch,Girls} = 6.5$	$\overline{x}_{Sch} = 7.75$
Adolescents	$\overline{x}_{Adl,Boys} = 7$	$\overline{x}_{Adl,Girls} = 4$	$\overline{x}_{Adl} = 5.5$
Group means:	$\overline{x}_{Boys} = 8.67$	$\overline{x}_{Girls} = 6.5$	$\overline{x}_{G} = 7.42$

factor) and the group of adolescents (chronological age or developmental maturity is the factor) as illustrated in table 7.1. The data in cells are values of a dependent variable, say, "confidence," although these have been summarized by means in table 7.1. (The means are made up, but the trends they represent are real; see Beal, 1994). Take paper and pencil and plot these means as in figure 7.1, putting confidence on the vertical axis and maturity on the horizontal, and drawing one curve for boys and another for girls. Do you see an interaction?

Recall that the one-way analysis of variance divides sample variance, s^2, into components, one due to noise and one that represents the effect of a factor. The levels of a factor, *A1,A2,A3*, are represented as columns in a table, each with its own mean, $\overline{x}_1$, $\overline{x}_2$, and $\overline{x}_3$. The deviation of datum k in group j from the grand mean of all the data, $\overline{x}_G$, is divided into two parts: $(x_{j,k} - \overline{x}_G) = (x_{j,k} - \overline{x}_j) + (\overline{x}_j - \overline{x}_G)$, the deviation of $x_{j,k}$ from its own group mean, plus the deviation of the group mean from the grand mean. When squared and summed over levels of factor A, $(x_{j,k} - \overline{x}_j)$ and

$(\overline{x}_j - \overline{x}_G)$ are interpreted as the effect of noise and the effect of A respectively, on the grounds that the deviations of a datum within a group are not affected by A because all data within the group have the same level of A, whereas the deviations of groups from the grand mean must represent the effect of whatever differentiates the groups, namely, A.

The two-way analysis of variance follows the same logic, except that the deviation of a datum from the grand mean is now represented as the sum of four influences. Consider an individual, say, Fred from the group of adolescent boys. The deviation of Fred from the grand mean, denoted $(x_{Adl,Boys,Fred} - \overline{x}_G)$ comprises: The deviation between Fred's confidence and the mean confidence of boys $(x_{Adl,Boys,Fred} - \overline{x}_{Boys})$, the deviation between Fred and adolescents $(x_{Adl,Boys,Fred} - \overline{x}_{Adl})$, Fred's deviation from the mean of his group of adolescent boys $(x_{Adl,Boys,Fred} - \overline{x}_{Adl,Boys})$, and a "leftover" component. These components are squared and summed as in the one-way analysis of variance and they are given these interpretations: The first two sums of squares are *main effects*, that is, independent effects of the two factors. The squared, summed deviation of individual data from their cell means are the effect of noise because the variation within a cell is not due to either maturity or gender. The squared, summed leftover component represents the effect that is not due to either factor or noise; it is interpreted as the effect of the *interaction* of the factors.

As in the one-way analysis of variance, sums of squares are divided by degrees of freedom yielding mean squares. Ratios of mean squares yield F statistics that indicate significant effects if they deviate much from unity. Generally, we calculate four mean squares: MS_{rows}, $MS_{columns}$, $MS_{interaction}$, and MS_{within}. F statistics for two main effects and the interaction effect are obtained by dividing MS_{rows}, $MS_{columns}$, and $MS_{interaction}$ by MS_{within}. If the experiment design is not factorial—if some levels of one factor are not crossed with all levels of another—or if the design involves repeated measures (e.g., if the same task is presented in different conditions), slightly different calculations are required (see section 7A).

Interactions are what make two-way analysis of variance indispensable. If the effects of factors were always additive, that is, independent, then they could be studied one at a time with one-way analyses. But effects are generally not additive. Indeed, sometimes several factors interact, as we will see.

7.2.2   Two-Way Analysis of Phoenix Data

Three analyses of the Phoenix planner serve to illustrate two-way and three-way analysis of variance. All use *AreaBurned* as the dependent variable and *WindSpeed* as one of the factors. Because Phoenix is a simulation, one can control the time the

Table 7.2   A two-way analysis of variance for the acreage lost at three wind speeds and two thinking speeds.

Source	df	Sum of squares	Mean square	F	p value
WindSpeed	2	194931.77	97465.88	82.27	.0001
RTK	1	71318.141	71318.141	60.19	.0001
WindSpeed × RTK	2	45701.23	22850.62	19.29	.0001
Within	337	399252.64	1184.726		

planner is allowed to think relative to the rate at which fires burn. This parameter, called *RTK* or thinking speed, exerts time pressure on the planner. Although *RTK* had seven levels in our original experiment (Hart and Cohen, 1992), it is partitioned into just two levels, called adequate and inadequate for the purpose of analysis.

Table 7.2 shows the results of a two-way factorial analysis of variance in which three levels of *WindSpeed* are crossed with two levels of *RTK*, yielding six experimental conditions. The results are organized in the same kind of tableau as characterized the one-way analysis (section 6.3.2). It shows large main effects of the two factors (i.e., large *F* values and extremely small *p* values), thus all wind speeds do not result in the same acreage loss, and thinking speed does influence acreage loss. Of course, one could get these results from a pair of one-way analyses, but the two-way analysis shows in addition that the effect of wind speed on area burned depends on thinking speed; conversely, the difference between adequate and inadequate thinking speeds (measured in lost acreage) gets worse as wind speed increases. Thus, the effects of thinking speed and wind speed on lost acreage are not additive.

We have not described how to calculate the entries in the analysis of variance tableau, nor will we, here. Interested readers will find a complete description of the process in section 7A.

The effects from this example are evident in figure 7.2: The lines' positive slopes indicate the effect of wind speed, and the vertical separation between the lines represents the effect of thinking speed. The interaction effect is indicated by nonparallel lines, which show the influence of *WindSpeed* on *AreaBurned* is not independent of *RTK* and vice versa. Interaction is a symmetric relationship; *RTK* might mediate the influence of *WindSpeed* on *AreaBurned* or vice versa. Figure 7.2 therefore has a twin, a graph with *RTK* on the horizontal axis and a separate line for each level of *WindSpeed*. It's often helpful to plot means both ways.

Some other examples of plots of means are shown in figure 7.3. See whether you can identify main effects and interaction effects in some of the examples. The

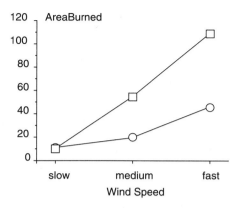

Figure 7.2 A plot of mean acreage lost at three wind speeds.

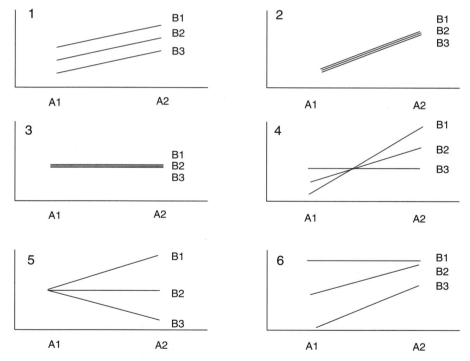

Figure 7.3 Examples of main effects and interaction effects in two-way analyses of variance.

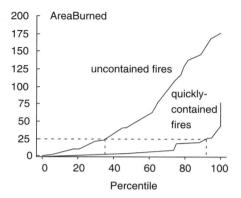

Figure 7.4 Percentile plots of *AreaBurned* for two groups of fires.

first example shows main effects of factors *A* and *B*—the former indicated by the positive slopes, the latter by the vertical separation of the lines—and no interaction effect. Example 2 shows a main effect of *A*, no effect of *B*, and no interaction effect. Example 3 shows no effects whatsoever, no slope and no separation between the lines. A more interesting case is example 4, which shows no main effect of factor *B* (the average of the two *B1* cell means is the same as the averages of the *B2* and *B3* means). On the other hand, there is a main effect of factor *A* and also an interaction effect, indicated by the nonparallel lines. The pattern is reversed in example 5: There is a main effect of factor *B* and an interaction effect, but no effect of factor *A*. Finally, example 6 is like the Phoenix example described earlier: Both factors have effects and they also interact.

7.2.3   Three-Way Analysis of Phoenix Data

If a fire isn't contained in a hurry, the Phoenix planner can lose control. When we ran our experiment (Hart and Cohen, 1992), we aborted thirty-seven trials after 120 simulated hours, fifty-eight trials after 150 hours, and six trials after 200 hours. Thus "quickly contained" fires were contained in less than 120 hours and "uncontained" fires were not contained after 120 (or 150, or 200) hours. The mean time to contain a quickly contained fire was 38.7 hours. Figure 7.4 shows a *percentile plot* of *AreaBurned* for these groups. More than 90% of quickly contained fires burned twenty-five acres or less, while more than 60% of uncontained fires burned twenty-five acres or more. Thus, nearly all quickly-contained fires are small while many uncontained fires are out of control.

Table 7.3 A two-way analysis of variance for acreage burned by contained and uncontained fires at three wind speeds.

Source	df	Sum of squares	Mean square	F	p value
Wind Speed	2	145793.5	72896.7	97.6	.0001
Containment	1	190958.9	190958.9	255.8	.0001
Wind Speed × Containment	2	55933.3	27966.7	37.5	.0001
Within	337	251552.3	746.4		

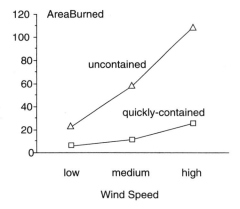

Figure 7.5 Main and interaction effects on the amount of area burned by wind speed and speed of fire containment.

The effect of this factor, called *Containment*, interacts with wind speed as shown in figure 7.5. The graph shows obvious main effects of wind speed and containment, and, because the lines have different slopes, we see fires that ultimately are not contained grow faster with increasing wind speed than fires that eventually are contained. This impression is confirmed by a two-way analysis of variance (table 7.3), which shows strong main effects of wind speed and containment and a highly significant interaction effect.

The next step is clearly to look at all these factors—*Containment, RTK* and *Wind-Speed*—together in a three-way analysis. Three-dimensional graphs are difficult to interpret, so figure 7.6 shows the cell means for this analysis in a pair of two-dimensional graphs, differentiated by *RTK*. The one on the left looks almost identical to the previous two-way analysis (figure 7.5) but it isn't, quite. The graph on the

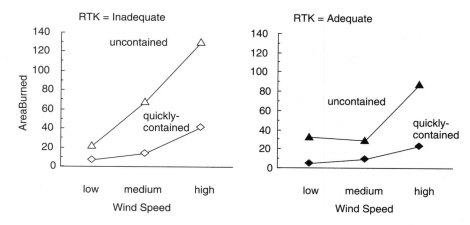

Figure 7.6   Cell means for all experimental conditions, differentiated by *RTK*.

right is clearly different. Of the four *performance profiles*, three seem to degrade gracefully and one is quite nonlinear. (A performance profile is a lineplot of the dependent variable for levels of one independent variable, e.g., the dependent variable at different levels of *WindSpeed*.)

These effects are apparent but they need the support of an analysis of variance. Why? Here are two broad hints, unequal cell sizes and variance. It might appear that the mean area burned is higher when thinking speed is inadequate because most of the six means in the leftmost graph in figure 7.6 are higher than the six means on the right. But what if we had collected only a few data for each condition on the left and ran dozens of trials in each condition on the right? What if the means in the left graph each represented just three trials and the highest mean on the right represented three hundred? In this case, the mean area burned might be greater when *RTK = adequate*, appearances notwithstanding. Even with equal cell sizes, however, the apparent differences between the means might not be significant if the within-cell variances are high.

To test these effects, however, the two-way analysis of variance needs extending to accommodate three or more factors. The logic of the analysis is not changed, and the sums of squares and mean squares are no less straightforward to compute. One looks for seven results instead of three: There's a main effect for each factor, of course, and also three two-way interactions and one three-way interaction. The interpretation of the three-way interaction is sometimes difficult, but in abstract terms it is just like a two-way interaction except the things that interact are not main effects but, rather, interactions. Whereas a two-way interaction says

Table 7.4   Three-way analysis of variance for the data shown in figure 7.6.

Source	df	Sum of squares	Mean square	*F*	*p* value
RTK	1	9994.3	9994.3	14.6	.0002
Containment	1	94601.5	94601.5	138.4	.0001
WindSpeed	2	98712	49356	72.2	.0001
RTK × Containment	1	2257.5	2257.5	3.3	.07
RTK × WindSpeed	2	8015.5	4007.8	5.9	.0031
Containment × Windspeed	2	24883.6	12441.8	18.2	.0001
RTK × Containment × WindSpeed	2	4157.6	2078.8	3.04	.0491
Within	331	226256.823	683.6		

the effect of one factor on the dependent variable is mediated by another factor, the three-way interaction says a two-way interaction effect is mediated by another factor.

Table 7.4 is a three-way analysis of the apparent effects in figure 7.6. First, note that all the factors have significant main effects. On average, more area was burned when the planner had inadequate time to think ($p \leq .0002$); less area was burned by quickly contained fires ($p \leq .0001$); and more area was burned at higher wind speeds ($p \leq .0001$). The interaction between *RTK* and *Containment* is not significant at the conventional .05 level ($p \leq .07$), which means the effect of *RTK* on *AreaBurned* is not significantly different for quickly contained and uncontained fires. On the other hand, *RTK* and *WindSpeed* interact ($p \leq .0031$) as do *Containment* and *Windspeed* ($p \leq .0001$). (These interactions aren't surprising given the results of our earlier two-way analyses.) Moreover, the *Containment* × *Windspeed* interaction is different for *RTK = inadequate* and *RTK = adequate*, as you can see in figure 7.6. In the former case, the area of uncontained fires grows more quickly with wind speed than that of quickly contained fires; but in the latter case, the relationship is murkier. The area of uncontained fires actually drops (relative to quickly contained fires) and then increases. This is why the three-way interaction is significant. When the two-way interaction between *WindSpeed* and *Containment* depends on a third factor, *RTK*, you get a significant—although in this case not very significant—three-way interaction ($p \leq .0491$).

7.3   Explaining Performance with Analysis of Variance

The analysis of variance is wonderfully versatile. This section surveys three common aspects of the technique; other more specialized methods are discussed in textbooks devoted to the subject (see section 7.3.4).

7.3.1   Looking for No Effect

In many experiments one hopes or expects to find an interaction effect, but in others, one hopes to demonstrate that two factors, though both influential, have independent influences. A good illustration of the latter comes from the experiment by Liane Acker and Bruce Porter (1994) described at length in chapter 6. To review, Acker and Porter built a system called the View Retriever that generated explanations called viewpoints. Human judges gave coherence scores to viewpoints—high scores for coherent explanations, lower scores for less coherent ones. Acker and Porter demonstrated that View Retriever viewpoints were indistinguishable from those written by humans (called textbook viewpoints) and superior to corrupted versions of View Retriever viewpoints (called degraded and random viewpoints). A contingency table analysis (section 6.8) showed another effect: The human judges were not equally stringent. The stingiest judge assigned a mean score of 1.93 points, and the most lax assigned a mean score of 4.444. (The minimum score was one point, the maximum, five.) It is not necessarily bad that the judges were more or less biased, nor could it be easily avoided. But it would weaken Acker and Porter's results considerably if the main effect they reported—View Retriever viewpoints are equal to textbook viewpoints and better than degraded and random viewpoints—depended on their choice of judges.

An example of the kind of result Acker and Porter wouldn't want is shown in figure 7.7. The stingy judge prefers random viewpoints to View Retriever viewpoints, but assigns them both relatively low scores, whereas the lax judge has the opposite preference and assigns high scores. There's a main effect of the type of viewpoint, because the mean coherence score for View Retriever viewpoints is higher than the mean score for random viewpoints. And clearly, there is a large main effect of judge. Unfortunately, the nonparallel lines also indicate an interaction effect, so the main effect must be qualified: The preference for View Retriever viewpoints is not a universal one, but rather, it depends on who is judging. In contrast, figure 7.8 shows a result that Acker and Porter would want: The stingy judge agrees with the lax judge, albeit less enthusiastically, so the preference for View Retriever viewpoints need not

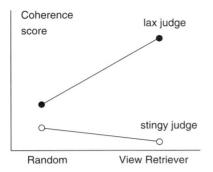

Figure 7.7   An undesirable interaction effect, suggesting that the main effect must be qualified.

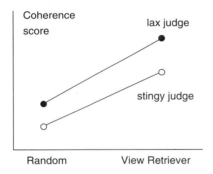

Figure 7.8   In the absence of an interaction effect, one can claim that View Retriever viewpoints are preferred irrespective of who judged them.

be qualified. If Acker and Porter's results looked like figure 7.8, they could claim their results are independent of their choice of judges.

We will analyze Acker and Porter's data as a factorial design without repeated measures, one in which all combinations of factors are present and each judge sees each kind of viewpoint, but no particular viewpoint is seen by more than one judge. In reality the design was quite complicated; for starters, many viewpoints were seen by more than one judge, so viewpoints were repeated across conditions. Analyzing a repeated measures design as one without repeated measures reduces the sensitivity of the *F* tests; it's more conservative. (Recall, one may analyze a paired-sample *t* test as an ordinary two-sample test, but one loses the opportunity to eliminate variance due to tasks that are repeated across the two groups. The same principle holds for analyzing repeated measures designs as if they involve no repeated measures.)

Table 7.5 A two-way analysis of variance for viewpoint rating by judge shows two main effects but no significant interaction effect.

Source	df	Sum of squares	Mean square	F	p value
Judge	9	75.69	8.41	6.31	.0001
Viewpoint	3	87.47	29.15	21.87	.0001
Judge × Viewpoint	27	45.76	1.69	1.27	.1757
Within	225	300	1.33		

Returning to the question at hand: Are coherence scores the sum of independent effects of judge and viewpoint, or do the effects of judge and viewpoint interact? A two-way analysis of variance (table 7.5) resolves the question. As expected, it shows main effects of viewpoint and judge, but no interaction effect ($p \leq .1757$, *n.s.*). Therefore, the preference for one type of viewpoint over another does not depend significantly on who is judging.

Negative and Positive Evidence for No Effect

An earlier discussion of Acker and Porter's experiment urged caution when applying statistical tests to demonstrate an absence of effects, because the conclusion one wants—no interaction effect—can always be achieved by making the critical value for rejecting the null hypothesis arbitrarily large (section 6.3.6). Clearly, the *F* statistic in table 7.5 for the interaction effect is unusual ($p \leq .176$), it just isn't unusual enough to reject the null hypothesis. Thus, the claim that judge and viewpoint are independent is supported by negative evidence. The factors seem to be independent because the available evidence does not lead us to believe they interact. In addition it would be nice to have some positive evidence of independence.

Positive evidence is provided by a plot of mean coherence scores, as shown in figure 7.9. Each line of four dots represents a single judge; for example, the "stingy" judge assigns scores of 4.7, 2.0, 1.2, and 1.0 to textbook, View Retriever, degraded and random viewpoints, respectively, and is represented by the lowest line in the figure. All the judges had pretty much the same preferences: Textbook viewpoints were judged as most coherent, followed by View Retriever, degraded, and random viewpoints in that order. Some judges deviated from this order (indicated by line segments with non-negative slope), but the deviations were minor and few. Earlier we said interaction effects show up as nonparallel lines in plots of means, and the lines

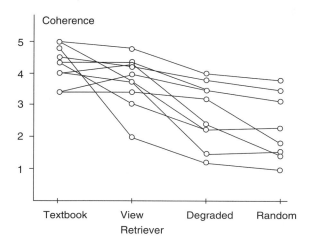

Figure 7.9   A plot of mean coherence scores by category assigned by each of ten judges. (From Acker and Porter's experiment, 1994.)

in figure 7.9 are certainly not parallel. They are nearly so, however, especially given the background variance in the judges' scores. In addition to the negative evidence of the *F* statistic for interaction, then, a plot of means shows substantially similar preferences for all the judges.

Random Factors and Generalization

Acker and Porter can claim that their results do not depend on who is judging because judge is a *random factor*. The ten judges were among hundreds who might have served; they constitute a random sample of those willing to serve. Thus, their responses may be taken as representative of a population, much the way polling results usually represent the voting behavior of a larger population. In contrast, *WindSpeed* in the earlier Phoenix experiment is not a random factor. When we designed the experiment we knew that Phoenix could not fight fires at wind speeds much in excess of those selected. Wind speed is a *fixed factor* because the levels of wind speed were not determined by random sampling from a population of wind speeds, but, rather, were fixed at levels we expected to be informative. Consequently, we cannot claim our results are general with respect to wind speed. (See chapter 9 for a more extensive discussion of generalization.)

   In experiments with humans and other animals, the choice of individuals is usually a random factor, thus the experiment results are thought to hold for all individuals in the population. In experiments with AI systems, on the other hand, the best candidate for a random factor is probably the choice of tasks or problems. For example, Lehnert and McCarthy (1993) ran their word-tagging system, OTB, on test sentences selected randomly from a corpus, so the sentences were a random factor, and the results were viewed as general with respect to the corpus (section 6.9). Analysis of variance proceeds the same way whether the factors are fixed or random. Random factors are often nested within fixed factors, however, resulting in mixed designs, and these are analyzed slightly differently (see section 7A).

7.3.2   Getting a Clearer Picture by Reducing Variance

Recall that an F statistic is a ratio of the mean square for an effect over the mean square within, which means that reducing the mean square within will increase F and, perhaps, push the statistic over a significance threshold. For concreteness, suppose you run a one-way analysis of variance on a factor, A, and find to your disappointment that $F = MS_{between}/MS_{within}$ is not large enough to be significant. Perhaps this is because another factor, B, is at work in your experiment, a factor you didn't include in the analysis, but that adds a lot of variance to MS_{within}. If you run a two-way analysis of variance, including both factors, you might find that the variance within cells is much lower, so MS_{within} is smaller. Moreover, because the mean square for factor A is calculated from the marginal means in your data table, it is unaffected by the inclusion of factor B. To illustrate this point, take another look at table 7.1. Clearly, $\bar{x}_{Boys}$ would not change if all the data in the *Boys* column was collapsed into a single cell, so, conversely, if a group of boys is partitioned by another factor into preschool, school age and adolescents, the marginal mean $\bar{x}_{Boys}$ won't change. If the mean square for factor A doesn't change when factor B enters the analysis, but the mean square error decreases, then adding B might boost the main effect of A to significance. Thus, you can get rid of variance (specifically, within-cell variance) by adding another factor to your analysis.

This is exactly what we did in a small study of computer-assisted planning (Oates and Cohen, 1994). We had built a simulator of ships and ports, docks and cargo, in which batches of cargo were transported from one port to another. Because the simulator is nondeterministic, shipping schedules slip, and, eventually, traffic between the ports becomes unevenly distributed and bottlenecks develop. We built an agent to predict bottlenecks before they occur and advise human users about how to avoid them. The most important of several performance measures was the total number of cargo-days required to deliver every piece of cargo to its destination. In one experiment, we asked whether humans performed better, according to this criterion,

Table 7.6   A one-way analysis of the effect of *Advice*.

Source	df	Sum of squares	Mean square	F	p value
Advice	1	78111	78111	1.967	.171
Within	30	1191433	39714		

Table 7.7   A two-way analysis of *Advice* and *Scenario*.

Source	df	Sum of squares	Mean square	F	p value
Advice	1	78111	78111	4.416	.0463
Scenario	3	734329	244776	13.84	.0001
Advice × Scenario	3	32629	10876	0.615	.612
Within	24	424475	17686		

with or without the advice of the agent. We got four volunteers, trained them to use the simulator, and put them through eight trials, each. The trials were drawn from four scenarios that involved different numbers of ships, cargo, and ports.

We wanted to show that the agent's advice would improve human performance, so we ran a one-way analysis of variance on the *Advice* factor. The mean number of cargo-days for the no-advice condition was 2849.438 and the mean for the advice condition was 2750.625: happy results, because advice reduces cargo-days, but unfortunately, not significant results. The tableau for the one-way analysis is shown in table 7.6.

To boost the significance of the *Advice* factor, we included another factor, *Scenario*, in the analysis. The tableau for this analysis is shown in table 7.7. The test statistic for *Advice* increased to a more satisfactory $F = 4.416$ ($p < .05$). Notice, too, that *Scenario* is highly significant; in fact, the scenario—the number of ships and ports and cargo—influenced our subjects' performance more than whether they enjoyed the assistance of our agent. Still, by removing variance due to *Scenario* from MS_{within}, the effect of *Advice* is seen more clearly. It's interesting to follow the redistribution of this variance. Notice that $SS_{within} = 1191433$ in table 7.6, whereas

$$SS_{Scenario} + SS_{Scenario \times Advice} + SS_{within} = 1191433$$

in table 7.7. The within-cell variance in the one-way analysis has been reapportioned, with some going to the main effect of *Scenario* and some to the interaction between *Advice* and *Scenario*. The sum of squares for the main effect of *Advice* doesn't change, as noted earlier. A similar reapportionment happens when new predictors are added to multiple regression models; see section 8A.6.

7.3.3   Explaining Nonlinear Effects: Transforming Data

Analysis of variance is based on a linear, additive model of effects; for the two-way analysis the model is something like this: $x_{i,j,k} = \mu + \xi_{i,\bullet} + \xi_{\bullet,j} + \xi_{i,j} + \varepsilon$. That is, each datum is the sum of five influences: the grand mean over all conditions (μ), the effect of being at level i of one factor ($\xi_{i,\bullet}$), the effect of being at level j of the other ($\xi_{\bullet,j}$), an interaction effect of being in the particular combination of levels ($\xi_{i,j}$), and a random component (ε). The hypothesis of no interaction can be represented as $\xi_{i,j} = 0$.

Suppose some researchers have developed a model of how an algorithm performs, a model that predicts no interaction between two factors. An analysis of variance can test this prediction, as described in section 7.3.1. But suppose the model isn't linear, so it doesn't map to the model of effects that underlies analysis of variance. In this case an interaction effect might appear even though the factors in the model don't interact. To avoid spurious results like this one, the model should be transformed before running the analysis.

For instance, we developed a model of the rate at which one process interrupts another: $\text{IR} = (1/y) - (\lambda/x\mu)$. In this model, x and y denote factors manipulated in an experiment, and λ and μ are constants (Anderson et al., 1991). We believed x and y would have additive effects on interruption rate, that is, no special costs or benefits of particular combinations of x and y were expected in our data. But an analysis of variance disclosed an interaction effect. This would be evidence against our model, were it not for the fact that the model involves nonlinear effects of x and y on IR. To linearize these effects we rewrote the model in terms of the reciprocals of x and y, resulting in $\text{IR} = y' + x'(\lambda/\mu)$, and we transformed the data, y to y' and x to x'. A new analysis showed no interaction effect between x' and y' on IR, so the effects of x' and y' were apparently independent, as the model predicts. Transformations of data are described in more detail when we discuss modeling, in chapter 8.

7.3.4   Summary: Analysis of Variance

The analysis of variance rests on some assumptions. First, it's assumed that the populations from which each cell sample is drawn are normal. Second, the variances of these populations are equal. Third, the within-cell error components are independent of each other, and between cells as well. If sample sizes are relatively large (e.g., ten items per cell), then the first two assumptions probably won't cause trouble. The third assumption is important, however. It can be violated by a repeated-measures design in which there's some "carryover" between conditions, typically due to learning (see section 7A.5). Keppel (1973, pp. 395–400) provides a good discussion of carryover effects.

If you remember the discussions of comparisons and orthogonal contrasts in section 6.4 and section 6A.2, you're probably wondering whether those methods extend to two-factor and higher designs. Indeed they do, although they aren't discussed here. Good resources include Keppel (1973, chapter 12) and an insightful book by Rosenthal and Rosnow (1985) on contrast analysis.

Factorial designs without repeated measures are common, versatile, and easily understood and analyzed. They are like peasant loaves: robust, sustaining, and perfectly alright for most meals. But sometimes one wants delicate, complex confections, the sort of thing one serves with raspberries. In the hands of an expert, the analysis of variance can be configured to examine subtle hypotheses in complex experiments. These analyses follow the same basic principles as the ones we've seen, just as a delicate brioche is made essentially the same way as peasant bread. All analyses partition variance and calculate ratios of mean squares—that's the flour, yeast and water—but some deal with repeated measures, some with incompletely crossed levels of factors, some with random factors, and so on. Three common variants are described in section 7A, yet this only touches the surface of the subject.

At this point, having introduced two- and three-way analysis of variance, our focus shifts from the analysis of amounts—whether one statistic is numerically bigger than another—to the analysis of frequencies or counts.

7.4   Dependencies among Categorical Variables: Analysis of Frequencies

Some studies focus not on the magnitudes of events, but on their frequencies. Contingency tables are a natural representation for joint distributions of events, and contingency table analysis provides answers to questions like these:

- Can one discover dependencies between parts of speech in a sentence? Do nouns follow determiners more often than they follow adverbs, for instance?

- A case-based planner relies heavily on a handful of plans, but sometimes the chosen plan fails and another must be tried. Do some plans fail more often, proportionally, than others? Is there a dependency between the *Plan* factor and the *Outcome* factor?

- Many control algorithms are based on a "Markov principle," which says the future state of a system depends on its current state but no earlier state. If the Markov principle governed the weather, then tomorrow's weather depends on today's but not yesterday's, or last week's, weather. Does the Markov principle govern the behaviors of agents in a robot's environment, that is, are the frequencies of "tomorrow's" behaviors independent of their frequencies "yesterday"?

Two of these examples deal with joint distributions of events in sequences, an interesting prospect if you want to analyze the behavior of programs over time. This section focuses on *execution traces*, which are time series of labels that correspond to behaviors. For example, a robot exploring its environment might generate this trace:

```
go-forward, stop, look-around, turn-left, go-forward...
```

Note that the level of abstraction of these labels is much higher than the machine instructions required to implement them. The appropriate level of abstraction obviously depends on what an experiment is designed to show.

One might look for many kinds of patterns in execution traces:

- **tit-for-tat** whenever behavior A occurs, behavior B follows;

- **mediation** behavior B follows behavior A if both take place in the context of environmental event E (or, perhaps, another behavior, C);

- **action at a distance** behavior B is observed uncommonly often when it is preceded by no more than, say, ten minutes, by behavior A;

- **escalation** a behavior happens with increasing frequency over time.

One general procedure is sufficient to find all but the last kind of pattern. It was developed by Adele Howe to analyze execution traces of failure recovery in the Phoenix planner. A simple version of the procedure is described briefly at the end of chapter 2. Here, it is shown capable of finding more complex dependencies.

7.5   Explaining Dependencies in Execution Traces

In the context of execution traces, a *dependency* is an unexpectedly frequent or infrequent co-occurrence. For example, let A, B and C be actions in a plan, and consider the execution trace

B A B C C C B B C B A B A B C A B A C

One thing you will notice is that A almost never occurs without B following it immediately (only the last occurrence of A is followed by C). This co-occurrence can be summarized with a contingency table as follows:

	B	$\overline{B}$	Totals
A	4	1	5
$\overline{A}$	3	10	13
Totals	7	11	18

The rows of the table are labeled with precursors and the columns with successors; for instance, scanning the execution trace from left to right, A precedes B (conversely, B is the successor of A) four times. The table shows also that A was followed by something other than B (denoted $A\overline{B}$) just once. Similarly, the execution trace contains three occurrences of $\overline{A}B$ and ten occurrences of $\overline{A}\overline{B}$. The table is unspecific about dependencies between C and the other actions, and it does not summarize the tendency of A to follow B. It was set up solely to test the hypothesis that B follows A more often than one would expect by chance. To test other hypotheses, one constructs other tables.

The row frequencies in the contingency table above certainly appear heterogenous and nonindependent: The ratios are 4:1 in the first row and 3:10 in the second. Said differently, when A occurs, B seems to follow more often than one would expect if A and B were independent. A *G* test (or a chi-square test) will lend weight to this impression. The test statistic is:

$$G = 2 \sum_{\text{cells}} f_{ij} \ln \left(\frac{f_{ij}}{\hat{f}_{ij}} \right), \tag{7.1}$$

where f_{ij} is the number of occurrences, or frequency, in the cell i,j, and $\hat{f}_{ij}$ is the expected frequency for cell i,j. Recall that expected frequencies can be arrived at two ways: They can be specified extrinsically (as we might specify that the expected frequency of males to females in a sample is one to one) or they can be calculated from the contingency table under the assumption that the row and column variables are independent. In the first case, the *G* test is a test of goodness of fit to an extrinsic frequency distribution; in the second, it is a test of independence or heterogeneity (section 6.13). Dependency detection relies primarily but not exclusively on heterogeneity tests.

To test whether B depends on A in the execution trace just discussed, first construct a contingency table, as shown, then calculate expected frequencies under the null hypothesis that A and B are independent. The expected frequency for a cell in row i and column j, is $\hat{f}_{ij} = f_{i\bullet} f_{\bullet j} / f_{\bullet\bullet}$, or the row margin $f_{i\bullet}$ times the column margin, $f_{\bullet j}$, divided by the sum of all the cells, $f_{\bullet\bullet}$ (section 6.13). Substituting expected and actual frequencies into equation 7.1 yields a heterogeneity measure, G_H, for the contingency table:

$$G_H = 2 \left[4 \ln \left(\frac{4}{\frac{5 \cdot 7}{18}} \right) + 1 \ln \left(\frac{1}{\frac{5 \cdot 11}{18}} \right) + 3 \ln \left(\frac{3}{\frac{7 \cdot 13}{18}} \right) + 10 \ln \left(\frac{10}{\frac{11 \cdot 13}{18}} \right) \right] = 5.007.$$

For a contingency table with R rows and C columns, the significance level of G_H is found by comparing it to a chi-square distribution with $(R - 1) \times (C - 1)$ degree of freedom. The probability of obtaining $G_H \geq 5.007$ given that A and B are independent is less than .03. One can safely conclude that B depends on A.

Actually, the previous test does not itself support the asymmetry of this conclusion. Significant values of G_H show that B and A are associated—much as correlation does for continuous data—not that one depends on or causes the other. The asymmetric interpretation of the association is allowed only because contingency tables compiled from execution traces represent the propensity of one thing to follow another. Because B follows A unexpectedly often, we do not say A depends on B but rather, B depends on A. Even so, "depends on" has a pretty limited connotation; for instance, it doesn't mean "caused by," it means "associated in one direction in a sequence."

7.6   Explaining More Complex Dependencies

Although the dependency between A and B is probably not spurious, it is not the only one in the execution trace, and is perhaps not as easy to explain as others that might subsume it. Note, for example, that the longer subsequence B*B occurs four times, three of which have A in place of the wildcard *. Perhaps the execution trace is telling us that B tends to be followed after an intervening action by itself, and, by chance, A is the intervening action three times out of four. The question is whether B*B subsumes AB, that is, whether AB occurs primarily as a subsequence of BAB, or whether, instead, AB has some independent existence. Subsumption is but one relationship that may occur in longer sequences of actions. If an execution trace contains an unexpectedly large number of sequences BAB, for example, one must consider three possibilities:

1. There is a dependency between A and B, but the dependency does not depend on the preceding action, B.

2. There is a dependency between B and B separated by one action, but the dependency does not depend on the intervening action, A.

3. There is a dependency between B, A and B.

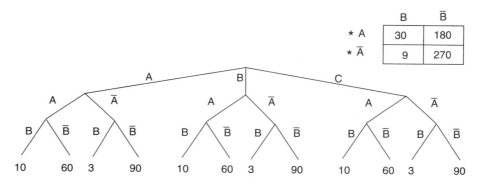

Figure 7.10   An example of a dependency between A and B, where the dependency does not depend on the previous action.

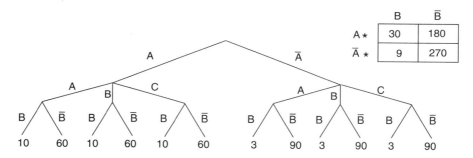

Figure 7.11   An example of a dependency between A and B separated by one action, where the dependency does not depend on the intervening action.

An example of the first kind is shown in figure 7.10. The lower levels of the tree represent the four two-action sequences studied earlier: AB, A$\overline{\text{B}}$, $\overline{\text{A}}$B, $\overline{\text{A}}\overline{\text{B}}$, and the upper level represents three possible precursors, A, B, and C, of these sequences. A tree like this shows whether a dependency between A and B itself depends on a precursor. In figure 7.10, at least, the odds of seeing B after A are 1:6, whereas the odds of seeing B after $\overline{\text{A}}$ are 1:30, and these ratios do not depend on which action precedes the two-action subsequences. In other words, figure 7.10 shows a strong *AB dependency that is not subsumed by AAB, BAB, or CAB.

Figure 7.11 shows an example of the second kind, an A*B dependency that does not depend on which intervening action is substituted for the wildcard. In this case, the odds of seeing A*B are 1:6, whereas the odds of seeing $\overline{\text{A}}$*B are 1:30, and these odds do not depend on whether the intervening action is A, B, or C.

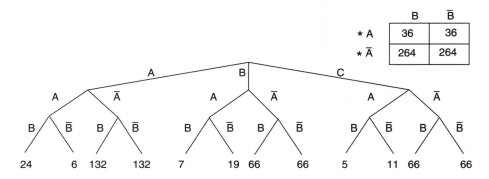

Figure 7.12   Although the contingency table shows no *AB dependency, B shows a strong propensity to follow A in AAB, and the opposite effect holds for BAB and CAB.

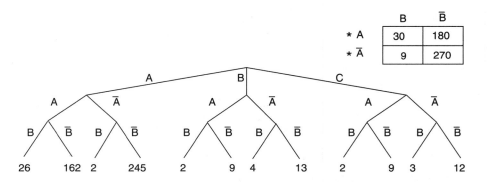

Figure 7.13   The AB dependency appears only when the previous action is A.

Sometimes, dependencies can cancel each other out. Figure 7.12 shows a case in which there is a strong propensity for B to follow AA in the three-action sequence AAB, and a propensity for B to not follow A in the sequences BAB and CAB. The overall contingency table shows no dependency between A and B: The probability of B following A is .5 and the probability of B following $\overline{A}$ is also .5.

Lastly, Figure 7.13 shows a case in which the AB dependency shows up only when the first actions of a three-action sequence are AA, and this dependency dominates the data. There is no evidence in figure 7.13 for a general two-action AB dependency, because B does not appear to depend on A in three-action sequences BAB and CAB.

G tests can differentiate the cases illustrated in figures 7.10, 7.11, 7.12, and 7.13. The procedure (Howe and Cohen, 1995) involves a sequence of three tests:

Table 7.8 The figure 7.13 contingency table

	B	$\overline{B}$	Totals
*A	30	180	210
*$\overline{A}$	9	270	279
Totals	39	450	489

Procedure 7.1   Dependency Detection for Two-Item Precursors

i.   Test the "packed" contingency table for heterogeneity (a packed table is one in which the precursors contain asterisks). This will disclose a dependency between an incompletely specified precursor (e.g., *A) and a successor (e.g., B).

ii. Build a new table by unpacking the first row of the packed table. Unpacking means creating a new row for each possible instantiation of an asterisk in the precursor. Test this unpacked table for heterogeneity. This assesses whether the completely specified predecessors (e.g., AA, BA, CA) influence differently the probabilities of B and $\overline{B}$ as successors.

iii. Test the goodness of fit of each row in the unpacked table to the marginal column frequencies of the packed table. This will show the extent to which each completely specified predecessor influences the result of the first test.

The cases in figures 7.10 and 7.11 show up as significant dependencies in the first test but not the second. In the case of cancelling dependencies (figure 7.12) the pattern is reversed: an insignificant result in the first test and significant heterogeneity in the second. The case of one dependency dominating the others (figure 7.13) shows up as a significant result in the first test and only one significant result (of several possible) in the third test. This is a good place to begin because it illustrates many features of the dependency-detection procedure.

The first step in procedure 7.1, then, is a heterogeneity test on the packed table in figure 7.13, reproduced here as table 7.8. Because the G statistic (Eq. 7.1) is a sum, the heterogeneity test can be run in pieces, one row at a time. Expected frequencies are calculated as they always are for heterogeneity or independence tests: multiply the row and column margins and divide by the table total. Here's the G statistic for the *A row of table 7.8:

$$G_{*A} = 2 \left[30 \ln \left(\frac{30}{\frac{(210 \times 39)}{489}} \right) + 180 \ln \left(\frac{180}{\frac{(210 \times 450)}{489}} \right) \right] = 9.40.$$

The *G* statistic for the second row is calculated the same way:

$$G_{*\overline{A}} = 2 \left[9 \ln \left(\frac{9}{\frac{(279 \times 39)}{489}} \right) + 270 \ln \left(\frac{270}{\frac{(279 \times 450)}{489}} \right) \right] = 10.88.$$

The sum of these statistics is 20.28, which is the heterogeneity of the whole table. We denote this result, $G_{H*} = 20.28$, with an asterisk to remind us it is a heterogeneity test on a packed table. The critical value for $\alpha = .05$ for the chi-square distribution with one degree of freedom is 3.84, which is greatly exceeded by 20.28, so the incompletely specified precursor *A evidently influences the occurrence of the successor B.

A brief word about degrees of freedom for heterogeneity or independence tests, both *G* and chi-square tests. The row and column margin are fixed because they are used to estimate cell frequencies, as is the total sum for the table. So if a row contains *C* columns, only $C - 1$ values in the row are free to vary; the last being constrained to "make up" the row sum. Similarly, a column of *R* rows has $R - 1$ degrees of freedom. An $R \times C$ table therefore has $(R - 1) \times (C - 1)$ degrees of freedom; for example, table 7.8 has one, and table 7.9, below, has two degrees of freedom. Each test on a row has $C - 1$ degrees of freedom, because the row margin constrains one of the frequencies in the row. The tests of G_{*A} and $G_{*\overline{A}}$ each have one degree of freedom because our contingency tables have only two columns.

The second step in procedure 7.1 is to unpack the first row of table 7.8, to find out what effects, if any, may be attributed to the unspecified first item, *, in the precursor. To represent the frequencies in figure 7.13, the thirty occurrences of *AB in table 7.8 should be unpacked into twenty-six occurrences of AAB, two occurrences of BAB and two of CAB. The 180 occurrences of *A$\overline{B}$ are unpacked the same way, yielding table 7.9. You might wonder why we don't also unpack the second row of table 7.8. It's because we are looking for dependencies between increasingly specific precursors—*A, AA—and B. The precursor in the second row, $\overline{A}$ is not specific.

Table 7.9   The figure 7.13 contingency table with "unpacked" *A row.

	B	$\overline{B}$	Totals
AA	26	162	188
BA	2	9	11
CA	2	9	11
Totals	30	180	210

Now let's run a heterogeneity test on this table, one row at a time, as before:

$$G_{AA} = 2 \left[26 \ln \left(\frac{26}{\frac{(188 \times 30)}{210}} \right) + 162 \ln \left(\frac{162}{\frac{(188 \times 180)}{210}} \right) \right] = .032$$

$$G_{BA} = 2 \left[2 \ln \left(\frac{2}{\frac{(11 \times 30)}{210}} \right) + 9 \ln \left(\frac{9}{\frac{(11 \times 180)}{210}} \right) \right] = .1273$$

$$G_{CA} = 2 \left[2 \ln \left(\frac{2}{\frac{(11 \times 30)}{210}} \right) + 9 \ln \left(\frac{9}{\frac{(11 \times 180)}{210}} \right) \right] = .1273.$$

None of these G statistics is individually significant (each has one degree of freedom, and the critical value is 3.84, as noted earlier), nor is their sum, $G_H = .287$ significant. This means the rows in table 7.9, AA, BA, and CA, differ little among themselves—the ratios of their frequencies are similar. In fact, the ratio in row AA is 26:162, or roughly 1:6; whereas the ratios for rows BA and CA are 1:4.5.

At this point we know two things: B depends on the precursor ∗A, and the probability of observing B instead of $\overline{B}$ is roughly the same whether the precursor is AA, BA, or CA. These probabilities gloss over the raw row frequencies, however, and obscure the fact that B and $\overline{B}$ are much more likely to be observed following AA than any other precursor. This suggests the dependency between AA and B dominates the others, so if you were to give a concise rule for the data in figure 7.13 you would not say B depends on A but, rather, B depends on AA. There's strong evidence that B occurs unexpectedly often when it follows AA, but the evidence for dependencies between B and the other precursors is weak. These impressions are supported by a third sort of test.

Recall that $G_{*A} = 9.40$ for the packed, ∗A row of table 7.8. Because this test has one degree of freedom and a critical value (for $\alpha = .05$) of 3.84, we know that the ratio of B to $\overline{B}$ (30:180) is significantly different from the column marginal frequencies 39:450. Notice the slight shift in interpretation: Now we are using the column margins as expected frequencies and asking how well the ratio in row ∗A fits these frequencies. We are interpreting the G tests for each row—which sum to the heterogeneity test for the entire table—as tests of goodness of fit to the column margins 39:450. If we compare the unpacked frequencies in table 7.9 to the column margins from the packed table, 39:450, we can break $G_{*A} = 9.40$ into three components, one for each fully specified precursor. These tests constitute the third step in procedure 7.1. The first such test is:

$$G_{AA} = 2 \left[26 \ln \left(\frac{26}{\frac{(188 \times 39)}{489}} \right) + 162 \ln \left(\frac{162}{\frac{(188 \times 450)}{489}} \right) \right] = 7.327.$$

This result is significant, which means the ratio of B to $\overline{B}$ following AA is significantly different than 39:450. The remaining tests yield insignificant results:

$$G_{BA} = 2\left[2\ln\left(\frac{2}{\frac{(11\times 39)}{489}} \right) + 9\ln\left(\frac{9}{\frac{(11\times 450)}{489}} \right) \right] = 1.18.$$

Because the BA and CA rows are identical, $G_{CA} = 1.18$. The sum of these statistics, $G_T = 7.327 + 1.18 + 1.18 = 9.687$, does not equal $G_{*A} = 9.40$, but the heterogeneity of the three unpacked rows in table 7.9 makes the books balance:

$$G_T = G_{*A} + G_H$$

$$9.687 = 9.40 + .287.$$

That is, the summed deviations of the unpacked rows AA, BA and CA from the ratio 39:450, minus the internal heterogeneity of these rows, equals the deviation of the packed row *A from the ratio 39:450. The following table summarizes the results to this point:

Statistic	Value	Interpretation
G_{H*}	20.28	Significant: B depends on *A
G_{*A}	9.40	Significant: row *A differs from column margins
G_{AA}	7.327	Significant: row AA differs from column margins
G_{BA}	1.18	Not significant: Contributes little to G_{*A}
G_{CA}	1.18	Not significant: Contributes little to G_{*A}
G_H	0.287	Not significant: Ratio of B to $\overline{B}$ is independent of fully-specified precursor

Collectively these statistics support some informal impressions of figure 7.13. The dependency between A and B is not general but instead shows up only when the precursor is AA. Result 1 finds that B depends on whether the precursor is *A or *$\overline{A}$, and result 2 shows that a significant part of this dependency is due to the deviation of *A frequencies from the column marginal distribution 39:450. Result 3, in turn, shows that a significant part of result 2 is due to the deviations of AA frequencies from the marginal distribution, whereas results 4 and 5 are insignificant, which means the BA and CA frequencies can't be distinguished from the marginal distribution. Together, results 3,4, and 5 imply that B's dependence on *A is really a dependence on AA.

Other execution traces yield very different results; for example, here is the analysis of the trace represented by figure 7.10:

Statistic	Value	Interpretation
G_{H*}	20.28	Significant: B depends on *A
G_{*A}	9.40	Significant: *A differs from column margins
G_{AA}	3.133	Not significant: Contributes little to G_{*A}
G_{BA}	3.133	Not significant: Contributes little to G_{*A}
G_{CA}	3.133	Not significant: Contributes little to G_{*A}
G_H	0	Not significant: Ratio of B to $\overline{\text{B}}$ is independent of fully-specified precursor

Evidently B depends on *A and this effect is identical ($G_H = 0$) for all substitutions for *; it doesn't matter whether A, B, or C is the first item in the precursor. In fact, none of the individual three-action dependencies is significant. In short, when the second action of a precursor is A, the first action does not influence the occurrence of B.

The trace summarized in figure 7.11 yields identical G statistics and has a very similar interpretation to the data in figure 7.10. The only difference is that the precursors are AA, AB, and AC instead of AA, BA, CA; in other words, the dependency detection procedure tries but fails to find an effect of the middle item in three-item sequences.

Finally, consider the situation in which dependencies cancel each other out, shown in figure 7.12. The G statistics for this case are:

Statistic	Value	Interpretation
G_{H*}	0	Not significant: B doesn't depend on *A
G_{*A}	0	Not significant: *A doesn't differ from column margins
G_{AA}	11.565	Significant: AA differs from column margins
G_{BA}	5.754	Significant: BA differs from column margins
G_{CA}	2.306	Not significant: CA doesn't differ from column margins
G_H	19.625	Significant: B is more likely after AA, less likely after BA

When the precursor is AA, then the ratio of B to $\overline{\text{B}}$ in the subsequent action is significantly different from its expectation ($G_{AA} = 11.565$). The ratio also differs from its expectation when the precursor is BA, but no significant effect is found for precursor CA. Despite strong effects of two fully specified precursors, B doesn't depend on *A ($G_{*A} = 0$) because the dependencies of B on AA and BA cancel each other out. B follows AA unexpectedly often and BA unexpectedly rarely, and these opposing tendencies yield a highly heterogeneous table when the *A row is unpacked ($G_H = 19.625$), but of course they are invisible in the *A row itself.

In sum, for any ordered actions x, y, z in an execution trace, procedure 7.1 can differentiate three cases: z depends on y, irrespective of action x (figure 7.10); z depends on x, irrespective of action y (figure 7.11); and the dependency between z and y depends on x (figures 7.12 and 7.13). It's worth noting that other actions might occur between x, y, and z that would simply be ignored in the analysis; or in successive analyses, y could be each of several actions that fall between x and z. Procedure 7.1 has been extended to test "action at a distance" hypotheses of this kind (Howe and Fuegi, 1994). Another extension involves several execution traces instead of just one, or, equivalently, one execution trace of feature vectors. This technique is designed to find dependencies such as, "the temperature and humidity on wednesday depend on the level of rainfall and the wind speed on tuesday" (Oates et al., 1995).

A weakness of dependency detection is that it usually finds lots of statistically significant dependencies. As we have seen in other contexts, statistical significance isn't always synonymous with meaningful. For example, Adele Howe found dozens of dependencies between successive failures in execution traces of the Phoenix planner and dozens more dependencies between failure-recovery methods and subsequent failures. Relatively few of these were interesting, however. Here's one that was: Roughly 10 percent of 1183 failure-repair-failure sequences collected by Howe in her experiments involved back-to-back failures of type *prj*. This is striking. Imagine you're a doctor, treating infections with antibiotics. After a few years you discover a particular infection is highly recurrent—once a patient gets it, he or she is apt to get it again—and this pattern doesn't depend on which antibiotic the patient got. All are equally ineffective. This appears to be the story of the *prj* failure in Phoenix, which reoccurs alarmingly and with statistically-indistinguishable probability following all types of failure-recovery actions.

Although *prj* failures are interesting because of their seemingly chronic nature, it's difficult to know whether they say anything useful about the Phoenix planner. As it happens, *prj* failures occur when the state of the world isn't as the planner projected it to be. Their recurrence probably reflects the fact that the Phoenix environment changes in unpredictable ways, so no matter how plans are repaired, they are usually inadequate for a future state of the environment.

Thus, raw dependencies are interpreted, after which one can judge whether they are interesting and important. Of course, it's much easier to find dependencies than it is to interpret them. A remarkable contribution of Howe's work is a program she developed to interpret dependencies semi-automatically. The interpretations were used for debugging. For example, her program attributed some dependencies to incorrectly used shared variables in Phoenix's code. After she fixed the shared variable problem, the incidence of particular dependencies decreased in execution traces. This work provides a glimpse of a future in which programs will not merely perform statistical tests at the behest of human analysts, but will also run tests and interpret the results, autonomously.

7.7   General Patterns in Three-Way Contingency Tables

Dependency detection starts with a two-way contingency table—the rows representing precursors and the columns, successors—then unpacks one row into a second two-way table.   An alternative scheme would be to analyze a three-way table in which two dimensions correspond to items in a precursor, and the third corresponds to the successor.   One can test several related hypotheses with three-way contingency tables.   A concrete illustration is provided by the distribution of projects at the 1993 University of Massachusetts Region 1 Science Fair.   There were two divisions of students, junior and senior high school; five areas, biology, behavioral science, engineering, environmental science, and physical science; and, of course, there were male and female students.   Thus we have a two-by-five-by-two table.   Each cell contains the number of students who belong in the three categories; for example, fifteen junior girls presented biology projects.

Here are all the hypotheses we can test with such a table:

Complete Independence   Although it seems pretty unlikely, *Division, Area,* and *Gender* might be mutually independent.   Independence requires, among other things, that boys and girls are drawn in equal proportions to physics, that girls are equally likely to participate at the junior and senior levels, and that psychology is equally popular at both levels.

One-Factor Independence   If the three factors are not mutually independent, then at least two of them are dependent, but the third might be independent of the others. For example, although gender and area are dependent (girls tend to focus on biology and psychology, boys on physics and engineering) this pattern might be found at both the junior and senior divisions.   If so, *Division* is independent of *Area* and *Gender*; said differently, the dependence between *Area* and *Gender* isn't influenced by *Division*. Note that although there is only one hypothesis of complete independence, you can test three hypotheses of one-factor independence.

Conditional Independence   If one-factor independence doesn't hold, it does not mean the three factors are necessarily mutually dependent.   Rather, two factors might be conditionally independent given the third.   Imagine that *Gender* and *Area* are not independent, and that their relationship is not independent of *Division*. This could happen if *Division* and *Area* are dependent—if psychology is very popular at the senior level but not at the junior level, for instance—and yet *Gender* and *Division* might remain independent, given *Area*. For instance, boys might prefer physics to psychology and girls vice versa (i.e., *Gender* and *Area* are not independent) and senior students might like psychology more than junior students (i.e., *Division* and *Area* are not independent) but within each area, the ratio of boys to girls is the same at junior and senior levels (i.e., *Gender* and *Division* are independent given area). Note that three conditional independence hypotheses can be tested for a three-way table.

Homogenous Association   If no conditional independence relationships hold, the factors still needn't be mutually dependent. It could be that each pair of factors is dependent, but each of these dependencies is independent of the third factor. Said differently, the nature of the relationship between a pair of factors is the same—or homogenous—at every level of the "given" factor. Homogenous association is a pretty strong hypothesis because it requires all of the following statements to be true.

1. *Gender* and *Area* are not independent, but their association is unaffected by *Division*. For example, if boys favor physics and girls psychology, this relationship must be the same at junior and senior levels.

2. *Gender* and *Division* are not independent, but their relationship is unaffected by *Area*. For instance, if girls outnumber boys at the junior level but both appear in equal numbers at the senior level, then this pattern must hold for each of the five areas.

3. *Area* and *Division* are not independent, but *Gender* doesn't influence their relationship. For example, if psychology is more popular with boys at the senior level, it should be no more or less popular with senior girls.

Note that there is only one homogenous association hypothesis to test, although it has three conditions.

Complete Dependence   If homogenous association and all the other hypotheses fail, then the factors are mutually dependent. It isn't possible to test this "hypothesis" directly because expected frequencies for contingency tables are derived for hypotheses of independence, whereas here the hypothesis is that everything depends on everything else. Thus the "test" is to try all the other hypotheses— complete independence, one-factor independence, conditional independence, homogenous association—and if they all fail, then the three factors must be mutually dependent.

These hypotheses can be organized hierarchically in the sense that "higher" ones are suggested when lower ones fail. The *G* statistic from equation 7.1 is used to test

Table 7.10   Observed frequencies in a three-way contingency table

		Contained	Uncontained	Totals
RTK=adequate	*WindSpeed*=high	59	24	83
	WindSpeed=medium	53	26	79
	WindSpeed=low	57	21	78
Totals		169	71	240
RTK=inadequate	*WindSpeed*=high	4	19	23
	WindSpeed=medium	14	24	38
	WindSpeed=low	28	14	42
Totals		46	57	103

all these hypotheses, because all involve summing deviations between expected and observed frequencies, although expected frequencies for the different hypotheses are calculated differently.

7.7.1   A Three-Way Contingency Table Analysis

It is instructive to run a three-way contingency table analysis of the same factors that earlier illustrated a three-way analysis of variance, namely *WindSpeed* (with three levels, low, medium and high), *RTK* (adequate and inadequate), and *Containment* (contained and uncontained). A three-way contingency table is shown in two slices (split by *RTK*) in table 7.10. Each cell represents the number of times (in 343 trials) a particular combination of factors occurred; for example, fifty-nine fires were contained when thinking time was adequate and wind speed was high.

Complete Independence

Testing the hypothesis of complete independence is easy, a simple extension of the two-factor case. Under the null hypothesis that the factors are independent, the probability of a combination is just the product of their individual probabilities. For example, the probability that a fire will be contained when thinking time is adequate and wind speed is high, is

$$Pr(Containment = contained, RTK = adequate, WindSpeed = high)$$

$$= Pr(Containment = contained) \times Pr(RTK = adequate)$$

$$\times Pr(WindSpeed = high).$$

Table 7.11   Expected frequencies for the complete independence hypothesis.

		Contained	Uncontained
RTK=adequate	*WindSpeed*=high	46.49	27.68
	WindSpeed=medium	51.32	30.55
	WindSpeed=low	52.63	31.33
RTK=inadequate	*WindSpeed*=high	19.95	11.88
	WindSpeed=medium	22.02	13.11
	WindSpeed=low	22.59	13.45

These individual probabilities are estimated from marginal frequencies; for example, $23 + 83 = 106$ trials involve high wind speed, and there are 343 trials in all, so $Pr(WindSpeed = high) = 106/343 = .31$. The expected frequency for a cell is just its probability times the total number of trials, so the expected frequency of fires contained when thinking time is adequate and wind speed is high, is:

$$\hat{f}_{contained,adequate,high} = \frac{169 + 46}{343} \times \frac{169 + 71}{343} \times \frac{83 + 23}{343} \times 343 = 46.49.$$

More generally, the expected frequency for level i of factor A, level j of factor B and level k of factor C is:

$$\hat{f}_{ijk} = \frac{f_{i\bullet\bullet} \times f_{\bullet j\bullet} \times f_{\bullet\bullet k}}{f^2_{\bullet\bullet\bullet}},$$

where $f_{i\bullet\bullet}$, say, is the marginal frequency of level i of factor A (e.g., $f_{contained\bullet\bullet} = 215$) and $f_{\bullet\bullet\bullet}$ is the total count for the table (e.g., 343). The expected frequencies under the hypothesis of complete independence for table 7.10 are shown in table 7.11, and the G statistic to test this hypothesis is:

$$G = 2\left[59\ln\frac{59}{46.49} + 24\ln\frac{24}{27.68} + \cdots + 28\ln\frac{28}{22.59} + 14\ln\frac{14}{13.45}\right] = 43.08.$$

For a three-way table with a, b, and c levels of factors A, B, and C, respectively, a test of complete independence has $abc - a - b - c + 2$ degrees of freedom (Wickens, 1989, pp. 73–75), which for table 7.10 is seven. As in the test of two-way tables, G is compared to a chi-square distribution with the appropriate degrees of freedom. As it happens, the critical value that cuts off .001 of the chi-square distribution with seven degrees of freedom is 24.322, and $G = 43.08$ exceeds this by a lot. Hence, the probability of attaining $G = 43.08$ by chance given the null hypothesis that the three factors are independent is virtually zero.

Table 7.12   Contingency table for one-factor independence hypothesis

		Contained	Uncontained	Totals
RTK=adequate	*WindSpeed*=high	59	24	83
	WindSpeed=medium	53	26	79
	WindSpeed=low	57	21	78
RTK=inadequate	*WindSpeed*=high	4	19	23
	WindSpeed=medium	14	24	38
	WindSpeed=low	28	14	42
Totals		215	128	343

One-Factor Independence

Because the test of complete independence fails, it's appropriate to test three one-factor independence hypotheses. For brevity we will test only the hypothesis that *Containment* is independent of *WindSpeed* and *RTK*. The first step is to build a contingency table. The hypothesis is really that the joint distribution of *WindSpeed* and *RTK* is the same for both levels of containment, so the corresponding contingency table has rows representing the joint distribution and columns representing levels *Containment*, as shown in table 7.12. Expected frequencies are calculated from the margins, as with any test of independence in a two-way table. For example, the expected frequency of fires contained when thinking time is adequate and wind speed is high, is:

$$\hat{f}_{contained,adequate,high} = \frac{83}{343} \times \frac{215}{343} \times 343 = \frac{83 \times 215}{343} = 52.03.$$

By the same logic, the expected frequency of uncontained fires under the same conditions—adequate thinking time and high wind speed—is 30.97. Notice that these frequencies, 52.03 and 30.97, mirror the proportions of the column margins: $52.03/30.97 = 215/128$. The same is true for every row in table 7.12. Thus, if you expressed each frequency in a column as a percentage of the column margin, then the distributions in the columns would be identical. This is what we want: The expected frequencies reflect the hypothesis that the joint distribution of *WindSpeed* and *RTK* is identical for *Containment=contained* and *Containment=uncontained*. The expected frequencies for the entire analysis are shown in table 7.13; ignore the final column, labeled G_{row}, for now.

The *G* statistic for the analysis is

$$G = 2 \left[59 \ln \frac{59}{52.03} + 24 \ln \frac{24}{30.97} + \cdots + 28 \ln \frac{28}{26.33} + 14 \ln \frac{14}{15.67} \right] = 37.65$$

Table 7.13   Expected frequencies and G components for one-factor independence hypothesis

		Contained	Uncontained	G_{row}
RTK=adequate	*WindSpeed*=high	52.03	30.97	2.59
	WindSpeed=medium	49.52	29.48	0.67
	WindSpeed=low	48.89	29.11	3.78
RTK=inadequate	*WindSpeed*=high	14.42	8.58	19.95
	WindSpeed=medium	23.82	14.18	10.38
	WindSpeed=low	26.33	15.67	0.29

and the test has five degrees of freedom (i.e., $(rows - 1)(columns - 1)$). The critical value for the chi-square distribution (with 5 *dof*) to reject the null hypothesis at the $p \leq .001$ level is 20.515, so the joint distribution of *WindSpeed* and *RTK* is almost certainly not independent of *Containment*.

The individual components of this G statistic show where the joint distributions of *WindSpeed* and *RTK* deviate most from their expectations. The last column in table 7.13, G_{row}, contains the sum of the G components in each row; for example,

$$G_{adeq.,high} = 2\,[59 \ln(59/52.03) + 24 \ln(24/30.97)] = 2.596.$$

You can see that more than 80% of the total value of G is due to two rows of the table, where *RTK*=*inadequate* and *WindSpeed*=*(high, medium)*. In fact, the first of these rows accounts for 53% of the total G statistic, even though it contains only 6.7% of the data in the table. It's disturbing that so little data has such a large effect: it means this effect is unlikely to be as robust as the others. If you imagine adding noise to the cells in table 7.12 in accordance with the expected frequencies under the null hypothesis (e.g., the counts in the cells in the row in question are incremented with probabilities 14.42/23 and 8.58/23, respectively) then the G value for the *RTK*=*inadequate*, *WindSpeed*=*high* row will change more quickly than G for other rows.

There are two other one-factor independence hypotheses to test. Each test proceeds as shown previously, by constructing a two-way table with rows representing the joint distribution of two factors and columns representing levels of the third factor. Each hypothesis fails: neither *RTK* ($G = 37.63$, $p \leq .001$) nor *WindSpeed* ($G = 23.00$, $p \leq .001$) is independent of the joint distribution of the remaining factors.

Conditional Independence

Since one-factor independence tests fail, it's appropriate to test whether any two factors are conditionally independent given the third. The simplest way to think of conditional independence is this: when the value of the "given" factor is fixed, no association exists between the others. It is an unavoidable fact that shoe size and language skill are associated, because children with very small feet are not facile with language. We recognize this to be a spurious relationship that depends on a third, though unmentioned, factor. Age is responsible for the association between shoe size and language skill, so if age were fixed, the association would vanish. One way to fix age is to partition data into narrow age groups, so that the members of each group are roughly the same age. Then, if age is really responsible for the relationship between language skill and shoe size, these factors should be independent within an age group. This phenomenon is conditional independence: a relationship between two factors vanishes when a third (or, more generally, a set of factors) is fixed. Conditional independence is an important relationship (e.g., it plays a role in inferring causal relationships, see section 8.8) and it is tested in many ways. Conditional independence in contingency tables is perhaps the most intuitive of all such tests.

Suppose three factors, *A,B*, and *C* have a, b, and c levels, respectively. Then to test whether *A* and *B* are conditionally independent given *C*, one should simply "slice" the a-by-b-by-c contingency table into c tables, one for each level of *C*, and run an ordinary independence test on each a-by-b table. The null hypothesis is that *A* and *B* will not be associated in any of the two-way tables, so to test it, one sums the *G* statistics for each table. If the sum is large enough to reject the hypothesis it means that at least one of the tables shows a significant association between *A* and *B*, or perhaps no individual table is significant but several show a weak association.

Consider the hypothesis that *Containment* and *WindSpeed* are conditionally independent given *RTK*. If true, then *WindSpeed* doesn't influence whether a fire is contained at a given level of thinking speed. The first step is to slice the original three-way contingency table into two *Containment* by *WindSpeed* tables, one for *RTK= adequate* and the other for *RTK= inadequate*. (In fact, table 7.10 represents the original table this way, as two slices.) Next, calculate expected frequencies for each slice from its row and column margins. For example the expected frequency for *RTK=adequate*, *Containment=contained* and *WindSpeed=high* is $(169 \times 83)/240 = 58.45$, because there are 240 trials in the *RTK=adequate* slice. Next, calculate the test statistic for the first slice, $G = 0.70$. This isn't remotely significant: When thinking time is adequate, *WindSpeed* doesn't affect *Containment*. For the second slice, however, the test statistic is significant, $G = 16.87$.

The sum of these statistics is 17.57, which measures the total association between *Containment* and *WindSpeed* given *RTK*. Slicing a table of size a-by-b-by-c by factor *C* produces c tables, each of which has $(a-1)(b-1)$ degrees of freedom. Each of these tables could show some dependence between *A* and *B*, hence, the total degrees of freedom for the conditional independence test is $(a-1)(b-1)c$. For the current example, this is $(2 - 1)(3 - 1)2 = 4$. The $\alpha = .005$ critical value for a chi-square distribution with four degrees of freedom is 14.86, which is exceeded by $G = 17.57$, so *Containment* is almost certainly not conditionally independent of *WindSpeed* given *RTK*. Recall that we can test three conditional independence hypotheses in a three-way table (each factor can be the "given" factor); for completeness, the two remaining conditional independence hypotheses also fail.

Homogenous Association

If conditional independence fails it means that A and B are associated given C, but there's always the possibility that the nature of the association is the same at all levels of C. Unfortunately, no closed form exists for the expected frequencies for this analysis. The frequencies can be found, however, with a simple, iterative algorithm (see e.g., Wickens, 1989 or Sokal and Rohlf, 1981).

Let's discuss the logic of the homogenous association test and see whether we can anticipate its outcome when applied to our ongoing example. We have already seen that *WindSpeed* affects *Containment* when *RTK=inadequate*. If the relationship between *WindSpeed* and *Containment* is essentially the same at the other level of thinking speed, *RTK=adequate*, then homogenous association obtains. But we know this is false because we found no significant dependency between *WindSpeed* and *Containment* when *RTK=adequate*. Clearly, two relationships cannot be homogenous when one is a highly significant dependency ($G = 16.87$) and the other shows no evidence whatsoever of dependence ($G = .7$). Thus we expect the homogenous association test to fail, which, in fact, it does.

7.8   Conclusion

The methods in this chapter and the next are organized around two simple distinctions: independent versus dependent variables, and continuous versus categorical variables. In manipulation experiments, independent variables are the ones we manipulate and dependent variables are the ones we measure. In observation experiments, we don't manipulate the independent variables, but we still regard them as causally "prior" to dependent variables, at least provisionally, and for the purpose of statistical analysis. When the independent and dependent variables are continuous, we can develop functional models to relate them, using techniques such as multiple regression, as discussed in the next chapter. When independent variables are categorical (or ordinal) and not too numerous, and the dependent variable is continuous, the analysis of variance is a powerful, flexible method. And when both independent and dependent variables are categorical, then contingency table analysis is the method of choice.

7.9   Further Reading

The analysis of variance literature is vast; you would do well to begin with Winer 1971 and Keppel 1973, two excellent sources aimed at psychological research. A very interesting and unorthodox presentation, which emphasizes the geometry of analysis of variance, is Box et al. 1978. Hays 1973 and Olson 1987 provide accessible, general discussions. Comparisons and contrasts for two- and three-way analyses are discussed in Keppel 1973, and Rosenthal and Rosnow 1985.

Contingency table analysis is presented thoroughly and accessibly in Wickens 1989; Sokal and Rohlf 1981 provide a readable, brief introduction to two- and three-way analyses.

Appendix : Experiment Designs and Analyses

One reason for the success of the analysis of variance is its intimate connection to experiment design. Analysis of variance decomposes the variance in an experiment, and a well-designed experiment is one for which the decomposition of variance is straightforward and the responsibility for variance is clear. This appendix describes three experiment designs and their associated analyses. These experiment designs illustrate principles that underlie more complex analyses.

The bridge between experiment design and analysis is the *design table*, a simple example of which is shown in table 7A.1. A single factor (*A*) has three levels, defining three conditions, and four data are collected in each condition. Data come from joint events in which a program works on a task in an environment, so table 7A.1 represents many possible experiment designs. One program might produce all the data, and factor *A* might represent an aspect of the program's environment such as its degree of unpredictability. Alternatively, the levels of factor *A* might represent three classes of tasks, such as planning tasks with independent, serializable, and laboriously serializable subgoals (Barret and Weld, 1994). Or, factor *A* might represent three different programs, or three different versions of one program; for example, three levels of roughening of MYCIN's certainty factors (section 6.7).

Several data in a cell are often called *replicates*, just as repetitions of experiments are called replications. This is no etymological accident if you take the perspective

Table 7A.1   A one-factor design with three levels and no repeated measures.

	Factor A	
A_1	A_2	A_3
$d_{1,1}$	$d_{2,5}$	$d_{3,9}$
$d_{1,2}$	$d_{2,6}$	$d_{3,10}$
$d_{1,3}$	$d_{2,7}$	$d_{3,11}$
$d_{1,4}$	$d_{2,8}$	$d_{3,12}$

of the data within a cell. Each datum "sees" exactly the same experiment, or, the experiment is repeated for each datum.

In a one-factor design, a datum is denoted $d_{i,j}$, where i is a level of the factor and j is an event that produced the datum. Referring again to table 7A.1, $d_{1,1}$ could denote the first task presented to the first program in a comparative study of three programs. By convention, the last item in a subscript always denotes the event that produced the datum; for example, $d_{1,4}$ could be the fourth task encountered by the first program in a comparative study. What, then, is $d_{2,8}$? It is the fourth task encountered by the second program, but the notation tells us that the first and second programs did not attempt the same four tasks: Program 1 worked on tasks 1 to 4, program 2 addressed tasks 5 to 8, and program 3 attempted tasks 9 to 12. Because no task appeared in more than one condition, this design is called *one-factor without repeated measures*. The one-way analysis of variance described in chapter 6 is the appropriate method.

Often, however, we want to test different programs working on the same tasks. In such a design, programs 1, 2, and 3, would each attempt tasks 1,2,3 and 4. This is called a *one-way repeated measures design* because the task is repeated for each program. Although it is a one-way design, it is usually analyzed with a two-way analysis of variance, treating *Task* and *Program* as factors. But if *Task* is a factor, then our design table includes $p \times t$ cells—where p and t are the numbers of programs and tasks in the design, respectively—and each cell contains just one datum. This raises the interesting question of how to estimate within-cell variance, a question deferred until later in this section.

A more straightforward two-way design involves two factors and several data collected in each condition. For example, one factor might be *Program* and the other *Task*, and each program tackles ten instances of each task. Obviously, this design makes sense only if a program's performance on task instances is expected to vary. For example, the tasks might involve parsing sentences with different structures: One task might involve sentences with embedded relative clauses, the other, sentences with anaphora. Then each program would be asked to parse ten sentences of each type.

You can analyze this experiment two ways, in fact, depending on whether you regard the *Program* and *Task* factors as fixed or random. The distinction is this: If you imagine running an experiment not once but twice, and you would use the same levels of a factor both times, then that factor is fixed, otherwise it is random. Suppose your experiment evaluates two parsers, *P1* and *P2*, on a variety of difficult sentence structures. You run the experiment with two kinds of structures, embedded relative clauses and anaphora, ten instances of each. Now imagine running the experiment again: You would probably use the same parsers because the purpose of the experiment is to compare them, but you might not use embedded relative clauses and anaphoric sentences. Instead you might select other types of difficult structures, such as compound noun phrases and pronominal references. If so, *Structure* is a random factor, and the design is called a *mixed design* because it mixes fixed and random factors. On the other hand, if you really want to know how *P1* and *P2* handle relative clauses and anaphora, then you wouldn't change these types of structures when you run the experiment again, and *Structure* would be a fixed factor. The variance in a *fixed-factor design* is decomposed the same way as in a mixed design, but it is interpreted and analyzed differently, as shown in the following sections.

7A.1   Two-Way Fixed Factorial Design without Repeated Measures

In a *factorial* design each level of one factor is crossed with each level of the other. Assume that each cell in the design table contains several data and, because unequal cell sizes complicate the analysis, each cell contains the same number of data. Unequal cell sizes are not fatal, just complicating, especially if they aren't very unequal (see Keppel, 1973, for procedures to handle these cases). Assume also that each data-producing episode is unique; for example, each problem is solved by one program only, in one condition only. In table 7A.2, for example, problems 1 through 4 are solved in the *A1,B1* condition and no other. This is what we mean by "without repeated measures."

To make the presentation concrete, imagine a study of two search algorithms, the old workhorse A* search, and a new, potentially superior method, Q* search. Each is tested on three classes of problems: Traveling Salesman, Tower of Hanoi, and the Eight Tiles puzzle. Thus the experimental factors are *Algorithm* and *Problem*. In table 7A.3, four problems are presented in each condition and no problem is presented more than once. Thus the table as a whole contains data from $2 \times 3 \times 4 = 24$ unique

Table 7A.2   A two-way factorial design without repeated measures.

	A_1	A_2	A_3
B_1	$d_{1,1,1}$	$d_{2,1,5}$	$d_{3,1,9}$
	$d_{1,1,2}$	$d_{2,1,6}$	$d_{3,1,10}$
	$d_{1,1,3}$	$d_{2,1,7}$	$d_{3,1,11}$
	$d_{1,1,4}$	$d_{2,1,8}$	$d_{3,1,12}$
B_2	$d_{1,2,13}$	$d_{2,2,17}$	$d_{3,2,21}$
	$d_{1,2,14}$	$d_{2,2,18}$	$d_{3,2,22}$
	$d_{1,2,15}$	$d_{2,2,19}$	$d_{3,2,23}$
	$d_{1,2,16}$	$d_{2,2,20}$	$d_{3,2,24}$

Table 7A.3   An illustration of a two-way factorial analysis without repeated measures.

	A* Search	Q* Search
Traveling Salesman	501, 277, 673, 833	321, 541, 387, 603
Tower of Hanoi	771, 124, 173, 208	477, 595, 901, 911
Eight Tiles	991, 1021, 2011, 877	625, 782, 543, 910

Table 7A.4   Cell, row, and column means for the data in table 7A.3.

	A*	Q*	Row mean
TS	571	463	$\overline{x}_{\bullet,TS} = 517$
TH	319	721	$\overline{x}_{\bullet,TH} = 520$
8T	1225	715	$\overline{x}_{\bullet,8T} = 970$
Column mean	$\overline{x}_{A*,\bullet} = 705$	$\overline{x}_{Q*,\bullet} = 663$	$\overline{x}_G = 669$

instances of problems. The dependent variable is the number of nodes searched before a solution node is found; for instance, A* searched 501 nodes in its first Traveling Salesman problem.

Each cell in table 7A.4 contains the mean of the four items in the corresponding cell in table 7A.3, and the last cell in each row and column contains the mean of that row or column. Because the cells are of equal size, the grand mean of all the data is the mean of the six cell means:

$$\overline{x}_G = (571 + 3198 + 1225 + 463 + 721 + 715)/6 = 669.$$

The effects of a factor, say, *Algorithm*, are expressed in terms of the deviations of the column means from the grand mean:

$$\mathcal{E}_{A*,\bullet} = (\overline{x}_{A*,\bullet} - \overline{x}_G) = 705 - 669 = 36; \tag{7A.1}$$

$$\mathcal{E}_{Q*,\bullet} = (\overline{x}_{Q*,\bullet} - \overline{x}_G) = 633 - 669 = -36. \tag{7A.2}$$

Similarly, here are the effects of problem:

$$\mathcal{E}_{\bullet,TS} = (\overline{x}_{\bullet,TS} - \overline{x}_G) = 517 - 669 = -152; \tag{7A.3}$$

$$\mathcal{E}_{\bullet,TH} = (\overline{x}_{\bullet,TH} - \overline{x}_G) = 520 - 669 = -149; \tag{7A.4}$$

$$\mathcal{E}_{\bullet,8T} = (\overline{x}_{\bullet,8T} - \overline{x}_G) = 970 - 669 = 301. \tag{7A.5}$$

In general, the effects of the ith level of a column factor and the jth level of a row factor are

$$\mathcal{E}_{i,\bullet} = \overline{x}_{i,\bullet} - \overline{x}_G,$$

$$\mathcal{E}_{\bullet,j} = \overline{x}_{\bullet,j} - \overline{x}_G,$$

respectively. Note that the effects of a factor are constrained by the grand mean to sum to zero; for example, $\mathcal{E}_{A*,\bullet} + \mathcal{E}_{Q*,\bullet} = 0$. In general, for fixed factor designs,

$$\sum_i \mathcal{E}_{i,\bullet} = 0; \tag{7A.6}$$

$$\sum_j \mathcal{E}_{\bullet,j} = 0. \tag{7A.7}$$

If the effects of the factors were independent, then each cell mean would be the sum of the grand mean, the effect of algorithm and the effect of problem type. For example, the mean of the top-left $(A*,TS)$ cell in the previous table would be

$$\overline{x}_G + \mathcal{E}_{A*,\bullet} + \mathcal{E}_{\bullet,TS} = 669 + 36 - 152 = 553.$$

Because the actual cell mean, 571, is not 553, it's clear that $\overline{x}_{A*,TS}$ isn't the sum of the grand mean and the effects of the two factors. Something else, besides these factors, influences the cell mean. The strength of this effect, denoted $\mathcal{E}_{A*,TS}$, is just the "leftover" component after the effects of the grand mean and the factors are removed:

$$\mathcal{E}_{A*,TS} = \overline{x}_{A*,TS} - (\overline{x}_G + \mathcal{E}_{A*,\bullet} + \mathcal{E}_{\bullet,TS})$$

$$= 571 - 553 = 18.$$

This influence is called an *interaction effect*. For computational purposes, expand the terms for row and column effects and then simplify the expression:

$$\mathcal{E}_{i,j} = \bar{x}_{i,j} - \left(\bar{x}_G + \mathcal{E}_{i,\bullet} + \mathcal{E}_{\bullet,i}\right)$$
$$= \bar{x}_{i,j} - \bar{x}_G - (\bar{x}_{i,\bullet} - \bar{x}_G) - (\bar{x}_{\bullet,j} - \bar{x}_G)$$
$$= \bar{x}_{i,j} - \bar{x}_{i,\bullet} - \bar{x}_{\bullet,j} + \bar{x}_G.$$

In general, every cell mean is the sum of the grand mean, the effects of two factors, and the effect of the interaction of the factors:

$$\bar{x}_{i,j} = \bar{x}_G + \mathcal{E}_{i,\bullet} + \mathcal{E}_{\bullet,j} + \mathcal{E}_{i,j}.$$

If the factors do not interact, then all the interaction terms will be zero (except for sampling fluctuations). In fixed factor designs, these interaction effects are constrained to sum to zero across both rows and columns:

$$\sum_i \mathcal{E}_{i,j} = 0; \tag{7A.8}$$

$$\sum_j \mathcal{E}_{i,j} = 0. \tag{7A.9}$$

Moreover, these effects are assumed to sum to zero in the population. In a mixed design, the interaction effects in the sample data necessarily sum to zero, also, and the population interaction effects over all possible selections of levels of the random factor are assumed to sum to zero. The population interaction effects for the particular levels of the random variable that were sampled are not expected to sum to zero. This complicates the analysis of interaction effects, as discussed in section 7A.3.

Table 7A.5 decomposes the cell means from the previous table into main effects of factors and interaction effects. The only decomposition remaining is to subtract from each datum its cell mean, yielding a residual, $e_{i,j,k} = (x_{i,j,k} - \bar{x}_{i,j})$. Said differently, a residual is what remains when the effects of the grand mean, the row and column

Table 7A.5   The cell means from table 7A.4 decomposed into grand mean, row and column effects, and interaction effects.

A*	Q*		
$669 + 36 - 152 + 18 = 571$	$669 - 36 - 152 - 18 = 463$	$\bar{x}_{TS} = 517,\ \mathcal{E}_{\bullet,TS} = -152$	
$669 + 36 - 149 - 237 = 319$	$669 - 36 - 149 + 237 = 721$	$\bar{x}_{TH} = 520,\ \mathcal{E}_{\bullet,TH} = -149$	
$669 + 36 + 301 + 219 = 1225$	$669 - 36 + 301 - 219 = 715$	$\bar{x}_{8T} = 970,\ \mathcal{E}_{\bullet,8T} = 301$	
$\bar{x}_{A*} = 705,\ \mathcal{E}_{A*,\bullet} = 36$	$\bar{x}_{Q*} = 633,\ \mathcal{E}_{Q*,\bullet} = -36$		

factors, and the interaction have been removed. For example, the residual for 501, the first datum in table 7A.3, is

$$e_{A*,TS,1} = 501 - (669 + 36 - 152 + 18) = -70.$$

Now it is easy to decompose the deviation of an individual datum from the grand mean, $(x_{i,j,k} - \bar{x}_G)$, and, thus, decompose the total variance in a two-way table. All told, the deviation of a datum from the grand mean has four components:

$$
\begin{aligned}
(x_{i,j,k} - \bar{x}_G) = {} & e_{i,j,k} && \text{within-cell variance} \\
& + \mathcal{E}_{i,\bullet} && \text{effect of column factor} \\
& + \mathcal{E}_{\bullet,j} && \text{effect of row factor} \\
& + \mathcal{E}_{ij} && \text{interaction effect.}
\end{aligned}
$$

As we have seen, these components can be expressed as deviations from means:

$$
\begin{aligned}
(x_{i,j,k} - \bar{x}_G) = {} & (x_{i,j,k} - \bar{x}_{i,j}) && \text{within-cell variance} \\
& + (\bar{x}_{i,\bullet} - \bar{x}_G) && \text{effect of column factor} \\
& + (\bar{x}_{\bullet,j} - \bar{x}_G) && \text{effect of row factor} \\
& + (\bar{x}_{i,j} - \bar{x}_{i,\bullet} - \bar{x}_{\bullet,j} + \bar{x}_G) && \text{interaction effect.}
\end{aligned}
$$

The sums of squares for these components are easily specified. SS_{total} is the summed, squared deviations of each datum from the grand mean:

$$SS_{total} = \sum_i \sum_j \sum_k (x_{i,j,k} - \bar{x}_G)^2.$$

SS_{within} is the sum over all columns, rows, and items within a cell, of the residual for each item:

$$SS_{within} = \sum_i \sum_j \sum_k e_{i,j,k}^2 = \sum_i \sum_j \sum_k (x_{i,j,k} - \bar{x}_{i,j})^2.$$

The sum of squares for the column factor, $SS_{columns}$, is just the sum of the squared effects of the factor, or in terms of deviations, the sum of squared deviations of the column means from the grand mean. There are n_i data items in column i, and the effect $\mathcal{E}_{i,\bullet}$ is the same for each datum, so we multiply the effect by n_i to get the sum of squares:

$$SS_{columns} = n_i \sum_i (\mathcal{E}_{i,\bullet})^2 = n_i \sum_i (\bar{x}_{i,\bullet} - \bar{x}_G)^2.$$

We moved n_i outside the sum because we assumed equal cell sizes; in general it would stay inside the sum. The sum of squares for the row factor is derived the same way, except we sum across rows instead of columns:

$$SS_{rows} = n_j \sum_j (\mathcal{E}_{\bullet,j})^2 = n_j \sum_j (\bar{x}_{\bullet,j} - \bar{x}_G)^2.$$

Table 7A.6   The decomposition of variance in the fixed two-way analysis of variance

Source	df	MS
Column	$C-1$	$\frac{SS_{column}}{C-1}$
Row	$R-1$	$\frac{SS_{row}}{R-1}$
Interaction	$(C-1)(R-1)$	$\frac{SS_{interaction}}{(C-1)(R-1)}$
Within	$RC(n-1)$	$\frac{SS_{within}}{RC(n-1)}$
Total	$RCn-1$	$\frac{SS_{total}}{RCn-1}$

Finally, the sum of squares for the interaction is the sum, over cells, of the interaction effects. Because there are $n_{i,j}$ items in a cell, we multiply the effects by $n_{i,j}$ to get the sum of squares:

$$SS_{interaction} = n_{i,j} \sum_i \sum_j (\mathcal{E}_{i,j})^2 = n_{i,j} \sum_i \sum_j (\overline{x}_{ij} - \overline{x}_{i,\bullet} - \overline{x}_{\bullet,j} + \overline{x}_G)^2.$$

The mean squares for these effects are derived from the sums of squares much as they are for the one-way analysis: each sum of squares is divided by the appropriate number of degrees of freedom. If there are C levels of the column factor and R levels of the row factor, then the degrees of freedom and mean squares are shown in table 7A.6.

Three hypotheses are tested by the two-way fixed factorial analysis without repeated measures:

1. The column factor has no effect (i.e., $\forall i : \mathcal{E}_{i,\bullet} = 0$).
2. The row factor has no effect (i.e., $\forall j : \mathcal{E}_{\bullet,j} = 0$).
3. There is no interaction effect (i.e., $\forall i, j : \overline{x}_{ij} = \overline{x}_G + \mathcal{E}_{i,\bullet} + \mathcal{E}_{\bullet,j}$).

Recall that in the one-way analysis of variance MS_{within} is an unbiased estimate of population variance irrespective of whether the null hypothesis is true or false, whereas $MS_{between}$ is an unbiased estimate of population variance if the null hypothesis is true. The null hypothesis is therefore tested by calculating the ratio of $MS_{between}$ and MS_{within} and comparing it to the F distribution, the sampling distribution of the ratio of two variances under the null hypothesis that the variances are equal.

Exactly the same logic is followed to test hypotheses in the current analysis. If there is no effect of the column factor, then $MS_{columns}$ is an unbiased estimator of population variance. Similarly, if there is no effect of the row factor and no interaction effect, then

MS_{rows} and $MS_{interaction}$, respectively, are unbiased estimators of population variance. As before, MS_{within} is an unbiased estimator of population variance whether or not any of these null hypotheses are true. Thus, MS_{within} is the *error term* that goes in the denominator of the F statistic to test these hypotheses.

7A.2   A Numerical Example

A two-way analysis of the data in table 7A.3 begins with sums of squares. It will help to refer to table 7A.5, also, as it shows row, column and interaction effects. Let's start with the sum of squares for the column factor, *Algorithm*. The number of data items in each column is $n_i = 12$ so the sum of squares is:

$$SS_{Alg.} = n_i \sum_i (\mathcal{E}_{i,\bullet})^2$$
$$= 12 \left[36^2 + -36^2 \right]$$
$$= 31104.$$

Each row includes eight data items, so the sum of squares for the row factor, *Problem*, is:

$$SS_{Prob.} = n_j \sum_j (\mathcal{E}_{\bullet,j})^2$$
$$= 8 \left[-152^2 + -149^2 + 301^2 \right]$$
$$= 1087248.$$

The sum of squares for the interaction effect is derived from the interaction effects in table 7A.5; these are the fourth item in each sum, for instance, 18 in the $A*,TS$ cell. Each cell contains four data, so $n_{i,j} = 4$ and the sum of squares is:

$$SS_{Alg.\times Prob.} = n_{i,j} \sum_i \sum_j \mathcal{E}_{i,j}$$
$$= 4 \left[18^2 + -18^2 + -237^2 + 237^2 + 219^2 + -219^2 \right]$$
$$= 835632.$$

Finally, the summed, squared residuals, or SS_{within}:

$$SS_{within} = \sum_i \sum_j \sum_k e_{i,j,k}^2$$
$$= (501 - 571)^2 \quad + (277 - 571)^2 + (673 - 571)^2 + (833 - 571)^2$$
$$\cdots$$
$$(625 - 715)^2 \quad + (782 - 715)^2 + (543 - 715)^2 + (910 - 715)^2$$
$$= 1557356.$$

Table 7A.7   Two-way analysis of variance for nodes expanded by two search algorithms applied to classic search problems.

Source	df	Sum of squares	Mean square	F	p value
Algorithm	1	31104	31104	.36	.556
Problem	2	1087248	543624	6.283	.009
Algorithm × Problem	2	835632	417816	4.829	.042
Within	18	1557356	86519.778		

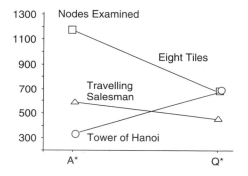

Figure 7A.1   Plot of cell means for the search problem data from table 7A.4.

Mean squares are simply sums of squares divided by the appropriate degrees of freedom. *F* statistics are mean squares for effects divided by the appropriate error term—the term that represents random variance in the table unassociated with any factors or interactions. In the current example, the appropriate error term is MS_{within} (other error terms will be described shortly).

The results of the analysis are shown in table 7A.7. It appears that *Algorithm* has no effect on the dependent variable ($F = .36$, $p > .5$), so there's little to choose between A* and Q*. The problem type, however, had a big effect ($F = 6.283$, $p \leq .009$), and the interaction between *Algorithm* and *Problem* was respectable ($F = 4.829$, $p \leq .042$).

In fact, this is a misleading account of the results. It is easy to misinterpret main effects when there is a significant interaction effect. Whenever you have an interaction effect, it's a good idea to plot the cell means, as we do in figure 7A.1. You can see that Q* performs better than A* on Eight Tiles and Traveling Salesman problems, but worse on Tower of Hanoi problems. You can also see that the previous interpretation of the noneffect of *Algorithm* is wrong. The algorithm does, in fact, influence the dependent variable, and the two algorithms do not perform identically on any of the problems. The main effect of *Algorithm* is insignificant because the average of the means for the A* algorithm, 705, is not very different from the average of the means for the Q* algorithm, 633. Yet A* is much better than Q* on Tower of Hanoi problems, and Q* wins handily on Eight Tiles problems; these are big effects, but they offset each other, leaving a small average difference. So when you see an insignificant main effect and a significant interaction, remember that the interaction may indicate offsetting effects, and that the "insignificant" factor might be quite influential.

7A.3   Two-Way Mixed Design without Repeated Measures

Mixed designs, which cross fixed and random factors, are extremely common in a wide range of research settings. Random factors, recall, are those with levels you might change in a repetition of an experiment. The paradigmatic random factor in social and biomedical research is *Subjects*—the people and organisms we test in an experiment. A biologist who tests the effects of alcohol on rats won't use the same rats when she replicates her experiment (they'll probably be dead), so *Rats* is a random factor. She probably will use the same levels of alcohol, making it a fixed factor. Analogously, a researcher in machine learning might test five techniques to prevent overfitting on classification problems, but he will select test problems randomly from a large corpus, and probably won't use the same problems if he repeats the experiment. In this case *Technique* is fixed and *Problem* is random. Another example of a mixed design is Acker and Porter's experiment with their View Retriever program. We analyzed their data as if it was a fixed-factor design in section 7.3.1, but actually, *Judge* is a random factor. The design is shown in table 7A.8. Each task involves the presentation of a viewpoint—a paragraph of text—to a judge who scores its coherence. Clearly, the viewpoints presented in the "textbook viewpoint" condition must be textbook viewpoints, not some other kind of viewpoint. Thus, tasks are nested within the viewpoint factor.

Each task is not confined to a single condition, however, because all judges see the same viewpoints of each type. Hence this is a *two-way mixed design with repeated measures*, and is slightly more complicated than mixed designs without repeated measures. Mixed designs are discussed further in Keppel (1973), Winer (1971), and Olson (1987). This discussion goes no further than mixed designs without repeated measures.

To illustrate such a design, suppose that in the previous experiment with algorithms A* and Q*, *Problem* was a random factor. This means we might have run the

Table 7A.8   The mixed, repeated measures design of Acker and Porter's experiment. Each judge sees ten viewpoints of four types, and all judges see the same viewpoints.

	Textbook viewpoints	ViewRetriever viewpoints	Degraded viewpoints	Random viewpoints
Judge 1	$d_{T,1,1}$	$d_{V,1,11}$	$d_{D,1,21}$	$d_{R,1,31}$
	$d_{T,1,2}$	$d_{V,1,12}$	$d_{D,1,22}$	$d_{R,1,32}$
	$d_{T,1,2}$	$d_{V,1,13}$	$d_{D,1,23}$	$d_{R,1,33}$
	$\vdots$	$\vdots$	$\vdots$	$\vdots$
Judge 2	$d_{T,2,1}$	$d_{V,2,11}$	$d_{D,2,21}$	$d_{R,2,31}$
	$d_{T,2,2}$	$d_{V,2,12}$	$d_{D,2,22}$	$d_{R,2,32}$
	$d_{T,2,3}$	$d_{V,2,13}$	$d_{D,2,23}$	$d_{R,2,33}$
	$\vdots$	$\vdots$	$\vdots$	$\vdots$
$\vdots$	$\vdots$	$\vdots$	$\vdots$	
Judge 10	$d_{T,10,1}$	$d_{V,10,11}$	$d_{D,10,21}$	$d_{R,10,31}$
	$d_{T,10,2}$	$d_{V,10,12}$	$d_{D,10,22}$	$d_{R,10,32}$
	$d_{T,10,3}$	$d_{V,10,13}$	$d_{D,10,23}$	$d_{R,10,33}$
	$\vdots$	$\vdots$	$\vdots$	$\vdots$

experiment with problems other than Traveling Salesman, Tower of Hanoi, and Eight Tiles. Said differently, these are merely one sample of types of problems, and a repetition of the experiment might include other types. To understand the far-reaching effects of this shift in perspective, it's necessary to retreat a few steps and ask, "What is an *F* test, really, and where does the variance in the analysis of variance come from?"

An *F* test, like any other statistical test, is a ratio of an observed effect divided by a measure of variance. Not any measure of variance, of course, but the standard error of the sampling distribution of the effect, derived under the null hypothesis of no effect. For example, in a two-sample *t* test, we divide the effect (the difference between two means) by an estimate of the variability of the distribution of all possible differences between means assuming the null hypothesis—that the means were drawn from the same population. The *F* statistic is no different. In the one-way analysis of variance, $MS_{between}$ is the average effect and MS_{within} is the error term, the variability of the distribution of effects given the null hypothesis (in fact, a one-way analysis

Table 7A.9 The population cell means for all possible problems, decomposed into grand mean, row and column effects, and interaction effects.

Problem	A*	Q*	
P1	$700 + 0 + 200 + 100 = 1000$	$700 + 0 + 200 - 100 = 800$	$\overline{x}_{P1} = 900,\ \mathcal{E}_{\bullet,P1} = 200$
P2	$700 + 0 + 300 - 200 = 800$	$700 + 0 + 300 + 200 = 1200$	$\overline{x}_{P2} = 1000,\ \mathcal{E}_{\bullet,P2} = 300$
P3	$700 + 0 - 200 - 200 = 300$	$700 + 0 - 200 + 200 = 700$	$\overline{x}_{P3} = 500,\ \mathcal{E}_{\bullet,P3} = -200$
P4	$700 + 0 - 300 + 300 = 700$	$700 + 0 - 300 - 300 = 100$	$\overline{x}_{P4} = 400,\ \mathcal{E}_{\bullet,P4} = -300$
	$\overline{x}_{A*} = 700,\ \mathcal{E}_{A*,\bullet} = 0$	$\overline{x}_{Q*} = 700,\ \mathcal{E}_{Q*,\bullet} = 0$	

of variance with two groups *is* a *t* test). In the two-way analysis with fixed factors, $MS_{columns}$ is the average effect of the column factor and MS_{within} is, again, the error term. But in a two-way mixed analysis, MS_{within} is not the right error term for the effect of the fixed factor. The reason, roughly speaking, is that levels of the random factor might be different in a repetition of the experiment, hence the random factor contributes to the variance of the effect of the fixed factor, and must therefore show up in the error term for the fixed factor.

We seek the standard error of the distribution of the average difference among the levels of a fixed factor, given the null hypothesis of no differences. For concreteness, let the fixed factor be *Algorithm*, with levels A* and Q*, as before. Assume also the null hypothesis; that is,

$$\mu_{A*} = \mu_{Q*} = \mu_G,$$

where μ_G is the population grand mean and μ_{A*} and μ_{Q*} are the population means for algorithms A* and Q*, respectively.

Now, assume we know all possible levels of the random factor, *Problem*. Suppose there are four levels, as shown in table 7A.9. Obviously, most random factors have many more levels, but four will suffice, here. Table 7A.9 represents *population* cell means, marginal means and grand mean; it represents the means of the joint distribution from which data are drawn in any experiment with *Algorithm* and *Problem*. These means are decomposed into the grand mean, column effects (which are zero), row effects, and interaction effects, as shown earlier in table 7A.5.

Suppose we define an experiment as follows: Select at random two kinds of problem from the set of four possible types. Then, generate twenty instances of each type, give ten of each to A*, and the rest to Q*. Because table 7A.9 represents the population means for all possible conditions, it follows that table 7A.10 represents the population means for an experiment with problem types *P1* and *P2*.

Table 7A.10   The population cell means for an experiment with problems of types *P1* and *P2*.

Problem	A*	Q*	
P1	1000	800	$\overline{x}_{P1} = 900$
			$\mathcal{E}_{\bullet, P1} = 200$
P2	800	1200	$\overline{x}_{P2} = 1000$
			$\mathcal{E}_{\bullet, P2} = 300$
	$\overline{x}_{A*(P1, P2)} = 900$	$\overline{x}_{Q*(P1, P2)} = 1000$	
	$\mathcal{E}_{A*(P1, P2), \bullet} = 200$	$\mathcal{E}_{Q*(P1, P2), \bullet} = 300$	

Table 7A.11   The population cell means for problems of types *P1* and *P2* decomposed into grand mean, row and column effects, and interaction effects.

Problem	A*	Q*	
P1	$700 + 200 + 200 - 100 = 1000$	$700 + 300 + 200 - 400 = 800$	$\overline{x}_{P1} = 900$
			$\mathcal{E}_{\bullet, P1} = 200$
P2	$700 + 200 + 300 - 400 = 800$	$700 + 300 + 300 - 100 = 1200$	$\overline{x}_{P2} = 1000$
			$\mathcal{E}_{\bullet, P2} = 300$
	$\overline{x}_{A*(P1, P2)} = 900,$	$\overline{x}_{Q*(P1, P2)} = 1000$	
	$\mathcal{E}_{A*(P1, P2), \bullet} = 200$	$\mathcal{E}_{Q*(P1, P2), \bullet} = 300$	

Note that the column marginal means in table 7A.10 aren't what they were in table 7A.9. In particular, $\overline{x}_{A*} - \overline{x}_{Q*} = 0$ when the algorithms are tested on all possible problems, but

$$\overline{x}_{A*(P1, P2)} - \overline{x}_{Q*(P1, P2)} = 900 - 1000 = -100 \tag{7A.10}$$

when the algorithms are tested on problem types *P1* and *P2*. Also, the effects of *Algorithm* are not individually equal to zero, as they are in table 7A.10. The effects are:

$$\mathcal{E}_{A*(P1, P2), \bullet} = \overline{x}_{A*(P1, P2)} - \overline{x}_G = 900 - 700 = 200;$$

$$\mathcal{E}_{Q*(P1, P2), \bullet} = \overline{x}_{Q*(P1, P2)} - \overline{x}_G = 1000 - 700 = 300.$$

Moreover, these effects do not sum to zero, as they must when both factors are fixed (equation 7A.7). The reason is simply that mean performance on a subset of problems will not generally equal mean performance on all possible problems.

Our chief concern, however, is the induced difference between A* and Q* in equation 7A.10. This difference is illusory in a sense, due entirely to the random choice of problems *P1* and *P2*. Different choices would yield different induced effects of *Algorithm*. Yet we know that in the long run, when A* and Q* are tested on all problem types, their mean performance will be equal. How then can we avoid concluding they are unequal on the basis of a single experiment, a single sample of problem types and its inevitable induced difference?

The answer is that induced main effects are offset exactly by induced interaction effects. Table 7A.11 shows the means from table 7A.10 decomposed as before into the grand mean, column and row effects, and interaction effects. Compare the top-left cells of table 7A.9 and table 7A.11. In the former, the effect of A* is zero and the interaction effect is 100; in the latter the effect of A* is 200 and the interaction effect is −100. The difference between the main effects, $200 − 0 = 200$, is exactly offset by the difference in the interaction effects, $−100 − 100 = −200$. This holds true for every cell in table 7A.11.

Thus, the sum of squares for a fixed factor in a mixed design, such as *Algorithm*, will include two effects: A true effect that holds when the algorithms are tested on all possible problems, and an induced effect that's due to the random selection of a subset of problems. The interaction effect, likewise, comprises a true interaction effect and an effect due to the random selection of problems. Under the null hypothesis that all levels of the fixed factor are equal, the only variance among these levels is induced by random selection of problems, and this variance is offset exactly by the variance in interaction effects. On the other hand, if the fixed factor truly has an effect, that is, if $\mu_{A*} \neq \mu_{Q*} \neq \mu_G$, then the variance among levels of the fixed factor will exceed the variance in the interaction effects. It follows that the proper error term for testing the effect of the fixed factor is the interaction effect; or, for a mixed design,

$$F_{FixedFactor} = \frac{MS_{FixedFactor}}{MS_{interaction}}.$$

The error terms for the random factor, *Problem*, and the interaction effect are both MS_{within}, as before. Table 7A.12 summarizes the degrees of freedom and F tests for the two-way, mixed design. The fixed factor is assumed arbitrarily to be the column factor.

7A.4   One-Way Design with Repeated Measures

A comparison between programs often seems more convincing when each program solves the same problems. A *one-way repeated-measures design* is shown in table 7A.13. It shows three conditions that for concreteness represent three algorithms, each of which solves the same four problems. You will recognize the paired-sample *t* test as a one-way repeated measures design in which one factor has just two levels

Table 7A.12   The decomposition of variance in the mixed two-way analysis of variance.

Source	df	MS	F
Column (fixed)	$C - 1$	$\frac{SS_{column}}{C-1}$	$\frac{MS_{columns}}{MS_{interaction}}$
Row (random)	$R - 1$	$\frac{SS_{row}}{R-1}$	$\frac{MS_{rows}}{MS_{within}}$
Interaction	$(C - 1)(R - 1)$	$\frac{SS_{interaction}}{(C-1)(R-1)}$	$\frac{MS_{interaction}}{MS_{within}}$
Within	$RC(n - 1)$	$\frac{SS_{within}}{RC(n-1)}$	
Total	$RCn - 1$	$\frac{SS_{total}}{RCn-1}$	

Table 7A.13   A one-way repeated measures design.

A_1	A_2	A_3
$d_{1,1}$	$d_{2,1}$	$d_{3,1}$
$d_{1,2}$	$d_{2,2}$	$d_{3,2}$
$d_{1,3}$	$d_{2,3}$	$d_{3,3}$
$d_{1,4}$	$d_{2,4}$	$d_{3,4}$

and each task is presented at each level. You will also remember the advantage of repeated-measures designs: by presenting the same problems in different conditions, the variance due to random variations among problems is minimized.

But it is precisely because the repeated measures design reduces variance that we must calculate its F statistics differently. As long as problems are randomly peppered over conditions (i.e., in designs without repeated measures) it didn't make sense to speak of "an effect of problem." Indeed, we used differences among problems within a condition to estimate random background variance. But in repeated measures designs, when the same problems appear in different conditions, differences in problem scores are no longer a good estimate of background variance. In fact, the choice of problems becomes a factor in a design. You can see this two ways: First, you could ask, whether all the problems are equally easy or difficult. This would involve calculating sums of squares for rows (each row representing a problem). Second, you could ask whether *Problem* interacts with the other factor in the design, for example, whether one program performs best on problems 1 and 2, while another performs poorly on these problems, but well on problems 3 and 4.

In short, a one-way analysis of variance with repeated measures looks awfully like a two-way analysis of variance in which the replicates (problems) are a factor. But

Table 7A.14   An example of a one-way repeated measures design.

	Abby	Beth	Carole	Vegetable means
Asparagus	6	8	4	6
Broccoli	3	4	2	3
Carrots	5	7	6	6
Daikon	5	6	4	5
Child means	4.75	6.25	4.0	5

the designs aren't the same: The former has just one datum per cell whereas the latter usually has several. If we treat *Problem* as a factor in table 7A.13, then $d_{1,1}$ is the only instance in which problem 1 is presented to program 1. How, then, should we estimate the background variance to which the effects of factors are compared? What error terms should be in the denominators of F statistics? Here's an even more basic question: Which effects can we test? Can we test the interaction effect, for example? The short answer is that we can test the main effect of the single (column) factor, and if we are willing to treat the replicates as fixed instead of random we can test their effects, too. We can't test the interaction effect unless we are willing to guess the level of random background variance. As to error terms, they follow from the assertion that a one-way repeated-measures design is actually a two-way design, albeit with only one replicate per cell.

Viewed this way, we calculate row and column effects as we did earlier, by subtracting the grand mean from each column mean to get column effects, and doing the same for the rows. For table 7A.14, which represents children's scores of how much they like particular vegetables, the column and row effects are:

$$\mathcal{E}_{Abby,\bullet} = -.25$$

$$\mathcal{E}_{Beth,\bullet} = 1.25$$

$$\mathcal{E}_{Carole,\bullet} = -1.$$

$$\mathcal{E}_{\bullet,Asparagus} = 1$$

$$\mathcal{E}_{\bullet,Broccoli} = -2$$

$$\mathcal{E}_{\bullet,Carrots} = 1$$

$$\mathcal{E}_{\bullet,Daikon} = 0.$$

Now, following the logic of the two-way analysis, treat each datum as a cell in a two-way table, and calculate "leftover" terms by subtracting from each cell value the sum of the grand mean and the corresponding column and row effects. For example, the leftover for the first cell in the *Asparagus* condition, is $6 - (5 - .25 + 1) = .25$. If this value was zero, we'd say Abby's liking for asparagus was determined by the grand mean and the row and column effects. As it is, we must acknowledge that these factors do not completely explain the data table. We can square and sum the leftover components, divide them by their degrees of freedom, and call them $MS_{interaction}$.

This statistic can be interpreted as the mean square for interaction effects, $MS_{interaction}$, or as the mean square residuals, MS_{within}. There's really no way to tease the interpretations apart. If we had several data per cell then we could estimate the within-cell variance and, hence, split it away from the interaction effects. But with only one datum per cell, the leftover component is open to interpretation. We can interpret the grand mean as the average child's taste for vegetables, and the column effects as the tastes of individual kids for the average vegetable, and row effects as the intrinsic appeal to children of particular vegetables, but how should we interpret the leftover effect? Apparently Abby has a special liking for asparagus over and above her baseline taste for vegetables. Is this an interaction effect or a fluke? If you asked Abby to taste asparagus again, and she gave the same response, we'd have an estimate of Abby's variance, and hence an estimate of her passion for asparagus in particular. But if she tastes asparagus only once, we cannot say whether her judgment was due to temporary insanity or a real affinity.

At this point you might be thinking, "error, interaction, who cares? As long as we can use $MS_{interaction}$ in the denominator of the F statistic." The good news is that you can do exactly this, but you might not be able to test the main effect of both *Vegetables* and *Children*. If both these factors are fixed, then the effects of asparagus and Abby will be the same if you run the experiment again, except for random error. Thus you can treat $MS_{interaction}$ for a single run as an estimate of random error and test both main effects, as in the two-way fixed factorial design. If, on the other hand, we view *Child* as a random factor, then we know the effect of, say, asparagus depends on the vegetable itself and the child who tastes it, so the effect we obtain is tested not against an estimate of random variation but against an estimated interaction effect. In this case, which parallels the two-way mixed design, we believe $MS_{interaction}$ estimates interaction, but then we have no estimate of error with which to test the effect of *Children*.

Usually, the repeated factor in a one-way repeated-measures design is a random factor—problems, children, or rats—and it doesn't make much sense to test a main effect of this factor in any case. It's no great loss that we cannot legitimately run the test. A more serious problem is that we cannot test interactions between, say, children and vegetables in a one-way repeated-measures design. Here we have only two options: Get more data or guess at the estimated background variance. The former option is clearly preferable but the latter should not be ruled out, especially if our experiment is a pilot study or otherwise exploratory.

Having raised the subject, let's also note the leeway we have in interpreting factors as fixed or random. Nowhere is it written that you must treat *Algorithm* and *Vegetable* as fixed factors and *Problem* and *Child* as random. You may treat factors as fixed or random, as you please, and analyze your data accordingly. Perhaps an effect will be significant under one interpretation and insignificant under the other, and you might choose to publish the significant one. This isn't cheating, provided you identify the experiment design, from which your readers will draw their own conclusions about whether your interpretation of a factor as fixed or random is reasonable.

The choice of error terms terrorizes statistics students and keeps them up late studying for exams. Many authors have systematized the problem (e.g., Cobb, 1984; Keppel, 1973), which helps if you remember that the choice of error terms is truly a choice. Nothing prevents you analyzing a design as if it were different. For example, you might have paired samples, but choose to run a two sample *t* test. This isn't very efficient—a paired-sample *t* test would be more sensitive because the error term is smaller—but nothing prevents you doing it. Still, it isn't very satisfying to be told, "analyze it however you like," especially when some choices of error terms are clearly better than others. To find appropriate error terms for designs other than those summarized here, you have three options: You may learn a good system such as Cobb's (1984), learn the underlying theory of expected mean squares (e.g., Winer, 1971), or simply look up the appropriate terms in a textbook. It seems someone, somewhere has worked out the details of the analysis of variance for any imaginable design.

7A.5   When Systems Learn

It is tempting to use a repeated-measures design to analyze *repeated trials*. Instead of asking Abby to taste asparagus, broccoli, carrots, and daikon, one might serve her asparagus on Monday, Tuesday, Wednesday and Thursday. The null hypothesis in such a case is that the taste for asparagus doesn't change over time. Or, Lehnert and McCarthy might assess the performance of their OTB system after 1, 10, 100, and 500 training sentences, testing the hypothesis that performance doesn't change with training (section 6.9).

A problem arises, however, if one of the factors is *Training*, or anything else that changes the knowledge or abilities of the system we're testing. The analysis of variance assumes *homogeneity of covariance* between pairs of treatment conditions. To illustrate, assume the dependent variable x is the proportion of slots in a frame filled correctly by OTB. Let $x_{i,t}$ be OTB's score on sentence i after t training sentences. Then,

$$\text{cov}\,(x_1, x_{10}) = \frac{\sum_{i=1}^{n}\left((x_{i,1} - \overline{x}_1)(x_{i,10} - \overline{x}_{10})\right)}{n - 1}$$

is the covariance of scores achieved by OTB after 1 and 10 training sentences. Homogeneity of covariance requires:

$$\text{cov}\,(x_1, x_{10}) = \text{cov}\,(x_{10}, x_{100}) = \text{cov}\,(x_1, x_{100}).$$

Covariance, recall, is related to correlation, so if we ignore the fact that the training conditions might have different variances, we can phrase homogeneity of covariance in terms of correlation. The correlation between scores after one training instance and ten training instances is the same as the correlation between scores after 10 and 100 instances and 1 and 100 instances. Scores for all pairs of levels of training are equally similar. This assumption is unlikely to hold. After all, the whole point of learning something is to make performance increasingly different from earlier levels of performance.

The effect of violating the homogeneity of covariance assumption is to inflate F values, so null hypotheses are incorrectly rejected more often than α levels suggest. Keppel (1973, p. 465) discusses a study in which α was fixed and hundreds of samples were drawn under the null hypothesis, so all significant results were spurious. When $\alpha = .05$, the null hypothesis of "no training effect" was actually rejected incorrectly 6.8 percent of the time, and the inflation associated with interaction effects is slightly higher. Other authors say the level of inflation is unpredictable and can be large (e.g., O'Brien and Kaiser, 1985).

Even so, one's conclusions are unlikely to be wrong if few levels of training are involved. Indeed, the problem formally disappears when the number of levels is two. And although F statistics might be inflated, I'm unwilling to give up a method that shows not only main effects of training, but also main effects of systems and interactions (i.e., different learning rates for different systems. I wouldn't trust a marginal F value, but if $p \leq .01$, say, I'd have no hesitation saying something significant is afoot, even though its level of significance is uncertain. Keppel discusses some corrections to the F statistic that are similar in spirit to Scheffé's correction for unplanned comparisons, but he concludes his discussion as follows:

A practical, but less precise, approach is to make no formal correction. ... We may actually be operating at $\alpha = .08$ when we base our decision rule on an uncorrected F nominally set at $\alpha = .05$. Most experimenters will still pay attention to an F that is significant at $\alpha = .06–.08$, which is probably the range of α levels that results from the usual violations of the homogeneity assumptions that we encounter in our research. ... In the absence of any other information, rigid decision rules, where we maintain α at an arbitrary level, make some sense. But if a finding is interesting theoretically, we should not ignore its presence merely because it fails to exceed the critical F value or its corrected value. (Keppel, 1973, p. 467)

8   Modeling

Cast your mind back to the beginning of this book where I said that the behavior of systems depends on their architectures, tasks, and environments. In the intervening chapters I presented methods for discovering and demonstrating how factors interact to influence behavior. Some factors are features of architectures (e.g., whether a part-of-speech tagger uses tag-repair heuristics) and some are features of tasks (e.g., whether one therapy will serve for several diseases). Increasingly, as AI systems become embedded in real-world applications, we must consider environmental factors, such as the mean time between tasks, noise in data, and so on. With the toolbox of methods from the previous chapters, we can detect faint hints of unsuspected factors and amplify them with well-designed experiments. We can demonstrate gross effects of factors and dissect them into orthogonal components; and we can demonstrate complex interactions between factors. Having done our reductionist best to understand individual and joint influences on behavior, we are left with something like a carefully disassembled mantle clock. We know the pieces and how they connect, we can differentiate functional pieces from ornamental ones, and we can identify subassemblies. We even know that the clock loses time on humid afternoons, and that humidity, not the time of day, does the damage. But we don't necessarily have an explanation of how all the pieces work and how humidity affects them. We need to complement reductionism with synthesis. Having discovered the factors that influence performance, we must explain how they all work together. Such explanations are often called models.

Different sciences have different modeling tools, of course, and some regard programs as models. For example, cognitive scientists offer programs as models of specific behaviors, such as verbal learning, or even as architectures of cognition (Newell, 1990; Anderson, 1983). It's difficult to think of a science that doesn't use computer-based models or simulations. But within AI we tend to view the behaviors of programs not as models of phenomena, but as phenomena in their own right. When we speak of models we mean models of architectures, tasks, and environments—models that explain how these interact to produce behavior.

To illustrate some essential features of models, consider one aspect of a "communications assistant," an agent that checks a remote server to see whether e-mail has arrived for you. Currently, it checks once per minute: You are concerned this frequency is too high. You can build a model of the optimal monitoring interval by making a few assumptions: First, the probability p of mail arriving during any one-minute interval doesn't change during the day. Second, at most one piece of mail will arrive during any one-minute interval. Third, the cost of checking for mail, c, is fixed. Fourth, the cost of waiting mail is a linear function of how long it waits, costing w per minute. Having made these assumptions you prove that the optimal interval between checks is $I = (2c/wp)^{.5}$ (Fatima, 1992). It isn't easy to put the costs c and w on a common scale, but suppose checking requires a long-distance telephone call that costs one dollar, and you assess yourself a penalty of one cent a minute for every message that you haven't read. Suppose, also, that the probability of getting a message in any given minute is .2. Then the optimal interval between checks is $((2 \cdot 100)/(1 \cdot .2))^{.5} = 31.62$. In other words, instead of checking every minute, your communications assistant should check every half hour.

Our model, $I = (2c/wp)^{.5}$, is in many ways typical. First, it is an abstraction of the monitoring interval problem that assumes some things and ignores others. It makes two assumptions about the arrival rate of messages and it ignores absolutely everything about the architecture of the communications assistant. In fact, from the standpoint of the model, the assistant is merely a device that checks whether something has happened. The model doesn't care whether the assistant has a fancy user interface, whether it is part of a larger "office management system," or whether it is implemented in Lisp or C. The model also doesn't care what the assistant is checking for. It might be the arrival of a bus, or whether a traffic light has turned green, or whether a book has been returned to a library. The model accomodates all these things, provided events have a constant probability of occurring, and they occur at most once in each time interval. Finally, the model doesn't care how costs are assessed, beyond requiring that one is a fixed cost, c, and the other is a rate, w.

Another typical aspect of our model is that it describes interactions. As p increases, I decreases—the probability of a message arriving influences the frequency of checking for messages—but if the cost of leaving a message unread decreases (w), it can offset the influence of p. Recalling the three basic research questions introduced in chapter 1, models can include terms for environmental influence, architectural decisions, and task features, and can describe or specify how these interact to produce behavior. For example, we might characterize w as a feature of the task and p and c as features of the environment, whereas I is the optimal behavior, the optimal monitoring interval.

In specifying what our agent *should* do, our model is normative. Normative models are not common in artificial intelligence, partly because optimality usually requires exhaustive search—an impossibility for most AI problems—and partly because our intellectual tradition is based in Simon's notion of *bounded rationality* and his rejection of normative models in economics. The models discussed in this chapter are performance models: They describe, predict, and explain how systems behave.

A good performance model is a compromise. It should fit but not overfit sample data, that is, it shouldn't account for every quirk in a sample if doing so obscures general trends or principles. A related point is that a good model compromises between accuracy and parsimony. For instance, multiple regression models of the kind described in section 8.6 can be made more accurate by adding more predictor variables, but the marginal utility of predictors decreases, while the number of interactions among predictors increases. These interactions must be interpreted or explained. Other compromises pertain to the scope and assumptions that underlie models. For example, the scope of our illustrative model $I = (2c/wp)^{.5}$ is just those situations in which the probability p of a message arriving is stationary, unchanging over time. But because a model for nonstationary probabilities is more complicated, we use the stationary model in nonstationary situations, where its accuracy is compromised but sufficient for heuristic purposes.

Good models capture essential aspects of a system. They don't merely simplify; they assert that some things are important and others are not. For example, our illustrative model asserts that only three quantities and a few assumptions are important, and every other aspect of any monitoring situation is unimportant. This is quite a claim. Quite apart from its veracity, we must appreciate how it focuses and motivates empirical work. It says, "find out whether the assumptions are warranted; see whether c, w and p are truly the only important factors." Lacking a model, what can we say of an empirical nature? That our communications assistant appears to work; that its users are happy; that its success might be due to anything. In short, as a model summarizes the essential aspects and interactions in a system, it also identifies assumptions and factors to explore in experiments.

Artificial intelligence researchers can be divided into those who use models and those who don't. The former group concerns itself with theoretical and algorithmic issues while the latter builds relatively large, complicated systems. I drew these conclusions from my survey of 150 papers from the Eighth National Conference on Artificial Intelligence (Cohen, 1991). I find them disturbing because surely architects and systems engineers need models the most. Think of any complicated artifacts—

airplanes, chemical processes, trading systems, and, no less complex, AI systems—and you see immediately the need to predict and analyze behavior. However, my survey found virtually no interaction between researchers who develop models that are in principle predictive and analytic and researchers who build systems. The problem is due in part to the predominance of worst-case complexity analysis, a pretty crude kind of model. Worst-case models usually don't predict actual computational effort. Furthermore, formal problems often don't represent natural ones. Perhaps models of AI systems and tasks have become more sophisticated and realistic, but in my 1990 survey, only eight of 150 papers described models sufficient to predict or explain the behavior of a system. Recent surveys (Churchill and Walsh, 1991; Lukowicz et al., 1994; Prechelt, 1994) present very similar results.

8.1   Programs as Models: Executable Specifications and Essential Miniatures

In a complicated system, some design decisions have theoretical weight while others are expedient. If you write a paper about your system or describe it to a colleague, you emphasize the important decisions. You say, "It's called 'case-based' reasoning, because it re-uses cases instead of solving every problem from first principles. The two big design issues are retrieving the best cases and modifying them for new problems." You don't talk about implementation details because, although they influence how your system behaves, you regard them as irrelevant. Allen Newell made this important distinction in his 1982 paper, *The Knowledge Level*:

The system at the knowledge level is the agent. *The components at the knowledge level are* goals, actions *and* bodies. . . . *The medium at the knowledge level is* knowledge *(as might be suspected). Thus, the agent processes its knowledge to determine the actions to take. Finally, the behavior law is the* principle of rationality: *Actions are selected to attain the agent's goals.*
. . .

The knowledge level sits in the hierarchy of systems levels immediately above the symbol level. . . .

As is true of any level, although the knowledge level can be constructed from the level below (i.e., the symbol level), it also has an autonomous formulation as an independent level. Thus, knowledge can be defined independent of the symbol level, but it can also be reduced to symbol systems. . . .

The knowledge level permits predicting and understanding behavior without having an operational model of the processing that is actually being done by the agent. The utility of such a level would seem clear, given the widespread need in AI's affairs for distal prediction, and also the paucity of knowledge about the internal workings of humans. . . . The utility is also clear in designing AI systems, where the internal mechanisms are still to be specified. To the extent that AI systems successfully approximate rational agents, it is also useful for predicting and understanding them. Indeed the usefulness extends beyond AI systems to all computer programs. (1982, pp. 98–108)

So, we should strive for knowledge-level models of AI systems, models that hide details and present the essential characteristics of a system. In what language should these models be framed? English and other natural languages have tremendous expressive power, but they are ambiguous. For example, we said case-based systems should retrieve the "best" cases, but what does this really mean? It probably doesn't mean finding optimum cases in a mathematical sense; it probably means striking a balance between search effort and the number and utility of the retrieved cases. It doesn't matter very much whether you call these the "best" cases or merely "good" cases—although the former connotes something you probably don't mean—neither word says what you do mean. Now, imprecision plays an important role in evolving theories, and connotation saves us the trouble of saying everything explicitly, as I discuss in chapter 9. Thus we shouldn't dismiss English as a modeling language, but we should consider some alternatives.

One alternative is that a program is its own model (Simon, 1993). It is, after all, a declarative, unambiguous, nonredundant, executable specification. For all these positive attributes, programs are hard to read, they obscure distinctions between essentials and implementation details, and their behaviors are difficult to predict.

Another alternative, called an *executable specification*, is based on the idea that although a program shouldn't be its own model, it can be modeled by another program. Cooper, Fox, Farringdon, and Shallice (1992) propose and develop this idea and illustrate it with an executable specification of the SOAR architecture (Newell, 1990). SOAR is itself a model of the human cognitive architecture but, as Cooper et al. point out, "there are many components of LISP SOAR that do not seem to have much theoretical force, such as the RETE algorithm [and] the algorithms employed to efficiently remove working memory elements on subgoal termination" (Cooper et al., 1992, p. 7). The designers of SOAR probably don't intend to claim that humans have RETE algorithms in their heads, but the SOAR code does not contain little disclaimers such as "the following procedure has no theoretical justification or implications." Cooper et al. allow that SOAR is an implementation of a theory, but they insist the muck of implementation details must be hosed away before the theory itself is clearly seen. Capitalizing on the hierarchical decomposition of functions, they draw an imaginary line: Above it are design decisions with theoretical force, below it are implementation decisions that have none. Then they introduce a modeling language called Sceptic with which they implement all above-the-line functions.

Sceptic is "an executable specification language in which we can describe a cognitive theory in a form that is (1) clear and succinct, and (2) is at the appropriate level of abstraction, (3) can be executed to permit direct observation of the behavior it predicts, (4) permits clear separation of the essential, theoretically-motivated components from the inessential but necessary algorithmic details" (Cooper et al., 1992, p. 8). Sceptic is syntactically very much like Prolog, and above-the-line components of Sceptic models are collections of Prolog-like rules. To illustrate, I will examine Sceptic rules for SOAR's elaboration phase: When SOAR gets some input from its environment, it puts tokens representing the input into working memory, after which it searches long term memory for productions that match the contents of working memory. In Sceptic, this phase is implemented as follows:

elaboration_phase:

       true

→   mark_all_wmes_as_old,

       input_cycle,

       continue_cycling_if_not_quiescent

continue_cycling_if_not_quiescent:

       not(quiescent)

→   elaboration_cycle,

       output_cycle,

       input_cycle,

       continue_cycling_if_not_quiescent

. . .

elaboration_cycle:

       generate_unrefracted_instantiation(Instantiation,FiringGoal),

       not(im_match(Instantiation,FiringGoal))

→   im_make(Instantiation,FiringGoal),

       fire_production(Instantiation,FiringGoal)

The first rule defines the elaboration phase: It marks all current working memory elements as old, then it gets input from the environment and adds it to working memory, and then it executes the rule `continue_cycling_if_not_quiescent`. This rule tests for quiescence (a state in which no new productions are triggered by the contents of working memory), and if quiescence has not been achieved it does several other things pertinent to instantiating and executing productions from long term memory. For instance, the elaboration cycle generates an instantiation and firing goal for a production and, if it is not already in instantiation memory (tested by `im_match`), it puts it there and then fires the production.

Five Sceptic rules are required to implement the above-the-line model of SOAR's elaboration phase, and several below-the-line functions must be supplied as well.

Checking whether an instantiation is in instantiation memory (im_match) is one function; it is called a *state tester* function. Testing for quiescence is another state-tester function. The work of identifying and instantiating productions prior to firing them is done by a below-the-line function called generate_unrefracted_instantiation. It is an example of a *generator* function. Finally, some functions are required to add elements to working memory, and to mark them. These are called *updater* functions. Thus, a Sceptic model comprises a list of Sceptic rules, which are the above-the-line specification of a system, and a collection of state-tester, generator, and updater functions, which implement the below-the-line specification. (See also Cooper, 1992a and 1992b, for examples of Sceptic models for other theories.)

Cooper et al. (1992) claim this division satisfies all their criteria for a good model. It is clear and concise, because Sceptic rules are declarative and relatively few are required. In fact, just twenty-eight above-the-line rules were needed to specify SOAR. Even with the below-the-line functions, the Sceptic model of SOAR is reported to be much smaller in terms of lines of code.

Sceptic models are "at the appropriate level of abstraction," not because Sceptic enforces a particular separation between above-the-line and below-the-line aspects of a system, but, rather, because it allows the model builder to draw the line at the level he or she finds appropriate. Similarly, Sceptic doesn't separate essential components from inessential ones, but it allows the model builder to do so.

Perhaps the most important feature of Sceptic models is executability: Sceptic models run. The resulting execution traces can be compared with traces from the target system; for example, Cooper et al. report. "Execution of the various versions of the program on published examples (e.g., monkeys and bananas, the eight puzzle, block stacking) has demonstrated that the behavior of the LISP and Sceptic versions are essentially identical" (1992, p. 25). Although these results are preliminary, they are significant: If a Sceptic model can reproduce SOAR's behavior on previously studied problems, then perhaps it can predict SOAR's behavior on new problems. This is a crucial test of the Sceptic approach. If Sceptic models do not make predictions, but only mimic what already exists in a target system, then neither engineers nor scientists will find them useful. On the other hand, if executable specifications can function as other engineering models do, predicting how components will interact in a range of conditions, then the implications for software engineering practice could be enormous. From a scientist's perspective, executable specifications must make interesting predictions if we are to accord them the status of theories. (In this context, interesting means not obvious, given the target system.) If this criterion is met—if executable specifications can make interesting predictions—then they might completely change how AI researchers discuss their theories and present their results. Time will tell.

An approximation to a Sceptic-like executable specification can be achieved by modeling a complicated system with a simpler one, called an *essential miniature*. The term "essential" comes from "Essential MYCIN," known widely as EMYCIN, the expert system shell that remained after all of MYCIN's medical knowledge was excised (van Melle, 1984). The term "miniature" was used first by Schank and Riesbeck to describe small versions of some of their early natural language programs (Schank and Riesbeck, 1981). An essential miniature, then, is a small version of a system that captures all the essential aspects of the system. Unfortunately, the implication of the EMYCIN example, that you get an essential miniature by throwing away inessential stuff, is wrong: It cost William van Melle a lot of effort to build EMYCIN, and the other examples we know of (e.g., Blumenthal, 1990) were likewise built largely from scratch.

Clearly, the technology for building predictive models of complex system behaviors is promising but nascent. On the other hand, if one is willing to settle for a model that predicts, say, the values of performance variables, then several well-established statistical techniques are available. Our focus for the rest of the chapter is *linear regression models*, including multiple regression and causal models. One can certainly find more sophisticated kinds of models, but it's hard to beat regression for versatility, ease of use, and comprehensibility.

8.2 Cost as a Function of Learning: Linear Regression

In chapter 6 we encountered Lehnert and McCarthy's study of their part-of-speech tagger, a system called OTB. We saw how OTB tagged the words "general motors corporation." The right answer is to tag "general" and "motors" as noun modifiers and "corporation" as a noun, but this is difficult because the first two words are also nouns. Although OTB got the right answer in chapter 6, it mistakenly tagged nouns as noun modifiers, and vice versa, in other examples. In this section we model the costs of these mistakes. A simple approach is to score OTB's performance by two criteria: The "stringent" one credits OTB with correct tags only if nouns are tagged as nouns and noun modifiers as noun modifiers; the "lax" criterion gives full credit if OTB tags nouns as noun modifiers and vice versa, but not if it tags either as, say, verbs. OTB was tested on batches of fifty sentences. The performance measure was the proportion of all the words in a batch that it tagged correctly, averaged over the number of batches. The mean proportion of words tagged correctly by the stringent and lax criteria are .738 and .892, respectively, and the mean difference is highly significant. Confusion between nouns and noun modifiers reduces OTB's mean proportion of correctly tagged words by a significant chunk, from .892 to .738.

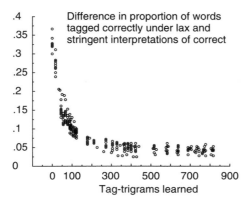

Figure 8.1   The cost of tagging errors as a function of the number of tag-trigrams learned.

Unfortunately, this result says little about how the confusion depends on other factors. For instance, OTB improved its performance by learning; did it learn to avoid confusing nouns and noun modifiers? Figure 8.1 shows, in fact, that the differences between lax and stringent scores were most pronounced when OTB had learned fewer than two hundred tag-trigrams. After that, the mean difference hovers around 5 percent. For simplicity, call the mean difference between lax and stringent scores the *cost* of noun/noun modifier tagging errors. We will derive a model that relates this cost to OTB's learning. Even though figure 8.1 shows clearly that the relationship is nonlinear, I will develop a linear model; later, I will transform Lehnert and McCarthy's data so a linear model fits it better.

8.2.1   Introduction to Linear Regression

Through the nightmares of statisticians run images like this: A hapless student is captured by an ogre who says, "I have before me a scatterplot, and I won't show it to you, but I will show you the distribution of *y* values of all the points. After you have studied this distribution, I will blindfold you, and then I will call out the *x* value of a randomly-selected point. You must tell me its *y* value. You'll be wrong, of course, and the difference between your guess and the point's true *y* value will be noted. We will play this game until I have selected all *N* points, after which I will square your errors, sum them, and divide the result by $N - 1$. Should this average be greater than it needs to be, a terrible penalty will be exacted!" Ominous? Not really. Whenever the ogre selects a point and calls out its *x* value, the student should respond with $\overline{y}$, the mean of all the *y* values. This way the student will never incur greater errors than necessary, and the ogre's terrible penalty will be avoided. It will come as no surprise

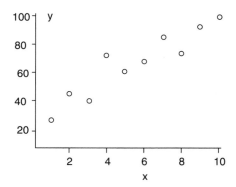

Figure 8.2   A scatterplot can be viewed as a guessing game.

that the student's mean squared error is the sample variance of the y scores, s_y^2. It should also be clear that s_y^2 is a lower bound on one's ability to predict the y value of a coordinate, given a corresponding x value. One's mean squared error should be no higher than s_y^2, and might be considerably lower if one knows something about the relationship between x and y variates.

For instance, after looking carefully at the scatterplot in figure 8.2, you guess the following rule:

Your Rule $\hat{y}_i = 7.27x_i + 27.$

Now you are asked, "What y value is associated with $x = 1$?" and you respond "$y = 34.27$." The difference between your answer and the true value of y is called a *residual*. Suppose the residuals are squared and summed, and the result is divided by $N - 1$. This quantity, called *mean square residuals* is one assessment of the predictive power of your rule. As you would expect, the mean square residuals associated with your rule is much smaller than the sample variance; in fact, your rule gives the smallest possible mean squared residuals. The line that represents your rule in figure 8.3 is called a *regression line*, and it has the property of being the *least-squares fit* to the points in the scatterplot. It is the line that minimizes mean squared residuals.

Parameters of the Regression Line

For simple regression, which involves just one predictor variable, the regression line $\hat{y} = bx + a$ is closely related to the correlation coefficient. Its parameters are:

$$b = r_{xy}\frac{s_y}{s_x}, \ a = \bar{y} - b\bar{x}, \tag{8.1}$$

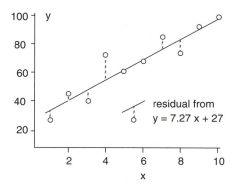

Figure 8.3   Residuals associated with the rule $\hat{y} = 7.27x + 27$.

where r_{xy} is the correlation between x and y, and s_x and s_y are the standard deviations of x and y, respectively. Note that the regression line goes through the mean of x and the mean of y. A general procedure to solve for the parameters of the regression line is described in section 8A.

Variance Accounted for by the Regression Line

As we saw earlier, without a regression line the best prediction of y is $\overline{y}$, yielding deviations $(y_i - \overline{y})$ and mean squared deviations $s_y^2 = \sum(y_i - \overline{y})^2 / (N - 1)$. Each deviation is a mistake—an incorrect stab at the value of y. Wanting a regression line, s_y^2 represents the "average squared mistake." The predictive power of the regression line is usually expressed in terms of its ability to reduce these mistakes.

Recall how one-way analysis of variance decomposes variance into a systematic component due to a factor and an unsystematic "error" component (see chapter 6). In an essentially identical manner, linear regression breaks deviations $(y_i - \overline{y})$ (and thus variance) into a component due to the regression line and a residual, or error component. This is illustrated in figure 8.4 for two points and their predicted values, shown as filled and open circles, respectively. The horizontal line is $\overline{y}$ and the upward-sloping line is a regression line. The total deviation $y_i - \overline{y}$ is divided into two parts:

$$(y_i - \overline{y}) = (\hat{y}_i - \overline{y}) + (y_i - \hat{y}_i).$$

If $(y_i - \hat{y}_i)$ was zero for all points, then all points would fall exactly on the regression line, that is, the filled and open circles in figure 8.4 would coincide.

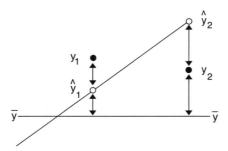

Figure 8.4   Decomposition of residuals from the mean.

The sum of squared deviations can also be broken into two parts:

$$SS_{total} = SS_{reg.} + SS_{res.}$$

$$\sum (y_i - \overline{y})^2 = \sum (\hat{y}_i - \overline{y})^2 + \sum (y_i - \hat{y}_i)^2.$$

In words, the total sum of squares comprises the sum of squares for regression plus the sum of squares residual. The proportion of the total variance accounted for by the regression line is

$$r^2 = \frac{SS_{total} - SS_{res.}}{SS_{total}} = \frac{SS_{reg.}}{SS_{total}}. \tag{8.2}$$

Remarkably, this proportion is the square of the correlation coefficient, r^2. When $SS_{res.} = 0$, all of the variance in data is accounted for or explained by the regression line. If $SS_{total} = SS_{res.}$ then the regression line is a horizontal line through $\overline{y}$, and has no more predictive power than the rule $\hat{y}_i = \overline{y}$. If $r^2 = 0.5$, then $SS_{res.}$ is half of SS_{total}, so one's squared, summed mistakes are half as costly by merit of the regression line.

8.2.2   Lack of Fit and Plotting Residuals

It is a simple matter to fit a regression line to Lehnert and McCarthy's data. The line is shown in the left panel in figure 8.5, which relates the number of tag-trigrams OTB has learned (horizontal axis) to the cost of noun/noun modifier tagging errors (vertical axis). Although this line is the best possible fit to the data (in the least-squares sense, see the appendix to this chapter), it accounts for only 44 percent of the variance in the cost of tagging errors.

   In general, when a model fails to account for much of the variance in a performance variable, we wonder whether the culprit is a systematic nonlinear bias in our data,

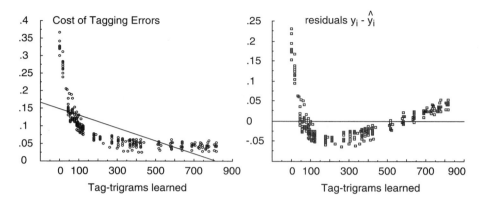

Figure 8.5   Linear regression and residuals for Lehnert and McCarthy's data.

outliers, or unsystematic variance. Systematic bias is often seen in a *residuals plot*, a scatterplot in which the vertical axis represents residuals $y_i - \hat{y}_i$ from the regression line and the horizontal axis represents the predictor variable x. The right panel of figure 8.5 shows a residuals plot for the regression line in the left panel. Clearly, there is much structure in the residuals. As it happens, the residual plot shows nothing that wasn't painfully evident in the original scatterplot: The regression line doesn't fit the data well because the data are nonlinear. In general, however, residuals plots often disclose subtle structure because the ranges of their vertical axes tend to be narrower than in the original scatterplot (e.g., see figure 8.11.e). Conversely, if a regression model accounts for little variance in y (i.e., r^2 is low) but no structure or outliers are seen in the residuals plot, then the culprit is plain old unsystematic variance, or noise.

8.3   Transforming Data for Linear Models

Linear models are so useful and linear regression so straightforward that we often want to apply regression to variables that aren't linearly related. In the previous sections we wanted to see the influence of learning on a performance variable, the difference between lax and stringent scoring of noun modifier errors, but this influence was clearly not linear. A solution is to transform one variable or the other to "straighten" the function relating them. Power transforms and log transforms are commonly used for this purpose. Both preserve order, which means if $a > b$ then $t(a) > t(b)$ for a transform t, but they compress or stretch scales at higher or lower values.

Thus they can change the shape of a function, even straightening a distinctly curved one.

Consider how to straighten Lehnert and McCarthy's data, reproduced in the top-left graph in figure 8.6. Let y denote the performance variable and x denote the level of learning. The function plunges from $y = .375$ to $y = .075$ (roughly) as x increases from 0 to 100, then y doesn't change much as x increases further. Imagine the function is plotted on a sheet of rubber that can be stretched or compressed until the points form a straight line. What should we do? Four options are:

- Compress the region above $y = .1$ along the y axis.
- Stretch the region below $y = .1$ along the y axis.
- Compress the region to the right of $x = 100$ along the x axis.
- Stretch the region to the left of $x = 100$ along the x axis.

A log transform stretches the distances between small values and compresses the distances between large ones; for example, $\log(20) - \log(10) = .3$ whereas $\log(120) - \log(110) = .038$, so a difference of ten for large values is compressed relative to the same difference between small values. Figure 8.6 shows three log transformations of y and x. The top-right graph shows a plot of x against $\log(y)$; as expected, points with smaller y values are spread out more along the y axis, and you can see more detail than when the points were scrunched together. A regression line fit to these data explains more of the variance, too. The regression of $\log(y)$ on x explains 66.5 percent of the variance in $\log(y)$. The bottom-left graph shows a regression of y on $\log(x)$. As expected, points with small x values are spread wider by the transformation, and points with large x values are compressed. Unfortunately, this creates a dense mass of points at the right of the graph, making it very difficult to see any details, although the variance in y accounted for by $\log(x)$ is pretty high, $r^2 = 82.3$ percent. Finally, we can transform both x and y, yielding the graph at the lower right of figure 8.6. Notice that the worrying clump of points has been spread apart along the y axis because they had low y values. Nearly 90 percent of the variance in $\log(y)$ is explained by $\log(x)$.

The log transform is but one of many used by data analysts for a variety of purposes. In addition to straightening functions, transformations are also applied to make points fall in a more even distribution (e.g., not clumped as in the lower left graph in figure 8.6), to give them a symmetric distribution along one axis, or to make the variances of distributions of points roughly equal. Some of these things are done to satisfy assumptions of statistical tests; for instance, regression and analysis of variance assume equal variance in distributions of y values at all levels of x. In his book,

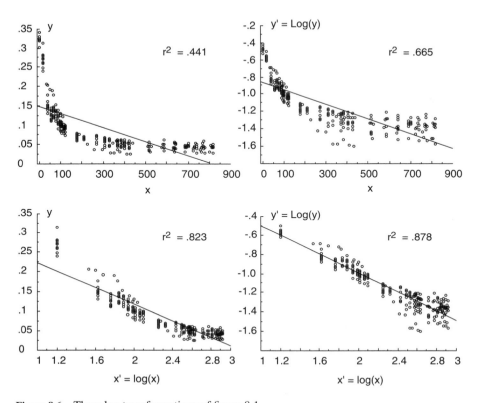

Figure 8.6   Three log transformations of figure 8.1.

Exploratory Data Analysis, Tukey (1977) introduces a *ladder of re-expressions.* Here are some steps on the ladder:

$$\ldots\; x' = x^2,\; x' = x^{1.5},\; x' = x,\; x' = \sqrt{x},\; x' = \log x,$$

$$x' = \frac{-1}{\sqrt{x}},\; x' = \frac{-1}{x},\; x' = \frac{-1}{x^2},\; \ldots$$

Figure 8.7 shows how these re-expressions (or transformations) stretch a function in different parts of its range. The straight line is, of course, $x' = x$. To pull apart large values of x but leave small values relatively unchanged, you would use a power function with an exponent greater than one, such as $x' = x^2$. You can see that the deviation between x and $x' = x^2$ increases with x; therefore, $x' = x^2$ spreads points further apart when they have big x values. Alternatively, to pull apart small values of x and make larger values relatively indistinguishable, you would

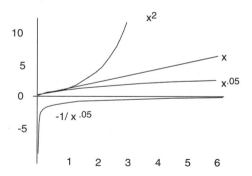

Figure 8.7 Graphing transformation functions illustrates their effects on different parts of the range.

use a transformation such as $x' = -1/x^{.5}$. Note that $x' = x^2$ and $x' = -1/x^{.5}$ are on opposite sides of the "null" transformation $x' = x$. Moving down the ladder (left of $x' = x$) stretches the scale for large values of x and moving up the ladder stretches the scale for small values of x. As you move further in either direction transformations become more radical. The log transformation, used earlier, is pretty gentle. Less radical yet are the power transformations $x' = x^{0.9}$, $x' = x^{0.8}$, ... Note that all the terms in the ladder of re-expressions can be negated and thus applied to curves that are reflections of those in figure 8.7. General guidance for applying re-expressions is provided by Tukey (1977), Emerson and Stoto (1983), and Gregory (1994).

8.4 Confidence Intervals for Linear Regression Models

One can derive confidence intervals (secs. 4.6, 5.2.3) for several parameters of regression equations, including

- the slope of the regression line
- the y intercept
- the population mean of y values.

Confidence intervals for the slope of the regression line will illustrate the general approach. See any good statistics text (e.g., Olson, 1987, pp. 448–452) for confidence intervals for other parameters.

8.4.1   Parametric Confidence Intervals

Confidence intervals describe how well a sample statistic, such as b, estimates a population parameter, which in the case of the slope of the regression line is denoted β (not to be confused with the probability of a type II error, nor with beta coefficients, discussed later). Not surprisingly, all confidence intervals for parameters of regression equations depend on $SS_{res.}$, the sum of squared residuals from the regression line.

Recall the parametric confidence interval for the population mean, μ:

$$\mu = \overline{x} \pm t_{.025}\hat{\sigma}_{\overline{x}}.$$

Here, $\overline{x}$ is the statistic that estimates μ and $\hat{\sigma}_{\overline{x}}$ is the estimated standard error of the sampling distribution of $\overline{x}$, which is a t distribution. Under the assumption that the predicted variable y is normally distributed with equal variance at all levels of the predictor variable x, confidence intervals for parameters of regression lines have exactly the same form. This is the 95 percent confidence interval for the parametric slope of the regression line, β:

$$\beta = b \pm t_{.025}\hat{\sigma}_b.$$

As always, the tricky part is estimating the standard error of the statistic. The estimate is:

$$\hat{\sigma}_b = \frac{\sqrt{SS_{res.}/(N-2)}}{\sqrt{SS_x}}.$$

$SS_{res.} = (1-r^2)SS_{total}$ (equation 8.2); SS_x is the numerator of the variance of x. The appropriate t distribution has $N-2$ degrees of freedom. Note that $\beta = b \pm t_{.025}\hat{\sigma}_b$ will produce an upper and lower bound on the 95 percent confidence interval for β, that is, two slopes, one steeper than b and one symmetrically more shallow. When you draw confidence intervals around a regression line, they look as shown in figure 8.8. All regression lines pass through $\overline{x}$ and $\overline{y}$ so the confidence intervals for β "fan out" around the regression line on either side of $\overline{x}$. Of course, $\overline{x}$ and $\overline{y}$ are also estimates of their true population values, so confidence intervals are often derived for them as well. In this case the confidence intervals for the slope of the regression line will not pass through a point, as in figure 8.8. Instead, the picture will look like the outline of an hourglass, where the width of the central aperture depends on uncertainty about the population means.

Incidentally, with the standard error $\hat{\sigma}_b$ we can test the hypothesis that m is the population value of the slope of a regression line, $H_0 : \beta = m$. The appropriate test statistic is $t = (b - m)/\hat{\sigma}_b$; degrees of freedom for this test are $N - 2$.

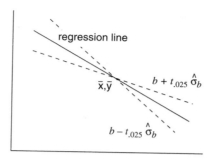

Figure 8.8   Confidence intervals for a regression line.

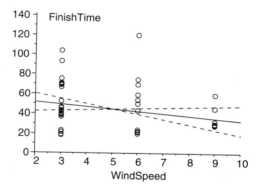

Figure 8.9   Scatterplot of *WindSpeed* and *FinishTime* showing heteroscedasticity. The solid line is the regression line for the sample of 48 points. The dotted lines are bootstrap confidence intervals on the slope of the regression line.

8.4.2   Bootstrap Confidence Intervals

The assumptions that underlie parametric confidence intervals are often violated. The predicted variable sometimes isn't normally distributed, and even when it is, the variance of the normal distribution might not be equal at all levels of the predictor variable. For example, figure 8.9 shows a scatterplot of *FinishTime* predicted by *WindSpeed* in forty-eight trials of the Phoenix planner. The variances of *FinishTime* at each level of *WindSpeed* are not equal, suggesting that they might not be equal in the populations from which these data were drawn (a property called heteroscedasticity, as opposed to homoscedasticity, or equal variances). This departure from the assumptions of parametric confidence intervals might be quite minor and unimportant, but even so, the assumptions are easily avoided by constructing a bootstrap confidence interval, as described in section 5.2.3. The procedure is:

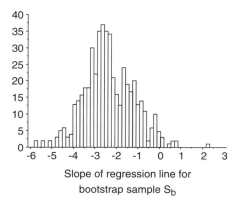

Figure 8.10   A bootstrap sampling distribution of the slope of the regression line. The original sample comprises 48 data shown in figure 8.9.

Procedure 8.1   Bootstrap Confidence Intervals on Regression Lines

Do i=1 to 500 times:

1. Select with replacement a bootstrap sample S_i^* of 48 points (keeping the x_i and y_i together as a unit) from the original sample S.
2. Compute and record b^*, the slope of the regression line for S_i^*.

The resulting distribution of b^* is shown in figure 8.10. Its mean, -2.36, is very close to the slope of the regression line of the original sample, -2.33. To find the 95 percent confidence intervals for the slope of the regression line, just find the cutoff values that bound the upper and lower 2.5 percent of the distribution in figure 8.10. These values are .17 and -4.644, respectively, and they are also the slopes of the dotted lines in figure 8.9.

8.5   The Significance of a Predictor

One assessment of the "goodness" of a predictor is r^2, introduced in section 8.2.1 as the proportion of the total variance accounted for by the regression rule:

$$r^2 = \frac{SS_{reg.}}{SS_{total}}.$$

However, r^2 leaves some doubt as to whether its value could be due to chance. In sections 4.5 and 5.3.3 I described tests of the hypothesis that the correlation is zero, asking, in effect, whether a particular correlation coefficient r_{xy} could have arisen from chance association between x and y. Clearly, we could use the same tests to assess whether a sample value of r^2 arose by chance. Conventionally, however, this question is framed as an F test:

$$F = \frac{MS_{reg.}}{MS_{res.}}.$$

The sum of squares for regression has just one degree of freedom (Hays, 1973, pp. 642–644), so $MS_{reg.} = SS_{reg.}$. The sum of squares for residuals has $N - j$ degrees of freedom where N is the sample size and j is the number of predictors, one for simple regression.

To illustrate this test, let's return to Lehnert and McCarthy's data, particularly the transformed data in the lower right of figure 8.6. First, we'll regress the logarithm of tagging errors against the logarithm of the number of tag-trigrams learned:

est. $\log(Errors) = -.49 \log(TrigramsLearned) - .03$

This regression fits the data very well: $r^2 = .878$. Now we'll test the hypothesis that the number of trigrams accounts for none of the variance in tagging errors. We need the sum of squares for the regression, which turns out to be $SS_{reg.} = 65.05$ and the sum of squares residual, which is $SS_{res.} = 9.01$. Lehnert and McCarthy's transformed sample included 255 data, so degrees of freedom for $SS_{res.}$ is 254, and the F statistic is:

$$F = \frac{65.05}{\frac{9.01}{254}} = 1832.95.$$

This is a huge value. The $\alpha = .01$ critical value for an F test with one and 254 degrees of freedom is roughly 6.7, so we can reject the hypothesis—with essentially no probability of error—that the number of trigrams learned predicts nothing about the number of tagging errors.

Sums of squares and F tests for regression analysis are usually provided by statistics packages; if not, a simple trick for calculating them by hand is described in section 8A.6.

8.6   Linear Models with Several Predictors: Multiple Regression

In *multiple linear regression* the predicted value of a performance variable $\hat{y}$ depends on several predictor variables $\{x_1, x_2, \ldots, x_n\}$, and the least-squares model is a plane or a hyperplane. Not surprisingly, multiple regression models generally account for more of the variance in the dependent variable than simple regression models: $SS_{res.}$, the summed, squared deviation between predicted and actual values, generally decreases as one adds predictors. Suppose you want to predict an athlete's time in a 1500-meter race, given data from her previous races. You might start with her average time and then add predictors that represent race conditions. For instance, a regression model might be

$$est.\ RunningTime = 221 + .1(Lane) + .0005(Altitude) +$$

$$.008(Temperature) - .0001(TimeOfDay) - .1(PositiveAttitude)$$

If our athlete draws Lane 8, and the race is held near Denver at 5,000 feet, at 2100 hours (9 p.m.) on a warm evening (70° F), and she's feeling terrific (i.e., *PositiveAttitude*=10) then her estimated running time is $221 + .8 + 2.5 + .56 - .21 - 1.0 = 223.65$ seconds. Each predictor in the regression model improves our estimate, some more than others. Note also that some predictors are correlated; for example, *Temperature* is correlated with *Altitude* and *TimeOfDay*. You might be tempted to add more predictors to the model, such as whether the athlete is running in new shoes or old, but you will find in this case (and in general) that a handful of predictors accounts for much of the variance in a dependent variable, and additional predictors are hardly worth the effort. More to the point, those additional predictors might serve better in another part of a larger model; for instance, old shoes might make our athlete feel comfortable, so the age of her shoes accounts for some of the variance in her attitude, more variance, perhaps, than in her running time. Models that include chains of predictors, such as

$$AgeOfShoes \rightarrow PositiveAttitude \rightarrow RunningTime$$

are sometimes called *structural equation models*, and are discussed in section 8.9.

The coefficients of predictors in a multiple regression model are called *regression coefficients*, and their values ensure that the model is optimal in the least-squares sense. To accomplish this, multiple regression solves a set of linear equations called the *normal equations* to find a set of weights $\{b_1, b_2, \ldots, b_n\}$ and a constant, a, that minimizes $SS_{res.}$. The normal equations are simple in form and they can be solved by straightforward computer algorithms, or by hand if you have nothing better to do (see section 8A.1).

The proportion of the variance in y accounted for by a linear model with several predictors is defined exactly as it is for one predictor, denoted with an uppercase "R" to distinguish it from r^2:

$$R^2 = \frac{SS_{total} - SS_{res.}}{SS_{total}} = \frac{SS_{reg.}}{SS_{total}}$$

$$= \frac{\sum(y_i - \overline{y})^2 - \sum(y_i - \hat{y}_i)^2}{\sum(y_i - \overline{y})^2}.$$

F tests for the significance of predictors are important in multiple regression because in general, some predictors do more to increase R^2 than others. In fact, some predictors may contribute almost nothing to R^2; these are caught by F tests. To understand F tests for multiple regression, it's necessary to understand how predictors partition $SS_{res.}$. These topics are discussed in sections 8A.6 and 8A.5.

A somewhat frustrating characteristic of regression is that the coefficients of predictors depend on the other predictors in a model, so adding and removing predictors can change coefficients dramatically and unpredictably. A practical consequence is that it's difficult to search the space of models. If you have very few predictors, you can toss them all into the model and be done with it; but if you intend to build a model from a proper subset of many predictors, you'll find there's no foolproof algorithm to find the subset with the best R^2, short of exhaustive search. A popular heuristic approach, called *stepwise multiple regression*, adds predictors that are highly correlated with the performance variable, provided F tests show them to be significant. Because the significance of a predictor depends on the others in the model, the algorithm also occasionally removes predictors that become insignificant. Stepwise multiple regression is discussed in (Draper and Smith, 1966). An alternative heuristic for selecting predictors is described in section 8.9.

Regression models are easier to interpret if regression coefficients are standardized. In the previous, unstandardized model, *Lane* has a relatively large coefficient but a relatively small effect on running times, whereas *Altitude* has the smallest coefficient and, potentially, the largest effect. This is apt to be confusing. The problem is that regression coefficients depend on the units of measurement of their associated factors. The solution is to standardize the factors so they are all measured on the same scale. We saw in chapter 4 how to standardize a variate x_i by subtracting its mean $\overline{x}$ and dividing by its standard deviation s:

$$X_i = \frac{x_i - \overline{x}}{s}. \tag{8.3}$$

We called these transformed variates *standard scores* or *Z scores* and denoted them with the letter Z; here we denote standardized variates with capital letters (e.g., X_i) and unstandardized ones with lowercase letters (e.g., x_i). A distribution of standardized variates has mean 0.0 and standard deviation 1.0, so standardizing variables puts them on the same scale and makes their coefficients comparable.

Let's leave our hypothetical athlete and build a regression model for the Phoenix planner. The dependent variable will be *FinishTime*, the amount of time it takes the planner to contain a simulated forest fire. We will regress *FinishTime* on four predictors: *WindSpeed*, *AreaBurned*, *NumPlans* (the number of plans that had to be tried before one succeeded), and *RTK* (the number of simulated minutes that the fire burns for every CPU second the planner is allowed to think). Two regression models are given next, the first with ordinary regression coefficients and second with standardized coefficients.

$$\text{est. } FinishTime = 16.553(NumPlans) + 0.779(AreaBurned)$$
$$- 0.727(WindSpeed) - 4.388(RTK) + 26.618$$

$$\text{est. } \text{FINISHTIME} = 0.623(\text{NUMPLANS}) + 0.369(\text{AREABURNED})$$
$$- 0.09(\text{WINDSPEED}) - 0.382(\text{RTK}).$$

You might be wondering what happened to the y intercept term of the standardized regression model. Just as regression lines go through the means of x and y (see section 8.2.1) regression planes and hyperplanes go through the means of all the predictor variables and the dependent variable. And because the means of standardized variables are zero the y intercept for standardized regression surfaces is zero, and is dropped from the model.

The unstandardized coefficients in the first model depend on scale; for example, *AreaBurned* is measured in acres, but if it was measured in square yards, its coefficient would be very much smaller. Because scale is arbitrary, we cannot compare the coefficients directly to see which variables have larger effects on *FinishTime*. Standardized coefficients are comparable, however. Imagine changing an unstandardized variable x enough to change the standardized variable X by one. How much is x changed? Equation 8.3 tells us that

$$X + 1 = \frac{x - \overline{x}}{s_x} + \frac{s_x}{s_x} = \frac{(x + s_x) - \overline{x}}{s_x},$$

so a unit increase in X corresponds to one standard deviation increase in x. Thus, if $Y = \beta_X X$, then β_X is the number of units by which Y changes for each unit change in X; alternatively, β_X is the number of units of s_y by which y changes for each s_x change in x. For example, FINISHTIME changes by .623 units for every unit that NUMPLANS changes. In contrast, increasing RTK by 1.0 decreases FINISHTIME by .382. Hence, RTK has roughly 60 percent of the influence on FINISHTIME that NUMPLANS has.

Coefficients of standardized variables are denoted β instead of b, and are called *beta coefficients*. In section 8A we show that the relationship between b coefficients and β is

$$\beta_x = b_x \frac{s_x}{s_y}. \tag{8.4}$$

This means we can run a regression with unstandardized variables and simply transform b coefficients into β coefficients, or we can standardize our variables before running the regression, in which case the b coefficients *are* β coefficients.

An interesting special case arises in simple regression (the regression of y on a single predictor variable x), which has the equation $\hat{y} = bx + a$. You might recall that b was given in terms of the correlation between y and x:

$$b = r_{xy} \frac{s_y}{s_x}. \tag{8.5}$$

Standardizing this involves multiplying by s_x/s_y, as shown in equation 8.4. The fractions cancel, which means that the standardized regression coefficient in simple regression is just the correlation:

$$Y = r_{xy} X.$$

8.7   A Model of Plan Adaptation Effort

A common argument for case-based planning is that it is usually cheaper to retrieve a plan from memory and adapt it to a novel situation than it is to generate a plan from scratch. This is at best a plausible intuition, however, and nobody really knows how much effort is saved by adapting old plans. The savings surely depend on many factors, such as the effort required to retrieve plans from memory, the cost of evaluating candidate plans before and after they are adapted, and the degree of mismatch between the retrieved plan and the novel situation. Hanks and Weld (1992) used multiple regression to build a model of the cost of adapting an old plan to a novel situation. Their model is interesting because it illustrates how multiple regression provides least-squares estimates of model parameters, and it shows how nonlinear terms are sometimes included in linear regression models.

Hanks and Weld modeled the costs incurred by their SPA plan-adaptation algorithm for one class of block-stacking problems. The initial state of each problem represents a handful of toy blocks on a table; no block is on top of any other block. The goal state represents a tower of blocks. For instance, the initial state of a 4BS problem has blocks *A*, *B*, *C*, and *D* on the table; the final state is a tower *ABCD* with *A* on the bottom and *D* on the top. A *library plan* to solve part of this problem—to build, say, a two-block tower *AB*—might be retrieved from memory and given to the SPA algorithm, which would adapt it by adding block-stacking actions to it. In the process, new partial plans are generated; for example, a partial plan involves adding block *D* to the tower *AB* (it won't work, of course, but it is considered). Given a retrieved plan, such as the plan to generate *AB*, the SPA algorithm searches systematically through the space of partial plans that extend the given plan until it finds one that achieves the original goal, namely, *ABCD*. If SPA is given no plan at all, its search through the space of possible extensions to this "null plan" is equivalent to planning from scratch. Hanks and Weld frame the question of the cost savings of plan adaptation thus: How much cheaper is it to search the space of extensions of a library plan, rather than the entire space of partial plans? Their answer is partly analytical, partly empirical; we will show how refinements of an empirical regression model suggest an analytical one.

Two factors that interest Hanks and Weld are the size of the goal (denoted *GoalSize*) and the size of the library plan that's retrieved and adapted to achieve the goal (denoted *LibPlanSize*). In the previous example, the size of the goal, *ABCD*, is 4, and the size of the library plan, which achieves *AB*, is 2.[15] Hanks and Weld measured the cost of adaptation in terms of processor time. They ran twenty-five trials of every combination of *LibPlanSize* and *GoalSize* such that the library plan was smaller than the goal; for example, given the goal *ABCDEFG*, they would give SPA library plans such as *ABCDEF*, *ABCDE*, . . . , and also no plan whatsoever (i.e., require SPA to plan from scratch).

A scatterplot of *GoalSize* against processor time showed a distinct nonlinearity: time increased exponentially with problem size. Hence, Hanks and Weld decided that their dependent variable would be the square root of time, which I denote as *t*. Regressing *t* on *GoalSize*, alone, yields the following model (with unstandardized coefficients):

$$\hat{t} = 30.8(GoalSize) - 82.9.$$

This model accounts for quite a lot of variance in *t*, $r^2 = .673$, but a plot of *Goal-Size* against the residuals (figure 8.11.a) shows some interesting structure. First,

---

15. Actually, Hanks and Weld define *LibPlanSize* as one plus the number of steps in the library plan, but this won't concern us here.

the variance of the residuals increases with *GoalSize*, with a range near 300 when *GoalSize* = 12 and a range less than 50 for small values. Second, the residuals appear to have a nonlinear, possibly quadratic component. With this in mind, we can add the term $(GoalSize)^2$ to the regression model; we expect this will eradicate the quadratic component of the residuals. The new regression model is:

$$\hat{t} = 2.258(GoalSize) + 1.807(GoalSize)^2 + 15.57,$$

which accounts for only a little more variance than the previous one, $R^2 = .69$. The standardized regression model is:

$$\hat{T} = .06(\text{GoalSize}) + .771(\text{GoalSize})^2,$$

which means the effect of $(\text{GoalSize})^2$ on T is more than ten times bigger than the effect of GoalSize on T. Said differently, when $(GoalSize)^2$ is in the model, *GoalSize* contributes almost nothing to our ability to predict t. Informally, this is because *GoalSize* and $(GoalSize)^2$ are correlated very highly ($r = .985$), and $(GoalSize)^2$ does a slightly better job of accounting for the variance in t (remember the quadratic component of the residuals) so *GoalSize* has little to offer.[16]   Because *GoalSize* contributes so little, we'll regress t on $(GoalSize)^2$, alone:

$$\hat{t} = 1.945(GoalSize)^2 + 23.701.$$

This model also accounts for 69 percent of the variance in t, confirming our suspicion that *GoalSize* contributed virtually nothing beyond what $(GoalSize)^2$ contributes. The residuals from this model are shown in figure 8.11.b. Again we see that the range of the residuals increases dramatically with $(GoalSize)^2$ (although the quadratic component from figure 8.11.a seems to be gone). Perhaps *LibPlanSize*, the size of the retrieved library plan, can account for some of this structure. When we regress t on $(GoalSize)^2$ and *LibPlanSize*, we get this model:

$$\hat{t} = 2.631(GoalSize)^2 - 23.275(LibPlanSize) + 68.163.$$

Now our model accounts for a gratifying 97.7 percent of the variance in t, and it is quite plausible. The time to adapt a plan to achieve a goal increases with the square of the size of the goal, and decreases with the size of the retrieved library plan, because bigger retrieved plans require less adaptation. The residuals from this model are shown

---

16. It is counterintuitive that *GoalSize* and $(GoalSize)^2$ are correlated so highly, but consider this, from Mosteller and Tukey 1977, p. 286: "if s is uniformly distributed over some interval $(0, A)$, then the correlation of x and x^2 is 0.97 for any choice of A."

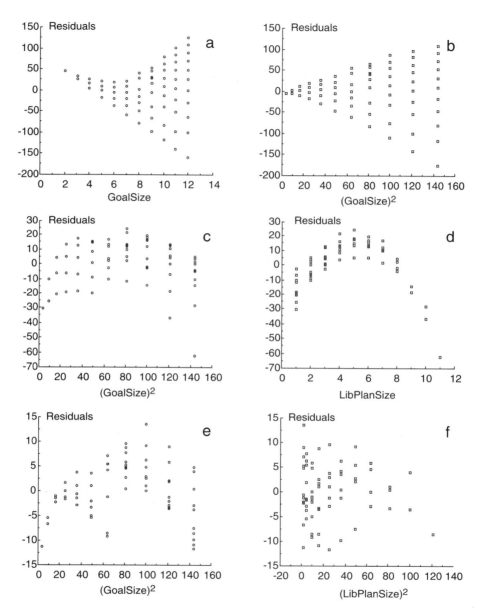

Figure 8.11   Residuals for successive regression models of Hanks and Weld's SPA algorithm.

in figures 8.11.c and 8.11.d. The former plots $(GoalSize)^2$ against the residuals; the pattern seems to be weakly nonlinear, perhaps a negative quadratic. This pattern is accentuated in figure 8.11.d, the plot of *LibPlanSize* against the residuals. Both plots suggest that $(LibPlanSize)^2$ might contribute something to the variance of t, so let's add it to the regression equation:

$$\hat{t} = 2.657(GoalSize)^2 - 3.529(LibPlanSize) - 1.968(LibPlanSize)^2 + 31.347.$$

With this addition, the model accounts for 99.7 percent of the variance in t; it's nearly perfect. As before, however, the standardized model tells us that *LibPlanSize* contributes little, relative to $(LibPlanSize)^2$:

$$\hat{T} = 1.134(\text{GOALSIZE})^2 - .093(\text{LIBPLANSIZE}) - .542(\text{LIBPLANSIZE})^2.$$

Thus, it's not surprising that the model

$$\hat{t} = 2.653(GoalSize)^2 - 2.289(LibPlanSize)^2 + 24.753$$

accounts for 99.6 percent of the variance in t. The plots of $(GoalSize)^2$ and $(LibPlanSize)^2$ against the residuals for this model are shown in figures 8.11.e and 8.11.f, respectively. They have less structure and smaller ranges of residuals than the previous plots, which corroborates the high R^2 score for the model.

From Hanks and Weld's data, we have derived a model of the time required to adapt a plan, as it is influenced by *GoalSize*, size of the goal, and *LibPlanSize*, the size of the plan that's retrieved and adapted to achieve the goal. The model is dominated by $(GoalSize)^2$ and $(LibPlanSize)^2$. Hanks and Weld themselves established a deterministic relationship between *GoalSize*, *LibPlanSize*, and the number of partial plans SPA dequeues from a list and examines:

$$n_{deq} = ((GoalSize)^2 - (LibPlanSize)^2) + (GoalSize - LibPlanSize) + 1.$$

The regression of n_{deq} on t accounts for 98.3 percent of the variance in n_{deq}. Although our empirical model is no substitute for Hanks and Weld's deterministic, analytical one, it's clear that the empirical exercise provides valuable information about the general form of the analytical model.

In sum, we have seen how multiple regression can help us find functional relationships in data even when those functions are nonlinear. The analysis of residuals suggests higher-order terms to include in the regression; for instance, if the residuals seem to be a quadratic function of a predictor variable x, one might include x^2 in the regression equation. We also saw how standardized regression coefficients can tell us which terms dominate functional relationships.

8.8   Causal Models

We often use unabashedly causal language to discuss regression models; for example, in a previous section, we not only asserted that *NumPlans affects FinishTime*, we even said the magnitude of *NumPlans*'s effect was twice that of *RTK*. What is the justification for this strong causal language? Everyone knows that correlation doesn't imply causation, so why should we believe regression does? Especially when, in simple regression, the standardized regression coefficient *is* the correlation. We are about to begin an excursion into the meaning of causal statements that will end with some techniques for causal modeling, but as with any expedition, it will help us to know the difficulties before we begin.

As you know, people with small feet, particularly small children, are not adept with language. Hence, the regression of language skill on shoe size could have a large standardized regression coefficient. Yet common sense tells us that the relationship between language skill and shoe size is due largely or entirely to a hidden or *latent* factor, namely, age. One compelling bit of evidence is that the relationship cannot be found in a sample of children who are between 100 and 101 weeks old. In other words, when age is held constant, the relationship between language skill and shoe size disappears. In general, we call a relationship between *a* and *b*, with *c* held constant, a partial relationship. If *a* and *b* are strongly related but their partial relationship with *c* held constant is weak, then *a*'s influence on *b* (or *b*'s influence on *a*) is probably mediated by or depends on *c*. The most common example of a partial relationship is the *partial correlation*:

$$r_{ab|c} = \frac{r_{ab} - r_{ac}r_{bc}}{\sqrt{1 - r_{ac}^2}\sqrt{1 - r_{bc}^2}}. \tag{8.6}$$

If the relationship between *a* and *b* depends on the relationship of each with *c*, then we'd expect r_{ac} and r_{bc} to be relatively large, and, thus, the partial correlation $r_{ab|c}$ will be small. For instance:

$$r_{language,shoe} = .7$$

$$r_{language,age} = .85$$

$$r_{shoe,age} = .8$$

$$r_{language,shoe|age} = \frac{.7 - .85 \times .8}{\sqrt{1 - .85^2}\sqrt{1 - .8^2}} = .06.$$

This pattern—a relationship between *a* and *b* that vanishes when *c* is controlled—is evidence that *a* and *b* are *conditionally independent* given *c*. (You can also find evidence for conditional independence in categorical data—you don't need continuous variables and correlations—see section 7.7.) Conditional independence, in turn, is often taken as evidence that *a* doesn't cause *b* and vice versa. Of course, if you want to know which factors are causally related, it's only a little help to know (or strongly suspect, anyway) which ones are not. The problem of when you can legitimately infer cause—the *causal induction problem*—is subtle and fascinating.

8.8.1 Why Causal Modeling Is Difficult

When *a* and *b* covary, how can we know they are not both influenced by another factor, *c*? Often, a controlled experiment will do the trick; for instance, we can control for age—by looking at children in a narrow age range—to see whether the relationship between language skill and shoe size disappears. Note that we can control for age in the experiment design or statistically, after the fact, when we analyze the results. Experimental control might involve sampling children in a narrow age range; *statistical control* looks at the partial relationship between shoe size and language skill with age held constant. Provided we think about age before we run the experiment and either sample in a narrow age range or record the age of each child, we can control for the effect of age. Problems arise, however, when we fail to measure a factor that explains an apparent relationship between others. An unmeasured factor that affects others in this way is called a *latent factor*. A fundamental problem for causal inference is to figure out that *a* does not cause *b* (or vice versa) when a latent factor affects both. We call it the *latent factor problem*. When latent factors are involved, the parallel between experimental and statistical control breaks down.

Suppose *c* causes both *a* and *b*, but *c* is obscure; something you can't imagine affecting *a* and *b* and something you don't measure. For example, *c* might be an obscure hormone that affects concentration and *a* and *b* might be an author's coffee intake and rate of typographical errors, respectively. Unknown to you, this hormone influences both coffee intake and typos, and, remarkably, coffee intake and typos are independent. You run an experiment in which you measure coffee intake and typos, but you don't measure the level of this hormone because you don't suspect its existence. At the end of the experiment you regress typos on coffee intake and obtain a nice high regression coefficient. But because the hormone is a latent factor, you cannot control for its effect statistically and you will never discover that coffee intake does not influence typing accuracy. Now consider running the experiment slightly differently. Instead of simply recording coffee intake and typos on each day, actively manipulate coffee intake and record the number of typos. In this design, you can solve the latent factor problem. You will find that when coffee intake is up, typos may go up or down, depending on the hormone, but you don't have to measure the hormone to observe this. Similarly, when coffee intake is down, typos go up or down, depending on the unmeasured hormone levels. Hence, coffee intake doesn't affect typing accuracy. So you see that experimental control can tell us that two factors are not really related but owe their covariance to another factor whether or not we measure that factor, but statistical control cannot disclose the effects of unmeasured (i.e., latent) factors.

These hypothetical experiments remind us of the distinctions in chapters 1 and 3 between manipulation and observation experiments. A manipulation experiment controls coffee intake and records the effects on typographical errors; an observation experiment records coffee intake and typos, but controls neither. Hence, data from manipulation experiments can solve the latent factor problem but data from observation experiments cannot. This is why some people insist manipulation experiments are the only "true" experiments (Shaffer, 1992; Holland, 1986). Unfortunately, many phenomena are not amenable to manipulation: You might observe that the murder rate is low in countries that don't impose the death penalty, and you might argue that one phenomenon is the cause of the other, but you can never be certain that other factors, say, religion, or level of education, aren't responsible for both phenomena, and you can't control either phenomenon to find out.

Another fundamental problem in causal inference is getting the causal direction right—the *causal ordering problem*. Even if the relationship between murder rates and the death penalty is genuine—even if it is not due to latent variables such as religion and education—we still don't know which causes which. Is the murder rate low because the death penalty is not imposed, or vice versa? When possible (and it isn't in this example) manipulation experiments can resolve the issue: To find out whether a causes b, or vice versa, or both, manipulate a and see whether b changes, then manipulate b and see whether a changes. Fortunately, manipulation isn't always necessary to solve the causal ordering problem. *Time stamped* data from observation experiments will sometimes suffice, because causal chains run forward in time. Hence, even if you cannot manipulate a and b, you are safe assuming that b cannot cause a if it happens after a.

Note that statistical control can tell us whether a measured variable accounts for some of the relationship between two others, but statistical control has nothing to say about causal order. By regressing language skill on both shoe size and age, we learned that the influence of shoe size on language skill when age was fixed was nearly zero.

This result does not tell us whether age causes language skill or vice versa. In fact, it does not differentiate three possible causal orderings:

1. shoe size $\rightarrow$ age $\rightarrow$ language skill;
2. shoe size $\leftarrow$ age $\leftarrow$ language skill;
3. shoe size $\leftarrow$ age $\rightarrow$ language skill.

You and I know that the third model is correct, but that's because we know neither language skill nor shoe size causes age. Statistical control alone, lacking this sort of exogenous domain knowledge, is insufficient to resolve causal ordering.

In sum, suppose the true state of affairs is

$$a \leftarrow c \rightarrow b$$

and we measure a, b, and perhaps c. If c is not measured, then manipulating a (or b) can tell us that a and b are not related. If c is measured, then observation experiments and statistical control can tell us the same thing. If c is manipulated, we can learn that it is causally "upstream" of b. And in an observation experiment, where c is not manipulated but is observed to occur before b, we can infer c is causally upstream of b.

The latent factor problem and the causal ordering problem are particularly difficult when we study humans because the obvious manipulation experiment is often unethical. The problems also arise, however, when we try to build causal models of AI programs. You might think we can look at a program and figure out what causes what, but it isn't so simple, and it can be difficult to manipulate programs for experimental control. Imagine a planner that often fails to accomplish a goal (call this failure f_1). After f_1 the planner takes a remedial action, a, and accomplishes its first goal, but later it fails to accomplish its second goal (call this failure f_2). How would you show that a causes f_2? You could manipulate the program to take a different action, b, after f_1, and see whether the frequency of f_2 changes. So far, so good: It is much less easy to test whether f_1 causes f_2, because you would have to control whether the program fails to achieve its first goal. It's one thing to control individual actions and quite another to control whether and when a program fails. Yet, to be certain that f_1 and not something else causes f_2, you must manipulate the occurrences of f_1 and observe the effects on f_2. Let's assume you do it: you modify the program so f_1 occurs no more, and you observe that f_2 also is eliminated. Unfortunately, this does not mean f_1 causes f_2. Whatever you did to eliminate f_1 probably also influenced f_2; in other words, you probably modified something that affected both failures. The latent factor problem strikes again. The causal ordering problem also arises, and knowing when events happen is often no help. A series of actions produced by loops, such as $ABCABCABCABC\ldots$, confound efforts to infer causal order from temporal order: Although it's true that A precedes B, the inverse is true almost as frequently.

Even when we can manipulate our programs, if we can't also manipulate their environments, we might be stuck with observation experiments. And even when we can manipulate environmental influences, they are sometimes diffuse, so it is difficult to point to a particular environmental event that preceded (and might have caused) a state of our program. For example, the Phoenix planner fails relatively often when the wind speed in its simulated environment is high, so we can say with some confidence that wind speed is a causal influence, but it's difficult to say exactly how wind speed affects performance. In sum, causal models of AI systems must sometimes be inferred from extensive observations of the systems running, because it is difficult to implement manipulation experiments. Unfortunately, observation experiments can't always resolve causal order or tell us unequivocally that an apparent effect is not due to a latent factor.

8.8.2 Regression Coefficients as Causal Strengths

Regression coefficients—standardized and unstandardized—are partial. Each can be interpreted as the influence of a predictor X_i on the dependent variable Y when the influences of all other predictors in the regression model are fixed (this is demonstrated in section 8A). Just as language skill has a low partial correlation with shoe size given age, so too does its coefficient drop when age enters the multiple regression model:

est. LanguageSkill $= .7(ShoeSize)$ before adding age as a predictor
est. LanguageSkill $= .055(ShoeSize) + .805(Age)$ with age as a predictor

The calculations of these coefficients follow from the normal equations in section 8A.

Because regression coefficients are partial, they can suggest that variables are not causally connected, as discussed earlier. If you decide by some means that some factors are connected, however, then regression coefficients may be interpreted as the strength of their causal relationship, provided you subscribe to one notion of what a "cause" is.

Suppes (1970) posits three requirements for a to cause b: a and b must covary, a must precede b, and other causes of b must be controlled. By these criteria, the previous regression models are causal models. First, age is a cause of language skill because age and language skill covary; adults are more fluent than children. Shoe size is also a cause of language skill by the covariance criterion, because shoe size and language skill covary. Second, age is a cause of language skill because in this model it predicts language skill. Models can be wrong and, in reality, the factor on the left in a regression equation might be a cause, and a factor on the right might be the effect. Even so, correct or not, a regression model implies precedence between factors. So, by the precedence criterion, the factors on the right of the equation are causes. Third, regression coefficients satisfy a statistical version of the control criterion. A high regression coefficient means its associated factor has a relatively big effect on the dependent variable when the effects of other factors in the model are fixed. Models can be wrong if apparent effects are due to latent factors. Even so, correct or not, a regression model estimates the strengths of causal influences between y and each predictor x_i in the model when the influences of other predictors in the model are controlled.

8.9   Structural Equation Models

Causal they might be, but regression models have one unsatisfying feature. Here is the regression of *FinishTime* on several factors in the Phoenix environment and planner design (the variables are standardized):

$$est.\ \text{FINISHTIME} = .609(\text{FIRELINEBUILT}) + 0.212(\text{AREABURNED})$$
$$+ 0.172(\text{NUMPLANS}) + 0.032(\text{FIRSTPLAN}) - 0.164(\text{RTK})$$
$$- 0.348(\text{WINDSPEED}).$$

This model is flat. Nothing in its structure tells us that the area burned by a fire is influenced by wind speed, nor that the amount of replanning (*NumPlans*) is influenced by the planner's relative thinking speed (*RTK*). Nothing in the structure of the regression equation distinguishes *independent variables*—those set by the experimenter—from *endogenous variables*, which are causally downstream of the independent variables. In fact, the regression model corresponds to a *one-level causal model* shown in figure 8.12. Each predictor variable has a direct effect on *FinishTime* and a correlation with every other predictor variable. The direct effects are the standardized regression coefficients from the previous equation.

A model that comes closer to our understanding of how Phoenix works, corresponding roughly to the causal story developed in chapter 2, is shown in figure 8.13. As a causal story, or at least a collection of causal hypotheses, it is more plausible. Not necessarily "correct," but more plausible: It places the independent variables, which we set in our experiment, causally upstream of the endogenous variables, which are measurements of the Phoenix planner's performance. It says *FirstPlan* influences

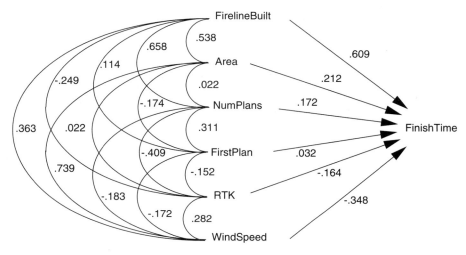

Figure 8.12   A flat regression model of *FinishTime*.

FirelineBuilt not directly but indirectly through the amount of area that it causes to be burned, and through replanning (*NumPlans*), which *FirstPlan* also influences. The model says *WindSpeed* has no direct effect on *FinishTime*, but influences *FinishTime* by increasing the area burned, the amount of fireline built, and the amount of replanning. We will return to other aspects of the model, particularly the links with very small weights, later.

This model is represented easily with a set of *structural equations*, for which the coefficients are found by multiple regression. For example, when *FinishTime* is regressed on *FirelineBuilt, NumPlans, Area*, and *RTK* we get the standardized coefficients in the first structural equation:

$$est.\ \text{FINISHTIME} = .499(\text{FIRELINEBUILT}) + 0.291(\text{NUMPLANS}) + 0.008(\text{AREA})$$
$$- .241(\text{RTK});$$

$$est.\ \text{FIRELINEBUILT} = .692(\text{NUMPLANS}) + .227(\text{WINDSPEED}) + .335(\text{AREA});$$

$$est.\ \text{NUMPLANS} = .25(\text{FIRSTPLAN}) - .361(\text{RTK}) - .038(\text{WINDSPEED});$$

$$est.\ (\text{AREA}) = .731(\text{WINDSPEED}) - .048(\text{FIRSTPLAN}).$$

Modeling generally has two phases, *specification* and *estimation*. In causal modeling, specification means saying which variables are causes and which are effects, and estimation means running a procedure such as multiple regression to find the

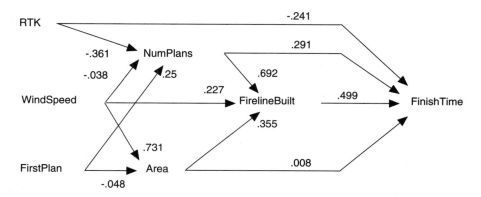

Figure 8.13   A structural equation model relating several factors.

strengths of specified causal relationships. From a formal standpoint, specification is a combinatorial nightmare: Allowing both causal and correlational links in a model, one can construct 2^{n^2-n} models for n variables—over one million models for just five variables. It helps, though not much, to exclude correlation links. Remarkably, several algorithms for specification are quite efficient (Spirtes et al., 1993; Pearl and Verma, 1991; Gregory and Cohen, 1994; Cohen et al., 1995), but they aren't our focus, here. Building models by hand is our focus—albeit with a little algorithmic help—because researchers usually know a lot about the systems they are modeling, so their hand-built models are more plausible than those built by algorithms. Here is a simple procedure for building causal models by hand:

1. Set M to be the dependent variable, denoted X_0 and let P to be all the other variables.

2. Dequeue each element X_i in M and

   (a) Filter the elements of P to get a set $\{X_q, X_r, \dots\}$
   (b) Write down a structural equation $X_i = \beta_q X_q + \beta_r X_r + \dots$
   (c) Regress X_i on $X_q, X_r, \dots$ to solve for $\beta_q, \beta_r, \dots$
   (d) Add $X_q, X_r, \dots$ to M.

This procedure assumes we're trying to build a causal model of a particular behavior or measure (e.g., *FinishTime*), and not merely searching the space of models for some that fit the data. The procedure produces a single model that we should regard as a "first draft." Clearly, the quality of this model depends on how we filter the elements of P. Many kinds of filtering knowledge might be introduced, but here we'll rely on four simple heuristics to decide whether a causal link $X_j \rightarrow X_i$ should be forged. Any link that makes it through these filters gets added to the model.

1. X_j shouldn't point to X_i if a directed path from X_i to X_j already exists (i.e., no cycles).

2. After regressing X_i on X_j and perhaps other variables, reject the link $X_j \rightarrow X_i$ if $|\beta_{ji}| \leq T_\beta$ (i.e., the standardized regression coefficient must exceed a threshold).

3. Assuming the previous regression, reject $X_j \rightarrow X_i$ if $R^2 \leq T_{R^2}$ (i.e., reject X_j and its fellow predictors if they don't account collectively for at least some threshold percentage of variance in X_i).

4. Assuming the previous regression, reject $X_j \rightarrow X_i$ if $|\omega_{ji}| \geq T_\omega$.

The omega (ω) statistic is defined as follows: $\omega_{ji} = (r_{ji} - \beta_{ji})/r_{ji}$. The beta coefficient, recall, measures the influence of X_j on X_i when the influences of all other predictors are held constant; and the correlation r_{ji} represents the total influence of X_j on X_i. Thus, $(r_{ji} - \beta_{ji})$ is the influence of X_j on X_i that is due to X_j's relationships with other predictors, and ω_{ji} is the proportion of X_j's influence on X_i that is not direct. If X_j has little direct influence on X_i relative to its indirect influence through, say, X_k, then X_k, not X_j, is heuristically more apt to be the direct cause of X_i (Gregory and Cohen, 1994; Cohen et al., 1995). Small values of ω are necessary but not sufficient to consider one variable a cause of another. This is because ω_{ji} will be very small if both r_{ji} and β_{ji} are small, but in this case the predictor X_j has little influence on X_i, direct or indirect, and should be discarded (it will be caught by the filters, previously mentioned). Even if the beta coefficients are relatively high, the regression of X_i on X_j and other variables might account for very little variance in X_i, so we discard X_j if it doesn't contribute enough (perhaps with other variables) to R^2 for X_i.

Following these heuristics gives us the "first draft" model of Phoenix in figure 8.13. Let's see how. We'll set $T_\omega = .8$, $T_\beta = .1$ and $T_{R^2} = .25$ and initialize M to be *Finish-Time* and P to {*RTK, WindSpeed, FirstPlan, NumPlans, AreaBurned, FirelineBuilt*}. Then we dequeue *FinishTime* from M and regress it on the elements in P, yielding beta coefficients, with which we calculate omega scores:

	RTK	WindSpeed	FirstPlan	NumPlans	FirelineBuilt	AreaBurned
r_{YX}:	−.484	−.053	.204	.718	.755	.277
β_{YX}:	−.164	−.348	.032	.172	.609	.212
ω_{YX}:	.662	−5.577	.841	.760	.193	.234

This regression accounts for much of the variance in *FinishTime* ($R^2 = .705$) so this set of predictors meets the T_{R^2} threshold. Four of the six predictors have ω scores lower than T_ω and absolute value β coefficients higher than T_β, so we write them into a structural equation and solve for coefficients by regression:

$$est.\ \text{FINISHTIME} = .499(\text{FIRELINEBUILT}) + 0.291(\text{NUMPLANS})$$

$$+ 0.008(\text{AREABURNED}) - .241(\text{RTK}).$$

Lastly, we enqueue these selected predictors on M. You can see immediately that our heuristics have allowed a poor predictor, *AreaBurned*, into the model, but the others have relatively strong coefficients. Next, we dequeue an element from M, say *FirelineBuilt*, and repeat the previous steps. We regress *FirelineBuilt* on the other variables in P, yielding these statistics:

	RTK	WindSpeed	FirstPlan	NumPlans	AreaBurned
r_{YX}:	−.249	.363	.114	.658	.538
β_{YX}:	−.050	.249	−.002	.676	.340
ω_{YX}:	.798	.314	1.014	−.027	.368

Four of the five predictors have absolute ω scores lower than T_ω, but *RTK* has a β coefficient lower than T_β, so *WindSpeed*, *NumPlans*, and *Area* are selected as *FirelineBuilt*'s predictors, which results in this structural equation:

$$est.\text{FIRELINEBUILT} = .692(\text{NUMPLANS}) + .227(\text{WINDSPEED})$$

$$+ .335(\text{AREABURNED}).$$

Then we enqueue *WindSpeed* on M (the other predictors are already there).

Repeating these steps until M is empty produces the model in figure 8.13. Is it a good model? That depends on our criteria.

If our goal is to predict *FinishTime* as accurately as possible then, no, it isn't the best model. It accounts for 70.5 percent of the variance in *FinishTime*, whereas the flat regression model in figure 8.12 accounts for 74.7 percent. In general (but not invariably) adding predictors to a regression equation will increase R^2; so removing predictors for use "further upstream"—as we removed, say, *WindSpeed*—generally reduces R^2. By the criterion of maximum predictive power, a flat regression model is almost always preferable to any multilevel model constructed from the same variables.

On the other hand, the difference in predictive power between the flat regression model and the multilevel one we just constructed is small, less than 5 percent. In compensation, the multilevel model elucidates some relationships among factors in a way that the regression model—in which all factors are simply correlated—cannot. Whereas the flat regression model credits *AreaBurned* with some small influence on *FinishTime* ($\beta = .212$), the multilevel model says *AreaBurned* has virtually no direct influence ($\beta = .008$) and can affect *FinishTime* only through its influence on *FirelineBuilt*. Whether or not this is correct, it is a plausible and explicit hypothesis about how Phoenix works, something we can verify, or test in future experiments. The multilevel model also says thinking time (*RTK*) doesn't have pervasive influences, as we thought it might, but rather influences *FinishTime* directly and through its effects on replanning (*NumPlans*). Again, this could be wrong, but it represents a moderately interesting hypothesis: The Phoenix planner reacts to time pressure by replanning. So, although the multi-level model accounts for slightly less variance in *FinishTime* than the flat regression model, it makes more explicit predictions. This seems a worthwhile trade.

8.10 Conclusion

There is a need in artificial intelligence for concise models that relate a system's behavior to its structure, its tasks, and the dynamics of its environment. Systems themselves are complex and many (perhaps most) system-level design decisions have no theoretical import. The distinction between "above the line" theories and "below the line" implementations has considerable appeal, and its implementation in the Sceptic methodology seems promising. We can also exploit statistical modeling methods, particularly linear regression, to build predictive models and even causal models of system behavior.

8.11 Further Reading

Good entrances into the huge literature on multiple regression are texts by Draper and Smith (1966) and Mosteller and Tukey (1977). Less intensive, but still very informative, is Hays' general text (1973). The appendix to this chapter lays out some basic theory. The branch of regression modeling that deals with structural equations is sometimes called *path analysis*. A good introduction in the biometric tradition is provided by Li (1975); see also Sokal and Rohlf's text (1981). The logic and practice of causal modeling, including path analysis, is debated in Shaffer 1992. See also Holland 1986. A scholarly introduction, including several algorithms and their mathematical justifications, is to be found in Spirtes et al. 1993. Pearl (Pearl and Verma, 1991; Pearl, 1988) has developed causal induction algorithms and their underlying theory.

Appendix: Multiple Regression

Recall that simple linear regression finds a least-squares line relating a single predictor variable x to a performance variable y. A least-squares line is one that minimizes the sum of squared deviations of predicted values from actual values, called the sum of squared residuals, or $SS_{res.}$. That is, simple linear regression finds a line $\hat{y}_i = bx_i + a$ to minimize

$$SS_{res.} = \sum_i \left(\hat{y}_i - y_i \right)^2 .$$

In this section we show how to find least-squares rules for more than one predictor variable, rules of the form $\hat{y}_i = b_1 x_{1_i} + \cdots + b_k x_{k_i} + a$. (Later we will derive a rule for a standardized regression model.)

For simplicity we will first develop a least-squares rule for just two predictor variables, x_1 and x_2. Our goal, then, is to find values of b_1 and b_2 in the rule

$$\hat{y}_i = b_1 x_{1_i} + b_2 x_{2_i} + a.$$

that minimize $SS_{res.}$. Recall that the deviation of $\hat{y}$ from y is but one component of the deviation of y from its mean: $(y_i - \overline{y}) = (y_i - \hat{y}_i) + (\hat{y}_i - \overline{y})$. We want our rule to minimize the summed squared deviations of $\hat{y}$ from y, but for the moment we will look at a single deviation $(y_i - \hat{y}_i)$. Rearranging the previous equation gives

$$(y_i - \hat{y}_i) = (y_i - \overline{y}) - (\hat{y}_i - \overline{y}). \tag{8A.1}$$

Let's focus on the last term of this equation, $(\hat{y}_i - \overline{y})$. We know that a simple regression line goes through the point $(\overline{x}, \overline{y})$, and, it turns out, the regression plane for two predictor variables goes through the point $(\overline{x}_1, \overline{x}_2, \overline{y})$. Therefore, $\overline{y}$ can be expressed in terms of the regression equation, $\overline{y} = b_1 \overline{x}_1 + b_2 \overline{x}_2 + a$, and the term $(\hat{y}_i - \overline{y})$ is

$$(b_1 x_{1_i} + b_2 x_{2_i} + a) - (b_1 \overline{x}_1 + b_2 \overline{x}_2 + a) = b_1(x_{1_i} - \overline{x}_1) + b_2(x_{2_i} - \overline{x}_2).$$

Substituting this result back into equation 8A.1 we get

$$(y_i - \hat{y}_i) = (y_i - \overline{y}) - b_1(x_{1_i} - \overline{x}_1) + b_2(x_{2_i} - \overline{x}_2). \tag{8A.2}$$

Note that three of the terms on the right are deviations from means. To simplify the expression, let $Y_i = (y_i - \overline{y})$, $X_{1_i} = (x_{1_i} - \overline{x}_1)$, $X_{2_i} = (x_{2_i} - \overline{x}_2)$:

$$(y_i - \hat{y}_i) = Y_i - b_1 X_{1_i} + b_2 X_{2_i} .$$

Then the sum of squared deviations that we're trying to minimize is

$$\mathcal{Q} = \sum_i (y_i - \hat{y}_i)^2 = \sum_i (Y_i - b_1 X_{1_i} + b_2 X_{2_i})^2.$$

The minimum is found by taking the partial derivatives $\partial \mathcal{Q}/\partial b_1$, $\partial \mathcal{Q}/\partial b_2$ and setting them to zero, yielding two *normal equations*:

$$\sum_i (Y_i - b_1 X_{1_i} + b_2 X_{2_i}) X_{1_i} = 0;$$

$$\sum_i (Y_i - b_1 X_{1_i} + b_2 X_{2_i}) X_{2_i} = 0.$$

Multiplying through and rearranging terms, we get

$$b_1 \sum_i X_{1_i}^2 + b_2 \sum_i X_{2_i} X_{1_i} = \sum_i Y_i X_{1_i};$$ (8A.3a)

$$b_1 \sum_i X_{1_i} X_{2_i} + b_2 \sum_i X_{2_i}^2 = \sum_i Y_i X_{2_i}.$$ (8A.3b)

Now, the sum of the products of deviations is just the numerator of the covariance:

$$\text{COV}(x, y) = \frac{\sum_i (x_i - \bar{x})(y_i - \bar{y})}{N} = \frac{\sum_i X_i Y_i}{N}$$

and the covariance of a variable with itself is just the variance, so $(\sum_i X_i^2)/N = s^2$. Thus, equation 8A.3a can be written:

$$N \left(b_1 \frac{\sum_i X_{1_i}^2}{N} + b_2 \frac{\sum_i X_{2_i} X_{1_i}}{N} \right) = N \left(\frac{\sum_i Y_i X_{1_i}}{N} \right)$$

or, in terms of variance and covariances:

$$N \left((b_1 \cdot s_1^2) + (b_2 \cdot \text{COV}(x_1, x_2)) \right) = N \left(\text{COV}(x_1, y) \right).$$

Finally, dividing by N, this normal equation and its twin (derived from eq. 8A.3b) are written:

$$b_1 s_1^2 + (b_2 \cdot \text{COV}(x_1, x_2)) = \text{COV}(x_1, y);$$ (8A.4a)

$$(b_1 \cdot \text{COV}(x_1, x_2)) + b_2 s_2^2 = \text{COV}(x_2, y).$$ (8A.4b)

For a given set of data, we can easily calculate the variances and covariances in 8A.4a and 8A.4b and solve for b_1 and b_2. The values we derive minimize $SS_{res.} = \sum_i (\hat{y}_i - y_i)^2$. That is, b_1 and b_2 give us a least-squares plane, analogous to the least-squares line in simple regression.

8A.1   Normal Equations

We can generalize the preceding procedure to any number of predictor variables. We will always end up with k normal equations in k unknowns. For simplicity, let's designate our variables with numbers, $y = 0$, $x_1 = 1$, $x_2 = 2$, ..., and denote the covariance of two variables, say y and x_1, as s_{01}. Then the general form for the normal equations is

$$b_1 s_1^2 + b_2 s_{12} + b_3 s_{13} + \cdots + b_k s_{1k} = s_{01} \tag{8A.5a}$$

$$b_1 s_{21} + b_2 s_2^2 + b_3 s_{23} + \cdots + b_k s_{2k} = s_{02} \tag{8A.5b}$$

$$b_1 s_{31} + b_2 s_{32} + b_3 s_3^2 + \cdots + b_k s_{3k} = s_{03} \tag{8A.5c}$$

$$\vdots \quad \vdots$$

$$b_1 s_{k1} + b_2 s_{k2} + b_3 s_{k3} + \cdots + b_k s_k^2 = s_{0k}. \tag{8A.5k}$$

Solving these equations yields values for $b_1 \ldots b_k$ that guarantee that

$$\hat{y}_i = b_1 x_{1_i} + \cdots + b_k x_{k_i} + a \tag{8A.6}$$

is a least-squares rule.

8A.2   Standardized Coefficients

The nice thing about standardized regression (beta) coefficients is that they are comparable: Each coefficient is the number of units by which Y changes for a unit change in a predictor variable, X. The relationship between b coefficients and beta coefficients is

$$\beta_x = b_x \frac{s_x}{s_y}. \tag{8A.7}$$

We know from equation 8A.2 that

$$(\hat{y}_i - \overline{y}) = b_1(x_{1_i} - \overline{x}_1) + b_2(x_{2_i} - \overline{x}_2).$$

Dividing each side by s_y standardizes the left hand side:

$$\hat{Y} = \frac{(\hat{y} - \overline{y})}{s_y} = \frac{b_1(x_1 - \overline{x}_1)}{s_y} + \frac{b_2(x_2 - \overline{x}_2)}{s_y}.$$

We dropped the subscript i for simplicity. Dividing the last two terms by s_{x_1}/s_{x_1} and s_{x_2}/s_{x_2} respectively gives

$$\hat{Y} = \frac{(\hat{y} - \overline{y})}{s_y} = b_1 \cdot \frac{s_{x_1}}{s_y} \cdot \frac{(x_1 - \overline{x}_1)}{s_{x_1}} + b_2 \cdot \frac{s_{x_2}}{s_y} \cdot \frac{(x_2 - \overline{x}_2)}{s_{x_2}}.$$

Now you can see that two of the ratios on the right are standardized variables, and the other terms, $b_k(s_k/s_y)$, are beta coefficients, as defined in equation 8A.7:

$$\hat{Y} = \beta_1 X_1 + \beta_2 X_2.$$

This, then, is the form of the standardized regression equation. To solve for the standardized regression coefficients we can, of course, solve the normal equations 8A.3a and 8A.3b to get b coefficients, then derive beta coefficients as shown in equation 8A.7. Or we can standardize our variables first, in which case $b_i = \beta_i$.

8A.3   Normal Equations for Standardized Variates

Even though one rarely solves normal equations by hand, it is worth looking at the form they take when variables are standardized. They have have an interesting causal interpretation. We will now show how to transform the normal equations 8A.3a and 8A.3b so they can be solved for beta coefficients. Here again is one of the normal equations, derived earlier:

$$b_1 s_1^2 + (b_2 \cdot \mathrm{COV}(x_1, x_2)) = \mathrm{COV}(x_1, y). \tag{8A.8}$$

Note that covariances are transformed to correlations by dividing by the product of standard deviations:

$$r_{xy} = \frac{\mathrm{COV}(x, y)}{s_x s_y}.$$

Here is equation 8A.8 after dividing through by $s_{x_1} s_y$:

$$b_1 \frac{s_1^2}{s_{x_1} s_y} + b_2 \frac{\mathrm{COV}(x_1, x_2)}{s_{x_1} s_y} = r_{x_1 y}.$$

Now multiply the first term on the left hand side by s_1/s_1 and the second by s_2/s_2:

$$b_1 \frac{s_{x_1}}{s_{x_1}} \cdot \frac{s_{x_1}^2}{s_{x_1} s_y} + b_2 \frac{s_{x_2}}{s_{x_2}} \cdot \frac{\mathrm{COV}(x_1, x_2)}{s_{x_1} s_y} = r_{x_1 y}.$$

Multiplying through, we get

$$b_1 \frac{s_{x_1}}{s_y} \cdot \frac{s_{x_1}^2}{s_{x_1}^2} + b_2 \frac{s_{x_2}}{s_y} \cdot \frac{\mathrm{COV}(x_1, x_2)}{s_{x_1} s_{x_2}} = r_{x_1 y},$$

which simplifies to

$$b_1 \frac{s_{x_1}}{s_y} + b_2 \frac{s_{x_2}}{s_y} r_{x_1 x_2} = r_{x_1 y}.$$

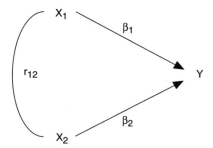

Figure 8A.1   Path model corresponding to two-predictor normal equations.

The term $b_k(s_k/s_y)$ is a beta coefficient, β_k. In terms of beta coefficients and correlations, then, the normal equations 8A.5a through 8A.5k have this form:

$$\beta_1 \quad + \beta_2 r_{12} + \beta_3 r_{13} + \cdots + \beta_k r_{1k} = r_{01}$$
$$\beta_1 r_{21} + \beta_2 \quad + \beta_3 r_{23} + \cdots + \beta_k r_{2k} = r_{02}$$
$$\beta_1 r_{31} + \beta_2 r_{32} + \beta_3 \quad + \cdots + \beta_k r_{3k} = r_{03}$$
$$\vdots \qquad \vdots \qquad \vdots \qquad\quad \vdots \qquad \vdots$$
$$\beta_1 r_{k1} + \beta_2 r_{k2} + \beta_3 r_{k3} + \cdots + \beta_k \quad = r_{0k}.$$

Once again, we have k normal equations in k unknowns, which, when solved, yield beta coefficients that guarantee that

$$\hat{Y} = \beta_1 X_1 + \beta_2 X_2 + \cdots + \beta_k X_k$$

is a least-squares rule.

8A.4   A Causal Interpretation of Regression: Path Diagrams

One interpretation of the normal equations for standardized variables is that they partition the correlations between predictor variables X and dependent variable Y into causal components. This can be seen by looking at the normal equations for just two predictor variables, X_1 and X_2:

$$\beta_1 \quad + \beta_2 r_{12} = r_{Y1}$$
$$\beta_1 r_{21} + \beta_2 \quad = r_{Y2}.$$

Graphically we can represent these equations as a *path diagram*, as in figure 8A.1. Each normal equation corresponds to a set of paths from X_1 (or X_2) to Y; for example, the first equation corresponds to the direct path from X_1 to Y and the indirect path from X_1 to X_2 to Y.

It is easy to see the genesis of the ω heuristic (section 8.9) in terms of path diagrams. For each predictor variable, the normal equations tell us how much of its total influence on Y is direct and how much is indirect through other predictor variables. For example, the total influence of X_1 on Y is r_{Y1}, of which β_1 is direct influence and $\beta_2 r_{12}$ is indirect. The ω heuristic implements the idea that X_i is likely to be a cause of Y if its direct effect is large, relative to its indirect effect. Conversely, if X_i's indirect influence on Y is a large fraction of r_{Yi}, then X_i "goes through" another variable to influence Y, so probably isn't a direct cause of Y.

Perhaps you are wondering why we need path diagrams and rules for reading them if we have normal equations and multiple regression. What do path diagrams add to our understanding of our data? First, path diagrams are graphic, so they help us interpret the results of regression analysis. Second, a causal interpretation of arrows and their weights is clear. The weights are standardized partial regression coefficients, so they satisfy Suppes' three criteria for cause: covariance, precedence, and control (section 8.8.2).

Third, path diagrams show that correlations are sums of influences. To illustrate this point, recall a surprising result from chapter 2: In our study of the Phoenix planner, the correlation between *WindSpeed* and *FinishTime* is nearly zero ($r = -.053$). How can this be, when *WindSpeed* affects *FirelineBuilt*, which in turn affects *FinishTime*? A path model of the three variables suggests another factor is lurking in the background (figure 8A.2). Although the path model doesn't identify this factor (we later discovered it was a sampling bias, see section 3.3), the model does estimate its strength: To be consistent with the empirical correlations between *FirelineBuilt* and *FinishTime* ($r = .755$), and between *WindSpeed* and *FirelineBuilt* ($r = .363$), the regression coefficients must be .892 for *FirelineBuilt* and $-.377$ for *WindSpeed*. (You can derive these numbers for yourself: Plug the empirical correlations into the normal equations for two predictors, shown previously, and solve for the betas.) We interpret this model to mean *WindSpeed* somehow has a negative influence on *FinishTime* that is roughly equal to its positive influence on *FirelineBuilt*. Keep in mind that the model and its coefficients would change if we introduce other variables, but in this model, at least, we interpret the surprisingly low correlation between *WindSpeed* and *FinishTime* as the sum of two influences, one positive and one negative.

Path diagrams and the causal interpretation of regression have a long history (Li, 1975; Shaffer, 1992; Spirtes et al., 1993; Glymour et al., 1987; Pearl and Verma, 1991; Bohrnstedt and Knoke, 1988). Sewall Wright worked out the rules for calculating estimated correlations between variables and R^2 from path diagrams, in the 1920s. More recently, path models have been called *structural equation models*, because, as we showed in section 8.9, they can be represented as sets of equations.

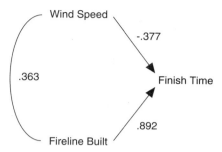

Figure 8A.2   Path model showing that *WindSpeed* does in fact influence *FinishTime*.

8A.5   Regression Coefficients Are Partial

The coefficients in multiple regression models are *partial*: for a dependent variable y and predictor variables $x_1, x_2, \ldots, x_k$, the partial regression coefficient $b_{y1 \cdot 2 \ldots k}$ represents the effect of x_1 on y regardless of any relationships that might hold between x_1 and $x_2, \ldots, x_k$. This isn't to imply that adding or dropping x_i's from the list of predictors won't influence the regression coefficient. Quite the contrary. But having fixed a set of predictors, the regression coefficients measure each one's individual contribution. Informally, the key to this important property is that each predictor accounts for just the part of y's variance that isn't accounted for by another predictor; or, more accurately, the part of a predictor that's independent of all other predictors accounts for the part of y's variance that isn't accounted for by another predictor. Let's see how.

A residual, recall, is the difference between the value predicted by the regression equation and the actual value of a datum. We'll denote these quantities $\tilde{y}_i = \hat{y}_i - y_i$. Residuals tell us what a regression equation does not predict; they tell us that some aspect of our data is not modeled adequately by a straight line. Consider a simple regression model, $\hat{y}_i = bx_i + a$. The residuals for this model are independent of the values of the predictor variables; that is, $r_{x\tilde{y}} = 0$, the correlation between the predictor and the residuals is zero. Subject to one condition, this means that a rule that explains the residuals is independent of the regression equation that generated the residuals. To see this, let $\hat{y}_i = f(x_i)$ be our regression equation and $\hat{r}_i = g(z_i)$ be a rule that predicts residuals. Because $y_i = f(x_i) + r_i$, we can estimate y by estimating residuals: $\hat{y}_i = f(x_i) + g(z_i)$. Our estimate of y is the sum of two functions, hence these functions contribute independently to the estimate, under the condition that z and x are independent.

Now imagine we have two predictor variables, x_1 and x_2, and we regress y on x_1, giving us $\hat{y}_i = f(x_{1_i})$. If we use x_2 to predict the residuals from this equation, then x_2 would explain some (or all) of the variance in y that isn't explained by x_1. That is, if $\hat{r}_i = g(x_{2_i})$, then we could estimate y in terms of the contributions of both x_1 and x_2 as follows: $\hat{y}_i = f(x_{1_i}) + g(x_{2_i})$. The only problem with this scheme is that x_1 and x_2 might not be independent. The solution is to regress x_2 on x_1 and use the residuals from this regression, which are independent of x_1, to estimate the residuals from the first regression.

This all sounds complicated, but it is pretty straightforward. We regress y on x_1:

$$\widehat{y_{[1]}} = b_{y1}(x_1) + a_1. \tag{8A.9}$$

We have dropped the subscript i for clarity, and denoted the fact that y is predicted by x_1 as $\widehat{y_{[1]}}$. This regression leaves some stuff, the residuals, to be explained,

$$res.\ y_{[1]} = \widehat{y_{[1]}} - y, \tag{8A.10}$$

and we seek a rule based on x_2 that will do the explaining. Because x_1 and x_2 will generally not be independent, we first regress x_2 on x_1:

$$\widehat{x_{2[1]}} = b_{21}(x_1) + a_2, \tag{8A.11}$$

which produces residuals that *are* independent of x_1:

$$res.\ x_{2[1]} = \widehat{x_{2[1]}} - x_2. \tag{8A.12}$$

Now we can use these residuals to predict or "mop up" the residuals from the regression of y on x_1:

$$\widehat{res.\ y_{[1]}} = b_{y2\cdot1}(res.\ x_{2[1]}). \tag{8A.13}$$

Regressions on residuals usually don't have y-intercept terms. The regression coefficient $b_{y2\cdot1}$ denotes the influence of x_2 on y independent of x_2's relationship with x_1.

From these components we can build a multiple regression model that has both x_1 and x_2 as independent predictors of y. Because $y = \hat{y}_{[1]} - res.\ y_{[1]}$ we can substitute eq. 8A.9 for $\hat{y}_{[1]}$; and eq. 8A.13 provides an independent estimate of $res.\ y_{[1]}$ based on x_2:

$$\widehat{y_{[12]}} = \left[b_{y1}(x_1) + a_1\right] - \left[b_{y2\cdot1}(res.\ x_{2[1]})\right]. \tag{8A.14}$$

Substituting eqs. 8A.12 and 8A.11 in succession for $res.\ x_{2[1]}$ we get:

$$\widehat{y_{[12]}} = \left[b_{y1}(x_1) + a_1\right] - \left[b_{y2\cdot1}\left((b_{21}(x_1) + a_2) - x_2\right)\right]. \tag{8A.15}$$

Rearranging terms:

$$\widehat{y_{[12]}} = (b_{y1} - b_{y2\cdot1}b_{21})x_1 + (b_{y2\cdot1})x_2 + (a_1 + (b_{y2\cdot1})a_2). \tag{8A.16}$$

In the original regression, with only x_1 as a predictor, the regression coefficient was b_{y1}; in the multiple regression we just constructed, this coefficient is "corrected" by $b_{y2\cdot1}b_{21}$. The correction amounts to subtracting the extent to which x_1 predicts x_2 times the independent influence of x_2.

You can certainly build a multiple regression model as described here but you needn't. Solving the normal equations for two variables will yield coefficients $b_{y1\cdot2} = (b_{y1} - b_{y2\cdot1}b_{21})$ and $b_{y2\cdot1}$. The purpose of our construction here is simply to show the sense in which regression coefficients are partial. The part of x_2 that's independent of x_1 can "mop up" or explain the part of y that x_1 leaves unexplained.

The order in which predictors enter the regression equation does not affect their final coefficients. This seems counterintuitive given our characterization of one predictor mopping up the variance that remains after another has done its best to predict y. The normal equations show us that these mopping up calculations happen simultaneously, however, so the order of introducing predictors doesn't matter. Although our construction was limited to two predictors, our conclusions generalize to any number of predictors. Each mops up some fraction of the variance that isn't explained by the others.

Finally, note that the previous demonstration might have been done with standardized variables, in which case the b coefficients would be standardized β coefficients. It follows, then, that standardized coefficients are partial. Another way to look at it is that standardizing a coefficient b_x involves multiplying it by the ratio of two standard deviations, s_x/s_y, an operation that cannot render coefficients dependent.

8A.6   Testing the Significance of Predictors

When building models incrementally, adding or deleting predictors one at a time, F tests for the significance of predictors can provide guidance about which predictors should be in a model. The F test of the significance of a single predictor is the ratio of the mean square due to regression (which is just $SS_{reg.}$ because it has one degree of freedom) to the mean square for residuals:

$$F = \frac{SS_{reg.}}{MS_{res.}}.$$

These terms result from a decomposition of the total sum of squares:

$$SS_{total} = SS_{reg.} + SS_{res.}. \tag{8A.17}$$

$$\sum(y_i - \overline{y})^2 = \sum(\hat{y}_i - \overline{y})^2 + \sum(y_i - \hat{y}_i)^2. \tag{8A.18}$$

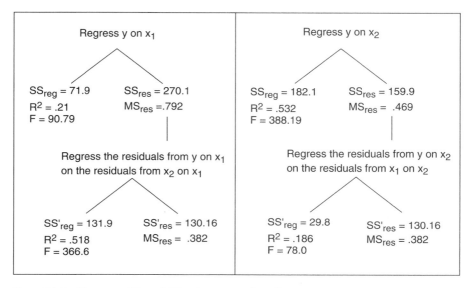

Figure 8A.3   Decomposition of $SS_{res.}$ by a second predictor.

The deviations in this expression are illustrated in figure 8A.3. The mean square residual, $MS_{res.}$ is, as one would expect, $SS_{res.}$ divided by degrees of freedom for the residual, which is the sample size minus the number of predictors.

In the previous section we said a new predictor mops up some of the variance a model doesn't explain. Said differently, a new predictor partitions $SS_{res.}$ into two parts: $SS'_{reg.}$ and $SS'_{res.}$. An F test can be run on the new predictor by dividing $SS'_{reg.}$ by $MS'_{res.}$, as illustrated in figure 8A.3. The statistics in this figure are from a dataset of $N = 343$ records; y is the performance variable and x_1 and x_2 are predictors. Suppose we regress y on x_1 to get the model $\hat{y} = b_1 x_1 + a_1$. It accounts for 21 percent of the variance in y. Because we have just one predictor, $MS_{res.} = 270.1/(N - 2) = .792$ and $F = 71.9/.792 = 90.79$. This is highly significant: x_1 clearly accounts for a significant fraction of the total variance in y. Recalling the previous section, suppose we regress x_2 on x_1 to get residuals that are independent of x_1, and suppose we use these residuals to predict the residuals from the regression of y on x_1. The effect is to partition $SS_{res.} = 270.1$ into two parts: $SS'_{reg.} = 131.9$, which is the part x_2 explains, and $SS'_{res.} = 130.16$, the part x_2 doesn't explain. Although our model now includes two variables, only one, x_2, is being used to predict the residuals of the other, so $MS'_{res.} = SS'_{res.}/(N - 2) = .382$, and $F = 131.9/.382 = 366.6$. This, too, is highly significant, so we can be virtually certain that x_2 mops up a significant fraction of the residuals from the model $\hat{y} = b_1 x_1 + a_1$. If our first predictor had been x_2 and then we'd added x_1, the partitioning of the total sum of squares would have proceeded as shown in the right-hand panel of figure 8A.3. Notably $SS'_{res.} = 130.16$ in both cases: x_1 and x_2 leave the same variance in y unexplained irrespective of the order in which we build the regression model.

Because our variables, y, x_1, and x_2, are standardized, the total sum of squares equals the total degrees of freedom: $SS_{total} = N - 1$. This observation leads to a simple trick for calculating F values without calculating sums of squares. Because $R^2 = SS_{reg.}/SS_{total}$, it follows that $SS_{reg.} = R^2(N-1)$, and, thus,

$$F = \frac{R^2(N-1)}{\frac{(1-R^2)(N-1)}{N-2}}.$$

9   Tactics for Generalization

Empirical research in artificial intelligence and other fields tends to produce specific results that provide researchers with raw material for generalizations. Generalizations emerge from analysis informed by empirical results, and empirical work lends credibility to general theories by testing important predictions, but empirical methods do not somehow create general theories. We researchers (and sometimes our programs) create theories; empirical methods only provide data. This chapter discusses empirical methods that support theorizing and generalization.

Many of the methods in this book support *statistical generalization* in the sense of inferring characteristics of populations given samples. In principle, random sampling is our guarantor of generality: If a sample is selected randomly from a population, then conclusions about the population are probabilistically bounded by conclusions about the sample. Unfortunately, statistical generalization is more limited than it first appears, not because it is statistical, but because random sampling is hard to achieve. If a sample or the levels of a factor are not selected randomly, then in principle the scope of our results is limited to the particular sample or levels. Moreover, every sample represents fixed levels of some factors, so when we speak of generalizing our results to other situations we really mean situations corresponding to all possible values of factors that were allowed to vary randomly in the original sample and identical values of factors that were not allowed to vary. Perhaps our algorithm was tested on random chess endgame problems involving a king and a knight on one side and a king and a bishop on the other (KK,KB problems) where the KK side moves first. Our results then would generalize to unseen KK,KB problems, but not to problems involving other pieces or problems where the KB side moves first. Nor would our results generalize to samples of KK,KB problems selected by systematic criteria, such as KB positions in which the king is not on the bishop's rank.

These are "in principle" arguments. Because it's difficult to ensure that a sample is random, generalization is, in principle, impossible or at least limited. A more pragmatic characterization is that some samples are constructed in a way that under-mines confidence in the generality of results; this is also a more accurate characteri-zation because it is researchers, not samples, who decide whether results are credible. Thus an ideal random sample makes claims of generality more credible, but we often will accept a less perfect guarantee. If we sample all possible levels of a factor (e.g., males and females, or all brands of breakfast cereal) then we might believe a result is general even if we didn't sample the levels in their exact population proportions. Or, we might sample only three levels of a continuous factor such as wind speed, and yet believe our results generalize to levels interpolated between those we sampled and perhaps by extrapolation to levels beyond but "near" those we sampled. You might be wondering why we wouldn't simply treat wind speed as a random factor and save ourselves the cost—in terms of credibility—of interpolation. Left to vary randomly, wind speed might introduce so much variance into our data that effects cannot be dis-cerned, and even if this isn't a concern, we often select levels systematically because we want to ensure a particular range of levels is covered.

So you see we often have good reasons to sample systematically, but we also rely on tactics such as interpolation (when they are credible) to boost the generality of results. In sum, we decide what's general, based on experimental evidence and other arguments. Even with random sampling, we can't be sure that all levels of all latent factors are randomly distributed over our experimental conditions. In practical terms, this means generalizations are provisional. We believe them until we find reason not to.

By any standards, generalizing results to unseen KK,KB chess problems or to unseen values of wind speed is a modest accomplishment, not what we think of as the "generalization problem" in AI. Three generalization problems, really, seem particularly challenging.

The Problem of Representative Samples   Knowing something about a population, we can draw a sample that is representative in the senses described earlier—a random sample of problems and factor levels, a random sample of problems for all levels of factors, or a random sample of problems at representative levels of factors, between which we can interpolate. But if we do not know anything about a population, how can we draw a sample? What is the population of "planning" problems? Researchers in planning want to know. What is the population of "classification" problems? Re-searchers in machine learning maintain a sizeable corpus of classification problems, but it obviously doesn't exhaust nature's corpus and there is no way to tell whether it represents her corpus faithfully. The animals flocked to Noah's ark two by two until Noah had them all, but the Almighty has not assured AI researchers that nature is so perfectly represented in our samples. Sampling randomly from nature provides some assurance, but we always worry that our little sample is from an unrepresentative little corner of nature's realm. Rob Holte discovered that almost all the classification problems in the machine learning community's corpus could be solved by attending to a single feature (section 3.2.1); fungi, for instance, could be classified as poisonous or benign by their odor. Does this mean that almost all of nature's classification problems are so easily solved, or does it mean that the corpus is unrepresentative?[18] Until we have theories that explain the distributions of tasks in populations, we can only guess at answers to this kind of question.

The Problem of Other Versions   If we demonstrate something about a program, can we still believe it after we modify the program? Most AI programs are under development for most of their lives, so if we cannot generalize results across versions, we cannot believe anything published about the last one. To some extent this problem is ameliorated by finding the right degree of specificity for descriptions of system behavior; for example, we say, "wind speed has an nonlinear effect on the time required by the Phoenix planner to contain a fire," not, "the mean times to contain fires at 3, 6, and 9 kph., were 5.1, 8.2, and 13.6 hours, respectively." The latter statement is unlikely to remain true in the next version of the system; we might hope the former would, if only because it admits more results. But we cannot know whether the next modification of the system will erase even our weak "nonlinear effect" result. Until we have theories that explain interactions between features of programs and features of their environments, we can only guess the scope of our results.

The Problem of Other Systems   If we frame results in system-specific terms, they are irrelevant to other systems. Consider again the assertion in the previous paragraph. What does it say about the time required by other planners to contain simulated forest fires? Nothing. As before, it will help to find the right degree of specificity for our results. For instance, the Phoenix planner searches memory for a skeletal plan, then fills in some details that are unique to each fire, and begins to fight the fire. These initial steps require a significant but roughly constant amount of time, during which the area of the fire to be fought grows quadratically as a function of wind speed. To state the nonlinear effect result in terms that are not specific to Phoenix we might say that because the difficulty of solving unattended problems changes nonlinearly with an environmental parameter, and our planner delayed working on problems for a constant period, it experienced a nonlinear effect on performance of that parameter. This result is easily transformed into a simple theory that explains the interaction of defining features of a class of planners (those that delay working on problems) and

---

18. Professor Bruce Porter drew this question to my attention.

defining features of a class of tasks (those that get worse over time). Until we have such theories, we can only guess at the general import of system-specific results.

Each of the preceding paragraphs states a problem and a solution. We can try to get a representative sample by getting many instances, but we would prefer a theory of the distribution of instances in the population. We can try to claim a result is general if it is preserved across many versions of a system, but we would prefer a theory that relates the structure of the system to its behavior. We can try to claim that a result generalizes across systems if we find lots of other systems for which it holds, but we prefer a theory that defines the equivalence class of systems for which the result holds. Why do we prefer theories to lists of instances? Because a theory is more than a list: It tells us what the instances have in common and implies that these common features are responsible for something, so unseen instances with these features should fall within the scope of the theory. Theories don't grow on trees, however. Many, perhaps most, grow out of lists of instances. In the following sections I will describe a procedure—empirical generalization—for developing theories, as well as tactics for expanding and bounding the scope of the theories we have.

9.1   Empirical Generalization

Let's begin with a familiar result, discussed in chapter 6: Bill Clancey and Greg Cooper discovered that MYCIN's certainty factors, which were in the range -1000 to 1000, could be mapped onto coarser ranges without seriously affecting MYCIN's performance. In reporting this result, Buchanan and Shortliffe say:

Degradation of performance was only pronounced when the number of intervals changed to three (all CFs mapped onto 0, 333, 666, and 1000—and their negative counterparts). But even here five of the ten cases had the same organism list and therapy. It wasn't until CFs were changed to 0, 500, and 1000 that a dramatic effect occurred; and even with nine new organism lists, we find that seven of the ten cases had the same therapy. The fact that the organism list did not change radically indicates that MYCIN's rule set is not fine-tuned and does not need to be. The rules use CFs that can be modified by ± 0.2, showing that there are few deliberate (or necessary) interactions in the choice of CFs. The observed stability of therapy despite changing organism lists probably results because a single drug will cover for many organisms, a property of the domain.   (Buchanan and Shortliffe, 1984, p. 219)

If CFs are modified by ± 0.2 or less, MYCIN's performance is essentially unaffected; if the modifications are more extreme, then an intermediate stage of MYCIN's performance suffers (identifying organisms) but the final stage (therapy recommendation) still works moderately well. These results are specific to MYCIN but their implications are more general. One implication is, when building a system like MYCIN, you needn't worry about the accuracy of the CFs you acquire from experts; if the CFs are in the right ballpark, the system will work.

Getting from the specific result to the general implication was a simple speculative exercise, but getting from the implication to a general theory requires us to say what we mean by "a system like MYCIN." We can identify classes of systems in at least three ways:

Listing   Here you simply list the systems for which a behavior has been demonstrated. The class of systems for which ballpark CFs work is just the class for which ballpark CFs have been shown to work.

Featural Characterization   Here you describe the features of systems that exhibit the behavior of interest. You don't always know which of these features are responsible for the behavior in a single system, or whether they account for comparable behaviors in several systems, but they often co-occur with the behavior. For example, the MYCIN knowledge engineers tried hard to keep CFs independent across rules,[19] and perhaps this feature accounts for the result that ballpark CFs work. Or perhaps the reason is that MYCIN did exhaustive search; had it used CFs to prune its search, more accuracy might have been required.

Causal Explanation   If in addition to a featural characterization you know how features interact to produce behavior, then you have a causal explanation, and you can form an equivalence class of systems based on the explanation. My reading of the Clancey and Cooper result is that they understand some of MYCIN's features that might explain why it works with ballpark CFs, but they haven't developed and tested a causal explanation of why the organism list did not change radically.

Lists of systems are not general theories, nor are lists of features of systems, but both are important steps along the way. Time and again we see an *empirical generalization* strategy at work in science. Find a lot of examples of a behavior of interest, find out what the cases have in common, then build a causal explanation around these common features. Note that these steps correspond to the "understanding" dimension in figure 9.1 (reproduced from chapter 1), but now our focus is not a single system but classes of systems. Empirical enumeration is sufficient for a descriptive generalization, featural characterizations are predictive, and causal explanations are predictive

---

19. "Just as Bayesians who use their theory wisely must insist that events be chosen so that they are independent . . . we must insist that dependent pieces of evidence be grouped into single rather than multiple rules." (Buchanan and Shortliffe, 1984, p. 259).

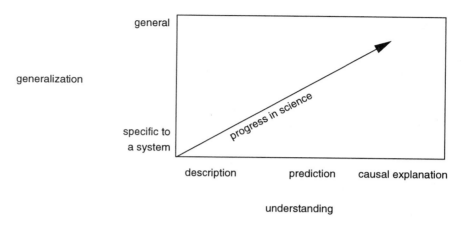

Figure 9.1   Two dimensions, generalization and understanding, define a space of versions of the basic research questions.

and, of course, explanatory. Inevitably, things don't go this smoothly and one finds oneself rethinking the salient features of a class (thus revising class membership) and also one's explanations. Still, empirical generalization is an efficient search process because one's explanations need to incorporate only those features that are common to a class, and the class needs to include only those systems that produce behaviors of interest.

Empirical generalization is even more efficient when we can work with examples and counterexamples of an interesting behavior. In his doctoral dissertation, Doug Lenat demonstrated that a program called AM could discover mathematical concepts by "mutating" other concepts; for instance, the concept "multiplication" had two arguments, x and y, and by mutating it so its arguments were x and x, AM derived the concept of "square." AM relied on heuristics to say which mutations were worth doing. Its performance was ultimately limited by its heuristics, so Lenat naturally wondered whether the same mutation strategy might produce new heuristics. He built a program called Eurisko that tried to explore the space of heuristics (a process Lenat called Heuretics) in much the way that AM explored the space of mathematical concepts. It didn't work very well. At this point in the story, Lenat had a successful example (AM) and an unsuccessful one (Eurisko), and with J. S. Brown, he puzzled out a featural characterization of the result.

It was only because of the intimate relationship between Lisp and Mathematics that the mutation operators (loop unwinding, recursion elimination, composition, argument elimination, function substitution, and so on) turned out to yield a high "hit rate" of viable, useful new math concepts when applied to previously-known, useful math concepts—concepts represented as

Lisp functions. But no such deep relationship existed between Lisp and Heuretics, and when the basic automatic programming (mutations) operators were applied to viable, useful heuristics, they almost always produced useless (often worse than useless) new heuristic rules.   (Lenat and Brown, 1983, p. 237)

In other words, if you represent mathematical concepts in Lisp, then syntactic mutations often produce meaningful results, but if you represent heuristics in Lisp then syntactic mutations produce junk. It still is not clear why this happens, but the observed "deep relationship" between Lisp and mathematical concepts will clearly play a role in any explanation.

Taking account of examples and counterexamples, then, the empirical generalization strategy goes like this:

Find examples and counterexamples of behaviors of interest, and common and discriminating features of architectures, tasks, and environments; then build causal explanations around these features.

Note the explicit recognition that we can generalize over tasks and environments, not just architectures. Generalizing over tasks is one of the great accomplishments of complexity theory; in fact, we are beginning to see AI problems associated with complexity classes (e.g., Chapman, 1987). I am not convinced, however, that the complexity of a task provides enough information for us to design programs to perform it, to predict performance accurately, or to explain performance. We should keep our eyes open for other features of tasks (and architectures and environments) that are predictive and explanatory.

A specific explanatory task feature is mentioned in the last sentence of the previous Buchanan and Shortliffe excerpt: "The observed stability of therapy despite changing organism lists probably results because a single drug will cover for many organisms, a property of the domain." As before, we can form equivalence classes of tasks "like MYCIN's" that can be accomplished with ballpark CFs:

Listing   Here you simply list tasks. The class of tasks for which ballpark CFs work is just the class for which ballpark CFs have been shown to work.

Featural Characterization   Here you describe the features of an equivalence class of tasks that can be accomplished with ballpark CFs. One feature is that many items (e.g., organisms that make us sick) are covered by a single action (e.g., a therapy). Features like this are thought to be responsible for the fact that ballpark CFs work, and this result holds or is expected to hold in other tasks with these features.

Causal Explanation   It is possible to form an equivalence class of tasks based on a causal explanation of how tasks lead to behavior. An example, elaborated later, goes like this: If the task is to select actions (therapies) for items (organisms), and the role of ranking (by CFs) is to determine which items need to be covered (the item list), and if most actions cover several items including those not on the item list, then the importance of accurate ranking is minimized.

Note that listing and featural characterizations can focus on tasks, alone, but it is difficult to explain a behavior without any reference to a system or class of systems.

We can also form equivalence classes based on the environments in which behaviors are observed; for example, one often hears that people in an organization are convivial while resources are plentiful, but when resources become tight their behavior changes. As before, we can do this by enumeration, or by describing the features of these environments, by a causal explanation of how a class of environments leads to the behaviors. (MYCIN doesn't provide us with an example because its environment was modest and had no impact on Clancey and Cooper's results.)

If we can describe classes of systems, tasks and environments, we can also try to describe intersections of these classes. Theories, then, are about the behaviors of systems performing tasks in environments. For example, we can have a theory that explains why systems in the class "backward chaining production systems with inaccurate CFs" perform well on tasks in the class "select actions to cover items," when the environment has the feature "time enough for exhaustive search." Not a profound theory, perhaps, but a useful one. I can't explain why such theories are rare in artificial intelligence.

9.2 Theories and "Theory"

Our focus will be featural theories, those that predict and explain the behavior of a system or a class of systems given architecture features, and features of tasks and environments. Theories are statements of the form:

A system with

architectural features $A_1, A_2, \ldots, A_l$ and
task features $T_1, T_2, \ldots, T_m$
in an environment with features $E_1, E_2, \ldots, E_n$,

will exhibit

behavior with features $B_1, B_2, \ldots, B_p$,

because

Sometimes the "because" clause is missing, in which case we have a predictive but not explanatory theory. For example, here's the Clancey and Cooper theory, again:

A system with

an architecture that includes a **list of items ordered** by a **parameter** (such as CFs), and a **set of actions** (such as therapies) that **cover** items, where **most actions cover several items,**

a task that involves **selecting actions to cover** the members of the item list,

will exhibit

action selection performance that is **robust against inaccuracies** in the parameter that orders the members of the item list.[20]

As stated, this theory is predictive but not explanatory. Salient features of the architecture, task, and behavior are highlighted in boldface. The rule is general because it applies to a class of systems with the highlighted features; it certainly is not specific to MYCIN.

The rule is not explanatory because it doesn't describe the mechanism by which the architecture and task features interact to produce behavior. An explanatory model is easily developed. Imagine a function is given a set of actions and a ranked list of items, and it returns a subset $\{A\}$ of the actions and a subset $\{I\}$ of the items. It chooses $\{A\}$ and $\{I\}$ to maximize a coverage score:

$$c = \frac{\sum_{i \in \{I\}} \frac{1}{rank(i)}}{|\{A\}|}.$$

In this case, the score will be higher if highly ranked items (e.g., rank=1,2,...) are covered, and lower as more actions are required. If the actions $\{A\}$ cover all the given items, then inaccuracies in rank will not affect the coverage score. For example, assume the given item list is $\{i_1, i_2, i_3, i_4, i_5\}$ and the actions $\{A\} = \{a_1, a_2\}$ cover all these items. The ranking of the items might be inaccurate, but the true ranking could be any permutation of the five without changing the coverage score. Thus ranking does not influence the coverage score given an item list, but it can influence the composition of the item list. For example, perhaps the list should have included item i_6, but its rank was too low for it to make the cut. This is actually the only situation in which the clause in our theory, most actions cover several items, is necessary. If an item is dropped from the item list because its rank is incorrect, then, because most

---

20. This rule includes no "environment" clause because MYCIN's environment was modest and placed few constraints upon its performance.

actions cover several items, the item will probably be covered even if it isn't on the item list.[21]

Theories have three parts: *scope*, *mechanism*, and *behavior*. The scope includes the architecture, task, and environment of a system. We want the scope of a theory to be as broad as possible and the behavior to be quite specific, so that the theory applies to a wide range of architectures, tasks, and environments, but makes specific predictions. At the same time, we want to predict the behavior of all the systems in the scope, so behavior should not be described in system-specific terms. Descriptions of behaviors should be specific enough to be strong predictions, but general enough to allow other researchers to see the relevance of the predictions to their own systems. Said differently, if you are going to expand the scope of a theory, its specification of behavior should include terms general enough to accommodate all the systems, tasks, and environments in the scope. There seems to be no clear line beyond which a theory is too general. Even extremely general specifications of behavior, for example, "performance" serve in general rules, such as, "As the amount of knowledge increases, performance improves." These rules fairly beg for researchers to find counterexamples, interpretations of "performance" for which the rule is not true.

It is difficult to say whether the theoretical branch of artificial intelligence would endorse our theory of MYCIN's behavior as such. If "theory" means "formal," then our theory isn't one, but if "theory" means "propositions from which we can derive testable hypotheses," then it is. Some theoreticians, perhaps most, acknowledge the second interpretation, For example, in a paper called "On The Role of 'Theory' in Artificial Intelligence, Ron Brachman, David Etherington, and Marc Vilain said:

We note that rigor, per se, does not imply formalism. The mere presence of axioms and "proofs" does not prevent sloppy work. In the worst case, it may even encourage it, by allowing sloppiness to hide behind impenetrable notational walls. Nor does rigorous and well-executed research presuppose formal logic....In [one] context, rigor depends on the quality of the design of... experiments and the analysis of their results. (Brachman et al., 1992, p. 17)

The authors discuss five contributions of "theory" to AI, only one of which is "classical, predictive theory...theories about phenomena in the world that predict behavior" (1992, p. 5). The other contributions are formalizations of existing work; the development of abstract frameworks and models for, say, nonmonotonic reasoning or learnability; analysis, particularly complexity analysis; and "mathematics, plain

---

21. This example takes liberties with what Clancey and Cooper claimed. They did not conclude that coverage scores are robust against inaccuracies in CFs. Rather, they concluded that action sets were robust, that MYCIN would prescribe the same therapies even if CFs were slightly inaccurate.

and simple." One can imagine all these activities giving rise to predictive theories, but this is not their principle aim and, in fact, Brachman et al. observe that "empirically testable theoretical hypotheses seem to be quite rare in AI" (1992, p. 5). In short, the connection between theoretical AI and theories is less well-developed than many researchers, theorists included, would like.

One can also make the argument that the hallmark precision of theoretical AI is most helpful after a certain amount of empirical generalization, and it impedes the development of theories if it is wielded too soon. This argument reminds us of an earlier point, that although exploratory data analysis has weak standards for "convincing results" relative to statistical hypothesis testing, we want suggestive, tantalizing, surprising results, not necessarily convincing results, early in a research project. The rush to precision, particularly in definitions, can have the same sort of chilling effect as the rush to hypothesis testing. This point is discussed further in section 9.6, where we consider the virtues of theories of ill-defined behavior.

9.3   Tactics for Suggesting and Testing General Theories

As I said earlier, experiments produce data, not generalizations, so it is up to us to generalize experimental results. Nobody is quite sure how we do this, although researchers in machine learning have developed many promising techniques. Some have proposed straightforward heuristic search as a model of scientific discovery (e.g., Langley et al., 1987) but others have challenged this model on empirical grounds; it often doesn't work with real experimental data (Schaffer, 1990). Most researchers agree, however, that generalization hinges on introducing terms to account for regularities in data. Hence our earlier characterization of empirical generalization: Find lots of examples, counterexamples, and common and discriminating features (terms), then build causal explanations around these features.

An early example of empirical generalization was Clancey's identification of *heuristic classification* as a task for expert systems. Clancey observed that many expert systems were doing essentially the same thing: classifying data into one or more known categories such as diseases, geological structures, types of ships and submarines, and so on (Clancey, 1984; Clancey, 1985). He developed a language in which to describe all these specific systems as instances of a single class. At roughly the same time, Chandrasekaran (1986) was developing a more inclusive taxonomy, one that included design and a variety of constraint-satisfaction problems. As a result of these efforts we saw that some expert tasks were superficially different but actually very similar, and although these classifications of tasks made no strong predictions, they did explain at least one observed phenomenon. Classification expert systems were much more common than systems for "design-like" or "synthetic" tasks. It became clear that the structure of most expert system knowledge bases—a list of rules—was well-suited to classification because the left-hand sides of rules could "recognize" something and the right-hand sides could assert a classification or an intermediate conclusion. Unfortunately, the Achilles heel of rule-based systems was control—figuring out which rules to fire when—and the asynchronous control of design and synthesis tasks, which feature backtracking and constraint propagation, was difficult to achieve in forward- or backward-chaining rule-based systems. Hence, fewer of these systems were built than classification systems.

Stronger predictions and explanations have more recently been forthcoming from several quarters in artificial intelligence, particulary in the machine learning community. Let us sample some results that illustrate tactics for empirical generalization.

9.3.1   A Theory about Task and Architecture Features

Minton showed that explanation-based learning (EBL) could acquire knowledge that would speed up problem solving for a program called Prodigy. EBL sometimes failed to speed up Prodigy's performance. Etzioni identified a single feature of the problems that are facilitated by EBL. He showed that if the problem to be solved has a *recursive structure*, then EBL learns rules that slow down problem solving:

A system with

an architecture that includes a problem-solver and an EBL component,
a task with a recursive structure,

will exhibit

problem solving slowdown as a result of rules learned by EBL,

because

EBL will learn many rules instead of just one when tasks have recursive structure, and requires time to find and apply the appropriate rule

Etzioni's example of a recursive structure is taken from the ubiquitous Blocksworld. Imagine you want to clear a block that is under a stack of other blocks. This is a recursive problem. You would like a single rule that says, "Unstack blocks by applying the unstack operator as many times as necessary to uncover the bottom block." Instead, EBL learns separate rules, one for two-block stacks, one for three-block stacks, and so on. Moreover, the effort required to find and apply these rules grows fast enough to offset any problem solving speedup that the rules could provide.

Etzioni ran a classical controlled experiment to test this hypothesis. He realized that it was not sufficient to generate recursive problems and demonstrate problem-solving slowdown; he also had to generate nonrecursive problems and show no slowdown. Better yet, to control for the possibility that his result was somehow specific to EBL learning in the Prodigy system, he showed that rules could be acquired directly by a different system from the search spaces associated with nonrecursive problems, and these rules match Prodigy/EBL's performance:

First I showed that Prodigy/EBL's performance degrades in the augmented Blocksworld, a problem space robbed of its nonrecursive [structure]. Second, I showed that a program that extracts nonrecursive explanations directly from the [problem space structure] matches Prodigy/EBL's performance.... Both experiments lend credence to the claim that Prodigy/EBL's primary source of power is nonrecursive problem space structure. (Etzioni, 1990, p. 921)

Notably, the second phase of Etzioni's experiment provided the basis for generalization. By showing that a program other than Prodigy/EBL could learn rules that performed in the same manner as Prodigy/EBL on nonrecursive problems, Etzioni showed that it was the acquisition of rules by explanation-based learning, not some other aspect of Prodigy/EBL, that was sensitive to the recursive structure of problems. This result is general to explanation-based learning: "Problem spaces that yield only recursive explanations ... will challenge Prodigy/EBL, Soar, and a wide range of EBL systems" (Etzioni, 1990, p. 919).

Let's sketch Etzioni's tactics in abstract terms.

- When a program performs well on some tasks but not others, find a feature of the tasks, T_i, that predicts performance.

- To demonstrate that T_i is responsible for performance, show that performance is good on problems with T_i and bad on problems without it (or vice versa).

- To show that a particular feature of the architecture, A_j, interacts with T_i to produce good (or bad) performance, show that a different architecture A' with this feature also performs well (or poorly) on problems with T_i.

To reiterate, the third tactic generalizes the result that task feature i and architecture feature j interact to produce good (or poor) performance.

9.3.2   Bounding the Scope of Theories and Predicted Behavior

The scope of a theory is the architecture, task, and environment that interact to produce behaviors. Often, a researcher can develop theories with broad scope that make fairly weak predictions about behavior as well as theories with narrower scope that make stronger predictions. We need tactics to specialize broad, weak theories. One example is due to John Allen, Pat Langley, and Stan Matwin (1992, p. 7). They specialized the weak theory that domain-specific knowledge facilitates planning:

> *Researchers have explored three broad approaches to using domain-specific knowledge in the planning process. . . . In this paper we present* TALUS, *a system that can use domain-specific plan knowledge in each of these modes. This lets us compare the three approaches experimentally to determine the conditions under which each is most appropriate. . . . We propose hypotheses about the relationship among these methods, characteristics of planning domains, and the behavior of the methods in such domains.*

The methods to which the authors refer are macro-operators, search control, and analogy. The key to their work was identifying a feature of tasks and a feature of the architecture that defined "the conditions under which each [approach] is most appropriate." Thus, the authors echo Etzioni in looking for features that will predict differential performance. Allen, Langley, and Matwin (1992, pp. 4–6) offer two hypotheses:

Hypothesis 1 Macro-operator methods are desirable in regular domains, search-control methods are desirable in nonregular domains, and analogical methods are desirable in domains of medium regularity.

Hypothesis 2 Macro-operator methods are desirable in the presence of considerable plan knowledge, search-control methods are desirable when little knowledge is available, and analogical methods are desirable in the presence of medium levels of knowledge.

Regularity is defined as follows (Allen et al., 1992, p. 5): "Highly regular domains are ones in which a small percentage of the possible problem types actually occur . . . nonregular domains are ones in which most of the possible problems actually occur."

The authors propose Hypothesis 1 because in regular domains, macro-operators can be learned for the few problem types that actually occur; whereas in nonregular domains, general search control knowledge has greater coverage and thus utility. Similarly for hypothesis 2: If much knowledge is available, then you'd prefer it to be specific macro-operators instead of general (and weak) search control knowledge; whereas if little knowledge is available, you'd prefer it to be general. Analogy, which is intermediate between weak search control knowledge and specific macro-operators is assumed to have medium "desirability" in both hypotheses.

By building one system that could use all three kinds of knowledge, Allen, Langley, and Matwin (1992) solved a tricky problem of experimental control. They wanted to be sure that differences in performance were due to interactions between the type of knowledge it used (an architecture feature) and domain regularity (a task or environment feature) or the amount of knowledge it had (another architecture feature). This problem could not be solved easily by comparing extant systems on a variety of tasks because any pair of systems will differ in many ways, each of which might be the true cause of differential performance. In sum, the author's hypotheses were borne out (although they didn't run a two-way analysis of variance to demonstrate interactions between memory size and domain regularity). Their study illustrates three tactics for reducing the scope of theories and improving the specificity of predictions of behavior:

- If several researchers conclude that different methods all achieve a good outcome, but these methods have been tested in different tasks, environments, and with different measures of behavior, then build one system that incorporates all the methods and facilitates their comparison and the discovery of differential behavior.

- Find features of architecture A and task T that predict differential behavior of other aspects of the architecture, namely, problem solving methods.

- Look for interactions between A and T in differential performance of the methods.

Theories often make fairly gross predictions of behaviors. For example, complexity theory predicts the order statistics of algorithms for solving particular problems, but the actual time or space requirements depend on unknown constant factors. Just as we want to bound the scope of theories, we also want to bound the behaviors they predict and explain.

A common technique for getting a lower bound on performance is to implement random behavior. For example, many machine learning algorithms classify data as instances of one concept or another, and machine learning researchers often report the level of performance achieved by the "default rule" of classifying by randomly selecting among the concepts. Similarly, stock-picking algorithms have been evaluated by comparing their performance to algorithms that pick stocks randomly.

Upper bounds on performance are sometimes obtained by writing programs that perform exhaustive search. Similarly, upper bounds can be obtained by giving a system all the information it needs and all the time it needs to process the information.

A parallel approach is to find lower bounds on performance by reducing the capabilities of a program, that is, setting up a "worst case version" of a program. One example, suggested by Bruce Porter, makes use of a result developed by Rob Holte that I mentioned earlier. Holte discovered that many data sets commonly used by the machine learning community can be learned by a very weak algorithm (Holte, 1993; section 3.2.1). In particular, Holte's algorithm uses just a single feature of each data set to form classification rules, yet classification accuracy is surprisingly high. Bruce Porter suggests that Holte's algorithm could be used as a worst-case version of any classification algorithm. If you want to know a lower bound on the performance of your classification algorithm, run Holte's first.

9.3.3   Bounding Task Difficulty with Marker Methods

Holte's algorithm also provides a measure of the difficulty of a classification task. This suggests a *marker method* for assessing task difficulty. Run a standard algorithm on the task and see how it performs. Just as antibodies can act as markers by binding to particular sites on cells, so, too, is Holte's algorithm a marker for a particular feature of tasks. If the algorithm achieves high classification accuracy, then classification can be achieved by a single feature of the data (such as whether fungi smell bad). I suppose one could design marker algorithms for any task or environment feature, and marker tasks for any architecture or environment feature, and so on. Yet marker methods are not common; for example, task difficulty is usually bounded analytically. To provide empirical evidence for analytical bounds (or in lieu of them), marker methods appear promising.

9.3.4   Noticing Analogous Features in the Literature

Concept size is defined by Larry Rendell and Howard Cho (1990, p. 271) as follows: "Concept size is the positive volume (integral of the class membership function) divided by the volume of the whole space." Compare this with Allen, Langley, and Matwin's (1992, p. 5) definition of domain regularity: "Highly regular domains are ones in which a small percentage of the possible problem types actually occur." Are concept size and domain regularity the same feature? They appear to be analogous, at least. Rendell and Cho ask us to consider a multidimensional space in which subspaces are positive instances of a concept; concept size is essentially the ratio of the volume of the subspaces to the volume of the entire space. If you replace the idea of problem types that occur with the idea of positive instances, then Allen, Langley, and Matwin's definition of highly regular domains is Rendell and Cho's definition of small concept size. This in turn means that the results of the two sets of studies are comparable. To the extent they corroborate, the results can increase the scope of theories about concept size (or domain regularity); conversely, if they disagree, the studies might suggest further experiments to limit the scope of theories. As it happens, Rendell and Cho's study looked at a different task than Allen, Langley, and Matwin's, and it is difficult to see any sense in which their results are comparable. Still, we must recognize that researchers will sometimes give different names to features of tasks (or architectures or environments) that are actually very similar, and thus present us with an opportunity to generalize.

9.4   Which Features?

Because featural characterization is a crucial bridge between lists of instances and theories, the choice of features is all-important. In this context it is instructive to compare two similar efforts in machine learning. We already mentioned Rendell and Cho's identification of concept size as a feature of classification problems. In a much more ambitious study, called Statlog, a large group of researchers in machine learning, statistics, and neural networks compared the behavior of sixteen algorithms on a dozen real-world classification problems (Feng et al., 1995). For the purpose of this discussion, the interesting thing about the study is how these problems were characterized by the Statlog investigators. In their own words: "An important objective in Statlog is to investigate why certain algorithms do better on some datasets. We have used several statistical measures on the datasets which will help to explain our findings." The measures were homogeneity of covariances, mean absolute correlation coefficient, canonical discriminant correlations, variation explained by the first four canonical discriminants, and univariate skewness and kurtosis. I list these without explanation because, from what I can tell, they don't contribute much to the Statlog investigators' understanding of why particular algorithms do well and poorly on particular datasets. Interesting results are in abundance, and explanations, too, but few explanations mention homogeneity of covariance, canonical discrimination correlations, and so on. Those that do are weak; for example, high skew and kurtosis tell us that a distribution of data is not multivariate normal, which explains why symbolic classification algorithms that don't assume multivariate normal data performed a little better than some statistical algorithms. Contrast this with Rendell and Cho's explanation of the interaction of concept size (the proportion of concept space covered by positive instances) and attribute error (random substitution of attribute values):

. . . The effect of attribute error is greatest if the concept covers about 50% of the space. . . . whereas attribute error has a lesser effect in either small or large concepts. . . . Let the relative size of the concept be p $(0 \leq p \leq 1.0)$. Hence, p is the probability that a random corrupted event x is positive. If attribute corruption is random, the probability that x will (incorrectly) land in a negative region of instance space is $1 - p$. Similarly, the probability that x is negative is $1 - p$, and the probability that it will (incorrectly) land in a positive region is p. In either

case, the probability that x will become incorrect is $P = p(1 - p)$. By differentiating and setting the result to zero, we find that P has a maximum at $p = 1/2$.   (Rendell and Cho, 1990, p. 279)

Here we have a somewhat surprising result—the effect of attribute error is greatest when half the instances in the space are positive—that seems to be completely and concisely explained. Attribute error and concept size are good features because they explain something about the performance of classification algorithms; homogeneity of covariances seems to be a bad feature because it doesn't explain much about the performance of classification algorithms. Although the Statlog project has the same goals as Rendell and Cho, it appears at this juncture that Rendell and Cho chose more explanatory features. Ongoing analyses of the voluminous Statlog data might reverse this impression. For now, at least, the comparison between the projects is striking evidence of the importance of features.

9.5   Finding the "Same" Behavior in Several Systems

One tactic for demonstrating generality is to find features that don't affect behavior. For example, the preference for male children is strong among men and women, from rich and poor nations, be they Christians, Buddhists, Hindus, Muslims, or Jews; it is a general preference in the sense that gender, wealth, and religion do not affect it (Beal, 1994). These factors affect the degree of the preference (e.g., fathers prefer boys more than mothers do) but not the preference itself. Said differently, no group defined by levels of gender, wealth, and religion prefers female offspring to males. The preference for boys isn't precisely the same across groups, but this doesn't stop us asserting a general preference. Let's review. One way to demonstrate generality is to find a feature that doesn't affect a behavior of interest. Of course, this feature will usually have some effect on behavior, so you must decide whether the behaviors you observe at different levels of the factor are "essentially the same." Here's an illustration.

Many agents monitor their environments, and the most common monitoring strategy is periodic. Despite its prevalence, periodic monitoring isn't the strategy of choice for humans in a wide range of situations. For example, in an experiment with ten- and fourteen-year-old children, Ceci and Bronfenbrenner (1985) identified the *cupcake problem*: Each child was instructed by an older sibling (who served as a confederate in the experiment and collected the data) as follows: "We are going to put some cupcakes in the oven and they will be done in thirty minutes. You can play PacMan while you wait, but you mustn't forget to take the cupcakes out of the oven. To help you remember, there's a clock on the wall." Cleverly, the clock was put behind the child, so the sibling could easily see when the child turned around to monitor the time. In this way, Ceci and Bronfenbrenner obtained latencies between monitoring events. For our purposes two results are notable. First, all the children monitored quite frequently for the first few minutes; Ceci and Bronfenbrenner interpret this as a period of "calibration," getting one's internal clock in synch with real time. Second, ten-year-old children monitored approximately periodically for the remainder of the trial, but fourteen-year-olds monitored infrequently after the initial calibration, and increased the frequency of monitoring as the deadline approached. We call this an *interval reduction* strategy because the interval between monitoring events is reduced as the deadline approaches.

To demonstrate the generality of the interval reduction monitoring strategy, Marc Atkin and I adopted the tactic discussed earlier. We showed that the preference for interval reduction doesn't depend on features of the agent architecture (Cohen et al., 1994). For starters, we implemented a video game version of the cupcake problem and replicated Ceci and Bronfenbrenner's result, except we used computer science graduate students. We also built two environments for simulated robots and wrote genetic algorithms to evolve monitoring strategies. In both cases, fitness was determined by how often the robot monitored (less was better) and how close it came to a target (close was better). In some trials, the robot's estimate of the position of the target was corrupted by sensor noise, in others it got accurate sensor information but its effectors were sloppy. One algorithm learned a simple monitoring function of the form $N = ct + b$, where N is the intended movement before the next monitoring event and t is the sensed distance to the goal. If the genetic algorithm evolves a function with $c = 0$ and $b > 0$, then it has learned a periodic monitoring strategy; whereas $0 < c < 1$ is a special case of the interval reduction strategy called *proportional reduction*, which causes the agent to move a fixed proportion of the remaining distance before monitoring. In all our experiments with this algorithm, the fittest strategies were always versions of proportional reduction.

The second genetic algorithm evolved small programs. The salient parts of one program are shown in figure 9.2. After turning itself towards the goal via TURN-TOGOAL, the agent enters a loop, within which it will measure the distance to the goal (MONITOR: OBJECT_DISTANCE) and then loop over this distance divided by ten. Because it executes four MOVE commands for every ten distance units, it moves 40 percent of the distance remaining after each monitoring action. The program will terminate after monitoring five times. Note the extra MOVE instruction within the outermost loop; this distorts the pure proportional reduction strategy very slightly. We ran tens of thousands of trials, varying many aspects of the environment, the

```
Main program:
 TURNTOGOAL
 MOVEQUICK
 LOOP 5 time(s):
   MOVE
   MONITOR: object distance
    LOOP (object distance)/10+1 times:
     LOOP 2 time(s):
       MOVE
       MOVE
```

Figure 9.2   A proportional reduction strategy generated by LTB.

available sensory information, the costs and penalties of monitoring and moving; in all cases, interval reduction was the fittest strategy.

Next, we developed a simple statistical model of the cupcake problem and proved that if monitoring events are independent and there are no monitoring costs, then interval reduction is the best strategy. A more general solution, with monitoring costs and penalties for missing the target, as well as nonindependent monitoring events, required dynamic programming solutions, but they, too, were interval reduction strategies.

In sum, it doesn't matter whether our agents are humans or programs, whether strategies are encoded in a simple linear function or a rudimentary programming language, or whether strategies are derived analytically, evolved genetically, or constructed by dynamic programming. Interval reduction always emerges. It isn't exactly the same strategy in all these conditions. Humans tend to monitor more frequently than the optimal dynamic programming strategy in some cases, and too infrequently in others. But these differences are matters of degree. In all cases, agents monitor more frequently as they approach a goal. This behavior is the "same" across conditions and doesn't depend on the agent architecture or on the parameters of individual cupcake problems, such as initial distance to the goal.

9.6   The Virtues of Theories of Ill-Defined Behavior

All the examples of the previous section dealt with precisely defined measures of behavior such as classification accuracy. In fact, the behaviors and their measured indicators were identical. Clancey's characterization of "heuristic classification" expert systems is different. He introduced heuristic classification to AI not with a precise definition but with lots of examples. He didn't need to say exactly what heuristic classification entailed because everyone had a pretty good idea of what it meant—good enough, certainly, to differentiate heuristic classification systems from other kinds. We can often recognize phenomena long before we can define them, and many important phenomena have been studied for years without benefit of a consensual definition. Arguments develop over definitions, certainly, but only when something other than the definition itself is at stake. For instance, tobacco companies argue that tobacco doesn't meet the definition of "drug," but the argument isn't really about the definition, it's about whether the U.S. government should regulate tobacco. It's a waste of time to argue about a definition unless changing it has ramifications. Thus a definition should be refined and made more precise not for precision's sake but because we have some stake in a distinction. If little is at stake, then we shouldn't be afraid to include ill-defined terms in our theories. In fact, they can speed our progress, as we will see shortly.[22]

AI researchers have a justly maligned tendency to define behavior as "what my program does." Drew McDermott calls this problem *wishful mnemonics* in his insightful and wickedly funny paper, "Artificial Intelligence Meets Natural Stupidity":

A major source of simple-mindedness in AI programs is the use of mnemonics like "UNDER-STAND" or "GOAL" to refer to programs and data structures. If a researcher tries to write an "understanding" program, it isn't because he has thought of a better way of implementing this well-understood task, but because he thinks he can come closer to writing the first *implementation. If he calls the main loop of his program "UNDERSTAND," he is (until he is proven innocent) merely begging the question. He may mislead a lot of people, most prominently himself, and enrage a lot of others.*

What he should do instead is refer to this main loop as "G0034" and see if he can convince *himself or anyone else that G0034 implements some part of understanding. Or he could give it a name that reveals its intrinsic properties, like* NODE-NET-INTERSECTION-FINDER, *it being the substance of his theory that finding intersections in networks of nodes constitutes understanding.* (McDermott, 1981, p. 144)

By defining behavior as what one's program does, we make generalization difficult. A "theory" of this kind might be:

A system with

an architecture identical to my system's architecture,
a task identical to my system's task,
an environment identical to my system's environment,

will exhibit

"understanding," which is behavior identical to my system's behavior

---

22. I am indebted to Professor Bruce Porter, of the University of Texas at Austin, for the discussions that are summarized here.

Such a theory is obviously not general and the path to generalization is unclear. Still, defining "understanding" as "what my system does" has two great, related advantages: It provides a concrete example of the behavior and it liberates us from the difficult task of defining a behavior without any examples. Let me illustrate these points with my favorite example.

For two decades the artist Harold Cohen has been working on a program called AARON, which draws pictures. Cohen writes: "AARON began its existence some time in the mid-seventies, in my attempt to answer what seemed then to be—but turned out not to be—a simple question, 'What is the minimum condition under which a set of marks will function as an image?'" (Cohen, 1994). Imagine what would have happened if Cohen had started his study by trying to define "image," or, worse yet, "art." It's a good bet that he would never have emerged from his armchair. Instead he decided to build a program to make images, trusting in his ability to recognize reliably that a set of marks does or doesn't function as an image. Then, with the program running, he had something to study, and insights came relatively rapidly. For example, "the earliest versions of AARON could do very little more than distinguish between figure and ground, closed forms and open forms, and to perform various simple manipulations of these structures. On that basis it succeeded in producing moderately complex systems of marks that, to judge from the responses of art-museum audiences, functioned as images." In other words, surprisingly few distinctions and operations are sufficient to produce marks that were recognized not only by Cohen, but also by the general public, as images. (Figure 9.3 is a reproduction of one such image, dated 1980; the cover of this book is from a reproduction of a recent image.) Again, imagine how events would have unfolded had Cohen refined his definitions instead of AARON. His discourse would have been abstract, presumably with other artists and critics instead of museum audiences, and absolutely all of it would have been speculative. You don't have to define something to study it, and, in fact, defining can be so excruciatingly difficult that no other work gets done. If you can reliably recognize instances of what you are studying, then you can study them even if you cannot define the class to which they belong. Eventually you will try to define the class in terms of features—this is just empirical generalization as I described it earlier—but it is often impossible or unproductive to attempt to define the class in the absence of any instances.

Let's say your goal is not to generate evocative images, but, rather, to generate "coherent" explanations, as it was for Acker and Porter (chapter 6). You are pretty sure that coherence is a real characteristic of explanations because you have heard and read explanations that you regard as more or less coherent. Coherence is not an imaginary characteristic, nor are coherence judgments capricious or peculiar. Rather,

Figure 9.3   A drawing by AARON, a program written by the artist Harold Cohen.

let's suppose your judgments are consistent and, compared with judgments of your colleagues, consensual.

Examining a program's explanations, you and your colleagues might agree that "coherent explanations" are just what the program produces. But wait! This is McDermott's wishful mnemonic problem: You might all agree, but that doesn't mean you understand coherence. You don't necessarily know why you judged some explanations more coherent than others. McDermott worried that words such as "coherent" encourage us to believe we understand things we don't, so he suggested we shouldn't use them. This advice throws the baby out with the bathwater. We need such words. If the problem is that we don't understand them, the solution is not to avoid them but to develop our understanding. In other words, we should flirt with the wishful mnemonic problem but avoid it deftly in the following procedure.

Procedure for Generating and Testing Theories about Coherent Explanations

1. Build a program that produces explanations that are judged coherent.
2. Figure out what the program is doing to make its explanations coherent.

3. Manipulate the features or causal mechanisms identified in (2) to see whether coherence judgments are affected as predicted.

4. Generalize the causal mechanisms.

Step 1 requires a good idea, a hunch, or a crude hypothesis. For example, you might believe (as Liane Acker and Bruce Porter did) that explanations will be judged as coherent if they are generated by a filtering mechanism called *viewpoints* (Acker and Porter, 1994). This step doesn't matter very much because all you want, at this stage, is a program that produces behaviors that are consensually judged coherent. Viewpoints may or may not be a good idea; the point is to study not viewpoints but coherence. If viewpoints generate explanations that are judged incoherent, then we will modify viewpoints until we get better judgments. This is not to disparage the ingenuity of viewpoints or any other solution, but simply acknowledges that one solution is as good as another until we show why it isn't, so the emphasis must be on producing behavior and studying it.

In step 2, two kinds of refinement happen simultaneously. The definition of "coherent" is refined, and so are the conditions under which coherent explanations are apt to arise. One tactic for step 2 is to interview the people who judged the coherence of viewpoint-generated explanations. You can ask them what they like and don't like about the explanations. If this debriefing goes well, you will get a list of features of explanations that can be used to classify them as coherent and not-so-coherent. Let's say that one feature is "preserves causal order," or PCO. An explanation preserves causal order if it explains the steps of a process in the order that they happen; for example, "people go to the polls to vote, the votes are counted, and the winner is announced and then inaugurated." With features such as PCO, we can form hypotheses and test them in step 3. Here is a theory:

A system with

a task of generating explanations,
an architecture that includes a representation of processes as causal orders of events, and generates explanations by describing events in their causal order,

will exhibit

explanations that are consensually judged to be coherent

It is easy to design an experiment to test this theory. Have the program generate some explanations preserving causal order and some (ideally of the same material) not preserving causal order, and see which gets the higher coherence scores.

Finally, in step 4 we generalize the theory or apply some of the other tactics from earlier in this chapter to bound the scope or the behavior described in the theory. For example, we might be inclined to expand its scope to cover any text or, generalizing further, any presentation, including lectures, book chapters, and so on. Alternatively, to bound the scope of the theory, we might test the hypothesis that PCO is strongly correlated with coherence in explanations of physical processes such as plant reproduction, but doesn't predict the coherence of explanations of affective processes such as falling in love. To bound the scope of the behavior we might try to refine the notion of coherence, differentiating senses of the word such as "answering the question that was asked" and "answering the question without introducing irrelevant material."

In sum, the procedure we have been discussing starts with an ill-defined behavior and builds a program that is judged consistently and consensually to demonstrate the behavior. Next, features of the program (and its task and environment) are hypothesized to affect the behavior, and experiments are run to test the hypotheses. At the end of the day the behavior might still be ill-defined, but we will understand the conditions under which it arises. More often, we will tighten up the definition of the behavior as we bound the conditions in which it is observed. There is some danger that in our haste to be precise we find ourselves studying something that has but little connection to the behavior that interested us originally, but if we can avoid this pitfall, we may hope to gain a better understanding of a better-defined behavior.

Artificial intelligence was not always so leery of ill-defined terms as it is today (otherwise McDermott would not have written his article) and I cannot help thinking we were better off when we pursued them, however clumsily. I think ill-defined terms such as graceful degradation, coherence, opportunism, cooperation, altruism, aggressive, expectation-driven, robust, and the like, denote traits of intelligent behavior and should be our focus. These terms have *open texture*. They are difficult to define precisely with necessary and sufficient conditions, but they have rewarding scope, generality, and longevity. Legal scholars attribute the scope and longevity of the U.S. Constitution to the fact that it is open to interpretation. It puts in general terms the principles that guide the behavior of citizens, states, and government. I would like to see some statements of general principles of how AI programs behave. In their famous Turing Lecture, Newell and Simon called these *Laws of Qualitative Structure*:

All sciences characterize the essential nature of the systems they study. These characterizations are invariably qualitative in nature, for they set the terms within which more detailed knowledge can be developed. Their essence can often be captured in very short, very general statements. One might judge these general laws, because of their limited specificity, as making relatively little contribution to the sum of a science, were it not for the historical evidence that shows them to be results of the greatest importance.   (Newell and Simon, 1981, p. 83)

Simon identified several laws of qualitative structure for AI in his keynote address to the Fourteenth National Conference on Artificial Intelligence. One is due to Lenat and Feigenbaum (1987, p. 1173):

"The Knowledge Principle: A system exhibits intelligent understanding and action at a high level of competence primarily because of the specific *knowledge that it can bring to bear."*

Note the "understanding" word, again, the same one that earlier drew McDermott's ire. Lenat and Feigenbaum haven't defined it, nor should they, because they want all the denotations and connotations of understanding to fall within the scope of their law. Had a hypothetical researcher followed McDermott's advice and called his algorithm G0034, he would have lost the connection to what other researchers call understanding, and he probably would not have formulated the Knowledge Principle. Had the algorithm been called G0034, Lenat and Feigenbaum would not have recognized it as an opportunity to test the Knowledge Principle. A researcher can certainly use a word two ways: precisely, where its denotation is a particular system's behavior (e.g., "understanding" is precisely what my system does) and imprecisely, intending all its meanings. My point is that we must use words imprecisely to formulate general laws and identify evidence for and against them.

The path to general laws has two fatal forks, and an astonishing amount of AI research takes one or both of them. Early on, we might try to define terms that we should leave ill-defined. If we make it past this hazard and build a program that is judged to produce a desired (if ill-defined) behavior, we might stop to rest—it's hard work building programs that do the things we care about in AI—and as we sleep we might dream of other things we'd like to build, so that when we awaken we do not continue on the path to understanding. We don't discover features of our program (or its task or environment) that account for its behavior, and we don't test theories or bound their scope, but rather, we veer off the path and build another system.

General laws begin with ill-defined terms like "understand." After the hard work of building a system that understands in one sense, we have one precise denotation for the word. We won't forget its ill-defined ancestor, for it is our connection to other research on understanding. Now we ask, why does our system understand so well? We will characterize our system (and its tasks and environment) in terms of features that have precise denotations in our own work but are also vague and evocative, features like "immediate cause" and "consistent domain model." In time, we will publish our results, unafraid to use vague terms because they also refer to precise structures and behaviors in our own studies. Another researcher will make a connection and perhaps bring our theory of understanding within her own. Another will differentiate the senses in which we and he use the word. Eventually, someone will formulate general principles of understanding, and we will have the satisfaction of knowing that we have helped the science of artificial intelligence move forward.

References

Acker, Liane, and Porter, Bruce. 1994. Extracting viewpoints from multifunctional knowledge bases. In *Proceedings of the Twelfth National Conference on Artificial Intelligence*, Menlo Park, CA. AAAI/MIT Press. 547–592.

Allen, John A.; Langley, Pat; and Matwin, Stan. 1992. Knowledge regularity in planning. Technical Report FIA-92-24, NASA Ames Research Center, Moffett Field, CA.

Anderson, John Robert. 1983. *The Architecture of Cognition*. Harvard University Press, Cambridge, MA.

Anderson, Scott D.; Hart, David M.; and Cohen, Paul R. 1991. Two ways to act. Technical Report 91–67, Computer Science Department, University of Massachusetts, Amherst, MA.

Anscombe, F. J. 1973. Graphs and statistical analysis. *The American Statistician* 27(1):17–21.

Barret, Anthony, and Weld, Daniel S. 1994. Partial-order planning: Evaluating possible efficiency gains. *Artificial Intelligence* 67(1):71–112. Shorter version available as University of Washington Computer Science and Engineering Technical Report number 92-05-01.

Beal, Carole R. 1994. *Boys and Girls: The Development of Gender Roles*. McGraw Hill, New York, NY.

Blumenthal, Brad. 1990. Empirical comparisons of some design replay algorithms. In *Proceedings of the Eighth National Conference on Artificial Intelligence*, Menlo Park, CA. AAAI/MIT Press. 902–907.

Bohrnstedt, George W., and Knoke, David. 1988. *Statistics for Social Data Analysis*. F. E. Peacock Publishers, Itasca, IL.

Bower, Gordon H., and Clapper, John P. 1990. Experimental methods in cognitive science. In Posner, Michael I., editor 1990, *Foundations of Cognitive Science*. MIT Press, Cambridge, MA. chapter 7, 245–300.

Box, George E. P.; Hunter, William G.; and Hunter, J. Stewart. 1978. *Statistics for Experimenters: An Introduction to Design, Data Analysis and Model Building*. John Wiley and Sons, New York, NY.

Brachman, Ronald J.; Etherington, David W.; and Vilain, Marc. 1992. On the role of "theory" in artificial intelligence. Unpublished.

Buchanan, Bruce B., and Shortliffe, Edward H., editors. 1984. *Rule Based Expert Systems: The MYCIN Experiments of the Stanford Heuristic Programming Project.* Addison-Wesley, Reading, MA.

Campbell, Donald T., and Stanley, Julian C. 1963. *Experimental and Quasi-Experimental Designs for Research.* Rand McNally & Company, Chicago, IL.

Ceci, S.J., and Bronfenbrenner, U. 1985. Don't forget to take the cupcakes out of the oven: Prospective memory, strategic time-monitoring, and context. *Child Development* 56:152–164.

Chandrasekaran, B. 1986. Generic tasks in Knowledge-Based Reasoning: High-Level Building Blocks for Expert System Design. *IEEE Expert.* 3(1) 23–30.

Chapman, David. 1987. Planning for conjunctive goals. *Artificial Intelligence* 32(3):333–377.

Chinchor, Nancy; Hirschman, Lynette; and Lewis, David D. 1993. Evaluating message understanding systems: An analysis of the Third Message Understanding Conference (MUC-3). *Computational Linguistics* 19(3):410–449.

Churchill, Elizabeth, and Walsh, Toby. 1991. Scruffy but Neat? *AISB Quarterly.*

Clancey, William J. 1984. Classification problem solving. In *Proceedings of the Fourth National Conference on Artificial Intelligence*, Menlo Park, CA. AAAI Press/MIT Press. 49–55.

Clancey, William J. 1985. Heuristic classification. *Artificial Intelligence* 27:289–350.

Cobb, George W. 1984. An algorithmic approach to elementary anova. *The American Statistician* 38(2):120–123.

Cohen, Clifford A. Jr. 1959. Simplified Estimators for the Normal Distribution When Samples are Singly Censored or Truncated. *Technometrics.* 217–237.

Cohen, Harold. 1994. The further exploits of AARON, painter. *Stanford Humanities Review* 4(2).

Cohen, Paul R. 1991. A survey of the Eighth National Conference on Artificial Intelligence: Pulling together or pulling apart? *AI Magazine* 12(1):17–41.

Cohen, Paul R., and Feigenbaum, Edward A., editors. 1982. *The Handbook of Artificial Intelligence, Vol. III.* Addison-Wesley, Reading, MA.

Cohen, Paul R.; Greenberg, Michael L.; Hart, David M., and Howe, Adele E. 1989. Trial by Fire: Understanding the Design Requirements for Agents in Complex Environments, *AI Magazine* 10(3):32–48.

Cohen, Paul R., and Kim, John B. 1993. A bootstrap test for comparing performance of programs when data are censored, and comparisons to Etzioni's test. Technical Report 93–52, Computer Science Department, University of Massachusetts, Amherst, MA.

Cohen, Paul R.; Atkin, Marc S.; and Hansen, Eric A. 1994. The interval reduction strategy for monitoring cupcake problems. In *Proceedings of the Third International Conference on Simulation of Adaptive Behavior: From Animals to Animats 3*, Cambridge, MA. The MIT Press. 82–90.

Cohen, Paul R.; Gregory, Dawn E.; Ballesteros, Lisa A.; and Amant, Robert St. 1995. Two algorithms for inducing structural equation models from data. In *Proceedings of the Fifth International Workshop on Artificial Intelligence and Statistics*, 129–139.

Cook, T. D., and Campbell, D. T. 1979. *Quasi-Experimental Design*. Houghton Mifflin, Boston, MA.

Cook, R. Dennis, and Weisberg, Sanford. 1982. *Residuals and Influence in Regression*. Chapman and Hall, New York, NY.

Coombs, Clyde H.; Dawes, Robyn M.; and Tversky, Amos. 1970. *Mathematical Psychology*. Prentice-Hall, Inc., Englewood Cliffs, NJ.

Cooper, Lynn A., and Shepard, Roger N. 1973. Chronometric Studies of the Rotation of Mental Images. *Visual Information Processing*. Ed. William G. Chase, Academic Press, New York, 75–176.

Cooper, Richard. 1992a. A Sceptic specification of Johnson-Laird's "mental models" theory of syllogistic reasoning. Technical Report UCL-PSY-ADREM-TR4, University College, London.

Cooper, Richard. 1992b. A Sceptic Specification of Sloman's Motive Processing Engine and its Application in the Nursemaid Scenario. Technical Report UCL-PSY-ADREM-TR4a, University College, London.

Cooper, Richard; Fox, John; Farrington, Jonathan; and Shallice, Tim. 1992. Towards a systematic methodology for cognitive modelling. Technical Report UCL-PSY-ADREM-TR5, University College; Imperial Cancer Research Fund, London.

Cox, D. R., and Oakes, D. 1984. *Analysis of Survival Data*. Cambridge University Press.

Diaconis, Persi, and Efron, Bradley. 1983. Computer-intensive methods in statistics. *Scientific American* 248:116–130.

Dietterich, Thomas G. 1990. Editorial: Exploratory Research in Machine Learning. *Machine Learning* 5(1):5–9.

Draper, N. R., and Smith, H. 1966. *Applied Regression Analysis*. John Wiley & Sons, New York, NY.

Eddy, David M. 1982. Probabilistic reasoning in clinical medicine: Problems and opportunities. In Kahneman, Daniel; Slovic, Paul; and Tversky, Amos, editors 1982, *Judgment Under Uncertainty: Heuristics and Biases*. Cambridge University Press, Cambridge, England. 249–267.

Efron, Bradley, and LePage, Raoul. 1992. Introduction to bootstrap. In LePage, Raoul and

Billard, Lynne, editors 1992, *Exploring the Limits of Bootstrap.* John Wiley & Sons, New York, NY. 3–10.

Efron, Bradley, and Tibshirani, Robert. 1986. Bootstrap methods for statistical errors, confidence intervals, and other measures of statistical accuracy. *Statistical Science* 1(1):54–57.

Efron, Bradley, and Tibshirani, Robert. 1991. Statistical data analysis in the computer age. *Science* 253:390–395.

Efron, Bradley, and Tibshirani, Robert J. 1993. *An Introduction to the Bootstrap.* Chapman and Hall, New York, NY.

Emerson, John D., and Hoaglin, David C. 1983. Resistant lines for x versus y. In Hoaglin, David C.; Mosteller, Frederick; and Tukey, John W., editors. 1983, *Understanding Robust and Exploratory Data Analysis.* John Wiley & Sons, New York, NY. 129–165.

Emerson, John D., and Stoto, Michael A. 1983. Transforming data. In Hoaglin, David C.; Mosteller, Frederick; and Tukey, John W., editors 1983, *Understanding Robust and Exploratory Data Analysis.* John Wiley & Sons, New York, NY. chapter 4, 97–128.

Emerson, John D., and Strenio, Judith. 1983. Boxplots and batch comparison. In Hoaglin, David C.; Mosteller, Frederick; and Tukey, John W., editors 1983, *Understanding Robust and Exploratory Data Analysis.* John Wiley & Sons, New York, NY. 58–96.

Etzioni, Oren. 1990. Why PRODIGY/EBL works. In *Proceedings of the Eighth National Conference on Artificial Intelligence*, Menlo Park, CA. AAAI Press/MIT Press. 916–922.

Etzioni, Oren, and Etzioni, Ruth. 1994. Statistical methods for analyzing speedup learning experiments. *Machine Learning* 14:333–347.

Falkenhainer, Brian C., and Michalski, Ryszard S. 1986. Integrating quantitative and qualitative discovery: The ABACUS system. *Machine Learning* 1:367–401.

Fatima, Sameen S. 1992. The boxes experiment: Learning an optimal monitoring interval. Technical Report 92-38, Computer Science Department, University of Massachusetts, Amherst, MA.

Fayyad, Usama M., and Irani, Keki B. 1990. What should be minimized in a decision tree? In *Proceedings of the Eighth National Conference on Artificial Intelligence*, Menlo Park, CA. AAAI Press/MIT Press. 749–754.

Feng, C.; King, R.; and Sutherland, A. 1995. Statlog: Comparison of machine learning, statistical and neural network classification algorithms. Forthcoming.

Glymour, Clark; Scheines, Richard; Spirtes, Peter; and Kelly, Kevin. 1987. *Discovering Causal Structure: Artificial Intelligence, Philosophy of Science, and Statistical Modeling.* Academic Press, Orlando, FL.

Gregory, Dawn E. 1994. Power transformations: An approach to improving linear relationships in data. EKSL Memo #31, Dept. of Computer Science, University of Massachusetts, Amherst, MA.

Gregory, Dawn E., and Cohen, Paul R. 1994. Two algorithms for inducing causal models from data. In *Working Notes of the Knowledge Discovery in Databases Workshop: Twelfth National Conference on Artificial Intelligence*. AAAI Press, Menlo Park, CA. 73–84.

Hand, D. J. 1993. Measurement scales as metadata. In Hand, D. J., editor. 1993, *Artificial Intelligence Frontiers in Statistics: AI and Statistics III*. Chapman & Hall, London. chapter 6, 54–64.

Hanks, Steven, and Weld, Daniel S. 1992. The systematic plan adaptor: A formal foundation for case-based planning. Technical Report TR 92-09-04, University of Washington: Dept. of Computer Science, Seattle, WA.

Hanks, Steven; Pollack, Martha; and Cohen, Paul R. 1993. Benchmarks, testbeds, controlled experimentation, and the design of agent architectures. *AI Magazine* 14(4):17–42.

Hart, David M., and Cohen, Paul R. 1992. Predicting and explaining success and task duration in the phoenix planner. In *Artificial Intelligence Planning Systems: Proceedings of the First International Conference*, San Mateo, CA. Morgan Kaufmann Publishers, Inc. 106–115.

Hart, David M.; Cohen, Paul R.; and Anderson, Scott D. 1990. Envelopes as a vehicle for improving the efficiency of plan execution. In Sycara, Katia P., editor 1990, *Proceedings of the Workshop on Innovative Approaches to Planning, Scheduling and Control*, San Mateo, CA. Morgan Kaufmann Publishers, Inc. 71–76.

Hays, William L. 1973. *Statistics for the Social Sciences, 2nd Edition*. Holt, Rinehart, and Winston, New York, NY.

Holland, Paul W. 1986. Statistics and causal inference. *Journal of the American Statistical Association* 81(396):945–970.

Holte, Robert C. 1993. Very simple classification rules perform very well on most commonly-used datasets. *Machine Learning* 11:63–91.

Howe, Adele E. 1992. Analyzing failure recovery to improve planner design. In *Proceedings of the Tenth National Conference on Artificial Intelligence*, Menlo Park, CA. AAAI Press/MIT Press. 387–392.

Howe, Adele E., and Cohen, Paul R. 1991. Failure recovery: A model and experiments. In *Proceedings of the Ninth National Conference on Artificial Intelligence*, Menlo Park, CA. AAAI Press/MIT Press. 801–808.

Howe, Adele E., and Fuegi, Aaron D. 1994. Methods for finding influences on program failure. In *Proceedings of the Sixth International Conference on Tools with Artificial Intelligence*, IEEE Computer Society Press. 764–767.

Howe, Adele E., and Cohen, Paul R. 1995. Understanding Planner Behavior. *Artificial Intelligence Journal*. To come.

Keppel, Geoffrey. 1973. *Design and Analysis: A Researcher's Handbook*. Prentice-Hall, Inc., Englewood Cliffs, NJ.

Kibler, Dennis, and Langley, Pat. 1988. *Machine Learning as an Experimental Science*. Pitman Publishing Ltd., London.

Langley, Pat; Simon, Herbert A.; Bradshaw, Gary L.; and Zytkow, Jan M. 1987. *Scientific Discovery: Computational Explorations of the Creative Process*. MIT Press, Cambridge, MA.

Lehnert, Wendy G. 1991. Symbolic/subsymbolic sentence analysis: Exploiting the best of two worlds. In Pollack, J. and Barnden, J., editors 1991, *Advances in Connectionist and Neural Computation Theory, Vol. 1*. Ablex Publishing, Norwood, NJ. 135–164.

Lehnert, Wendy G.; McCarthy, Joseph; Soderland, Stephen; Riloff, Ellen; Cardie, Claire; Peterson, Jonathan; Feng, Fang Fang; Dolan, Charles; and Goldman, Seth 1993. Umass/Hughes: Description of the CIRCUS system as used for MUC-5. In *Proceedings of the Fifth Message Understanding Conference*, San Mateo, CA. Morgan Kaufmann Publishers, Inc. 277–291.

Lenat, Douglas B., and Brown, John S. 1983. Why AM and EURISKO appear to work. In *Proceedings of the Third National Conference on Artificial Intelligence*, Menlo Park, CA. AAAI Press/MIT Press. 236–240.

Lenat, D. B., and Feigenbaum, E. 1987. On the thresholds of knowledge. In *Proceedings of the Tenth International Joint Conference on Artificial Intelligence*, Los Altos, CA. Morgan Kaufmann Publishers, Inc. 1173–1182.

Li, C.C. 1975. *Path Analysis: A Primer*. Boxwood Press, Pacific Grove CA.

Lukowicz, Paul; Heinz, Ernst A.; Prechelt, Lutz, and Tichy, Walter F. 1994. Experimental Evaluation in Computer Science: A Quantitative Study. University of Karlsruhe, Karlsruhe, Germany, 17/94.

McDermott, Drew. 1981. Artificial intelligence meets natural stupidity. In Haugeland, John, editor 1981, *Mind Design*. Bradford Books, Montgomery, VT. chapter 5, 143–160.

Mosteller, Frederick, and Tukey, John W. 1977. *Data Analysis and Regression: A Second Course in Statistics*. Addison Wesley, Reading, MA.

Proceedings of the Third Message Understanding Conference (MUC-3), San Mateo, CA. Morgan Kaufmann Publishers, Inc.

Neisser, Ulric. 1976. *Cognition and Reality*. W. H. Freeman, San Francisco, CA.

Newell, Allen, 1973. You can't play 20 questions with nature and win. In Chase, William G., editor 1973, *Visual Information Processing*. Academic Press, New York. chapter 6, 283–308.

Newell, Allen, 1975. A Tutorial on Speech Understanding Systems. In Reddy, D. R., editor 1975, *Speech Recognition: Invited Papers Presented at the 1974 IEEE Symposium*, Academic Press, New York. 3–54.

Newell, Allen. 1982. The knowledge level. *Artificial Intelligence* 18(1):87–127.

Newell, Allen. 1990. *Unified Theories of Cognition*. Harvard University Press, Cambridge, MA.

Newell, Allen, and Simon, Herbert A. 1981. Computer science as empirical inquiry: Symbols and search. In Haugeland, John, editor 1981, *Mind Design*. Bradford Books, Montgomery, VT. chapter 1, 35–66.

Nordhausen, Bernd, and Langley, Pat. 1990. A robust approach to numeric discovery. In *Proceedings of the Seventh International Conference on Machine Learning*, San Mateo, CA. Morgan Kaufmann Publishers, Inc. 411–418.

Noreen, Eric W. 1989. *Computer-Intensive Methods for Testing Hypotheses: An Introduction*. John Wiley & Sons, New York, NY.

Norman, Donald A., and Daniel G. Bobrow. 1974. On Data-limited and Resource-limited Processes. Technical Report CSL 74-2. Mimeo, Palo Alto Research Center, Palo Alto.

Oates, Tim, and Cohen, Paul R. 1994. Toward a plan steering agent: Experiments with schedule maintenance. In *Proceedings of the Second International Conference on Artificial Intelligence Planning Systems*, Menlo Park, CA. AAAI Press. 134–139.

Oates, Tim; Gregory, Dawn; and Cohen, Paul R. 1995. Detecting dependencies in categorical data. In *Proceedings of the Fifth International Workshop on Artificial Intelligence and Statistics*, 417–423.

O'Brien, Ralph G., and Kaiser, Mary Kister, 1985. MANOVA Method for analyzing repeated measures designs: An extensive primer. *Psychological Bulletin* 97(2):316–333.

Olson, Chester. 1987. *Statistics: Making Sense of Data*. Allyn and Bacon, Newton, MA.

Pearl, Judea, and Verma, T. S. 1991. A theory of inferred causation. In James A. Allen, Richard Fikes and Sandewall, E., editors. 1991, *Principles of Knowledge Representation and Reasoning: Proceedings of the Second International Conference*, San Mateo, CA. Morgan Kaufmann Publishers, Inc. 441–452.

Pearl, Judea. 1988. *Probabilistic Reasoning in Intelligent Systems: Networks of Plausible Inference*. Morgan Kaufmann Publishers, Inc., San Mateo, CA.

Pollack, Martha E., and Ringuette, Marc. 1990. Introducing the Tileworld: Experimentally evaluating agent architectures. In *Proceedings of the Eighth National Conference on Artificial Intelligence*, Menlo Park, CA. AAAI Press/MIT Press. 183–190.

Porter, Bruce. 1991. AI methodologies. Unpublished talk presented at AI Methodology Workshop, Northampton, MA.

Prechelt, Lutz, 1994. A study of Experimental Evaluations of Neural Network Learning Algorithms: Current Research Practice. University of Karlsruhe, in Progress, 19/94.

Rao, R. Bharat; Yu, Stephen C-Y.; and Stepp, Robert E. 1991. Knowledge-based equation discovery in engineering domains. In *Proceedings of the Eighth International Workshop on Machine Learning*, San Mateo, CA. Morgan Kaufmann Publishers, Inc. 630–634.

Rendell, Larry, and Cho, Howard. 1990. Empirical learning as a function of concept character. *Machine Learning* 5(3):267–298.

Rosenthal, Robert, and Rosnow, Ralph L. 1985. *Contrast Analysis: Focused Comparisons in the Analysis of Variance*. Cambridge University Press, Cambridge, England.

Rudd, Andrew, and Clasing, Henry K. Jr. 1982. *Modern Portfolio Theory: The Principles of Investment Management*. Dow Jones-Irwin, Homewood, IL.

Schaffer, Cullen. 1990. A proven domain-independent scientific function-finding algorithm. In *Proceedings of the Eighth National Conference on Artificial Intelligence*, Menlo Park, CA. AAAI Press/MIT Press. 828–833.

Schaffer, Cullen. 1991. On evaluation of domain-independent scientific function-finding systems. In Piatetsky-Shapiro, Gregory and Frawley, William J., editors 1991, *Knowledge Discovery in Databases*. AAAI Press, Menlo Park, CA. chapter 5, 93–104.

Schank, Roger C., and Riesbeck, Christopher K., editors. 1981. *Inside Computer Understanding*. Lawrence Erlbaum Associates, Hillsdale, NJ.

Shaffer, Juliet Popper, editor. 1992. *The Role of Models in Nonexperimental Social Science: Two Debates*. American Educational Research Association and American Statistical Association, Washington DC.

Shrager, Jeff, and Langley, Pat, editors. 1990. *Computational Models of Scientific Discovery and Theory Formation*. Morgan Kaufmann Publishers, Inc., San Mateo, CA.

Simon, Herbert A. 1993. Artificial intelligence as an experimental science (Keynote Address). In *Proceedings of the Eleventh National Conference on Artificial Intelligence*, Menlo Park, CA. AAAI Press/MIT Press. 853. To appear in *Artificial Intelligence*, 1995.

Sokal, Robert R., and Rohlf, F. James. 1981. *Biometry*. W. H. Freeman, San Francisco, CA.

Spirtes, Peter; Glymour, Clark; and Scheines, Richard 1993. *Causation, Prediction and Search*. Springer Verlag, New York, NY.

Sundheim, Beth M. 1991. Overview of the third message understanding evaluation and conference. In *Proceedings of the Third Message Understanding Conference (MUC-3)*, San Mateo, CA. Morgan Kaufmann Publishers, Inc. 3–16.

Suppes, Patrick. 1970. *A Probabilistic Theory of Causality*. North Holland, Amsterdam.

Suppes, Patrick, and Zinnes, Joseph L. 1963. Basic measurement theory. In Luce, R. Duncan; Bush, Robert R.; and Galanter, Eugene, editors 1963, *Handbook of Mathematical Psychology*. John Wiley & Sons, New York, NY. chapter 1, 1–76.

Tufte, E. R. 1983. *The Visual Display of Quantitative Information*. Graphics Press, Cheshire, CT.

Tufte, Eward R. 1990. *Envisioning Information*. Graphics Press, Cheshire, CT.

Tukey, John W. 1958. Bias and confidence in not-quite large samples (abstract). *Annals of Mathematics and Statistics* 29:614.

Tukey, John W. 1977. *Exploratory Data Analysis*. Addison-Wesley, Reading, MA.

van Melle, William. 1984. The structure of the MYCIN system. In *Rule-Based Expert Systems: The MYCIN Experiments of the Stanford Heuristic Programming Project*. Addison-Wesley, Reading, MA. 67–77.

Velleman, Paul F., and Hoaglin, David C. 1981. *Applications, Basics, and Computing of Exploratory Data Analysis*. Duxbury Press, Boston, MA.

Velleman, Paul F., and Wilkinson, Leland. 1993. Nominal, ordinal, interval and ratio typologies are misleading. *The American Statistician* 47(1):65–72.

Weiss, Sholom M., and Kulikowski, Casmir A. 1989. *Computer Systems That Learn*. Morgan Kaufmann Publishers, Inc., San Mateo, CA.

Wickens, Thomas D. 1989. *Multiway Contingency Tables Analysis for the Social Sciences*. Lawrence Erlbaum Associates, Hillsdale, NJ.

Winer, B. J. 1971. *Statistical Principles in Experimental Design*. McGraw Hill, New York, NY.

Winkler, Robert L., and Hays, William L. 1975. *Statistics: Probability, Inference and Decision*. Holt, Rinehart and Winston, New York, NY.

Zytkow, J. M. 1987. Combining many searches in the FAHRENHEIT discovery system. In *Proceedings of the Fourth International Workshop on Machine Learning*, San Mateo, CA. 281–287.

Index

Italics indicate definitions.

accuracy
  of classification, 82, 93, 222
  of parameter estimates, 132
Acker, L., 187–189, 192, 194, 196, 198, 205,
    208, 210, 226, 242, 260, 262, 263, 298, 380
agents, 9–10, 64, 102, 251, 265, 268, 310,
    376, 378
Allen, J.A., 371, 372, 374
alternative hypothesis, 128
analysis of variance, *192–194*, 210
  additive model, 292
  and experiment design, 287–308
  mixed without repeated measures, 298–302
  one-way, 195, 235–241
  one-way repeated measures, 288, 302–308
  three-way, 256–260
  two-way, 251–256, 262, 265
  two-way without repeated measures, 289–
    298
anomalous value, 18
anova. *See* analysis of variance
Anscombe, F. J., 51
architecture, 309–313, 365–368, 371, 372,
    374, 375, 377–379, 382
arrangements, 173
assessment studies, 6–8, 186
assistant. *See* agent
association, 48–51, 53, 62
  linear, 45, 48, 50–51, 54, 310, 317
  nonlinear, 21, 23, 46, 48, 258, 266, 317, 320,
    321, 333, 361

strength of, 50, 52–53
without causal direction, 28, 29, 49, 52, 270,
    337
assumptions
  analysis of variance, 194, 266, 306
  bootstrap tests, 164
  F test, 206
  nonparametric tests, 180
  t test, 126, 169, 326
Atkin, M., 377
autocorrelation, 61–63
  confounded by trend, 62

Beal, C.R., 72, 252, 376
behavior, 2–6, 268, 309–312
  ill-defined, 378
β coefficient, 330–332, 350–356
between-group variance, *193*, 236–238
bin, 20, 24
bin size, 21–24
binning, 45
blocking, 224
bootstrap, 153–164, 217
  compared with randomization, 175–177
  confidence interval, 161–163, 326–327
  cross-validation, 217
  normal approximation method, 158–159
  one-sample tests, 157, 177–178
  sampling distribution, *153*, 156
  shift method, 157–158
  two-sample tests, 159–161
bootstrap-randomization hybrid, 160
bounded rationality, 311